TAKING SIDES

Clashing Views in

Science, Technology, and Society

EIGHTH EDITION

TAKING SIDES

Clashing Views in

Science, Technology, and Society

EIGHTH EDITION

Selected, Edited, and with Introductions by

Thomas A. Easton
Thomas College

McGraw-Hill
Higher Education

Boston   Burr Ridge, IL   Dubuque, IA   New York   San Francisco   St. Louis
Bangkok   Bogotá   Caracas   Kuala Lumpur   Lisbon   London   Madrid   Mexico City
Milan   Montreal   New Delhi   Santiago   Seoul   Singapore   Sydney   Taipei   Toronto

McGraw-Hill
Higher Education

TAKING SIDES: CLASHING VIEWS IN SCIENCE, TECHNOLOGY,
AND SOCIETY, EIGHTH EDITION

This book is printed on recycled, acid-free paper containing
10% postconsumer waste.

1 2 3 4 5 6 7 8 9 0 DOC/DOC 0 9 8 7

MHID: 0-07-351512-4
ISBN: 978-0-07-351512-0
ISSN: 1098-5417

Managing Editor: *Larry Loeppke*
Production Manager: *Beth Kundert*
Senior Developmental Editor: *Jill Peter*
Editorial Assistant: *Nancy Meissner*
Production Service Assistant: *Rita Hingtgen*
Permissions Coordinator: *Lori Church*
Senior Marketing Manager: *Julie Keck*
Marketing Communications Specialist: *Mary Klein*
Marketing Coordinator: *Alice Link*
Project Manager: *Jane Mohr*
Design Specialist: *Tara McDermott*
Senior Administrative Assistant: *DeAnna Dausener*
Senior Operations Manager: *Pat Koch Krieger*
Cover Graphics: *Maggie Lytle*

Compositor: ICC Macmillan Inc.
Cover Image: Space Telescope Science Institute/NASA

Library of Congress Cataloging-in-Publication Data

Main entry under title:
    Taking sides: clashing views in science, technology, and society/selected, edited, and with
    introductions by Thomas A. Easton.—8th ed.

    Includes bibliographical references and index.
    1. Science—Social aspects. 2. Technology—Social Aspects. I. Easton, Thomas A., *comp.*
                                                                306.45

www.mhhe.com

Preface

T hose who must deal with scientific and technological issues—scientists, politicians, sociologists, business managers, and anyone who is concerned about energy policy, genetically modified foods, government intrusiveness, expensive space programs, or the morality of medical research, among many other issues—must be able to consider, evaluate, and choose among alternatives. Making choices is an essential aspect of the scientific method. It is also an inescapable feature of every public debate over a scientific or technological issue, for there can be no debate if there are no alternatives.

The ability to evaluate and to select among alternatives—as well as to know when the data do not permit selection—is called critical thinking. It is essential not only in science and technology but in every other aspect of life as well. *Taking Sides: Clashing Views in Science, Technology, and Society* is designed to stimulate and cultivate this ability by holding up for consideration 19 issues that have provoked substantial debate. Each of these issues has at least two sides, usually more. However, each issue is expressed in terms of a single question in order to draw the lines of debate more clearly. The ideas and answers that emerge from the clash of opposing points of view should be more complex than those offered by the students before the reading assignment.

The issues in this book were chosen because they are currently of particular concern to both science and society. They touch on the nature of science and research, the relationship between science and society, the uses of technology, and the potential threats that technological advances can pose to human survival. And they come from a variety of fields, including computer and space science, biology, environmentalism, law enforcement, and public health.

Organization of the book For each issue, I have provided an *issue introduction,* which provides some historical background and discusses why the issue is important. I then present two selections, one pro and one con, in which the authors make their cases. Each issue concludes with a *postscript* that brings the issue up to date and adds other voices and viewpoints. I have also provided relevant Internet site addresses (URLs) on the *Internet References* page that accompanies each part opener. At the back of the book is a listing of all the *contributors to this volume,* which gives information on the scientists, technicians, professors, and social critics whose views are debated here.

Which answer to the issue question—yes or no—is the correct answer? Perhaps neither. Perhaps both. Students should read, think about, and discuss the readings and then come to their own conclusions without letting my or their instructor's opinions (which perhaps show at least some of the time!) dictate theirs. The additional readings mentioned in both the introductions and the postscripts should prove helpful. It is worth stressing that the issues covered in this book are all *live* issues; that is, the debates they represent are active and ongoing.

Changes to this edition   This eighth edition represents a considerable revision of its predecessor. There are three completely new issues: "Should the Internet Be Neutral?" (Issue 3); "Are Genetically Modified Foods Safe to Eat?" (Issue 11); and "Should the World's Libraries Be Digitized?" (Issue 17). The issue on manned space exploration (Issue 14) has been retitled and given two new essays. The issues on the search for extraterrestrial life (Issue 13), on Internet impacts on community (Issue 15), and on cloning (Issue 19) have been retitled and given one new essay each to reflect changes in the focus of the debates.

In addition, for seven of the issues retained from the previous edition, one reading has been replaced to bring the debate up to date: "Should Government Restrict the Publication of Unclassified But 'Sensitive' Research?" (Issue 2); "Should Society Act Now to Halt Global Warming?" (Issue 4); "Will Hydrogen Replace Fossil Fuels for Cars?" (Issue 6); "Should DDT Be Banned Worldwide?" (Issue 9); "Should Potential Risks Slow the Development of Nanotechnology?" (Issue 10); "Does the Spread of Surveillance Technology Threaten Privacy?" (Issue 16); and "Is the Use of Animals in Research Justified?" (Issue 18). One issue has had both essays replaced: "Is It Time to Revive Nuclear Power?" (Issue 5). In all, there are 20 new selections. The book's introduction and the issue introductions and postscripts in the retained issues have been revised and updated where necessary.

A word to the instructor   An *Instructor's Resource Guide with Test Questions* (multiple-choice and essay) is available through the publisher for the instructor using *Taking Sides* in the classroom. It includes suggestions for stimulating in-class discussion for each issue. A general guidebook, *Using Taking Sides in the Classroom,* which discusses methods and techniques for integrating the pro-con approach into any classroom setting, is also available. An online version of *Using Taking Sides in the Classroom* and a correspondence service for *Taking Sides* adopters can be found at http://www.mhcls.com/usingts/.

Taking Sides: Clashing Views in Science, Technology, and Society is only one title in the Taking Sides series. If you are interested in seeing the table of contents for any of the other titles, please visit the Taking Sides Web site at http://www.mhcls.com/takingsides/.

Thomas A. Easton
Thomas College

Contents In Brief

Contents

Law professor Lawrence Lessig argues that imposing network-access fees on content providers would unduly interfere with innovation in an important area of the economy. Building network neutrality into law would thus keep major network companies from imposing fees and slowing the economy. Kyle D. Dixon, director of the Federal Institute for Regulatory Law & Economics at the Progress & Freedom Foundation, argues that lacking demonstrated abuses, a network neutrality law would unfairly limit corporate investment and innovation and thereby reduce consumer welfare.

UNIT 2   THE ENVIRONMENT   69

Nicholas Stern, head of the British Government Economics Service, reports that although taking steps now to limit future impacts of global warming would be very expensive, the economic and social impacts of not doing so will be much more expensive. The Bush administration's plan for dealing with global warming insists that short-term economic health must come before reducing emissions of greenhouse gases. It is more useful to reduce "greenhouse gas intensity" or emissions per dollar of economic activity than to reduce total emissions.

Michael J. Wallace argues that because the benefits of nuclear power include energy supply and price stability, air pollution control, and greenhouse gas reduction, new nuclear power plant construction—with federal support—is essential. Karen Charman argues that nuclear power's drawbacks and the promise of clean, lower-cost, less dangerous alternatives greatly weaken the case for nuclear power.

more effective and less environmentally harmful methods. She maintains that DDT should be banned or reserved for emergency use. Donald R. Roberts argues that the scientific evidence regarding the environmental hazards of DDT has been seriously misrepresented by anti-pesticide activists. The hazards of malaria are much greater and, properly used, DDT can prevent them and save lives.

Radio astronomer and SETI researcher Seth Shostak argues that if the assumptions behind the SETI search are well grounded, signals of extraterrestrial origin will be detected soon, perhaps within the next generation. Peter Schenkel argues that SETI's lack of success to date, coupled with the apparent uniqueness of Earth, suggest that intelligent life is probably rare in our galaxy and that the enthusiastic optimism of SETI proponents should be reined in.

Astronomer Neil deGrasse Tyson argues that large, expensive projects such as space exploration are driven only by war, greed, and the celebration of power. The dream of colonizing space became a delusion as soon as we beat the Russians to the Moon, and it remains so. President George W. Bush argues for his vision of renewed and expanded manned space travel because it improves our lives and lifts the national spirit.

UNIT 5   THE COMPUTER REVOLUTION   283

Denise M. Carter argues that the Internet enhances or adds to social relationships. In fact, the trust essential to successful relationships may be easier to develop online than offline. Jonathon N. Cummings, Brian Butler, and Robert Kraut maintain that online communication is less valuable for building strong social relationships than more traditional face-to-face and telephone communication.

Julian Sanchez argues that new technologies make it astonishingly easy
to detect transgressions of laws regarding traffic, drugs, weapons, and
illegal computer files. Ordinary expectations of privacy are seriously
threatened, and we face the need for difficult tradeoffs. Stuart Taylor, Jr.,
contends that those who object to surveillance—particularly government
surveillance—have their priorities wrong. Curbing "government powers
in the name of civil liberties [exacts] too high a price in terms of
endangered lives."

Brendan Rapple argues that as Google scans, indexes, and makes
available for online searching the books of the world's major libraries, it
will increase access, facilitate scholarship, and in general benefit human
civilization. Keith Kupferschmid argues that there is no justification in law
for Google's massive copying of books. If the Google Print Library
Project is allowed to continue, the interests of publishers, authors, and
creators of all kinds will be seriously damaged.

Journalist Josie Appleton contends that a proper relationship to animals
means using them for human ends, for humans are the measure of all
things. Philosopher Tom Regan argues that any attempt to define what it
is about being human that gives all humans moral rights must also give
animals moral rights, and that therefore we have no more right to use
animals as research subjects than we have to use other humans.

Julian Savulescu, director of the Ethics Program of the Murdoch Institute at the Royal Children's Hospital in Melbourne, Australia, argues that it is not only permissible but morally required to use human cloning to create embryos as a source of tissue for transplantation. Physician David van Gend argues that not only is the cloning of embryonic stem cells morally indefensible, but recent progress with adult stem cells makes it unnecessary as well.

Introduction

Analyzing Issues in Science and Technology

As civilization enters the twenty-first century, it cannot escape science and technology. Their fruits—the clothes we wear, the foods we eat, the tools we use—surround us. They also fill us with both hope and dread for the future, for although new discoveries promise us cures for diseases and other problems, new insights into the wonders of nature, new gadgets, new industries, and new jobs (among other things), the past has taught us that technological developments can have unforeseen and terrible consequences.

Those consequences do *not* belong to science, for science is nothing more (or less) than a systematic approach to gaining knowledge about the world. Technology is the application of knowledge (including scientific knowledge) to accomplish things we otherwise could not. It is not just devices such as hammers and computers and jet aircraft, but also management systems and institutions and even political philosophies. And it is of course such *uses* of knowledge that affect our lives for good and ill.

We cannot say, "for good *or* ill." Technology is neither an unalloyed blessing nor an unmitigated curse. Every new technology offers both new benefits and new problems, and the two sorts of consequences cannot be separated from each other. Automobiles provide rapid, convenient personal transportation, but precisely because of that benefit, they also create suburbs, urban sprawl, crowded highways, and air pollution, and even contribute to global climate change.

Optimists vs. Pessimists

The inescapable pairing of good and bad consequences helps to account for why so many issues of science and technology stir debate in our society. Optimists focus on the benefits of technology and are confident that we will be able to cope with any problems that arise. Pessimists fear the problems and are sure their costs will outweigh any possible benefits.

Sometimes the costs of new technologies are immediate and tangible. When new devices—steamship boilers or space shuttles—fail or new drugs prove to have unforeseen side-effects, people die. Sometimes the costs are less obvious.

The proponents of technology answer that if a machine fails, it needs to be fixed, not banned. If a drug has side-effects, it may need to be refined or its permitted recipients may have to be better defined (the banned tranquilizer thalidomide is famous for causing birth defects when taken early in pregnancy; it is apparently quite safe for men and nonpregnant women).

Certainty vs. Uncertainty

Another root for the debates over science and technology is uncertainty. Science is by its very nature uncertain. Its truths are provisional, open to revision.

Unfortunately, most people are told by politicians, religious leaders, and newspaper columnists that truth is certain. They therefore believe that if someone admits uncertainty, their position is weak and they need not be heeded. This is, of course, an open invitation for demagogues to prey upon fears of disaster or side-effects or upon the wish to be told that the omens of greenhouse warming and ozone holes (etc.) are mere figments of the scientific imagination.

Is Science Just Another Religion?

Science and technology have come to play a huge role in human culture, largely because they have led to vast improvements in nutrition, health care, comfort, communication, transportation, and humanity's ability to affect the world. However, science has also enhanced understanding of human behavior and of how the universe works, and in this it frequently contradicts what people have long thought they knew. Furthermore, it actively rejects any role of God in scientific explanation.

Many people therefore reject what science tells us. They see science as just another way of explaining how the world and humanity came to be; in this view, science is no truer than religious accounts. Indeed, some say science is just another religion, with less claim on followers' allegiance than other religions that have been divinely sanctioned and hallowed by longer traditions. Certainly, they see little significant difference between the scientist's faith in reason, evidence, and skepticism as the best way to achieve truth about the world and the religious believer's faith in revelation and scripture. This becomes very explicit in connection with the debates between creationists and evolutionists. Even religious people who do not favor creationism may reject science because they see it as denying both the existence of God and the importance of "human values" (meaning behaviors that are affirmed by traditional religion). This leads to a basic antipathy between science and religion, especially conservative religion, and especially in areas—such as human origins—where science and scripture seem to be talking about the same things but are contradicting each other. This point can be illustrated by mentioning the Italian physicist Galileo Galilei (1564–1642) who in 1616 was attacked by the Roman Catholic Church for teaching Copernican astronomy and thus contradicting the teachings of the Church. Another example arose when evolutionary theorist Charles Darwin first published *On the Origin of Species by Means of Natural Selection* in 1859. Mano Singham notes in "The Science and Religion Wars," *Phi Delta Kappan* (February 2000), that "In the triangle formed by science, mainstream religion, and fringe beliefs, it is the conflict between science and fringe beliefs that is usually the source of the most heated, acrimonious, and public debate." Michael Ruse takes a more measured tone when he asks "Is Evolution a Secular Religion?" *Science* (March 7, 2003);

his answer is that, "Today's professional evolutionism is no more a secular religion than is industrial chemistry" but there is also a "popular evolutionism" that treads on religious ground and must be carefully distinguished. In recent years, efforts to counter "evolutionism" by mandating the teaching of creationism or "intelligent design" (ID) in public schools have made frequent appearances in the news, but so have the defeats of those efforts. One of the most recent defeats was in Dover, Pennsylvania, where the judge declared that "ID is not science." See Jeffrey Mervis, "Judge Jones Defines Science—And Why Intelligent Design Isn't," *Science* (January 6, 2006), and Sid Perkins, "Evolution in Action," *Science News* (February 25, 2006).

Even if religion does not enter the debate, some people reject new developments in science and technology (and in other areas) because they seem "unnatural." For most people, "natural" seems to mean any device or procedure to which they have become accustomed. Very few realize how "unnatural" are such ordinary things as circumcision and horseshoes and baseball.

Yet new ideas are inevitable. The search for and the application of knowledge is perhaps the human species' single most defining characteristic. Other creatures also use tools, communicate, love, play, and reason. Only humans have embraced change. We are forever creating variations on our religions, languages, politics, and tools. Innovation is as natural to us as building dams is to a beaver.

Voodoo Science

Public confusion over science and technology is increased by several factors. One is the failure of public education. In 2002, the Committee on Technological Literacy of the National Academy of Engineering and the National Research Council published a report (*Technically Speaking: Why All Americans Need to Know More about Technology*) that said that although the United States is defined by and dependent on science and technology, "its citizens are not equipped to make well-considered decisions or to think critically about technology. As a society, we are not even fully aware of or conversant with the technologies we use every day."

A second factor is the willingness of some to mislead. Alarmists stress awful possible consequences of new technology without paying attention to actual evidence, they demand certainty when it is impossible, and they reject the new because it is untraditional or even "unthinkable." And then there are the marketers, hypesters, fraudsters, activists, and even legitimate scientists and critics who oversell their claims. Robert L. Park, author of *Voodoo Science: The Road from Foolishness to Fraud* (Oxford University Press, 2002) lists seven warning signs "that a scientific claim lies well outside the bounds of rational scientific discourse" and should be viewed warily:

- The discoverer pitches his claim directly to the media, without permitting peer review.
- The discoverer says that a powerful establishment is trying to suppress his or her work.

- The scientific effect involved is always at the very limit of detection.
- Evidence for a discovery is only anecdotal.
- The discoverer says a belief is credible because it has endured for centuries.
- The discoverer has worked in isolation.
- The discoverer must propose new laws of nature to explain an observation.

The Soul of Science

The standard picture of science—a world of observations and hypotheses, experiments and theories, a world of sterile white coats and laboratories and cold, unfeeling logic—is a myth of our times. It has more to do with the way science is presented by both scientists and the media than with the way scientists actually do their work. In practice, scientists are often less orderly, less logical, and more prone to very human conflicts of personality than most people suspect.

The myth remains because it helps to organize science. It provides labels and a framework for what a scientist does; it may thus be especially valuable to student scientists who are still learning the ropes. In addition, it embodies certain important ideals of scientific thought. It is these ideals that make the scientific approach the most powerful and reliable guide to truth about the world that human beings have yet devised.

The Ideals of Science: Skepticism, Communication, and Reproducibility

The soul of science is a very simple idea: *Check it out.* Scholars used to think that all they had to do to do their duty by the truth was to say "According to . . . " some ancient authority such as Aristotle or the Bible. If someone with a suitably illustrious reputation had once said something was so, it was so. Arguing with authority or holy writ could get you charged with heresy and imprisoned or burned at the stake.

This attitude is the opposite of everything that modern science stands for. As Carl Sagan says in *The Demon-Haunted World: Science as a Candle in the Dark* (Random House, 1995, p. 28), "One of the great commandments of science is, 'Mistrust arguments from authority.'" Scientific knowledge is based not on authority but on reality itself. Scientists take nothing on faith. They are *skeptical*. When they want to know something, they do not look it up in the library or take others' word for it. They go into the laboratory, the forest, the desert—wherever they can find the phenomena they wish to know about—and they ask those phenomena directly. They look for answers in the book of nature. And if they think they know the answer already, it is not of books that they ask, "Are we right?" but of nature. This is the point of "scientific experiments"—they are how scientists ask nature whether their ideas check out.

This "check it out" ideal is, however, an ideal. No one can possibly check everything out for himself or herself. Even scientists, in practice, look things up in books. They too rely on authorities. But the authorities they rely on are other scientists who have studied nature and reported what they learned. In principle, everything those authorities report can be checked. Observations in the lab or in the field can be repeated. New theoretical or computer models can be designed. What is in the books can be confirmed.

In fact, a good part of the official "scientific method" is designed to make it possible for any scientist's findings or conclusions to be confirmed. Scientists do not say, "Vitamin D is essential for strong bones. Believe me. I know." They say, "I know that vitamin D is essential for proper bone formation because I raised rats without vitamin D in their diet, and their bones turned out soft and crooked. When I gave them vitamin D, their bones hardened and straightened. Here is the kind of rat I used, the kind of food I fed them, the amount of vitamin D I gave them. Go thou and do likewise, and you will see what I saw."

Communication is therefore an essential part of modern science. That is, in order to function as a scientist, you must not keep secrets. You must tell others not just what you have learned by studying nature, but how you learned it. You must spell out your methods in enough detail to let others repeat your work.

Scientific knowledge is thus *reproducible* knowledge. Strictly speaking, if a person says, "I can see it, but you can't," that person is not a scientist. Scientific knowledge exists for everyone. Anyone who takes the time to learn the proper techniques can confirm it. They don't have to believe in it first.

≈⟨◉⟩≈

As an exercise, devise a way to convince a red-green colorblind person, who sees no difference between red and green, that such a difference really exists. That is, show that a knowledge of colors is reproducible, and therefore scientific, knowledge, rather than something more like belief in ghosts or telepathy.

Here's a hint: Photographic light meters respond to light hitting a sensor. Photographic filters permit light of only a single color to pass through.

≈⟨◉⟩≈

The Standard Model of the Scientific Method

As it is usually presented, the scientific method has five major components. They include *observation, generalization* (identifying a pattern), stating a *hypothesis* (a tentative extension of the pattern or explanation for why the pattern exists), and *experimentation* (testing that explanation). The results of the tests are then *communicated* to other members of the scientific community, usually by publishing the findings. How each of these components contributes to the scientific method is discussed briefly below.

Observation

The basic units of science—and the only real facts the scientist knows—are the individual *observations*. Using them, we look for patterns, suggest explanations, and devise tests for our ideas. Our observations can be casual, as when we notice a black van parked in front of the fire hydrant on our block. They may also be more deliberate, as what a police detective notices when he or she sets out to find clues to who has been burglarizing apartments in our neighborhood.

Generalization

After we have made many observations, we try to discern a pattern among them. A statement of such a pattern is a *generalization*. We might form a generalization if we realized that every time there was a burglary on the block, that black van was parked by the hydrant.

Cautious experimenters do not jump to conclusions. When they think they see a pattern, they often make a few more observations just to be sure the pattern holds up. This practice of strengthening or confirming findings by *replicating* them is a very important part of the scientific process. In our example, the police would wait for the van to show up again and for another burglary to happen. Only then might they descend on the alleged villains. Is there loot in the van? Burglary tools?

The Hypothesis

A tentative explanation suggesting why a particular pattern exists is called a *hypothesis*. In our example, the hypothesis that comes to mind is obvious: The burglars drive to work in that black van.

The mark of a good hypothesis is that it is *testable*. The best hypotheses are *predictive*. Can you devise a predictive test for the "burglars use the black van" hypothesis?

Unfortunately, tests can fail even when the hypothesis is perfectly correct. How might that happen with our example?

Many philosophers of science insist on *falsification* as a crucial aspect of the scientific method. That is, when a test of a hypothesis shows the hypothesis to be false, the hypothesis must be rejected and replaced with another.

The Experiment

The *experiment* is the most formal part of the scientific process. The concept, however, is very simple: An experiment is nothing more than a test of a hypothesis. It is what a scientist—or a detective—does to check an idea out.

If the experiment does not falsify the hypothesis, that does not mean the hypothesis is true. It simply means that the scientist has not yet come up with the test that falsifies it. The more times and the more different ways that falsification fails, the more probable it is that the hypothesis is true. Unfortunately, because it is impossible to do all the possible tests of a hypothesis, the scientist can never *prove* it is true.

Consider the hypothesis that all cats are black. If you see a black cat, you don't really know anything at all about all cats. If you see a white cat, though, you certainly know that not all cats are black. You would have to look at every cat on Earth to prove the hypothesis. It takes just one to disprove it.

This is why philosophers of science say that *science is the art of disproving,* not proving. If a hypothesis withstands many attempts to disprove it, then it may be a good explanation of what is going on. If it fails just one test, it is clearly wrong and must be replaced with a new hypothesis.

However, researchers who study what scientists actually do point out that the truth is a little different. Almost all scientists, when they come up with what strikes them as a good explanation of a phenomenon or pattern, do *not* try to disprove their hypothesis. Instead, they design experiments to *confirm* it. If an experiment fails to confirm the hypothesis, the researcher tries another experiment, not another hypothesis.

Police detectives may do the same thing. Think of the one who found no evidence of wrongdoing in the black van but arrested the suspects anyway. Armed with a search warrant, he later searched their apartments. He was saying, in effect, "I *know* they're guilty. I just have to find the evidence to prove it."

The logical weakness in this approach is obvious, but that does not keep researchers (or detectives) from falling in love with their ideas and holding onto them as long as possible. Sometimes they hold on so long, even without confirmation of their hypothesis, that they wind up looking ridiculous. Sometimes the confirmations add up over the years and whatever attempts are made to disprove the hypothesis fail to do so. The hypothesis may then be elevated to the rank of a *theory, principle,* or *law.* Theories are explanations of how things work (the theory of evolution *by means of* natural selection). Principles and laws tend to be statements of things that happen, such as the law of gravity (masses attract each other, or what goes up comes down) or the gas law (if you increase the pressure on an enclosed gas, the volume will decrease and the temperature will increase).

Communication

Each scientist is obligated to share her or his hypotheses, methods, and findings with the rest of the scientific community. This sharing serves two purposes. First, it supports the basic ideal of skepticism by making it possible for others to say, "Oh, yeah? Let me check that." It tells those others where to see what the scientist saw, what techniques to use, and what tools to use.

Second, it gets the word out so that others can use what has been discovered. This is essential because science is a cooperative endeavor. People who work thousands of miles apart build with and upon each other's discoveries, and some of the most exciting discoveries have involved bringing together information from very different fields, as when geochemistry, paleontology, and astronomy came together to reveal that what killed off the dinosaurs 65 million years ago was apparently the impact of a massive comet or asteroid with the Earth.

Scientific cooperation stretches across time as well. Every generation of scientists both uses and adds to what previous generations have discovered. As

Isaac Newton said, "If I have seen further than [other men], it is by standing upon the shoulders of Giants" (Letter to Robert Hooke, February 5, 1675/6).

The communication of science begins with a process called "peer review," which typically has three stages. The first occurs when a scientist seeks funding—from government agencies, foundations, or other sources—to carry out a research program. He or she must prepare a report describing the intended work, laying out background, hypotheses, planned experiments, expected results, and even the broader impacts on other fields. Committees of other scientists then go over the report to see whether the scientist knows his or her area, has the necessary abilities, and is realistic in his or her plans.

Once the scientist has the needed funding, has done the work, and has written a report of the results, that report will go to a scientific journal. Before publishing the report, the journal's editors will show it to other workers in the same or related fields and ask whether the work was done adequately, the conclusions are justified, and the report should be published.

The third stage of peer review happens after publication, when the broader scientific community gets to see and judge the work.

This three-stage quality-control filter can, of course, be short-circuited. Any scientist with independent wealth can avoid the first stage quite easily, but such scientists are much, much rarer today than they were a century or so ago. Those who remain are the object of envy. Surely it is fair to say that they are not frowned upon as are those who avoid the later two stages of the "peer review" mechanism by using vanity presses and press conferences.

On the other hand, it is certainly possible for the standard peer review mechanisms to fail. By their nature, these mechanisms are more likely to approve ideas that do not contradict what the reviewers think they already know. Yet unconventional ideas are not necessarily wrong, as Alfred Wegener proved when he tried to gain acceptance for the idea of continental drift in the early twentieth century. At the time, geologists believed the crust of the Earth—which was solid rock, after all—did not behave like liquid. Yet Wegener was proposing that the continents floated about like icebergs in the sea, bumping into each other, tearing apart (to produce matching profiles like those of South America and Africa), and bumping again. It was not until the 1960s that most geologists accepted his ideas as genuine insights instead of hare-brained delusions.

The Need for Controls

Many years ago, I read a description of a wish machine. It consisted of an ordinary stereo amplifier with two unusual attachments. The wires that would normally be connected to a microphone were connected instead to a pair of copper plates. The wires that would normally be connected to a speaker were connected instead to a whip antenna of the sort we usually see on cars.

To use this device, one put a picture of some desired item between the copper plates. It could be a photo of a person with whom one wanted a date, a lottery ticket, a college, anything. One test case used a photo of a pest-infested cornfield. One then wished fervently for the date, a winning ticket, a college acceptance, or whatever else one craved. In the test case, that meant wishing that all the cornfield pests should drop dead.

Supposedly the wish would be picked up by the copper plates, amplified by the stereo amplifier, and then sent via the whip antenna wherever wish-orders have to go. Whoever or whatever fills those orders would get the message, and then. . . . Well, in the test case, the result was that when the testers checked the cornfield, there was no longer any sign of pests.

What's more, the process worked equally well whether the amplifier was plugged in or not.

I'm willing to bet that you are now feeling very much like a scientist—skeptical. The true, dedicated scientist, however, does not stop with saying, "Oh, yeah? Tell me another one!" Instead, he or she says something like, "Mmm. I wonder. Let's check this out." (Must we, really? After all, we can be quite sure that the wish machine does not work because if it did, it would be on the market. Casinos would then be unable to make a profit for their backers. Deadly diseases would not be deadly. And so on.)

Where must the scientist begin? The standard model of the scientific method says the first step is observation. Here, our observations (as well as our necessary generalization) are simply the description of the wish machine and the claims for its effectiveness. Perhaps we even have an example of the physical device itself.

What is our hypothesis? We have two choices, one consistent with the claims for the device, one denying those claims: The wish machine always works, or the wish machine never works. Both are equally testable, but perhaps one is more easily falsifiable. (Which one?)

How do we test the hypothesis? Set up the wish machine, and perform the experiment of making a wish. If the wish comes true, the device works. If it does not, it doesn't.

Can it really be that simple? In essence, yes. But in fact, no.

Even if you don't believe that wishing can make something happen, sometimes wishes do come true by sheer coincidence. Therefore, if the wish machine is as nonsensical as most people think it is, sometimes it will *seem* to work. We therefore need a way to shield against the misleading effects of coincidence. We need a way to *control* the possibilities of error.

Coincidence is not, of course, the only source of error we need to watch out for. For instance, there is a very human tendency to interpret events in such a way as to agree with our preexisting beliefs, our prejudices. If we believe in wishes, we therefore need a way to guard against our willingness to interpret near misses as not quite misses at all. There is also a human tendency not to look for mistakes when the results agree with our prejudices. That cornfield, for instance, might not have been as badly infested as the testers said it was, or a farmer might have sprayed it with pesticide whether the testers had wished or not, or the field they checked might have been the wrong one.

We would also like to check whether the wish machine does indeed work equally well plugged in or not, and then we must guard against the tendency to wish harder when we know it's plugged in. We would like to know whether the photo between the copper plates makes any difference, and then we must guard against the tendency to wish harder when we know the wish matches the photo.

Coincidence is easy to protect against. All that is necessary is to repeat the experiment enough times to be sure we are not seeing flukes. This is one major purpose of replication.

Our willingness to shade the results in our favor can be defeated by having someone else judge the results of our wishing experiments. Our eagerness to overlook "favorable" errors can be defeated by taking great care to avoid any errors at all; peer reviewers also help by pointing out such problems.

The other sources of error are harder to avoid, but scientists have developed a number of helpful *control* techniques. One is "blinding." In essence, it means setting things up so the scientist does not know what he or she is doing.

In the pharmaceutical industry, this technique is used whenever a new drug must be tested. A group of patients are selected. Half of them—chosen randomly to avoid any unconscious bias that might put sicker, taller, shorter, male, female, homosexual, black, or white patients in one group instead of the other—are given the drug. The others are given a dummy pill, or a sugar pill, also known as a placebo. In all other respects, the two groups are treated exactly the same. Drug (and other) researchers take great pains to be sure groups of experimental subjects are alike in every way but the one way being tested. Here that means the only difference between the groups should be which one gets the drug and which one gets the placebo.

Unfortunately, placebos can have real medical effects, apparently because we *believe* our doctors when they tell us that a pill will cure what ails us. We have faith in them, and our minds do their best to bring our bodies into line. This mind-over-body "placebo effect" seems to be akin to faith healing.

Single Blind.   The researchers therefore do not tell the patients what pill they are getting. The patients are "blinded" to what is going on. Both placebo and drug then gain equal advantage from the placebo effect. If the drug seems to work better or worse than the placebo, then the researchers can be sure of a real difference between the two.

Double Blind.   Or can they? Unfortunately, if the researchers know what pill they are handing out, they can give subtle, unconscious cues. Or they may interpret any changes in symptoms in favor of the drug. It is therefore best to keep the researchers in the dark too; since both researchers and patients are now blind to the truth, the experiment is said to be "double blind." Drug trials often use pills that differ only in color or in the number on the bottle, and the code is not broken until all the results are in. This way nobody knows who gets what until the knowledge can no longer make a difference.

Obviously, the double-blind approach can work only when there are human beings on both sides of the experiment, as experimenter and as experimental subject. When the object of the experiment is an inanimate object such as a wish machine, only the single-blind approach is possible.

With suitable precautions against coincidence, self-delusion, wishful thinking, bias, and other sources of error, the wish machine could be convincingly tested. Yet it cannot be perfectly tested, for perhaps it works only sometimes, when the aurora glows green over Copenhagen, in months without an "r," or when certain people use it. It is impossible to rule out all the possibilities, although we can rule out enough to be pretty confident as we call the gadget nonsense.

Very similar precautions are essential in every scientific field, for the same sources of error lie in wait wherever experiments are done, and they serve very much the same function. However, we must stress that no controls and no peer review system, no matter how elaborate, can completely protect a scientist—or science—from error.

Here, as well as in the logical impossibility of proof (experiments only fail to disprove) and science's dependence on the progressive growth of knowledge (its requirement that each scientist make his or her discoveries while standing on the shoulders of the giants who went before, if you will) lies the uncertainty that is the hallmark of science. Yet it is also a hallmark of science that its methods guarantee that uncertainty will be reduced (not eliminated). Frauds and errors will be detected and corrected. Limited understandings of truth will be extended.

Those who bear this in mind will be better equipped to deal with issues of certainty and risk.

Something else to bear in mind is that argument is an inevitable part of science. The combination of communication and skepticism very frequently leads scientists into debates with each other. The scientist's willingness to be skeptical about and hence to challenge received wisdom leads to debates with everyone else. A book like this one is an unrealistic portrayal of science only because it covers such a small fraction of all the arguments available.

Is Science Worth It?

What scientists do as they apply their methods is called *research*. Scientists who perform *basic or fundamental research* seek no specific result. Basic research is motivated essentially by curiosity. It is the study of some intriguing aspect of nature for its own sake. Basic researchers have revealed vast amounts of detail about the chemistry and function of genes, explored the behavior of electrons in semiconductors, revealed the structure of the atom, discovered radioactivity, and opened our minds to the immensity in both time and space of the universe in which we live.

Applied or strategic research is more mission-oriented. Applied scientists turn basic discoveries into devices and processes, such as transistors, computers, antibiotics, vaccines, nuclear weapons and power plants, and communications and weather satellites. There are thousands of such examples, all of which are answers to specific problems or needs, and many of which were quite surprising to the basic researchers who first gained the raw knowledge that led to these developments.

It is easy to see what drives the effort to put science to work. Society has a host of problems that cry out for immediate solutions. Yet there is also a need for research that is not tied to explicit need because such research undeniably supplies a great many of the ideas, facts, and techniques that problem-solving researchers then use in solving society's problems. Basic researchers, of course, use the same ideas, facts, and techniques as they continue their probings into the way nature works.

In 1945—after the scientific and technological successes of World War II—Vannevar Bush argued in *Science, the Endless Frontier* (Washington, DC: National Science Foundation, 1990) that science would continue to benefit society best if it were supported with generous funding but not controlled by society. On the record, he was quite right, for the next half-century saw an unprecedented degree of progress in medicine, transportation, computers, communications, weapons, and a great deal more.

There have been and will continue to be problems that emerge from science and its applications in technology. Some people respond like Bill Joy, who argues in "Why the Future Doesn't Need Us," *Wired* (April 2000), that some technologies—notably robotics, genetic engineering, and nanotechnology—are so hazardous that we should refrain from developing them. On the whole, however, argue those like George Conrades ("Basic Research: Long-Term Problems Facing a Long-Term Investment," *Vital Speeches of the Day*, May 15, 1999), the value of the opportunities greatly outweighs the hazards of the problems. Others are less sanguine. David H. Guston and Kenneth Keniston ("Updating the Social Contract for Science," *Technology Review*, November/December 1994) argue that despite the obvious successes of science and technology, public attitudes toward scientific research also depend on the vast expense of the scientific enterprise and the perceived risks. As a result, the public should not be "excluded from decision making about science." That is, decisions should not be left to the experts alone.

Conflict also arises over the function of science in our society. Traditionally, scientists have seen themselves as engaged in the disinterested pursuit of knowledge, solving the puzzles set before them by nature with little concern for whether the solutions to these puzzles might prove helpful to human enterprises such as war, health care, and commerce, among many more. Yet again and again the solutions found by scientists have proved useful. They have founded industries. And scientists love to quote Michael Faraday who, when asked by politicians what good the new electricity might be, replied: "Someday, sir, you will tax it."

Not surprisingly, society has come to expect science to be useful. When asked to fund research, it feels it has the right to target research on issues of social concern, to demand results of immediate value, and to forbid research it deems dangerous or disruptive.

Private interests such as corporations often feel that they have similar rights in regard to research they have funded. For instance, tobacco companies have displayed a strong tendency to fund research that shows tobacco to be safe and to cancel funding for studies that come up with other results, which might interfere with profits.

One argument for public funding is that it avoids such conflict-of-interest issues. Yet politicians have their own interests, and their control of the purse strings—just like a corporation's—can give their demands a certain undeniable persuasiveness.

Public Policy

The question of targeting research is only one way in which science and technology intersect the broader realm of public policy. Here the question becomes how society should allocate its resources in general: toward education or prisons? health care or welfare? research or trade? encouraging new technologies or cleaning up after old ones?

The problem is that money is finite. Faced with competing worthy goals, we must make choices. We must also run the risk that our choices will turn out, in hindsight, to have been wrong.

The Purpose of This Book

Is there any prospect that the debates over the proper function of science, the acceptability of new technologies, or the truth of forecasts of disaster will soon fall quiet? Surely not, for some of the old issues will forever refuse to die (think of evolution vs. creationism), and there will always be new issues to debate afresh. Some of the new issues will strut upon the stage of history only briefly, but they will in their existence reflect something significant about the way human beings view science and technology. Some will remain controversial as long as has evolution or the population explosion (which has been debated ever since Thomas Malthus' 1798 "Essay on the Principle of Population"). Some will flourish and fade and return to prominence; early editions of this book included the debate over whether the last stocks of smallpox virus should be destroyed; they were not, and the war on terrorism has brought awareness of the virus and the need for smallpox vaccine back onto the public stage. The loss of the space shuttle *Columbia* reawakened the debate over whether space should be explored by people or machines. Some issues will remain live but change their form, as has the debate over government interception of electronic communications. And there will always be more issues than can be squeezed into a book like this one—think, for instance, of the debate over whether elections should use electronic voting machines (discussed by Steve Ditlea, "Hack the Vote," *Popular Mechanics,* November 2004).

Since almost all of these science and technology issues can or will affect the conditions of our daily lives, we should know something about them. We can begin by examining the nature of science and a few of the current controversies over issues in science and technology. After all, if one does not know what science, the scientific mode of thought, and their strengths and limitations are, one cannot think critically and constructively about any issue with a scientific or technological component. Nor can one hope to make informed choices among competing scientific, technological, or political and social priorities.

Internet References . . .

Union of Concerned Scientists

The Union of Concerned Scientists is an independent nonprofit alliance of more than 100,000 concerned citizen and scientist advocates dedicated to building a cleaner, healthier environment and a safer world.

http://www.ucsusa.org/

Science and Technology Policy

The Federal Office of Science and Technology Policy advises the President on how science and technology affects domestic and international affairs.

http://www.ostp.gov/

SavetheInternet.Com

The SavetheInternet.com Coalition believes that the Internet is a crucial engine for economic growth and free speech and lobbies to preserve Network Neutrality.

http://www.savetheinternet.com

Hands Off the Internet

Hands Off the Internet opposes net neutrality legislation on the grounds that market forces are the next way to stimulate innovation.

http://www.handsoff.org

The Place of Science and Technology in Society

*T*he partnership between human society and science and technology is an uneasy one. Science and technology offer undoubted benefits, in both the short and long term, but they also challenge received wisdom and political ideology. They also present us with new worries, perhaps especially when they fall into the wrong hands. The issues in this section deal with whether public policy should follow science or ideology, whether access to scientific and technological information should be controlled, and whether commerce or freedom is a better foundation for regulation.

- Does Politics Come Before Science in Current Government Decision Making?

- Should Government Restrict the Publication of Unclassified but "Sensitive" Research?

- Should the Internet Be Neutral?

ISSUE 1

Does Politics Come Before Science in Current Government Decision Making?

YES: Union of Concerned Scientists, from *Scientific Integrity in Policymaking: An Investigation into the Bush Administration's Misuse of Science* (Union of Concerned Scientists, 2004)

NO: John H. Marburger III, from "Statement on Scientific Integrity in the Bush Administration" (April 2, 2004)

ISSUE SUMMARY

YES: The Union of Concerned Scientists argues that the Bush administration displays a clear pattern of suppression and distortion of scientific findings across numerous federal agencies. These actions have consequences for human health, public safety, and community well-being.

NO: Speaking for the Bush administration, John H. Marburger III argues that the Bush administration strongly supports science and applies the highest scientific standards in decision making, but science is only one input to the policy-making process.

T he history of science is also the history of struggle against those who insist—from religious, political, or other motives—that truth is what they say it is. Scientists insist on evidence and reason rather than creed or ideology, and the monuments on the field of battle between the two opposing forces include the tombstones of Galileo and Lysenko, among others.

Galileo Galilei used an early telescope to discover that Venus showed phases like Earth's moon and to find moons around Jupiter. The Roman Catholic Church, upset that Galileo's discoveries contradicted traditional teachings of the Church, demanded in 1633 that he recant. (See The Galileo Project at http://galileo.rice.edu/index.html.) Trofim Lysenko concluded that plants could be, in effect, trained to grow in inhospitable conditions. This view found favor with Soviet dictator Josef Stalin (whose ideology insisted on the "trainability" of human nature), who put Lysenko in charge of Soviet genetic and agricultural research and thereby set Soviet progress in these fields back by decades. (See http://www.wsws.org/articles/1999/feb1999/sov-gen.shtml.)

In the United States, science has enjoyed a very special relationship with government. Largely because science has generated answers to many pressing problems in areas ranging from war to medicine, the government has chosen to fund science with a liberal hand and, as well, to sponsor organizations such as the National Academies of Science, Engineering, and Medicine (http://www.nas.edu/) to provide objective advice to Congress and government agencies. Historically, the role of government has been to pose questions to be answered, or to offer money for research into specific problem areas. Government has *not* specified the answers sought or required that scientists belong to a particular political party or religion.

There have been exceptions. Robert Buderi, in "Technological McCarthyism," *Technology Review* (July/August 2003), reminds us that in 1954, J. Robert Oppenheimer, who played a crucial role in the development of the atomic bomb, was investigated for his opposition to the hydrogen bomb and for his "alleged left-wing associations." Oppenheimer lost his security clearance and was thereby barred from further work in his field. "Scientific McCarthyism" has become the term of choice for using a scientist's political or religious beliefs to judge their scientific work. It arises in connection with research into sexual behavior, AIDS, environmental science, and many other areas, notably where the conservative and religious right already "know" the answers the scientists seek in their research. (For example, do abstinence-only sex education programs keep young people from contracting HIV, or should they be taught about condoms?)

Another method of avoiding the scientific evidence and the need to make decisions that conflict with political or corporate agendas is to create the appearance of doubt. According to David Michaels, "Doubt Is Their Product," *Scientific American* (June 2005), "this administration has tried to facilitate and institutionalize the corporate strategy of manufacturing uncertainty," in part by putting industry representatives or industry-funded scientists on advisory panels. "Instead of allowing uncertainty to be an excuse for inaction," he says, "regulators . . . should use the best science available."

In February 2004, and again in March, the Union of Concerned Scientists (UCS) released a report that assembled numerous charges that the Bush administration had repeatedly and on an unprecedented scale used political "litmus tests" to choose members of scientific advisory panels, suppressed and distorted scientific findings, and otherwise tried to stack the scientific deck in favor of its policies, with important consequences for human health, public safety, and community well-being. In April 2004, the President's science advisor, John H. Marburger III, responded with a point-by-point rebuttal of the UCS report. He argued that the Bush administration strongly supports science and applies the highest scientific standards in decision making, but he also stressed that science is only one input in the policy process. He did not say that other factors can override scientific input, but that is an inescapable implication of his words.

Scientific Integrity in Policymaking: An Investigation into the Bush Administration's Misuse of Science

Executive Summary

Science, like any field of endeavor, relies on freedom of inquiry; and one of the hallmarks of that freedom is objectivity. Now more than ever, on issues ranging from climate change to AIDS research to genetic engineering to food additives, government relies on the impartial perspective of science for guidance.

—President George H.W. Bush, 1990

The U.S. government runs on information—vast amounts of it. Researchers at the National Weather Service gather and analyze meteorological data to know when to issue severe-weather advisories. Specialists at the Federal Reserve Board collect and analyze economic data to determine when to raise or lower interest rates. Experts at the Centers for Disease Control examine bacteria and viral samples to guard against a large-scale outbreak of disease. The American public relies on the accuracy of such governmental data and upon the integrity of the researchers who gather and analyze it.

Equally important is the analysis of fact-based data in the government's policy-making process. When compelling evidence suggests a threat to human health from a contaminant in the water supply, the federal government may move to tighten drinking water standards. When data indicate structural problems in aging bridges that are part of the interstate highway system, the federal government may allocate emergency repair funds. When populations of an animal species are found to be declining rapidly, officials may opt to seek protection for those animals under the federal Endangered Species Act.

Given the myriad pressing problems involving complex scientific information—from the AIDS pandemic to the threat of nuclear proliferation—the American public expects government experts and researchers to provide more data and analysis than ever before, and to do so in an impartial and accurate way.

However, at a time when one might expect the federal government to increasingly rely on impartial researchers for the critical role they play in gathering and analyzing specialized data, there are numerous indications that the opposite is occurring. A growing number of scientists, policy makers, and technical specialists both inside and outside the government allege that the current Bush administration has suppressed or distorted the scientific analyses of federal agencies to bring these results in line with administration policy. In addition, these experts contend that irregularities in the appointment of scientific advisors and advisory panels are threatening to upset the legally mandated balance of these bodies.

The quantity and breadth of these charges warrant further examination, especially given the stature of many of the individuals lodging them. Toward this end, the Union of Concerned Scientists (UCS) undertook an investigation of many of the allegations made in the mainstream media, in scientific journals, and in overview reports issued from within the federal government and by non-governmental organizations. To determine the validity of the allegations, UCS reviewed the public record, obtained internal government documents, and conducted interviews with many of the parties involved (including current and former government officials).

Findings of the Investigation

1. *There is a well-established pattern of suppression and distortion of scientific findings by high-ranking Bush administration political appointees across numerous federal agencies. These actions have consequences for human health, public safety, and community well-being.* Incidents involve air pollutants, heat-trapping emissions, reproductive health, drug resistant bacteria, endangered species, forest health, and military intelligence.

2. *There is strong documentation of a wide-ranging effort to manipulate the government's scientific advisory system to prevent the appearance of advice that might run counter to the administration's political agenda.* These actions include: appointing under-qualified individuals to important advisory roles including childhood lead poisoning prevention and reproductive health; applying political litmus tests that have no bearing on a nominee's expertise or advisory role; appointing a non-scientist to a senior position in the president's scientific advisory staff; and dismissing highly qualified scientific advisors.

3. *There is evidence that the administration often imposes restrictions on what government scientists can say or write about "sensitive" topics.* In this context, "sensitive" applies to issues that might provoke opposition from the administration's political and ideological supporters.

4. *There is significant evidence that the scope and scale of the manipulation, suppression, and misrepresentation of science by the Bush administration are unprecedented.*

Restoring Scientific Integrity to Federal Policymaking

This report calls on the president, Congress, scientists, and the public to take immediate steps to restore the integrity of science in the federal policymaking process.

The president should immediately request his science advisor to prepare a set of recommendations for executive orders and other actions to prohibit further censorship and distortion of scientific information from federal agencies, and put an end to practices that undermine the integrity of scientific advisory panels.

Congress should ensure that this administration and future administrations reverse this dangerous trend. To this end, Congress should: hold oversight hearings to investigate and assess the allegations raised in this report; ensure that the laws and rules that govern scientific advisory appointments require that all appointees meet high professional standards, and protect against the domination of such panels by individuals tied to entities that have a vested interest at stake; guarantee public access to government scientific studies and the findings of scientific advisory panels; and re-establish an organization able to independently assess and provide guidance to Congress on technical questions that have a bearing on public policy, similar to the former Office of Technology Assessment.

Scientists must encourage their professional societies and colleagues to become engaged in this issue, discuss their concerns directly with elected representatives, and communicate the importance of this issue to the public, both directly and through the media. And the *public* must also voice its concern about this issue to its elected representatives, letting them know that censorship and distortion of scientific knowledge are unacceptable in the federal government and must be halted.

Suppression and Distortion of Research Findings at Federal Agencies

> *Tinkering with scientific information, either striking it from reports or altering it, is becoming a pattern of behavior. It represents the politicizing of a scientific process, which at once manifests a disdain for professional scientists working for our government and a willingness to be less than candid with the American people.*

> —Roger G. Kennedy, Former Director of the National Park Service, Responding to the Doctoring of Findings on Yellowstone National Park.

Political partisans have long disagreed over each administration's politics and policy. But there is little disagreement about the need for elected and appointed officials to have access to rigorous, objective scientific research and analysis, and to fully understand its implications for addressing the problems they are trying to solve. To be sure, politics plays an unavoidable and, at times, valuable role in policymaking because many factors in addition to science and technology must be weighed in decision making. To make policy choices, government officials must frequently balance the needs of one constituency against another. Consider, for instance, the policy quandary over nuclear waste from the nation's nuclear power plants. Politics and science both play a crucial role as policy makers try to balance the risk to public health and the environment from the proposed spent fuel repository at Yucca Mountain in Nevada versus the long-term health risks to people living near one of the country's numerous current nuclear spent fuel storage facilities. In health care, decision makers must weigh the funding of research on rare serious diseases against broad public health issues such as funding cholesterol screening or childhood vaccinations.

There is, however, a crucial difference between political fights over policy and the manipulation of the scientific underpinnings of the policy-making process itself. Distorting that process runs the risk that decision makers will not have access to the factual information needed to help them make informed decisions that affect human health, public safety, and the well-being of our communities.

The following section details the results of a UCS investigation into numerous allegations that the current administration has undermined the quality of the science that informs policy making by suppressing, distorting, or manipulating the work done by scientists at federal agencies.

Distorting and Suppressing Climate Change Research

Since taking office, the Bush administration has consistently sought to undermine the public's understanding of the view held by the vast majority of climate scientists that human-caused emissions of carbon dioxide and other heat-trapping gases are making a discernible contribution to global warming.

After coming to office, the administration asked the National Academy of Sciences (NAS) to review the findings of the Intergovernmental Panel on Climate Change (IPCC) and provide further assessment of what climate science could say about this issue. The NAS panel rendered a strong opinion, which, in essence, confirmed that of the IPCC. The American Geophysical Union, the world's largest organization of earth scientists, has also released a strong statement describing human-caused disruptions of Earth's climate. Yet Bush administration spokespersons continue to contend that the uncertainties in climate projections and fossil fuel emissions are too great to warrant mandatory action to slow emissions.

In May 2002, President Bush expressed disdain for a State Department report to the United Nations that pointed to a clear human role in the accumulation of heat-trapping gases and detailed the likely negative consequences of climate change; the president called it "a report put out by the bureaucracy." In September 2002, the administration removed a section on climate change from the Environmental Protection Agency's (EPA) annual air pollution report, even though the climate issue had been discussed in the report for the preceding five years.

Then, in one well-documented case, the Bush administration blatantly tampered with the integrity of scientific analysis at a federal agency when, in June 2003, the White House tried to make a series of changes to the EPA's draft Report on the Environment.

A front-page article in *The New York Times* broke the news that White House officials tried to force the EPA to substantially alter the report's section on climate change. The EPA report, which referenced the NAS review and other studies, stated that human activity is contributing significantly to climate change. . . .

In a political environment now-departed EPA Administrator Christine Todd Whitman has since described as "brutal," the entire section on climate change was ultimately deleted from the version released for public comment. According to internal EPA documents and interviews with EPA researchers, the agency staff chose this path rather than compromising their credibility by misrepresenting the scientific consensus. Doing otherwise, as one current, high-ranking EPA official puts it, would "poorly represent the science and ultimately undermine the credibility of the EPA and the White House."

The EPA's decision to delete any mention of global warming from its report drew widespread criticism. Many scientists and public officials—Republicans and Democrats alike—were moved to decry the administration's political manipulation in this case. Notably, the incident drew the ire of Russell Train, who served as EPA administrator under Presidents Nixon and Ford. In a letter to *The New York Times*, Train stated that the Bush administration's actions undermined the independence of the EPA and were virtually unprecedented for the degree of their political manipulation of the agency's research. As Train put it, the "interest of the American people lies in having full disclosure of the facts." Train also noted that, "In all my time at the EPA, I don't recall any regulatory decision that was driven by political considerations. More to the present point, never once, to my best recollection, did either the Nixon or Ford White House ever try to tell me how to make a decision."

Were the case an isolated incident, it could perhaps be dismissed as an anomaly. On the contrary, the Bush administration has repeatedly intervened to distort or suppress climate change research findings despite promises by the president that, "my Administration's climate change policy will be science-based."

Despite the widespread agreement in the scientific community that human activity is contributing to global climate change, as demonstrated by the consensus of international experts on the IPCC, the Bush administration has sought to exaggerate uncertainty by relying on disreputable and fringe science reports and preventing informed discussion on the issue. As one current EPA scientist puts it, the Bush administration often "does not even invite the EPA into the discussion" on climate change issues. "This administration seems to want to make environmental policy at the White House," the government scientist explains. "I suppose that is their right. But one has to ask: on the basis of what information is this policy being promulgated? What views are being represented? Who is involved in the decision making? What kind of credible expertise is being brought to bear?"

Dr. Rosina Bierbaum, a Clinton administration appointee to the Office of Science and Technology Policy (OSTP) who also served during the first year of the Bush administration, offers a disturbing window on the process. From the start, Bierbaum contends, "The scientists [who] knew the most about climate change at OSTP were not allowed to participate in deliberations on the issue within the White House inner circle."

Through such consistent tactics, the Bush administration has not only distorted scientific and technical analysis on global climate change and suppressed the dissemination of research results, but has avoided fashioning any policies that would significantly reduce the threat implied by those findings. . . .

Censoring Information on Air Quality

Mercury Emissions from Power Plants

The Bush administration has long attempted to avoid issuing new standards to regulate mercury emissions by coal-fired power plants based on Maximum Achievable Control Technology (MACT), as required by the Clean Air Act. Mercury is a neurotoxin that can cause brain damage and harm reproduction in women and wildlife; coal-fired power plants are the nation's largest source of mercury air emissions, emitting about 48 tons annually.

As a prelude to the current debate, published accounts to date have documented that senior Bush officials suppressed and sought to manipulate government information about mercury contained in an EPA report on children's health and the environment. As the EPA readied the report for completion in May 2002, the White House Office of Management and Budget and the OSTP began a lengthy review of the document. In February 2003, after nine months of delay by the White House, a frustrated EPA official leaked the draft report to the *Wall Street Journal*, including its finding that including its finding that 8 percent of women between the ages of 16 and 49 have mercury levels in the blood that could lead to reduced IQ and motor skills in their offspring.

The finding provides strong evidence in direct contradiction to the administration's desired policy of reducing regulation on coal-fired power plants and was, many sources suspect, the reason for the lengthy suppression by the White House. On February 24, 2003, just days after the leak, the EPA's report was finally released to the public. Perhaps most troubling about this incident is that the report may never have surfaced at all had it not been leaked to the press. . . .

Distorting Scientific Knowledge on Reproductive Health Issues

Abstinence-only Education

Since his tenure as governor of Texas, President Bush has made no secret of his view that sex education should teach teenagers "abstinence only" rather than including information on other ways to avoid sexually transmitted diseases and pregnancy. Unfortunately, despite spending more than $10 million on abstinence-only programs in Texas alone, this strategy has not been shown to be effective at curbing teen pregnancies or halting the spread of HIV and other sexually transmitted diseases. During President Bush's tenure as governor of Texas from 1995 to 2000, for instance, with abstinence-only programs in place, the state ranked last in the nation in the decline of teen birth rates among 15- to 17-year-old females. Overall, the teen pregnancy rate in Texas was exceeded by only four other states.

The American Medical Association, the American Academy of Pediatrics, the American Public Health Association, and the American College of Obstetricians and Gynecologists all support comprehensive sex education programs that encourage abstinence while also providing adolescents with information on how to protect themselves against sexually transmitted diseases. In fact, a recent systematic analysis of pregnancy prevention strategies for adolescents found that, far from reducing unwanted pregnancies, abstinence programs actually "may increase pregnancies in partners of male participants."

The fact that the Bush administration ignores the scientific evidence, troubling though that is, is not the primary concern of this report. Rather, it is the fact that the Bush administration went further by distorting science-based performance measures to test whether abstinence-only programs were proving effective, such as charting the birth rate of female program participants. In place of such established measures, the Bush administration has required the government to track only participants' program attendance and attitudes, measures designed to obscure the lack of efficacy of abstinence-only programs.

In addition to distorting performance measures, the Bush administration has suppressed other information at odds with its preferred policies. At the behest of higher-ups in the Bush administration, according to a source inside the CDC, the agency was forced to discontinue a project called "Programs that Work," which identified sex education programs found to be effective in scientific studies. All five of the programs identified in 2002 involved comprehensive sex education for teenagers and none were abstinence-only programs. In ending the project, the CDC removed all information about these programs from its website. One scientist, recently departed from a high-ranking position at CDC, recounts that, on one occasion, even top staff scientists at the agency were required by the administration to attend a day-long session purportedly devoted to the "science of abstinence." As this source puts it, "out of the entire session, conducted by a nonscientist, the only thing resembling science was one study reportedly in progress and another not even begun." Despite the absence of supporting data, this source and others contend, CDC scientists were regularly reminded to push the administration's abstinence-only stance. As he puts it, "The effect was very chilling."

HIV/AIDS

Along similar lines, at the instigation of higher-ups in the administration, fact-based information on the CDC's website has been altered to raise scientifically questionable doubt about the efficacy of condoms in preventing the spread of HIV/AIDS.

A fact sheet on the CDC website that included information on proper condom use, the effectiveness of different types of condoms, and studies showing that condom education does not promote sexual activity was replaced in October 2002 with a document that emphasizes condom failure rates and the effectiveness of abstinence. When a source inside the CDC questioned the actions, she was told that the changes were directed by Bush administration officials at the Department of Health and Human Services.

Breast Cancer

Similarly, in a case *The New York Times* labeled "an egregious distortion of the evidence," information suggesting a link between abortion and breast cancer was posted on the National Cancer Institute website despite objections from CDC staff, who noted that substantial scientific study has long refuted the connection. After public outcry on the matter, the information has since been revised and no longer implies a connection. While the correct information is currently available on the website, it is troubling that public pressure was necessary to halt this promotion of scientifically inaccurate information to the public.

Suppressing Analysis on Airborne Bacteria

One particularly dramatic and well-documented case involves Dr. James Zahn, a research microbiologist at the USDA who asserts that he was prohibited on no fewer than 11 occasions from publicizing his research on the potential hazards to human health posed by airborne bacteria resulting from farm wastes.

Zahn's research had discovered significant levels of antibiotic-resistant bacteria in the air near hog confinement operations in Iowa and Missouri. But, as Zahn recounts, he was repeatedly barred by his superiors from presenting his research at scientific conferences in 2002. In at least one instance, a message from a supervisor advised Zahn that, "politically sensitive and controversial issues require discretion." . . .

Manipulation of Science Regarding the Endangered Species Act

A wide array of scientists, government officials, and environmental groups has charged that the Bush administration is engaged in a systematic attempt to weaken the Endangered Species Act. The administration has supported pending amendments before Congress that would make it harder to list threatened and endangered species, in particular by greatly limiting the use of population modeling. This technique is the most credible way to assess the likelihood that a small species population will survive in a given habitat. Perhaps most troubling, however, has been the way in which the Bush administration has suppressed or even attempted to distort the scientific findings of its own agencies to further its political agenda. These actions go well beyond a policy fight over the Endangered Species Act and represent a manipulation of the scientific underpinnings of the policymaking process itself. . . .

Manipulating the Scientific Process on Forest Management

In an incident involving the management of national forests, the Bush administration created a "review team" made up of predominantly nonscientists who proceeded to overrule a $12 million science-based plan for managing old-growth forest habitat and reducing the risk of fire in 11 national forests. This so-called Sierra Nevada Framework, which was adopted by the Clinton administration in 2001 after nine years of research by more than 100 scientists from the Forest Service and academia, had been viewed by the experts who reviewed it as an exemplary use of credible science in forest policy.

The Bush administration's proposed changes to the plan include harvesting more of the large trees, which may double or triple harvest levels over the first 10 years of the plan. Other changes call for relaxing restrictions on cattle grazing in some areas where the original plan significantly reduced grazing due to the potentially critical impact on sensitive species.

Forest Service officials justified these changes in part by stating that the original plan relies too much on prescribed burning and would fail to ". . . effectively protect the general forest areas from fire." Indeed, ecologically sustainable thinning that minimizes risks to threatened and endangered species may also be an appropriate tool for reducing risk of catastrophic fire in these forests. The Forest Service claims that these changes are "grounded in the best available scientific information." However, a scientific review panel put together by the Forest Service found that the revisions failed to consider key scientific information regarding fire, impacts on forest health, and endangered species. . . .

An Unprecedented Pattern of Behavior

No administration has been above inserting politics into science from time to time. However, a considerable number of individuals who have served in positions directly involved in the federal government's use of scientific knowledge and expertise have asserted that the Bush administration is, to an unprecedented degree, distorting and manipulating the science meant to assist the formation and implementation of policy. The following are accounts from a number of authoritative sources including political appointees from past Republican administrations, senior science advisors who have served both Republican and Democratic administrations, and long-term civil servants from federal agencies.

Disseminating Research from Federal Agencies

William Ruckelshaus, the first EPA administrator under President Nixon, and his successor, Russell Train, have spoken out about the matter. Specifically, Ruckelshaus told the press, "Is the analysis flawed? That is a legitimate reason for not releasing [a science-based analysis]. But if you don't like the outcome that might result from the analysis, that is not a legitimate reason." Train commented, "My sense is that, from the beginning of the Bush administration, the White House has constantly injected itself into the way the EPA approaches and decides the critical issues before it. The agency has had little or no independence. I think that is a very great mistake, and one for which the American people could pay over the long run in compromised health and reduced quality of life."

Scientific advisors to government also weigh in on this matter. Dr. Wolfgang K.H. Panofsky, a distinguished physicist who worked on the Manhattan Project and served on the Presidential Scientific Advisory Committee and in other high-level scientific advisory roles in the Eisenhower, Kennedy, Johnson, and Nixon administrations, states that the current administration has isolated itself from independent scientific advice to an unprecedented degree. Dr. Marvin Goldberger, a former president of the California Institute of Technology who has advised both Republican and Democratic administrations on nuclear weapons issues, compares the attitude of this administration to those he has served by stating, "Politics plays no role in scientists' search for understanding and applications of the laws of nature. To ignore or marginalize scientific input to policy decisions, where relevant, on the basis of politics is to endanger our national economic and military security."

According to Dr. Margaret Scarlett, a former CDC staff member who served in the agency for 15 years, most recently in the Office of HIV/AIDS Policy, "The current administration has instituted an unheard-of level of micromanagement in the programmatic and scientific activities of CDC. We're seeing a clear substitution of ideology for science and it is causing many committed scientists to leave the agency." Scarlett also points out that, "Ronald Reagan was very uncomfortable with the issue of sex education and the transmission of HIV, which was still largely stigmatized at the time. None-theless, with the help of CDC, his administration got factual information out to every household in the country about the problem. His actions stand in dramatic contrast to the sorry record of the current administration on informing the public about issues related to sex education and HIV transmission."

REP America, the national grassroots organization of Republicans for Environmental Protection, has also raised concerns about the administration's approach to scientific research: "Withholding of vital environmental information is getting to be a bad habit with the Bush administration."

Irregularities in Appointments to Scientific Advisory Panels

Donald Kennedy, editor of the journal *Science*, former president of Stanford University, and a former FDA commissioner, remarked in early 2003, "I don't think any administration has penetrated so deeply into the advisory committee structure as this one, and I think it matters. If you start picking people by their ideology instead of their scientific credentials you are inevitably reducing the quality of the advisory group."

Dr. D. Allan Bromley, science advisor in the first Bush administration, noted at a meeting of former OSTP directors that nominees are likely to face detailed questioning about their positions on issues ranging from global warming to stem cell research. "There are too many litmus tests," Bromley asserts.

Professor Lewis M. Branscomb is a highly regarded scientist who served as director of the National Bureau of Standards (now the National Institute of Standards and Technology) in the Nixon administration, vice president and chief scientist at IBM, and president of the American Physical Society. Dr. Branscomb recently stated, "I'm not aware that [Nixon] ever hand-picked ideologues to serve on advisory committees, or dismissed from advisory com-mittees very well-qualified people if he didn't like their views. . . . What's going on now is in many ways more insidious. It happens behind the curtain. I don't think we've had this kind of cynicism with respect to objective scientific advice since I've been watching government, which is quite a long time."

Dr. Lynn Goldman, a pediatrician and professor at the Bloomberg School of Public Health at Johns Hopkins University and former assistant administrator of the EPA, makes the same point emphatically about policymaking in the previous administration: "The Clinton administration did not do this. . . . They did not exclude people based on some sort of litmus test." She adds that this kind of activity represents "a threat to the fundamental principle that we want to make decisions based on the best available science."

Statement of the Honorable John H. Marburger, III On Scientific Integrity in the Bush Administration April 2, 2004

President Bush believes policies should be made with the best and most complete information possible, and expects his Administration to conduct its business with integrity and in a way that fulfills that belief. I can attest from my personal experience and direct knowledge that this Administration is implementing the President's policy of strongly supporting science and applying the highest scientific standards in decision-making.

The Administration's strong commitment to science is evidenced by impressive increases devoted to Federal research and development (R&D) budgets. With the President's FY 2005 budget request, total R&D investment during this Administration's first term will have increased 44 percent, to a record $132 billion in FY 2005, as compared to $91 billion in FY 2001. President Bush's FY 2005 budget request commits 13.5 percent of total discretionary outlays to R&D—the highest level in 37 years.

In addition to enabling a strong foundation of scientific research through unprecedented Federal funding, this Administration also believes in tapping the best scientific minds—both inside and outside the government—for policy input and advice. My office establishes interagency working groups under the aegis of the National Science and Technology Council for this purpose. In addition, this Administration has sought independent advice, most often through the National Academies, on many issues. Recent National Academies reviews of air pollution policy, fuel economy standards, the use of human tests for pesticide toxicity, and planned or ongoing reviews on dioxin and perchlorate in the environment are examples. The Administration's climate change program is based on a National Academies report that was requested by the Administration in the spring of 2001, and the National Academies continues to review our programs and strategic research planning in this field. The frequency of such referrals, and the high degree to which their advice has been incorporated into the policies of this Administration, is consistent with a desire to strengthen technical input into decision-making.

Statement on Scientific Integrity in the Bush Administration, April 2, 2004. Notes deleted.

Climate change has proven to be a contentious science-related issue. President Bush clearly acknowledged the role of human activity in increased atmospheric concentrations of greenhouse gases in June 2001, stating "concentration of greenhouse gases, especially CO_2, have increased substantially since the beginning of the industrial revolution. And the National Academy of Sciences indicates that the increase is due in large part to human activity." That speech launched programs to accelerate climate change science and technology to address remaining uncertainties in the science, develop adaptation and mitigation mechanisms, and invest in clean energy technologies to reduce the projected growth in global greenhouse gas emissions. In 2004, the U.S. will spend approximately $4 billion in climate change science and technology research.

The President created the new U.S. Climate Change Science Program (CCSP) to refocus a disorganized interagency activity into a cohesive program, oriented at resolving key uncertainties and enhancing decision making capabilities. The Strategy was heartily endorsed by the National Academies in its recent review. Their report, *Implementing Climate and Global Change Research— A Review of the Final U.S. Climate Change Science Program Strategic Plan*, stated "In fact, the approaches taken by the CCSP to receive and respond to comments from a large and broad group of scientists and stakeholders, including a two-stage independent review of the plan, set a high standard for government research programs. . . . Advancing science on all fronts identified by the program will be of vital importance to the Nation."

In this Administration, science strongly informs policy. It is important to remember, however, that even when the science is clear—and often it is not—it is but one input into the policy process.

Regulatory decisions provide the trigger for some of the most contentious policy debates. Science can play an important role in these policy decisions, and this Administration has sought to strengthen, not undermine, this role. In fact, the Office of Management and Budget (OMB) has for the first time hired toxicologists, environmental engineers, and public health scientists to review regulations and help agencies strengthen their scientific peer review processes. This increased attention to science in the regulatory process is providing a more solid foundation for regulatory decisions. As several recent examples demonstrate, emerging scientific data has prompted swift action by the Bush Administration to protect public health, strongly guided by advanced scientific knowledge:

- On May 23, 2003 the Environmental Protection Agency (EPA) proposed a new regulation to reduce by 90 percent the amount of pollution from off-road diesel engines used in mining, agriculture, and construction. This proposed rule stemmed from collaboration between EPA and OMB. Recent scientific data from the Harvard School of Public Health indicates that diesel engine exhaust is linked to the development of cardiopulmonary problems and also aggravates respiratory health problems in children and the elderly.
- On July 11, 2003 the Food and Drug Administration required that food labels for consumers contain new information on trans-fat content in

addition to existing information on saturated fat content. This rule, requested by the White House via a public OMB letter, responded to emerging scientific data indicating that intake of trans-fats (found in margarine and other foods) is linked to coronary heart disease.

- On December 29, 2003, the Department of Transportation requested public comment on ideas for potential reform of the CAFE program. Several potential reform ideas contained in that request for comment come directly from a 2002 National Academies report on the effectiveness of the current CAFE program.

Regarding the document that was released on February 18, 2004 by the Union of Concerned Scientists (UCS), I believe the UCS accusations are wrong and misleading. The accusations in the document are inaccurate, and certainly do not justify the sweeping conclusions of either the document or the accompanying statement. I believe the document has methodological flaws that undermine its own conclusions, not the least of which is the failure to consider publicly available information or to seek and reflect responses or explanations from responsible government officials. Unfortunately, these flaws are not necessarily obvious to those who are unfamiliar with the issues, and the misleading, incomplete, and even personal accusations made in the document concern me deeply. It is my hope that the detailed response I submit today will allay the concerns of the scientists who signed the UCS statement.

I can say from personal experience that the accusation of a litmus test that must be met before someone can serve on an advisory panel is preposterous. After all, President Bush sought me out to be his Science Advisor—the highest-ranking S&T official in the federal government—and I am a lifelong Democrat. . . .

Response to the Union of Concerned Scientists' February 2004 Document

I. The UCS' Claim of "Suppression and Distortion of Research Findings at Federal Agencies"

The UCS' Claims on "Distorting and Suppressing Climate Change Research"

- The UCS document claims that "the Bush administration has consistently sought to undermine the public's understanding of the view held by the vast majority of climate scientists that human-caused emissions of carbon dioxide and other heat-trapping gases are making a discernible contribution to global warming."

This statement is not true. In his June 11, 2001, Rose Garden speech on climate change, the President stated that the "[c]oncentration of greenhouse gases, especially CO_2, have increased substantially since the beginning of the Industrial Revolution. And the National Academy of Sciences indicate that the increase is due in large part to human activity. . . . While scientific uncertainties remain, we can now begin to address the factors that contribute to climate change." In this speech, the President cited the National Academy's Climate Change Science report that was initiated at the Administration's request, and launched a major, prioritized scientific effort to improve our understanding of global climate change.

Moreover, the President's Climate Change Science Program (CCSP) has developed its plans through an open and transparent process. In the development of its Strategic Plan, released in July 2003, the CCSP incorporated comments and advice from hundreds of scientists both from the U.S. and around the world. The CCSP Strategic Plan received a strong endorsement from the National Academy of Sciences in a February 2004 review, which commended the work of the CCSP.

- The UCS claims that the "Bush administration blatantly tampered with the integrity of scientific analysis at a Federal agency when, in June 2003, the White House tried to make a series of changes to the EPA's draft Report on the Environment."

This statement is false. In fact, the Administrator of the EPA decided not to include a short summary on climate change. An ordinary review process indicated that the complexity of climate change science was not adequately addressed in EPA's draft document. Instead, the final EPA report referred readers to the far more expansive and complete exposition of climate change knowledge, the Climate Change Science Program (CCSP) Strategic Plan. The Administration chose, appropriately, to present information in a single, more expansive and far more complete format. This choice of presentation format did not influence the quality or integrity of the scientific analysis or its dissemination.

- The UCS quotes an unnamed EPA scientist as saying that the Administration "does not even invite the EPA into the discussion" on climate change issues, and cites a previous Clinton Administration OSTP official, Dr. Rosina Bierbaum, as claiming that the Administration excluded OSTP scientists from the climate change discussions.

These accusations are wrong. The EPA, in fact, is a key participant in the development and implementation of climate change policy in the Bush Administration. The EPA participates in the development of Administration policy on climate change through the cabinet-level Committee on Climate Science and Technology Integration, which was created in February 2002. The EPA is also a member of subsidiary bodies, such as the Interagency Working Group on Climate Change Science and Technology, the Climate Change Science Program and the Climate Change Technology Program. (A table illustrating the Bush Administration's climate change program's organization can be found on page 9 of the CCSP Strategic Plan (2003)). Moreover, the EPA is a co-chair of the National Science and Technology Council's Committee on Environment and Natural Resources (CENR). CENR has oversight of and responsibility for the Subcommittee on Global Change Research. (This subcommittee holds the same membership and is functionally the same entity as the Climate Change Science Program, noted above.)

Dr. Bierbaum's claim refers to cabinet-level discussions that led to the development of the Administration's climate change organization described above. The cabinet-level discussions referenced by Dr. Bierbaum included numerous, respected Federal career scientists including Dr. David Evans, former Assistant Administrator for Oceanic and Atmospheric Research at NOAA, Dr. Ari Patrinos, Associate Director of the Office of Biological and Environmental Research at the Department of Energy, and Dr. Dan Albritton, Director of the Aeronomy Laboratory of Oceanic and Atmospheric Research at NOAA. Starting with these early discussions, the Bush Administration's climate change organization has fully involved climate change experts from throughout the Federal government.

As already noted, subsequent to its initial internal discussions, the Administration submitted the draft CCSP Strategic Plan to some of the Nation's most qualified scientists at the National Academy of Sciences for review. The Academy made numerous recommendations, which the CCSP incorporated. The CCSP then resubmitted its plans to the Academy for further review, and just recently, the NAS returned a highly favorable review. The Administration developed the climate change science strategic plan through an open, back-and-forth process. . . .

The UCS' Claims on "Censoring Information on Air Quality"

- The UCS claims that the Administration was withholding the publication of an EPA report on children's health and the environment in order to avoid the issue of mercury emissions by coal-fired power plants. The UCS also claims that the Administration suppressed and sought to manipulate government information about mercury contained in the EPA report.

This is not true. The interagency review of the EPA report on children's health and the environment occurred independently of the Administration's deliberations on mercury emissions from power plants. The interagency review process is the standard operating procedure for reports that include areas of scientific and policy importance to multiple agencies. As such, the report was reviewed by a number of scientists and analysts across Federal agencies. During this review, other agencies expressed concerns about the report. OSTP worked collaboratively with EPA staff on addressing interagency comments to make certain that the proposed indicators had a robust scientific basis and were presented in an understandable manner.

The report contained a statement that 8% of women of child-bearing age had at least 5.8 ppb of mercury in their blood in 1999–2000 and therefore children born to these women are at some increased risk. This information was available well before the EPA report both in raw form through the CDC and in an interagency analysis (CDC's Morbidity and Mortality Weekly Review, 2001) that indicated that approximately 10% of women of child-bearing age had blood mercury levels above the EPA reference dose, as opposed to the 8% level noted in EPA's report. The updated analysis in EPA's report and later published in the scientific literature (Journal of the American Medical Association, 2003) included an additional year of data and found the level to be 8%. These updated risk levels were used by the Administration in the preparation of its two regulatory proposals to reduce mercury emissions from coal-fired power plants.

The final report was released in February 2003, as soon as the interagency review process was completed.

- The UCS states that "the new rules the EPA has finally proposed for regulating power plants' mercury emissions were discovered to have no fewer than 12 paragraphs lifted, sometimes verbatim, from a legal document prepared by industry lawyers."

The UCS' implication that industry is writing government regulations is wrong. The reference here is to a preamble of a proposed EPA rule to control (for the first time) mercury emissions from power plants. The text in question is in the preamble, not the proposed rule itself. The preamble is intended to engage the public and encourage comments, including both assenting and dissenting viewpoints. All agencies, including EPA, openly seek public comment during rulemaking proceedings in order to obtain useful information and advice that is accepted or rejected or used in part.

Such direct use of submitted memoranda should not have occurred. However, the text at issue was taken from memoranda that were publicly presented to an advisory group made up of environmental activists, State officials, and industry representatives. These documents are openly available in the public docket. The UCS' allegations are based on text that had nothing to do with the integrity of the science used by EPA. . . .

The UCS' Claims on "Distorting Scientific Knowledge on Reproductive Health Issues"

- The UCS claims that the Administration distorted the U.S. Centers for Disease Control and Prevention's (CDC's) science-based performance measures to test whether abstinence-only programs were proving effective, and attempted to obscure the lack of efficacy of such programs.

This accusation is false. The UCS mischaracterizes the program, its performance measures, and the reasons behind changes that were made to those performance measures. There were no CDC science-based performance measures associated with this program. Currently, the Federal government funds abstinence-only education programs through the Health Resources and Services Administration, not CDC. The program was never designed as a scientific study, and so even if the original performance measures had been kept, little or no scientifically useable data would be obtained. However, other independent evaluation efforts are underway that *are* intended to address questions of the effectiveness of abstinence only programs.

- The UCS claims that a CDC condom fact sheet posted on its website was removed and replaced with a document that emphasizes condom failure rates and the effectiveness of abstinence.

This accusation is a distortion of the facts. The CDC routinely takes information off its website and replaces it with more up-to-date information. Recently updated topics include anthrax, West Nile Virus, and other health issues for which new information had become available. The condom fact sheet was removed from the website for scientific review and was subsequently updated to reflect the results of a condom effectiveness review conducted by the National Institutes of Health, as well as new research from other academic institutions. The condom information sheet was re-posted with the new information.

The "Programs That Work" website was also removed because the programs it listed were limited. CDC is exploring new and appropriate means to identify and characterize interventions that have scientifically credible evidence of effectiveness. In addition, CDC is currently working on a new initiative that is aimed at better addressing the needs of schools and communities by providing assistance in selecting health education curricula based on the best evidence available.

- The UCS alleges that information suggesting a link between abortion and breast cancer was posted on the National Cancer Institute (NCI) website despite substantial scientific study refuting the connection, and only revised after a public outcry.

This claim distorts the facts. The NCI fact sheet "Abortion and Breast Cancer" has been revised several times since it was first written in 1994. NCI temporarily removed the fact sheet from the website when it became clear that there was conflicting information in the published literature. In order to clarify the issue, in February 2003 a workshop of over 100 of the world's leading experts who study pregnancy and breast cancer risk was convened. Workshop participants reviewed existing population-based, clinical, and animal studies on the relationship between pregnancy and breast cancer risk, including studies of induced and spontaneous abortions. They concluded that having an abortion or miscarriage does not increase a woman's subsequent risk of developing breast cancer. . . . A revised fact sheet was posted on the NCI website shortly after the workshop reflecting the findings.

The UCS' Claims on "Suppressing Analysis on Airborne Bacteria"

- The UCS claims that a former Agricultural Research Service (ARS) scientist at Ames, Iowa, Dr. James Zahn, was prohibited on no fewer than 11 occasions from publicizing his research on the potential hazards to human health posed by airborne bacteria resulting from farm wastes.

This accusation is not true. Dr. Zahn did not have any scientific data or expertise in the scientific area in question. Dr. Zahn's assigned research project, as part of the Swine Odor and Manure Management Research Unit, dealt with the chemical constituency of volatiles from swine manure and ways to abate odors. In the course of this research, Dr. Zahn observed incidentally that when dust was collected from a hog feeding operation, some of the "dust" emitted from these facilities contained traces of antibiotic resistant bacteria. The recorded data were severely limited in scope and quantity, and did not represent a scientific study of human health threats.

In February 2002, Dr. Zahn was invited to speak at the Adair (Iowa) County Board of Health meeting in Greenfield, Iowa. Permission was initially granted by ARS management for Dr. Zahn to speak because it was thought that he was being invited to speak on his primary area of scientific expertise and government work, management of odors from hog operations. Permission for Dr. Zahn to speak representing the ARS at the meeting was withdrawn when it was learned that Dr. Zahn was expected to speak on health risks of hog confinement operations, an area in which Dr. Zahn did not have any scientific data or expertise.

The accusation of "no fewer than 11 occasions" of ARS denials to Dr. Zahn for him to present or publicize his research is not accurate. He was approved to report on his preliminary observations of dust borne antibiotic resistant bacteria at the 2001 meeting of the American Society of Animal Science and at a 2001 National Pork Board Symposium. He also was approved on numerous occasions to present and publish his research on volatiles and odors from swine manure. However, on five occasions he was not authorized to discuss the public health ramifications of his observations on the spread of resistant bacteria, because he had no data or expertise with respect to public health. Three of these occasions were local Iowa public community meetings; two others were professional scientific meetings.

- The UCS also claims that the USDA has issued a directive to staff scientists to seek prior approval before publishing any research or speaking publicly on "sensitive issues."

This is not true. USDA-ARS headquarters has had a long-standing, routine practice (at least 20 years) that has spanned several Administrations to require review of research reports of high-visibility topics (called the "List of Sensitive Issues"). ARS headquarters review, when required, do not censor, or otherwise deny publication of, the research findings, but may aid in the interpretation and communication of the results, including providing advance alert to others. The purpose of this review is to keep ARS Headquarters officials informed before publication and in an otherwise timely way of new developments on cutting-edge research, controversial subjects, or other matters of potential special interest to the Secretary's Office, Office of Communications, USDA agency heads (particularly those other agencies in USDA that depend on ARS for the scientific basis for policy development and program operations), scientific collaborators, the news media, and/or the general public. This practice deals with research reporting only and does not relate to the initial research priority setting process or to determining which studies will be undertaken. To the contrary, the "special issues" are mostly high-priority items and receive considerable research attention. . . .

The UCS' Claims on "Manipulation of Science Regarding the Endangered Species Act"

- The UCS claims that the Administration is attempting to weaken the Endangered Species Act.

This accusation is false. The current listing situation results from Fish and Wildlife Service (FWS) practices in place *before the Bush Administration took office.* The FWS listing budget is currently consumed by court-ordered listings and critical habitat designations. These court orders result from pre-2001 FWS decisions to list endangered species but not to designate associated critical habitat as required by the Act as well as to ignore pending petitions to list species. This practice resulted in a flood of litigation forcing FWS to act on petitions that had been languishing for years as well as to designate critical habitat for already listed species. Fulfilling the resulting court mandates expends all of FWS's listing budget (the Administration has taken steps to redirect additional funds to this budget account, and the President's FY05 Budget requests an increase of more than 50 percent). With respect to the critical habitat designations, officials from both the current and prior administrations have said that these lawsuits prevent FWS from taking higher priority actions such as listing new species. Moreover, without regard to the current court-driven budgetary situation, the number of new species listed as endangered during a particular time period varies over time for numerous reasons, and as such is not an appropriate measure of the success of the Act.

This Administration is committed to working in partnership with States, local governments, tribes, landowners, conservation groups, and others to conserve species through voluntary agreements and grant programs in addition to ESA procedures. For FY 2005, the President's proposed budget includes more than $260 million in the Interior Department budget alone for cooperative conservation programs for endangered species and other wildlife. The President created the new Landowner Incentive Program and the Private Stewardship Initiative grant programs to help private landowners conserve endangered species habitat on their property. In early March 2004, for example, Secretary Norton announced $25.8 million in cost-share grants to help private landowners conserve and restore the habitat of endangered species and other at-risk plants and animals. These grants are going to support projects in 40 states and the Virgin Islands.

Because the large majority of threatened and endangered species depend on habitat on private lands, this Administration believes it is vitally important that the Federal government provide incentives for landowners to engage in conservation efforts. The incentive programs implemented during this Administration have shown returns in the form of voluntary contributions of time and effort by landowners. These contributions provide far more to species conservation than the government could ever compel through regulatory action. This Administration is focusing on enhancing and restoring habitats of threatened and candidate species populations—thus keeping them off the list by preventing these species from becoming threatened in the first place. . . .

The UCS' Claims on "Manipulating the Scientific Process on Forest Management"

- The UCS claims that the USDA manipulated the scientific process on forest management, and used a "Review Team" made up primarily of non-scientists to "overrule" an existing forest management plan.

This claim is false. This case actually highlights how aggressive the Administration has been in using input from the scientific community to inform its forest management decisions. The UCS claim demonstrates a lack of understanding of the NEPA processes used to update the Sierra Nevada Forest Plan Amendment (SNFPA) Record of Decision. In fact, the Forest Service received over 200 appeals of the SNFPA and had to review and respond to them. To address these appeals, the Regional Forester (Region Five—California) established the five-person Review Team to evaluate any needed changes to the SNFPA Record of Decision. One scientist provided scientific support to this team. Once the Review Team completed its work, a Draft Supplemental EIS (DSEIS) was completed. This was developed using an interdisciplinary team of 31 people, which included four individuals with PhDs and nine additional individuals with master's degrees in scientific fields.

A Science Consistency Review (SCR) was conducted to assess the DSEIS from a scientific perspective. The Forest Service uses the SCR process infrequently and only when the additional level of thoroughness is judged necessary to ensure that decisions are consistent with the best available science. Controversy is not a consideration in the SCR process. The SCR is accomplished by judging whether scientific information of appropriate content, rigor, and applicability has been considered, evaluated, and synthesized in the draft documents that underlie and implement land management decisions. This SCR included 13 members, with 11 being scientists, nine external to the Forest Service and seven of these external to the government, including those from universities, the Nature Conservancy, and an independent firm. The results of the SCR were provided to a group of Forest Service professionals (including those experienced in NEPA, science, writing, and resource management) who prepared the final NEPA documents.

It would be highly unusual for all SCR comments to be reflected in the final NEPA documents, since these are prepared in the face of significant scientific uncertainty and a diversity of values. Nevertheless, the draft documents, the science consistency review, the response to the science consistency review, the responses to public comments, and the final SEIS are all available on the web so that scientific information used and the process that utilized this information is transparent. How uncertainty and risk are handled in the decision have both scientific and policy elements. In addition, a paper discussing the risk and uncertainty issues around the decision was developed by four additional university scientists. . . .

III. The UCS' Claims of "An Unprecedented Pattern of Behavior"

The UCS' Claims on "Disseminating Research from Federal Agencies"

Part III closes the UCS "investigation" and contains two sections—one on "Disseminating Research from Federal Agencies" and one on "Irregularities in Appointments to Scientific Advisory Panels." Here, the UCS does not provide a single instance of an actual suppression of agency research or an appointment irregularity occurring. Both sections consist entirely of quotations from various individuals and one organization.

Individual opinions are not actual events with facts that can be determined. With no context, one must assume these opinions are based upon the type of misinformation presented throughout the UCS document.

The stated opinions do not reflect the views of many outstanding scientists who have worked with this Administration. In particular, the National Academy of Sciences has been closely involved in various aspects of the Bush Administration's science policies. The Academy of Sciences has graciously accepted numerous requests to conduct research program reviews, and have gained first-hand knowledge of the Administration's commitment to independent scientific advice, a commitment that extends to all areas of science under Federal support. The most prominent example is the National Academy's review of the Climate Change Science Program's recently released Strategic Plan. If there has ever been an area of contention about this Administration's commitment to science, climate change science is it. Yet the Academy says about the Strategic Plan that:

> "The *Strategic Plan for the U.S. Climate Change Science Program* articulates a guiding vision, is appropriately ambitious, and is broad in scope. It encompasses activities related to areas of long-standing importance, together with new or enhanced cross-disciplinary efforts. It appropriately plans for close integration with the complementary Climate Change Technology Program. The CCSP has responded constructively to the National Academies review and other community input in revising the strategic plan. In fact, the approaches taken by the CCSP to receive and respond to comments from a large and broad group of scientists and stakeholders, including a two-stage independent review of the plan, set a high standard for government research programs. As a result, the revised strategic plan is much improved over its November 2002 draft, and now includes the elements of a strategic management framework that could permit it to effectively guide research on climate and associated global changes over the next decades. . . . Advancing science on all fronts identified by the program will be of vital importance to the nation."

POSTSCRIPT

Does Politics Come Before Science in Current Government Decision Making?

The Union of Concerned Scientists' report was followed by a number of press reports, including Jeffrey Brainerd, "How Sound Is Bush's 'Sound Science'?" *The Chronicle of Higher Education* (March 5, 2004), Eric Alterman and Mark Green, "The New Scopes Trials," *The Nation* (March 8, 2004) (which noted that "we risk an era of Lysenkoism in America"), and Andrew C. Revkin, "Bush vs. the Laureates: How Science Became a Partisan Issue," *The New York Times* (October 19, 2004). Robert Costanza, "When Scoundrels Rule," *Bioscience* (May 2005), notes in reviewing David W. Orr's *The Last Refuge: Patriotism, Politics, and the Environment in an Age of Terror* (Island Press, 2004), that "scientists abhor (as well they should) faith-based or politically driven conclusions to important questions of science and policy" and asks "But what happens when these rules of conduct are disrespected, as they have been in the last four years? What happens when religious beliefs and political power are allowed to influence science and policy?" See also Chris Mooney, *The Republican War on Science* (Basic Books, 2005).

In July 2004, the Union of Concerned Scientists published a riposte to Marburger's defense of the Bush administration's approach to science policy. *Scientific Integrity in Policy Making: Further Investigation of the Bush Administration's Misuse of Science* charged that "the White House document was filled with largely irrelevant information and arguments unrelated to the scientists' charges" and adduced new examples to support the UCS argument.

In April 2004, the U.S. Department of Health and Human Services (HHS) announced that henceforth, when the World Health Organization (WHO) invited scientists employed by the HHS (including scientists at the National Institutes of Health and the Centers for Disease Control), it could no longer send invitations directly to those scientists whom it deemed experts in particular fields (such as avian flu, carcinogenic chemicals, and SARS) and whose assistance it particularly desired. Instead, WHO must send invitations to the office of William Steiger, the HHS global health chief, who would then choose the appropriate experts. There was no suggestion that "appropriate" would mean anything other than scientific expertise, but Steiger did note in a letter to WHO that "regulations require HHS experts to serve as representatives of the U.S. government at all times and advocate U.S. government policies." See "Politics Manipulating Scientific Decisions, Recent Report Shows," *Nation's Health* (September 2004).

In the wake of the Union of Concerned Scientists report, as well as an earlier restriction in the number of government scientists allowed to travel to overseas scientific meetings on such topics as AIDS, there was immediate concern that the change in policy indicated an attempt to establish political control over what government scientists had the opportunity to tell the world. On April 28, 2005, the eleven Democrats on the House Science Committee sent a letter to the new HHS Secretary, Michael Leavitt, asking him to rescind or justify the "counterproductive" and "potentially dangerous" WHO-advisor policy (reported by Jocelyn Kaiser, "Democrats Protest Limits on WHO Advisory Panels," *Science* [May 6, 2005]).

About the same time, the Committee on Ensuring the Best Presidential and Federal Advisory Committee Science and Technology Appointments, of the National Academy of Sciences, National Academy of Engineering, and Institute of Medicine, published *Science and Technology in the National Interest: Ensuring the Best Presidential and Federal Advisory Committee Science and Technology Appointments* (National Academy Press, 2005) (see http://www.nap.edu/catalog/11152.html). This report stated that: "When a federal advisory committee requires scientific or technical proficiency, persons nominated to provide that expertise should be selected on the basis of their scientific and technical knowledge and credentials and their professional and personal integrity. It is inappropriate to ask them to provide nonrelevant information, such as voting record, political-party affiliation, or position on particular policies." The reason is simple:

> "The nation is in need of exceptionally able scientists, engineers, and health professionals to serve in executive positions in the federal government and on federal advisory committees. Such persons, when serving as presidential appointees, make key programmatic and policy decisions that will affect our lives and those of our children. Similarly, skilled scientists and engineers are needed for advisory committees to provide advice on the myriad issues with complex technologic dimensions that confront government decision makers. Our nation has long been served by its ability to draw qualified S&T candidates to government service because of the opportunities for intellectually challenging work that affects the world in which we live and that encourages and protects the scientific process. We must continue to enlist the best candidates for these important positions and ensure that the obstacles to their service are minimized."

Is science the only or chief factor to consider in making public policy decisions? John F. Kavanaugh, "The Values Vote," *America* (November 29, 2004), argues that there is a place for morality or ethics, but neither the Republicans nor the Democrats have suitable versions of either. Tibor R. Machan, "Faith and Public Controversy," *The Humanist* (May/June 2005), disagrees, arguing that resting public policy on faith "places it on wobbly foundations."

In December 2006, the Union of Concerned Scientists released a press release (http://www.ucsusa.org/news/press_release/10600-scientists-condemn.html) announcing that "A statement by Nobel laureates and other leading scientists calling for the restoration of scientific integrity to federal policy making has now been signed by 10,600 scientists from all 50 states. . . . The announcement came as the scientists' group released an 'A to Z' guide that documents dozens of recent allegations involving censorship and political interference in federal science."

ISSUE 2

Should Government Restrict the Publication of Unclassified but "Sensitive" Research?

YES: Lewis M. Branscomb, from "The Changing Relationship between Science and Government Post-September 11," in Albert H. Teich, Stephen D. Nelson, and Stephen J. Lita, eds., *Science and Technology in a Vulnerable World* (Committee on Science, Engineering, and Public Policy, American Association for the Advancement of Science, 2002)

NO: Ronald M. Atlas, from "Securing Life Sciences Research in an Age of Terrorism," *Issues in Science and Technology* (Fall 2006)

ISSUE SUMMARY

YES: Lewis M. Branscomb asserts that because the results of much scientific research have the potential to aid terrorists, there is a need to control the publication and distribution of "sensitive but unclassified" information.

NO: Ronald M. Atlas argues that voluntary measures now under development around the world will prevent misuse of life science research and help "avert government-imposed restrictions on information exchange that could be draconian in their impact."

The fall of 2001 was remarkable for two events. One was the al Qaeda use of hijacked airliners to destroy the World Trade Towers in New York City. The other was the still-mysterious appearance of anthrax spores in the mail. The two do not seem to have been related, but together they created a climate of fear and mistrust. Part of that fear and mistrust was aimed at science and technology, for the al Qaeda terrorists had used computers and the Internet for communicating with each other, and whoever was responsible for the anthrax scare obviously knew too much about anthrax. One response was the Bush administration's March 2002 declaration that some information—notably the results of scientific research, especially in the life sciences—might not be classified in the ways long familiar to researchers in nuclear physics (for instance), but it could still be considered "sensitive" and thus worthy of restrictions on publication and dissemination. The Department of Defence (DoD) announced—and promptly dropped—plans to restrict the use and spread of unclassified DoD-funded research. However, a National Academy of Sciences report on agricultural bioterrorism that contained no classified information was censored on the insistence of the Department of Agriculture "to keep potentially dangerous information away from enemies of the United States." National security experts warned "that the current system of openness in science could lead to dire consequences." [See Richard Monastersky, "Publish and Perish?" *Chronicle of Higher Education* (October 11, 2002).] However, many have objected to inventing and attempting to restrict the new "sensitive but unclassified" category of information.

In July 2002, researchers announced that they had successfully assembled a polio virus from biochemicals and the virus's gene map. Members of Congress called for more care in releasing such information, and the American Society for Microbiology (ASM) began to debate voluntary restrictions on publication. By August, the ASM had policy guidelines dictating that journal submissions that contain "information . . . that could be put to inappropriate use" be carefully reviewed and even rejected. The ASM policy has met surprisingly little active resistance, for though "New Antiterrorism Tenets Trouble Scientists," [Peg Brickley, *The Scientist* (October 28, 2002)], many researchers see the need for restraint. However, many say, there is a need for new rules to be very clear [see David Malakoff, "Researchers See Progress in Finding the Right Balance," *Science* (October 18, 2002)]. On the other hand, Charles M. Vest, in "Response and Responsibility: Balancing Security and Openness in Research and Education," *Report of the President for the Academic Year 2001–2002* (Massachusetts Institute of Technology, 2002), argued that openness in science must preempt fears of the consequences of scientific knowledge falling into the wrong hands. On October 7, 2004, the United Kingdom's Royal Society and Wellcome Trust released "Do No Harm: Reducing the Potential for the Misuse of Life Science Research," arguing for self-governance by the scientific community rather than new legislation.

In April 2002, the American Association for the Advancement of Science (AAAS) held its annual Colloquium on Science and Technology Policy. The papers in the resulting book [*Science and Technology in a Vulnerable World*, Albert H. Teich, Stephen D. Nelson, and Stephen J. Lita, eds. (AAAS, 2002)] included Lewis M. Branscomb's argument that because the results of much scientific research have the potential to aid terrorists, there is a need for government to control the publication and distribution of "sensitive but unclassified" information. Ronald M. Atlas argues that though anti-terrorism laws and biosafety/biosecurity regulations must be complied with, laws and regulations cannot keep up with the rapidly changing state of knowledge. Voluntary measures now under development around the world will better prevent misuse of life science research and help "avert government-imposed restrictions on information exchange that could be draconian in their impact."

YES

Lewis M. Branscomb

The Changing Relationship between Science and Government Post-September 11

The events of September 11, 2001 came as a great shock to the American people. But the anticipation of that day goes back a long time. Exactly 25 years ago Harvard professor Gerald Holton . . . describe[d] three kinds of terrorism. Type I is traditional terrorism by an individual or small group of people who are determined to wreak havoc for reasons of their own. It is not connected with any government. Type II terrorism is conducted by a dysfunctional state, unable to deal with the rest of the world through normal interstate relationships. This state engages in terrorism either against its own people or against others. Type III terrorism occurs when the Type I terrorist (a stateless terrorist group) finds that it can get resources and technical support from a Type II terrorist state.

We now face Type III terrorism. We must understand that the source of our vulnerability to terrorism is not the terrorists themselves. Our vulnerability is generated by our economic, social, and political systems. . . . If you have a highly competitive market economy, everyone is driven to greater efficiency. But the public also wants stability. Stability, with only small perturbations, is built into the system. But this does not work unless you have a peaceful, obedient society that does not threaten to exploit these vulnerabilities. This society cannot avoid threats to leverage that very hyper-efficiency.

University-Government Relationships

University-government relationships have changed with every major war. Before and during World War II, and even for some time after, everyone understood that you dropped what you were doing when your country needed you. The science and technology community was totally dedicated to defeating the enemy, which was known and identifiable. Everyone pulled together in the expectation of unconditional surrender by the enemy. The war would have an end point, after which there would be peaceful life and civil society again.

The Cold War was somewhat different, in that it was of indefinite duration. But it was similar because the opponent was a state, which was well-known and well-recognized. We produced an unresilient (but effective) strategy called mutually assured destruction (MAD). The military and foreign policy people had the responsibility to manage that problem. Society had to support it, but it did not really upset our civil life. The military-industrial complex ran the "war." Academic support was primarily through the basic research agencies (such as the Office of Naval Research, the Air Force Office of Scientific Research, the Army Research Office, and the Defense Advanced Research Projects Agency).

The war on terrorism is different. We have an unknown enemy in our midst, and the duration is indefinite. We are creating vulnerabilities all the time. Unless we do something different, it is going to get worse.

The universities need to support the nation in this war, building on their traditional values. But we need some significant changes. Catastrophic terrorism is the ultimate in asymmetric warfare. We depended on S&T [science and technology] to compensate for the asymmetry in the Cold War, when Soviet forces greatly outnumbered ours. We compensated by having our forces technically superior. But, now, each terrorist threat is in some ways a new war. Terrorists are technically competent and may be armed with weapons of mass destruction. To what extent can S&T compensate for this asymmetry? What is the role of and the effect on the universities? . . .

Countering Terrorism

There are three ways to counter terrorism. One, you can reduce the incentives that create and motivate terrorists. This approach clearly falls in the category of foreign and military policies, international relations and alliances, and intelligence. S&T can certainly contribute here, through technical means and gathering intelligence and through social science studies. The ideal solution would be to make this a peaceful world in which the number of individuals willing to kill themselves to destroy societies was greatly reduced. But that is very hard to do.

Another way is to detect and arrest the terrorists. This is essentially a police function. This may be the cheapest of the three, but it is the one that bears most heavily on civil rights and civil liberties.

The third way is to harden the target society, that is, make it more difficult for the terrorists to attack. We do this by detecting their preparations, intercepting their plans, making the targets less vulnerable, limiting the damage they can do, and enhancing the recovery. Industry has a role to play in this area. But we must motivate industry to reduce the vulnerabilities inherent in our society.

The Nature of the Vulnerabilities

We credit science and technology not only for creating an efficient economy, but also for creating the weapons that terrorists use. These weapons are based on the same technologies we use domestically for beneficial purposes. Our S&T

strategy to address this has to be very sophisticated. It has to use the very S&T that creates the vulnerabilities to lessen those vulnerabilities.

One of our biggest problems is that the critical elements of our infrastructure are deeply linked. When one part is attacked, we see a domino effect on the other parts. The three most obvious infrastructure elements are energy, communications, and transportation. If you bring down any one of these three, the other two are affected. For example, if you bring the energy sector down, you cannot communicate and you cannot travel. There is a lot you cannot do. Terrorists understand that, and we must deal with this reality. We have to consider the threat of multiple, simultaneous attacks on our infrastructure.

Another problem was brought on by deregulation, by getting the federal government out of the markets. Over the last decade, we have introduced more competition, particularly in the energy area, by deregulating. One result of that is a significant increase in vulnerability.

The threats are now more varied than simply the weapons of mass destruction. They include bioterrorism, chemical warfare, nuclear attack, and radiation contamination. All of these threats affect infrastructure issues. They come together in the cities where people are, because people are the targets. In cities we face the key issue of managing the warnings of an attack, as well as the attack itself. We also have to support the first responders.

And, finally, of course, our defense has to address the issues of intelligence and borders. One of the unfortunate characteristics of almost every feature of security and defense, whether security against crime or against minor acts of terrorism, is based on a single, thin wall. We try to check people coming into the country, but once they are legally in, they are in. We can put a fence around a critical facility, but if you can overcome it, you are in. That is characteristic of most of our systems, even in the computer area. Computer security has the same thin wall, and it does not work. We need a lot of technical tools to address this. They include sensor systems, data systems and networks, biomedical vaccines, chemical warfare treatments, and biometrics for efficient identification. Some of these involve cross-cutting issues and human factors-decision systems.

Terrorism, to a greater degree than any problem before, calls for a new way of thinking about the nature of the threats and how to deal with them. It calls for systems engineering and analysis. It calls for strategy-driven goals for the research program and the creation of new capabilities. Basic research will help us develop the strategy we need. It will not give us the answers to the current problem, but it will tell us how to change the questions.

Basic Research

Basic research, if it removes ignorance in critical areas, can give us a whole new way to approach this problem and make it easier to solve. That, in my view, is the critical role of basic research. But when you think about it, the government is not well-structured to do anything that is built on a systems strategy that cuts across all the current missions and areas of technical activity in the country. Countering terrorism is going to touch on every discipline in the universities, not just technical areas. Importantly, this time we have to pay attention to what the social sciences and humanities have to contribute.

Many different fields will need to address the many requirements of the war on terrorism. Developing sensors and dealing with hazardous materials will involve chemistry, physics, and engineering. Nuclear and radiological threats will be addressed by nuclear science. Bioterrorism will need the biomedical sciences and medical services. Threats against energy will be on the agenda of the physical facilities themselves, their infrastructure links, engineering, and information technology. Transportation and distribution are in the realm of engineering. Protecting our water, food, and agriculture will need people from biology and chemistry. Cyberattacks will be met by information science and engineering. Cities and people will be protected by the social and behavioral sciences. Infrastructure linkages will be taken care of by systems analysis and systems engineering people.

The political world has always been skeptical about the contributions of the social sciences and humanities. There are areas of which social science cannot give actionable advice, but there are many other areas where it absolutely can. Social scientists have studied the terrorism problem in great detail and have things to tell us that are very important.

R&D Capability and Mobilization

The big difficulty is that the government and the universities are "stovepiped," with different areas in technical work segregated into different organizations; financed by specific agencies. In the government, we do not have to create an S&T capability. We have fabulous S&T capability. It is nurtured by agencies born out of World War II and the Cold War. These agencies have massive capability to mobilize American science and technology. They are well-known: the National Institutes of Health [NIH], the National Science Foundation [NSF], the U.S. Departments of Energy (DOE), Defense and the National Aeronautics and Space Administration. These are big organizations devoted to a technical enterprise. But they do not, with the possible exception of the Department of Defense and some of DOE, have the mission of domestic security against terrorism. That mission is in agencies like the Federal Emergency Management Agency, the U.S. Customs Service, the Immigration and Naturalization Service, the U.S. Coast Guard, and the U.S. Department of Transportation. The latter is a technical agency, but it has never had a very strong research and development (R&D) capability. There are many other agencies, as well as state and local governments, in this situation. So the customers for science and technology are agencies with very little R&D experience.

Most of the U.S. R&D capability is in the hands of agencies that do not have the mission of countering terrorism. So how can we put all that together? When you go to the universities to get work done in physics, you know where to go. But if you want to solve a more complex problem, the universities are not internally structured, in most cases, to work on it. The implementation of any strategy depends on the federal government, which is capable of deploying most of the nation's capability (except that in the private sector).

We do not want to disrupt the present S&T capability. Instead, we are going to have to create an architecture for defining not only a strategy for using S&T in counterterrorism and managing its execution, but we also have to help the President manage that process. This requires linked-systems approaches and intersectional collaboration (involving the federal government, states, cities, and industry). It will be a challenge. We are not very experienced in this area. But most counterterrorism research must be interdisciplinary and in a systems context. We have our work cut out for us. As I said above, government science agencies tend to be stovepiped. Interdisciplinary work is hard to peer review. But many counterterrorism problems cut across agency lines. The university structure is also poorly adapted to a systems context and multidisciplinary work. We may need some institutional innovations, both in government and in the universities.

The universities have many resources. They have research capability for creating new options and competencies. They have links to local government and industry. They have access to students and colleagues around the world. And they have relevant capability in the social sciences and humanities. But the universities have needs too. They need more research resources. They need to continue to have access to foreign resources and students, the freedom to share technical information, and acceptable levels of security. They need to be able to admit students and collaborate with foreign scientists without irrational restrictions. And they need to be able to handle and deal with the very difficult and unclear question of how sensitive information should be handled in the research community.

Possible Effects of a New Strategy

Positive effects could come out of all this. . . . Important agencies of the government may learn how to use the research capacity of the country. We could also broaden the base of support, with new sources and levels of funding. . . .

[T]he right research strategy will benefit "dual use" technologies. We can define problems to address civil as well as security needs. For example, we could develop better ways to detect an infection prior to seeing clinical symptoms. We can also develop ways to make needed capabilities affordable. New probes and sensors that identify and track containers reduce costs in time and money in normal commercial shipping. This has wide application. We can also find new ways to deal with natural disasters. This would include advancements in communications, robotics, and even clothing for firefighters and hazardous materials specialists. We could also improve threat characterization for first responders. . . .

The good news is that basic research may emerge out of this to be seen as a strategic necessity. We may see a new balance between the physical and health sciences. Because the problem is so ill defined, we need an open-ended, imaginative, creative way of thinking about it. This will only come out of the basic research community, which has been substantially funded by the traditional civilian agencies (NSF, NIH, DOE, etc.).

The bad news is that as agencies re-label a large part of their programs as counterterrorism, they invite constraints. The research may be the same, but it may now be labeled as defending the country, and, therefore, critically important to national security. So Congress, knowing that the universities are so important, may put constraints on communication, publication, and the like, beyond what ought to be done. Legislation and agency policy may place information restrictions on grants. Indeed, counterterrorism is a preempting budget priority. So if you cannot re-label your program as counterterrorism, then that part of your budget may suffer. I hope this will not be the case.

We must look seriously at the government's inability to manage cross-cutting research programs. Counterterrorism requires a systems approach. The systems approach demands capability at the top level of government to develop national research programs. This will help with maximizing interdisciplinary research, but it is going to put additional burdens on the White House Office of Science and Technology Policy, the Office of Homeland Security, and others. But it is very important that we have a strong, visionary capability to lead the definition of how S&T can help in this area. If successful, we can apply this approach to sustainable development, climate change, and other areas that challenge our quality of life.

Control of Information

The control of sensitive information is a big issue. This is a quote from *The Economist,* which I think is very perceptive.

> Knowledge is power. Those who possess it have always sought to deny it to their enemies. . . . But exactly what knowledge needs to be controlled depends on who those enemies are. Nor is the control of knowledge without cost.
>
> A free society should regard it as a last resort. Scientists cannot build on each other's results if they do not know them. And governments are frequently tempted to hide not only what is dangerous, but also what is embarrassing. That can result in dangers of its own.[1]

Unfortunately, the present state of government controls on information is chaotic. The system of military secret classification is not adapted to the terrorist threat. The U.S. Department of Health and Human Services has no legal authority to classify information as "secret." This means that information that could be extraordinarily dangerous if it were publicly known to the terrorists is not protected. We have to protect this information in some way until the rules are worked out as to how this will be done routinely. The term "sensitive but unclassified" is likely to be applied to much university work, even though it has no clear definition. We see serious, legitimate dilemmas about what should, in fact, be published. Add to this the Patriot Act (PL 107-56), which authorizes intrusion into the Internet, servers, answering machines, and other telecommunication equipment. (It also requires colleges to turn over student records, and requires the National Center for Education Statistics to turn over data in response to a warrant.)

This poses the question, but it does not give the answer, of how this will be done. Ultimately, we need to resolve a lot of open issues with respect to the government's view of sensitive information.

Security and intelligence on university campuses is a much more difficult problem now than during the Cold War. Public interest in security lapses at universities, real or imagined, will be intense. Terrorist threats are extraordinarily diverse and of indefinite duration. The public will expect research universities to track students who may be perceived as threats.

Conclusion

I think the scientific community is going to have to engage in a long debate. It should have started before September 11 because this debate has to do with things besides terrorism. It has to do with the moral and ethical responsibility of individual scientists and engineers. We all must think about how they can relate our activity in science, our communication, and all the things we do in a way that we believe benefits the long-term public interest.

Must the culture of science evolve to discourage its misuse? If so, in what ways? Is there a consensus on the expectations scientists place on themselves now? I believe that thoughtful self-constraint is the only way to maintain the creativity of science and still protect the country.

Note

1. Secrets and lives. 2002. *The Economist,* March 9.

Ronald M. Atlas

Securing Life Sciences Research in an Age of Terrorism

The anthrax attacks that closely followed the 9/11 terrorist attacks helped create a sense that danger was everywhere. They also helped create a crisis for science. Government statements that the anthrax attacks had most likely been carried out by a U.S.-based microbiologist who had obtained the deadly Ames strain of Bacillus anthracis from a culture collection raised serious concerns about the security of potentially dangerous biological agents as well as the trustworthiness of scientists. The U.S. public began to take a dual view of the scientific community: capable of doing both great good (lifesaving medical treatments) and great harm (research that could be abused by terrorists).

In the five years since the attacks, the government has taken a number of sound steps to prevent the acquisition by terrorists of dangerous pathogens and toxins that could be used against civilian populations. It has also begun to deal with the more complex issue of how to secure new knowledge that could be misused to cause harm. In taking these actions, however, the government has raised fears among scientists that national security concerns will undermine scientific progress. So far, these fears have proven unfounded. Instead of a heavy-handed approach, the government has in large part supported a system of voluntary self-governance by scientists. Despite this, a significant part of the scientific community continues to oppose the additional government scrutiny for reasons ranging from a belief that it will not be effective to the larger concern that it could inhibit or even preclude scientific research that could lead to effective countermeasures against potentially dangerous bioagents.

But the potential for a more-intrusive government is not going away; indeed, there is a possibility, at least in the United States, that the government could become much more actively involved. We in the scientific community must work to ensure that reasonable laws are implemented and that the regulations imposed to date are fully complied with so that the government does not enact a regulatory system that isolates the U.S. life sciences community from its critical international collaborators. Most importantly, we must ensure that the self-governance structure works globally so that everything possible is done to minimize the risk that vitally important biological work could be misused to threaten public health or national security.

In the wake of the anthrax attacks, the government greatly increased funding for biodefense programs in a number of agencies. For example, the biodefense research budget at the National Institutes of Health (NIH) rose from $25 million in 2001 to about $1.5 billion in 2002 and is now being sustained at about $1.7 billion per year. Some of the funding is being spent to build the infrastructure needed to study infectious diseases, including highly secure laboratories. Other funds are being used to create a stockpile of vaccines and therapeutics.

Some critics have called the increased spending excessive, arguing that a biological attack is unlikely. Even if these critics were correct, this spending would still not be wasteful. In fact, it's likely to be highly beneficial, because much biodefense research complements the research that is being conducted to defend against naturally occurring infectious diseases. Biodefense research will help advance overall understanding of pathogenesis and the immune response, leading to the dual benefits of improved national security and enhanced global health. It is also highly likely that we will be better prepared to deal with a pandemic influenza as a result of investments in biodefense research. Because of the susceptibility of the world's populations to infectious diseases and the relative ease of bioterrorism, a continued investment in biodefense R&D is sound national policy.

Government faces a fundamental problem in trying to prevent dangerous biological agents from being acquired by terrorists: With the exception of smallpox virus, all other pathogenic microorganisms that are potential threats occur in nature. For example, anthrax occurs in African wildlife, and plague-causing bacteria are endemic to many animals, occasionally causing human infections. Cultures of these organisms are stored for research purposes in laboratories around the world, and there is always the possibility that they could be diverted for harmful purposes. Because it is impossible to eliminate these potential threats, the United States has sought to enhance the security of facilities that store them and to carefully control who has access to agents in quantities that can be used for bioterrorism.

Even before the anthrax attacks, there was a clear need to control access to dangerous human pathogens. In 1995, a member of the radical Aryan Nation tried to obtain Yersinia pestis, the bacterium that causes plague, from the American Type Culture Collection. At that time, there were no laws in the United States controlling the possession or domestic acquisition of dangerous pathogens, and for the most part, there was an openness and unquestioning willingness to share biological agents. As a result of the 1995 incident, practices for supplying microbial cultures to the research community began to change, with some collections refusing to supply potentially dangerous agents to anyone.

After the 2001 anthrax attacks, the federal government sought to establish a formal oversight system for the possession of microorganisms and toxins that could be used as weapons. Appropriately defined, such a system should ensure that pathogens and toxins would be available to legitimate researchers and denied to those who should not possess agents that could do mass harm. Initially, proposals surfaced that would have banned all foreigners from possessing the most dangerous pathogens in laboratories within the United States. Fortunately, such proposals were abandoned when it was recognized that such actions would isolate U.S. life scientists and impede collaborative research aimed at controlling infectious diseases and reducing the threat of bioterrorism. The aim of material-control efforts for the life sciences soon focused on ways to ensure that any individual given access to select agents was trustworthy and that these agents would be secure within each facility that housed them.

The USA Patriot Act of 2001 established restrictions on the possession of select agents only for people from countries designated as supporting terrorism and for individuals who are not permitted to purchase handguns. The act also made it a crime for a person to knowingly possess any biological agent, toxin, or delivery system of a type or in a quantity that, under the circumstances, is not reasonably justified by prophylactic, protective, bona fide research or other peaceful purpose. Even though terrorists may still be able to obtain biothreat agents from nature and from sources outside the United States, the prohibitions of the Patriot Act are appropriate measures that contribute to a web of protection. They are, however, subject to subjective determinations (for example, how to define what constitutes a bona fide reason for possessing a select agent) and hence are viewed with concern by some who worry about government intrusions into civil liberties and freedom of inquiry.

The provisions of the Patriot Act were subsequently incorporated into the Public Health Security and Bioterrorism Response Act, known as the Bioterrorism Act of 2002. This act added requirements for regulations governing the possession of select agents, including clearances by law enforcement. Clinical laboratories were granted a critical special exemption to permit them to legally isolate and identify (and thereby possess) select agents cultured from patients as part of the medical diagnostic process, even if they were not registered to possess select agents. This is essential for medical diagnoses in cases in which there is no way to predict what disease a patient might have, thereby precluding the ability to register for specific select agents. However, the clinical laboratories are mandated to destroy any select agents or transfer them to a registered laboratory that is permitted to possess that select agent within a few days, and they must also notify public health authorities whenever a select agent has been isolated and identified.

Because of the global distribution of pathogens that could be used for bioterrorism or biowarfare, it is also critical that other countries adopt appropriate regulatory oversight measures to ensure that individuals with access to agents that could be used for acts of bioterrorism are deemed trustworthy and that the agents are protected from potential misuse. The World Health Organization (WHO) has expanded its guidance for nations around the world to include biological security issues: "Security precautions should become a routine part of laboratory work, just as have aseptic techniques and other safe microbiological practices," according to the WHO statement. "Laboratory biosecurity measures should not hinder the efficient sharing of reference materials, clinical and epidemiological specimens and related information necessary for clinical or public health investigations. Competent security management should not unduly interfere with the day-to-day activities of scientific personnel or be an impediment to conducting research. Legitimate access to important research and clinical materials must be preserved. Assessment of the suitability of personnel, security-specific training and rigorous adherence to pathogen protection procedures are reasonable means of enhancing laboratory biosecurity. Checks for compliance with these procedures, with clear instructions on roles, responsibilities and remedial actions, should be integral to laboratory biosecurity programs and national standards for laboratory biosecurity." In essence, WHO has properly declared that the world's culture collections (biological resource centers) must not become mail-order sources for biothreat agents and that diagnostic laboratories must not carelessly become a source of bioweapons for terrorists.

As a result of the new U.S. laws, biological resource centers and individual scientists are now facing new scrutiny and regulatory requirements that limit their ability to supply certain microorganisms to research, educational, and domestic laboratories. Many members of the public and those in the security community see this oversight as prudent and a critical national security measure. Many in the scientific community agree that it is a necessary measure to retain the public trust. Others, though, feel that this scrutiny is ineffective and of little value, given that most of the pathogens of concern can be isolated from natural sources or are found in laboratories in developing countries that cannot afford biosecurity measures. Some in the scientific community believe that the imposition of biosecurity measures and the legal requirements imposed on the possession of select agents will inhibit the biomedical research needed for true biodefense.

In particular, many scientists object to the screening of researchers by the FBI that is now required in the United States in order to possess select agents. A few researchers have chosen to destroy their cultures of select agents rather than submit to the screening. There are also concerns that the restrictions will limit international collaborations in areas of critical biomedical research. NIH now requires that collaborative international projects meet the requirements of the select-agent regulations, including personnel screening and laboratory physical security and inspections.

The concern about potentially excessive regulations is heightened by the recognition that attempts to contain cultures of dangerous pathogens within biological resource centers will at best be imperfect, especially as advances are made in biotechnology. With synthetic biology, it is now at least theoretically possible to create virulent pathogenic viruses, including Marburg and Ebola. Although the select-agent regulations should be applicable to such genetic constructs, synthetic biology increases the possibility that terrorists could obtain bioweapons. According to an advisory committee of NIH, "Individuals versed in, and equipped for routine methods in molecular biology can use readily available starting material and procedures to derive some select agents de novo. It is now feasible to produce synthetic genomes that encode novel and taxonomically unclassified agents with properties equivalent to, or 'worse' than, current select agents. The rapid rate of scientific and technological advancements outpaces the development of list-based regulations, whereas policies and best practices can more readily accommodate new breakthroughs." Recognizing the danger, scientists, including pioneers in the synthetic biology field, have been working to develop a system of voluntary constraints.

Such voluntary systems of responsible conduct within the scientific community and commercial sector are critical components of the protective web against bioterrorism. This is especially true as the biothreats move beyond those pathogens and toxins that can be listed and subjected to regulatory controls. As pointed out in the 2006 National Research Council (NRC) report *Globalization, Biosecurity, and the Future of the Life Sciences,* "[We need to] recognize the limitations inherent in any agent-specific threat list and consider instead the intrinsic properties of pathogens and toxins that render them a threat and how such properties have been or could be manipulated by evolving technologies.' A broad array of mutually reinforcing actions, implemented in a manner that engages multiple stakeholder communities, will be required to reduce the biological threats facing society. To stay ahead of future biothreats, we need to enhance the scientific and technical expertise within the intelligence community and position the scientific and public health communities to respond appropriately.

To prevent future bioterrorism attacks, we will need to go beyond the issue of how to prevent terrorists from acquiring dangerous pathogens and toxins to the far more complex issue of the security of new knowledge that could be misused to cause harm. The fear that information from life science research might fall into the wrong hands has raised a great deal of anxiety within the scientific community and uncertainties among the public and policymakers as to how to balance national security with traditional scientific openness. We know now, for example, that the former biowarfare programs in Iraq and South Africa relied heavily on open-source literature to develop biological weapons. Both programs recruited some of the brightest graduate students in several different scientific fields and sent them to western universities for advanced studies, thereby subverting the graduate educational enterprise. There is legitimate concern that al Qaeda and other terrorist organizations or individuals could do the same, using the openly available scientific information available to them to plan and carry out a major bioterrorism attack.

Since the anthrax attacks, the most contentious debate has been over possible constraints on the use of unclassified information in the life sciences. Concerns were raised in the media about whether scientists were acting responsibly by openly providing information, especially in electronic formats, that could be misused. Some within the scientific community sought to eliminate the methods sections of the published literature so that experiments could not be repeated. Some openly asked whether there were areas of life sciences research that should be prohibited and/or specific scientific information that should not be communicated.

Meanwhile, the government has increasingly been restricting what it calls "sensitive but unclassified information." Information has been removed from Web sites and from public access in libraries. Despite the fact that the government still supports National Security Decision Directive 189, which states that research at academic institutions should be openly available to the maximum extent possible, some research contracts now permit the government to restrict the dissemination of information. Section 892 of the Homeland Security Act of 2002 requires the president to "prescribe and implement procedures under which relevant Federal agencies . . . identify and safeguard homeland security information that is sensitive but unclassified."

To try to deal with the pros and cons of changing the nature of scientific publication and related issues of communication within the life sciences, the National Academies held a workshop in January 2003, which was attended by members of the academic, security, and publishing communities. At a meeting of journal editors and publishers organized by the American Society for Microbiology that immediately followed, a statement was drafted in which the participants pledged to deal "responsibly and effectively with safety and security issues that may be raised by papers submitted for publication." It further stated: "We recognize that on occasions an editor may conclude that the potential harm of publication outweighs the potential societal benefits. Under such circumstances, the paper should be modified, or not be published." Several journals went on to adopt formal review processes. Some viewed such processes as self-censorship. Others considered them responsible citizenship. The controversy, however, did not disappear, perhaps because of the lack of guidance as to what constituted "forbidden knowledge."

The current situation is not the first time that life scientists have faced the challenge of assessing potential harm and the need to protect the public. The 1975 Asilomar conference, which was called to deal with concerns about recombinant DNA research, established the willingness of the scientific community to act responsibly to ensure that the emerging field of biotechnology did no harm. Responsibility for providing guidance to ensure the safe conduct of recombinant DNA research was subsequently assumed by NIH's Recombinant DNA Advisory Committee (RAC). The NIH guidelines were designed to ensure that any danger associated with a recombinant molecule or organisms was contained within the laboratory. Knowledge generated as a result of such research was to be freely disseminated. In contrast, in the current case of the threat of bioterrorism, the concern is largely focused on whether the knowledge itself might be dangerous and subject to misuse.

A 2004 NRC report, *Biotechnology Research in an Age of Terrorism*, tackled the critical question of how to define what is dangerous and how to design a system that contains that danger while allowing legitimate biomedical research to proceed in a manner acceptable to society. The NRC committee, chaired by Gerald Fink of the Massachusetts Institute of Technology, concluded that the release of some information could indeed be dangerous but that the United States should rely on self-governance by the scientific community to reduce the potential misuse of legitimate scientific inquiry and communication. The committee proposed a multistage system under which scientists would review experiments and their results to provide public reassurance that advances in biotechnology with potential applications for bioterrorism or bioweapons development were receiving responsible oversight. In essence, the committee adopted a bottom-up approach aimed at helping reduce the threat of misuse of the life sciences by mobilizing the scientific community to police itself.

In taking its self-governance approach, the Fink committee argued that government regulations work best when areas of concern can be objectively defined. Self-regulation was needed because one of the defining characteristics of potential dual-use research in biotechnology is the inability to set clear boundaries around the areas of concern. Because of this, the committee said, there is a need for extensive consultation between those trying to define the sphere of concern and those in the research community who can help figure out what is appropriate to be constrained. The committee recommended restrictions in only a very limited sphere of information in the life sciences and proposed a system modeled after the RAC to help guide the life sciences community.

The Fink committee concluded that research that would do any of the following would be a concern:

- Demonstrate how to render a vaccine ineffective
- Confer resistance to therapeutically useful antibiotics or antiviral agents
- Enhance the virulence of a pathogen or render a non-pathogen virulent
- Increase the transmissibility of a pathogen
- Alter the host range of a pathogen
- Enable evasion of diagnostic and detection modalities
- Enable the weaponization of a biological agent or toxin

The report did not suggest that research in these areas should not be conducted. Rather, it concluded that most proposed studies should go forward in an open environment because they likely would lead to the creation of beneficial knowledge. The report recognized, however, that some experiments might be readily misused and that those that might provide a roadmap for bioterrorists should be conducted in a classified environment or not at all.

The committee's proposed oversight system within the scientific community would have layers of filters that could help determine whether a particular study should be conducted and, if so, how the findings might best be published to avoid potential misuse. Journal editors and editorial boards would play a role in helping determine what information, if any, should not be published. Ultimately, the "secrecy" of information, though, would rest with the individual scientists who generated the data. Work in any of the areas where experiments might be of special concern would be subject to examination by institutional oversight committees to provide assurance that the benefits of that research would likely outweigh the dangers.

The type of system envisioned by the Fink committee has now been established at NIH. The National Science Advisory Board for Biosecurity (NSABB) will provide advice to federal departments and agencies on ways to minimize the possibility that knowledge and technologies emanating from vitally important biological research will be misused to threaten public health or national security. At the most general (strategic) level, the NSABB will serve as a point of continuing dialogue between the scientific and national security communities and as a forum for addressing issues of interest or concern. At the operational (tactical) level, the NSABB will provide case-specific advice on the oversight of research and the communication and dissemination of life sciences research information that is relevant for national security and bio-defense purposes. The NSABB has embraced both of these roles by developing generic guidelines for the definition of research of concern and offering case-specific advice (for example, on whether the papers on the reconstruction of the 1918 influenza virus should be published).

An important step taken by the NSABB has been to establish a committee that will refine the definition of "dual-use research of concern." This designation simply means that the research may warrant special consideration regarding conduct and oversight; it does not mean, a priori, that the work should not be performed or that the results should not be published. The committee has indicated that particular concern should be focused on research areas that are very similar to the Fink committee's list. The NSABB dual-use criteria are process-based rather than including categories based on specific organisms. It decided to specify that we must be concerned about agricultural as well as human pathogens. It included a category on enhancing the susceptibility of a host population. Because of concerns about the development of synthetic biology, it also added the generation of a novel pathogenic agent or toxin or the reconstitution of an eradicated or extinct biological agent as a dual-use category. Interestingly, though, it chose to omit as a concern enabling the weaponization of a biological agent or toxin. The NSABB did so presumably because it defined dual use as legitimate science that could be misused and assumed that legitimate scientists would not be involved in weaponization activities.

Recognizing that global security is at stake, scientists and policymakers are now working to establish worldwide voluntary measures to prevent the misuse of life science research, including the adoption of a code of ethics. These steps would contribute to the web of deterrence against bioterrorism and avert government-imposed restrictions on information exchange that could be draconian in their impact.

A common theme of the discussions to develop an ethics code is: First, do no harm. Beyond that, it is proving difficult to achieve consensus. However, a statement on biosecurity by the Interacademy Panel (IAP), a global network of science academies, provides key principles:

Awareness.   Scientists have an obligation to do no harm. They should always take into consideration the reasonably foreseeable consequences of their own activities. They should therefore always bear in mind the potential consequences—possibly harmful—of their research and recognize that individual good conscience does not justify ignoring the possible misuse of their scientific endeavor, and refuse to undertake research that has only harmful consequences for humankind.

Safety and security.   Scientists working with agents such as pathogenic organisms or dangerous toxins have a responsibility to use good, safe, and secure laboratory procedures, whether codified by law or common practice.

Education and information.   Scientists should be aware of, disseminate information about, and teach national and international laws and regulations, as well as policies and principles aimed at preventing the misuse of biological research.

Accountability.   Scientists who become aware of activities that violate the Biological and Toxin Weapons Convention or international customary law should raise their concerns with appropriate people, authorities, and agencies.

Oversight.   Scientists with responsibility for oversight of research or for the evaluation of projects or publications should promote adherence to these principles by those under their control, supervision, or evaluation and act as role models in this regard.

As recognized by the IAP, it is important that the scientific community assume responsibility for preventing the misuse of science and that it work with legal authorities, when appropriate, to achieve this end. Whistleblowing—the exposing of potential harms to authorities and/or the public—is an important ethical responsibility. Establishing a system of responsible authorities to whom concerns can be revealed and ensuring that whistleblowers can be protected from retribution, however, remain major challenges. Peer pressure within the scientific community will be needed to ensure full compliance with antiterrorism laws and biosafety/biosecurity regulations that are viewed by some as excessively restrictive and impeding legitimate science. Finally, further efforts to establish a culture of responsibility are needed to ensure fulfillment of the public trust and the fiduciary obligations it engenders to ensure that life sciences research is not used for bioterrorism or biowarfare.

POSTSCRIPT

Should Government Restrict the Publication of Unclassified but "Sensitive" Research?

$\mathbf{A}$ paper by Lawrence M. Wein and Yifan Liu, "Analyzing a Bioterror Attack on the Food Supply: The Case of Botulinum Toxin in Milk," on how terrorists might attack the U.S.'s milk supply and on how to safeguard it, was scheduled for the May 30, 2005, issue of the *Proceedings of the National Academy of Sciences* (*PNAS*) (see Lawrence M. Wein, "Got Toxic Milk?" *New York Times* [May 30, 2005], for an op-ed version of the paper). However, Stewart Simonson, assistant secretary of the Department of Health and Human Services, asked the NAS (National Academy of Sciences) not to publish the paper on the grounds that it provides "a road map for terrorists and publication is not in the interests of the United States." The journal put the paper on hold while it studied the issue; it appeared on-line (http://www.pnas.org/cgi/content/abstract/0408526102v1) on June 28, 2005, and in print in the July 12, 2005, issue of *PNAS*. The Department of Health and Human Services continues to believe publication is a mistake, for the "consequences could be dire."

In October 2005, scientists reassembled the deadly 1918 flu from synthesized subunits (see Phillip A. Sharp, "1918 Flu and Responsible Science" [Editorial], *Science*, October 7, 2005). In 2006, there were calls for authors, journal editors, and reviewers to do risk-benefit analysis before publishing "dual-use" work (see Yudhijit Bhattacharjee, "U. S. Panel Calls for Extra Review of Dual-Use Research," *Science*, July 21, 2006, and Robert F. Service, "Synthetic Biologists Debate Policing Themselves," *Science*, May 26, 2006). The relevance of the debate outside biology became clear when researchers omitted important details from a study of how a dirty-bomb attack could affect Los Angeles harbor (see Yudhijit Bhattacharjee, "Should Academics Self-Censor Their Findings on Terrorism?" *Science*, May 19, 2006).

It is a frustrating truth that science and technology offer both threat and promise, even in the context of terrorism. William B. Bonvillian and Kendra V. Sharp ["Homeland Security Technology," *Issues in Science and Technology* (Winter 2001–2002)] note that the need to detect terrorists before they can do damage requires "accelerated technology development and deployment." Yet the same science and technology, in the wrong hands, can aid the terrorists.

It is worth noting that "Even before the terrorist attacks of 2001, White House directives and agencies used the label SBU [sensitive but unclassified] to safeguard from public disclosure information that does not meet the standards for classification." [See Genevieve J. Knezo, "'Sensitive but Unclassified' and Other Federal Security Controls on Scientific and Technical Information:

History and Current Controversy" (Congressional Research Service Report for Congress, April 2, 2003).] Yet, says Ronald M. Atlas, ["National Security and the Biological Research Community," *Science* (October 25, 2002)], the controversy is far from settled and "is likely to continue until we have a national debate and reach consensus on how to balance the traditional openness of science with national security in the new age of bioterrorism." Early in 2003, the National Academies and the Center for Strategic and International Studies hosted a meeting that concluded researchers had better exercise self-restraint before the government imposes restraint. At the workshop, a group of editors and prominent scientists issued a "Statement on Scientific Publication and Security" that stressed that while both editors and authors bear responsibility to the public for the consequences of publication, scientific publication must include sufficient details for replication of the work; the very research that may be most helpful to terrorists is also likely to be most helpful to fighting terrorists; and when "on occasion an editor may conclude that the potential harm of publication outweighs the potential societal benefits . . . the paper should be modified, or not be published." [See Donald Kennedy, "Two Cultures" (editorial), *Science* (February 21, 2003).] In October 2003, the National Research Council issued a report calling for increased oversight of unclassified research with the potential to aid terrorists. Within a few months, one of the report's recommendations—a new advisory panel for the National Institutes of Health, the National Science Advisory Board for Biosecurity—was already being implemented. The government was "so far seeking only voluntary guidelines to control research and the dissemination of results that could conceivably aid bioterrorists." See Jennifer Couzin, "U.S. Agencies Unveil Plan for Biosecurity Peer Review," *Science* (March 12, 2004).

Are there other possible answers besides restricting—voluntarily or otherwise—publication of potentially hazardous work? John D. Steinbruner and Elisa D. Harris ["Controlling Dangerous Pathogens," *Issues in Science and Technology* (Spring 2003)] call for a global body that could oversee and regulate potentially dangerous disease research. When in March/April 2006, *Technology Review* published Mark Williams's "The Knowledge," which stressed the ominous implications of current knowledge and the ready availability of materials and equipment (DNA synthesizers can be bought on eBay!), it also published a rebuttal. Allison M. Macfarlane, "Assessing the Threat," *Technology Review* (March/April 2006), noted that turning biological agents of destruction into useful weapons is much harder than it seems and the real hazards are impossible to estimate without more research. For now, he thinks, it makes more sense to focus on more imminent threats, such as those involving nuclear weapons.

ISSUE 3

Should the Internet Be Neutral?

YES: Lawrence Lessig, from *Testimony before the Senate Committee on Commerce, Science and Transportation Hearing on "Network Neutrality"* (February 7, 2006)

NO: Kyle D. Dixon, from *Testimony before the Senate Committee on Commerce, Science and Transportation Hearing on "Network Neutrality"* (February 7, 2006)

ISSUE SUMMARY

YES: Law professor Lawrence Lessig argues that imposing network-access fees on content providers would unduly interfere with innovation in an important area of the economy. Building network neutrality into law would thus keep major network companies from imposing fees and slowing the economy.

NO: Kyle D. Dixon, director of the Federal Institute for Regulatory Law & Economics at the Progress & Freedom Foundation, argues that lacking demonstrated abuses, a network neutrality law would unfairly limit corporate investment and innovation and thereby reduce consumer welfare.

When the Internet was young—barely more than a decade ago—any content provider could send any kind of data they wished to any and all users. It was all bits—ones and zeroes—and from the standpoint of the computers or servers that accepted, transferred, and delivered the data, there was no difference between one stream of bits and another. The Communications Act of 1934, which regulated the phone companies that owned the wires over which almost all network traffic then ran, outlawed treating one kind of traffic or one source's traffic differently from any other. The result was that if one could figure out a way to turn a new kind of data into bits, or a new way to package the bits, or a new way to coordinate different bit streams, one could create a new business. It didn't matter whether one was a teenager in a bedroom in Indiana or a big business in New York. It also didn't matter whether the bits—or "content"—meant stock tips or porn. Everyone had a chance to innovate and make money.

The result was a virtual explosion of innovation. Today it is hard to imagine a world without e-mail, instant messaging, file sharing, Web pages, eBay,

PayPal, Google, blogging, MySpace, Monster, wireless connectivity, Web cameras, PDAs, Blackberries, Internet (VOIP) phones, and Web-enabled cell phones, among many other things. We have also gone from an Internet that ran on slow dial-up connections to one dominated by much faster broadband—DSL and cable—connections, which make it possible to deliver television and film over the Internet. Media and phone companies now deliver content, and at least some of them would like to facilitate the flow of their own content to their own customers and to interfere with the flow of content from other sources, unless those other sources pay a fee. Such a change has been likened to turning the open highway of the present Internet into a toll road. See Wendy M. Grossman, "Who Pays?" *Scientific American* (July 2006). At the same time, traffic on the Internet has increased tremendously, to the point where the flow of content is sometimes greatly slowed. Tom Giovanetti, "Network Neutrality? Welcome to the Stupid Internet," *Mercury News* (June 9, 2006), argues that a nonneutral Internet that gave priority to such things as VOIP (Internet phone) traffic from police and fire departments, 911 calls, and so on would be vastly preferable to a neutral Internet that did not.

Should the Internet be neutral? In the following selections, law professor Lawrence Lessig argues that imposing network-access fees on content providers would unduly interfere with innovation in an important area of the economy (fees on consumers who wish specific levels of service are another matter). Building network neutrality into law would thus keep major network companies from imposing fees and slowing the economy. Kyle D. Dixon, director of the Federal Institute for Regulatory Law & Economics at the Progress & Freedom Foundation, argues that a network neutrality law might be justified if the abuses that concern its proponents were actually happening, but those abuses are notably absent. Lacking demonstrated abuses, such a law would unfairly limit corporate investment and innovation and thereby reduce consumer welfare.

YES

Lawrence Lessig

Testimony before the Senate Committee on Commerce, Science and Transportation Hearing on "Network Neutrality"

Introduction

For the past decade I have been researching the relationship between technology and Internet policy, and in particular, the relationship between the architecture of the Internet and innovation. I am therefore happy to have the opportunity to address the question that this Committee is now considering—whether Congress should enact rules to protect network neutrality.

To answer that question, this Committee must keep in view a fundamental fact about the Internet: as scholars and network theorists have extensively documented, the innovation and explosive growth of the Internet is directly linked to its particular architectural design. It was in large part because the network respected what Saltzer, Clark and Reed called "the 'end-to-end' principle" that the explosive growth of the Internet happened. If this Committee wants to preserve that growth and innovation, it should take steps to protect this fundamental design.

In my view, the most important action that this government has taken to preserve the Internet's end-to-end design was the decision by Chairman Michael Powell to commit the FCC to enforce what he referred to as the Internet's four "Internet Freedoms." Building upon an idea first presented to this Committee by Microsoft's Craig Mundie in 2002, these "Internet Freedoms" established for the first time a federal policy to assure that network owners don't deploy technologies that weaken the environment for innovation that the Internet initially created. Those principles were relied upon by the FCC when it stopped DSL provider Madison River Communications from blocking Voice-over-IP services. That enforcement action sent a clear message to network providers that the Internet that they could offer must continue to respect the innovation-promoting design of end-to-end.

It is my view that Congress should ratify Powell's "Internet Freedoms," making them a part of the FCC's basic law. However, in the time since Chairman

From Testimony before the Senate Committee on Commerce, Science and Transportation Hearing on Network Neutrality, February 7, 2006.

Powell announced these principles, it has become clear that they are missing one important requirement. The now openly-stated intentions of AT&T and others to introduce access-tiering to the Internet threatens to undermine application competition on the Internet. Congress should act to avoid that result.

Access-tiering will create an obvious incentive among the effective duopoly that now provides broadband service to most Americans. By effectively auctioning off lanes of broadband service, this form of tiering will restrict the opportunity of many to compete in providing new Internet service. For example, there are many new user generated video services on the Internet, such as Google Video, YouAre.TV, and youTube.com. The incentives in a world of access-tiering would be to auction to the highest bidders the quality of service necessary to support video service, and leave to the rest insufficient bandwidth to compete. That may benefit established companies, but it will only burden new innovators.

To oppose access-tiering, however, is not to oppose all tiering. I believe, for example, that consumer-tiering should be encouraged. Network providers need incentives to build better broadband services. Consumer-tiering would provide those incentives.

Consumer-tiering, however, should not discriminate among content or application providers. There's nothing wrong with network owners saying "we'll guarantee fast video service on your broadband account." There is something wrong with network owners saying "we'll guarantee fast video service from NBC on your broadband account." And there is something especially wrong with network owners telling content or service providers that they can't access a meaningful broadband network unless they pay an access-tax.

I don't mean "wrong" in the sense of immoral, or even unfair. My argument is not about the social justice of Internet access. I mean "wrong" in the sense that such a policy will inevitably weaken application competition on the Internet, and that in turn will weaken Internet growth.

The Internet's growth is a crucial part of the Nation's economic growth. In my view, Congress should take steps to assure that the current concentration in broadband access does not translate into reduced application competition on the Internet. A "network neutrality" policy that combined Chairman Powell's "Internet Freedoms" with a requirement that network providers secure a level of basic internet service with only consumer-tiering would, in my view, promote that growth.

I. The End-to-End Internet Inspired A Wide Range of Innovation

The Internet has inspired a wide range of innovation. Because of its particular architectural design, that innovation has come primarily from the "edge" or "end" of the network through application competition. As network architects Jerome Saltzer, David Clark, and David Reed describe, the original Internet embraced an "end-to-end" design, meaning the network itself was to be as simple as possible, with intelligence for the network provided by applications that connected at the edge of the network.

One consequence of this design is that early network providers couldn't easily control the application innovation that happened upon their networks. That in turn meant that innovation for these network could come from many who had no real connection to the owners of the physical network itself. Indeed, if you consider some of the most important innovations in this history of the Internet—from the development of the World Wide Web by a Swiss researcher at CERN, to the first peer-to-peer instant messaging chat service, ICQ, developed by a young Israeli, to the first web based (or HTML-based) email, HoTMaiL, developed by an Indian immigrant—these are all innovations by kids or non-Americans: outsiders to the network owners.

This diversity of innovators is no accident. By minimizing the control by the network itself, the "end-to-end" design maximizes the range of competitors who can innovate for the network. Rather than concentrating the right to innovate in a few network owners, the right to innovate is open to anyone, anywhere. That architecture, in turn, has created an astonishing range of important and economically valuable innovation. Here, as in many other contexts, competition has produced growth. And that competition was assured by the network's design.

II. Concentrations in Broadband Access Threaten That End-to-End Neutrality

It was the assumption of many (including me) that competition in broadband access would prevent any compromise in end-to-end neutrality. That was the premise of the "open access" requirement imposed upon telecom providers. The assumption was that in a competitive market, no individual ISP would have the market power to successfully restrict the range of Internet applications. "Open access" thus sought to establish a competitive ISP market, which in turn was thought would protect network neutrality.

This assumption about competition protecting end-to-end neutrality has been drawn into doubt by recent scholarship. But given the increasing concentration in broadband provision, the question whether ISP competition could protect end-to-end neutrality is now effectively moot. Whether or not competition among ISPs is enough, America no longer has sufficient broadband ISP competition. In most markets, an effective duopoly controls access to high speed Internet.

This concentration has now led network owners to openly advocate changes in network policy designed to vest new control in the network owner over the applications and content that flow over their network. In the United States, there have been isolated incidents, for example, of DSL providers blocking Voice-Over-IP (VOIP) services. That policy has become the rule in a number of foreign jurisdictions. And as recently reported, network owners in the United States and Canada are now discussing adding access-tiering to their networks.

These changes, if allowed, would fundamentally alter the environment for innovation on the Internet. With a network that embeds the principle of end-to-end, there is no danger that an innovator's application or content will be blocked by the network owner. Consumers might not like the innovation. That risk is unavoidable. But an end-to-end network removes the risk that the network owner will interfere with an innovation, either because it competes with the network owners own business (e.g., VOIP), or because the owner wants to extract payment from the innovator. This threat-free environment induces more application innovation.

If the principle of end-to-end is abandoned, however, then innovators must now include in their calculation of risk the threat that the network owner might either block or tax a particular application. That increased risk will reduce application investment.

III. Powell's "Internet Freedoms" Are A Critical, Though Incomplete, Defense of Network Neutrality

This concern about the costs to innovation caused by network owners is not new. Since the 1996 Telecom Act, the FCC had been struggling to formulate policy that balanced both the need for new broadband investment against the risk that broadband operators would exercise too much control over network innovation. Former FCC Chairman Michael Powell finally resolved that policy struggle in February, 2004. In a speech given in Boulder, he outlined four principles that he promised would guide FCC policy. As Chairman Powell described, these "Internet Freedoms" were:

> (1) Freedom to Access Content. First, consumers should have access to their choice of legal content.

> Consumers have come to expect to be able to go where they want on high-speed connections, and those who have migrated from dial-up would presumably object to paying a premium for broadband if certain content were blocked. Thus, I challenge all facets of the industry to commit to allowing consumers to reach the content of their choice. I recognize that network operators have a legitimate need to manage their networks and ensure a quality experience, thus reasonable limits sometimes must be placed in service contracts. Such restraints, however, should be clearly spelled out and should be as minimal as necessary.

> (2) Freedom to Use Applications. [C]onsumers should be able to run applications of their choice.

> As with access to content, consumers have come to expect that they can generally run whatever applications they want. Again, such applications are critical to continuing the digital broadband migration because they can drive the demand that fuels deployment. Applications developers must remain confident that their products will continue to work without interference from other companies. No one can know for sure which "killer" applications will emerge to drive deployment of the next generation high-speed technologies. Thus, I challenge all facets of the industry to let the

market work and allow consumers to run applications unless they exceed service plan limitations or harm the provider's network.

(3) Freedom to Attach Personal Devices. [C]onsumers should be permitted to attach any devices they choose to the connection in their homes.

Because devices give consumers more choice, value and personalization with respect to how they use their highspeed connections, they are critical to the future of broadband. Thus, I challenge all facets of the industry to permit consumers to attach any devices they choose to their broadband connection, so long as the devices operate within service plan limitations and do not harm the provider's network or enable theft of service.

(4) Freedom to Obtain Service Plan Information. [C]onsumers should receive meaningful information regarding their service plans.

Simply put, such information is necessary to ensure that the market is working. Providers have every right to offer a variety of service tiers with varying bandwidth and feature options. Consumers need to know about these choices as well as whether and how their service plans protect them against spam, spyware and other potential invasions of privacy.

Powell's speech was an indication about enforcement strategy. In March, 2005, that strategy was demonstrated. In an extraordinarily swift manner, the FCC succeeded in securing a settlement with a DSL provider, Madison River Communications. That company had allegedly blocked VOIP on their DSL lines. In the settlement, Madison River agreed it would not use its power over the network to block legal applications on the network.

Powell's strategy, in my view, was a perfect mix of carrot and stick. His aim was to signal to network providers the kind of network service they could provide without fear of FCC intervention. But the Madison River case demonstrated that Powell's FCC would not hesitate to intervene when these basic principles were violated. Network providers thus knew the kind of business model that would steer clear of the FCC. That had an important effect upon investment incentives—both of network providers, and of application developers.

There is, however, one important hole in the "Internet Freedoms" that Powell articulated. And that risk is revealed in the recently revealed intentions of major network providers to begin to implement access-tiering for content and service providers on the Internet.

The motivation behind this sort of tiering is perfectly understandable. Network providers now have significant market power in the broadband market. They aim to leverage that power to maximize revenue. No doubt, some of that revenue will support new network provisioning. That provisioning will of course benefit everyone to the extent it increases the spread of broadband service.

But this form of tiering will also have consequences for the market for application and content innovation. That danger can be seen in a simple hypothetical.

Imagine a network owner with the ability to provision a network that is providing 6 Mbps to its customers. Initially, that capacity is the effective space for broadband application competition. Imagine then that the network begins to offer "speed lanes" to particular video providers. These channels effectively reduce the capacity for broadband application competition. In this context, video providers have the incentive both to secure for themselves sufficient bandwidth to guarantee quality service, and the incentive to guarantee that no one else, or at least, no one not paying the access fee, be able to provide that network service. Thus, working with the network provider, large video companies could secure sufficient provisioning to enable their content to be served while leaving insufficient bandwidth to other competitors.

Thus, for example, there are many new user-generated video sites appearing on the Internet. Google has one such site—Google Video—but others are being created by traditional Internet startups. Thus, youTube.com and YouAre.tv are two competitors to Google that are developing similar services to the Google Video service.

In a world with access-tiering, companies like Google in this context would have an incentive to secure sufficient bandwidth to enable its services while leaving competitors without enough bandwidth for their own. Access-tiering would thus become another barrier to entry for competitors, reducing application or content competition on the Internet.

This would represent a fundamental change in the environment for innovation on the Internet. For the first time, network owners would have a strategic capability, as well as incentive, to create barriers to entry for new innovators. We should remember that the current leaders in Internet innovation all began with essentially nothing. Google, eBay, Yahoo! and Amazon all started as simple websites providing limited, but fantastic, services. They had to pay no special access-tax to be on the Internet; there was no special channeling by Internet providers that disadvantage these competitors relative to any others. They succeeded because the product they offered was better than others. Competition on the merits thus drove this market.

That competition would be threatened by access-tiering. Existing content providers have an incentive to block competitors; access-tiering would be a means to effect that competitive advantage. And while these actions might not rise to the level of an antitrust violation, it is perfectly appropriate for Congress to select a network policy that it believes would maximize innovation and growth for the Nation. Adding toll booths to the Internet may well benefit those who own the roads; but it won't benefit application and content competition on the Internet, both of which drive economic growth.

To oppose access-tiering, however, is not to oppose all tiering. It is certainly valuable for network providers to offer consumers different tiers of service. Such differentiation will create incentives for network providers to improve network performance. The currently abysmal record of broadband provision in the United States demonstrates that they certainly need more incentives. Consumer-tiering could well provide more incentives.

But consumer-tiering would not create any of the anticompetitive effects that access-tiering would. So long as network owners offered neutral tiering—for example, offering high speed for video content, or simply higher speed for large file transfers—that "discrimination" would not harm application competition. The diversity of consumer wants would produce a general demand for faster, cheaper Internet service. That general demand would benefit application competition generally.

IV. Congress Should Ratify Powell's "Internet Freedoms" Along With A Restriction On Access-Tiering

In light of this emerging threat to application and content innovation, it is my view that Congress should enact legislation that clearly establishes the competitive baseline for broadband service in America. That legislation should first ratify Chairman Powell's "Internet Freedoms." These principles are an essential element to any "network neutrality" policy.

But in addition to these "Internet Freedoms," Congress should act to avoid the competitive costs that access-tiering could produce. There are two ways in which Congress could respond to this threat.

At a minimum, Congress could simply restrict access-tiering by network providers. That would leave network providers free to offer consumer-tiered service. But such tiering should not be allowed to turn upon the particular provider of network content. Instead, such tiering should be limited to either bandwidth guarantees (e.g., guaranteeing at least 10 Mbps) or service guarantees (e.g., guaranteeing fast 'video service' without specifying a particular provider).

A more ambitious regulation would require network providers to provide a "basic internet service" to all broadband customers. The FCC would define what "basic internet service" was. And the FCC's definition would turn upon a judgment about the capacity necessary to assure sufficient competition among application and service providers. In the current context, that could mean sufficient bandwidth to provide reasonable video services. But as the uses of the Internet develop, the scope of this "basic internet service" could change.

Conclusion

The Internet was the great economic surprise of the 20th century. No one who funded or initially developed the network imagined it would have the economic and social consequences that it has had.

But though the success of the network was a surprise, we have learned a great deal about why it was a success. Built into its basic design was a guarantee of maximum competition. A free market in applications was coded into its architecture. The growth of that network followed from this basic design. The world economy benefited dramatically from this growth.

The threat facing the Internet today is that network owners will convince regulators to go back on that original design. Through regulatory policies that permit broadband providers to act however their private interests dictate, these regulatory policies would threaten the economic potential of the network generally. New innovation always comes from outsiders. If insiders are given both technical and legal control over innovation on the Internet, innovation will be stifled.

Unlike many other industrialized nations, we in the United States have failed to preserve the extraordinary competition among ISPs that characterized early Internet growth. But despite that loss in access competition, the end-to-end principle, supported in part by the FCC, still provided significant opportunity for application and content competition. The changes now being spoken of by the effective duopoly of broadband providers will weaken that application and content competition.

It is my view that any policy that weakens competition is a policy that will weaken the prospects for Internet and economic growth. I therefore urge this Committee to secure and supplement the work of Chairman Powell, by enacting legislation that protects the environment for Internet innovation and competition that the original Internet produced.

Kyle D. Dixon

Testimony before the Senate Committee on Commerce, Science and Transportation Hearing on "Network Neutrality"

Thank you for the opportunity to speak* with you about whether Congress should mandate so-called "network neutrality." Such a mandate would constrain the ability of Internet access providers to make private arrangements with other companies that would differentiate among Internet applications, content or devices that rely on broadband network connections to consumers.

This issue confronts Congress with the most crucial regulatory decision for the broadband age. Remedies like a network neutrality mandate may be beneficial where evidence demonstrates that market power has been abused. But the more likely effect of a network neutrality mandate under current competitive conditions would be to reduce consumer welfare by undermining investment and innovation.

I. Consumer Welfare as the Touchstone for Resolving the Network Neutrality Debate

Network neutrality is hotly debated because it is so central to the economy and to our society. The Internet and broadband networks are permitting virtually any service or application—voice, video or data—to reach consumers over multi-purpose digital networks. Thus, if Congress decides to regulate how broadband providers work with content and other companies, it will affect the evolution of the converged communications and information technology industries dramatically.

Much ink already has been spilled in this debate, primarily by companies hoping to use the presence or absence of network neutrality mandates to their advantage in commercial negotiations. Yet too often the sound and fury of this rhetoric signifies little that cuts through to resolve this complex issue.

---

*The views expressed here are my own and may not reflect those of The Progress & Freedom Foundation, its Board, or its supporters.

From Testimony before the Senate Committee on Commerce, Science and Transportation Hearing, February 7, 2006.

As a former regulator, I recall being faced with this dilemma frequently. I learned then that the best way to resolve issues like this coherently and effectively was to return to first principles.

The touchstone for resolving network neutrality or any other regulatory debate is *consumer welfare*. Specifically, policymakers must balance many (and, inevitably, competing) interests to maximize benefits to consumers in the form of competition, investment and innovation. With this as a starting point, it becomes immediately clear what is known or apparent about the current status quo for consumer welfare, and what questions remain.

II. What We Know: The Status Quo for Consumer Welfare

A. Broadband Networks, Content, Applications and Devices Are All Critical to Maximizing Consumer Welfare

A quick Google search reveals that the Internet often is described as an ecosystem. Like nature, the Internet is highly *interdependent,* involving myriad collaborations among end users, broadband network providers, content and applications developers and so on. The Internet also resembles nature because it is *constantly changing and growing,* adding new users and uses continuously. This interdependence and dynamism account for the many benefits consumers already receive from the Internet, as well as the expectation that these benefits will expand. Conversely, this expansion of consumer benefits depends on maintaining healthy prospects for each of the Internet's components.

B. Content, Applications and Devices Are Thriving on the Broadband Internet

One need only consult advertisements, the news or most anyone with children to assess the vibrancy of the content, applications and device components of the broadband Internet. Consumers use "voice over Internet Protocol" services like Vonage to call cheaply across the country and around the globe. Virtual communities spring up daily as users create and share web logs, instant messages and other media, and as they compete in online video games. Companies fuel American productivity using business-to-business and business-to-consumer applications. Music and video programming lovers increasingly download or "stream" this content to iPods, TiVo boxes and other devices. The evolution of these components of the Internet continues unabated even in the absence of a network neutrality mandate.

C. Broadband Networks, Although Increasingly Ubiquitous and Competitive, Have not Reached Their Full Potential

Despite claims by network neutrality proponents that the market for "last mile" broadband connections is not competitive enough, this aspect of the Internet also shows promising signs:

- The FCC reports that nearly all zip codes are served by at least one broadband provider, and a solid majority is served by several.
- WiFi, WiMax, satellite and other emerging technologies continue to add customers, hoping to compete on a niche or wider basis with

existing cable and DSL offerings. Effective spectrum reform would dramatically improve these prospects, thus making such reform a top priority in bringing consumers the benefits of the broadband Internet.
- Industry analysts estimate that most Internet users have defected from "dial-up" Internet access to broadband and that this trend is accelerating.
- Cable modem, DSL and, increasingly, wireless and optical fiber-based networks compete on several bases, including price, speed and technology.

That said, neither the proponents nor opponents of network neutrality want the broadband market to stall at its current level of development. They agree that additional broadband deployment would bring consumers more of the benefits of competition and, hopefully, narrow the gap between the United States and other countries with respect to broadband usage. And although providers continue to make their networks faster, far more of this investment will be needed before high-value uses like streaming video can become commonplace. This, in turn, would initiate a "virtuous cycle" whereby bringing consumers more value would intensify demand for broadband investment.

III. Narrowing the Network Neutrality Debate

Given the importance and relative health of the broadband network, application, content and device components of the Internet, Congress can narrow the network neutrality debate to the following question:

> Would enacting a network neutrality mandate add to the benefits consumers *already enjoy,* or undermine those benefits?

In the continued absence of demonstrated market power abuses by broadband providers, I contend that network neutrality mandates would do more harm than good.

A. Network Neutrality Mandates Would not Improve (and Could Worsen) Conditions for Content and Applications Development

The broadband Internet already affords consumers unprecedented freedom in how they obtain, share and manipulate information. Other than a few incidents, broadband providers have not blocked or impaired consumers' use of the content, applications or devices of their choice. These incidents often alleged legitimate concerns about protecting consumers' Internet service quality from erosion by their neighbors' high intensive use of shared network capacity. In any event, these incidents generally were abandoned for business reasons or in response to FCC action.

Even as they experiment with business models to support their expensive network investments, broadband providers are not likely to change course in any way that reduces overall consumer welfare. This results from the current level of competition among broadband networks. There is no single, dominant broadband network provider and none seems likely to emerge in the immediate future. Instead, cable and phone companies vie to expand their respective, substantial market shares and to defend against wireless and other firms who hope to use less established technologies to enter new markets and expand existing footholds.

Nor does it seem likely that broadband providers will extract economically prohibitive terms from other firms any time soon. Companies hoping to earn a return on the billions of dollars they have invested or hope to invest in broadband networks understand that consumers pay a premium over dial-up service so they can access the diverse and exciting content and applications that the Internet offers. Although network owners may wish to bargain with other companies to share the revenues generated by this increased consumer value, they are unlikely to draw hard lines in the sand that risk losing existing or future customers to other networks.

Similarly, no broadband network owner is likely to acquire an "essential facility" without which rivals are effectively barred from the market. Whether a facility denied to a competitor is "essential" for competitive analysis largely turns on whether the competitor is unable, practically or reasonably, to duplicate the essential facility. In most cases, however, at least two firms already compete in the local broadband market, and consumers continue to sign up for additional technologies, such as wireless. Moreover, consumers have accelerated their switch from dial-up to broadband, raising the possibility that network owners entering the market can gain customers without having to entice them away from other broadband providers.

Finally, it seems unlikely that broadband providers can parlay their position in the market as leverage to constrain the market for complementary or "vertical" products, such as content, applications and devices. Leveraging and attempted monopolization theories, at a minimum, require that a company has a monopoly or is likely to be capable of acquiring one. Broadband providers probably will not satisfy this prerequisite anytime soon, for the reasons already stated. And to the extent broadband providers take actions that arguably might fit this theory in the future, attention to the goal of maximizing consumer welfare would need to make sure those actions were not justified as pro-competitive. This seems especially true to the extent providers act to preserve incentives for them (and thus others) to invest in broadband infrastructure.

Note that there is reason to expect that a network neutrality mandate actually might *weaken* the competitive vibrancy of the content, applications and device components of the Internet. For all its flexibility, the Internet cannot be all things to all uses. For example, Internet protocols (e.g., TCP/IP) route packets of digitized data over the Internet anonymously on "first come, first served" and "best effort" bases. This approach has worked well for applications or related devices that are not time-sensitive. This approach works poorly, however, for uses that depend on a steady transfer of data of networks, such as streaming media, online gaming and even voice over IP. An example of this type of application would include Internet delivery of high definition television programming. If Congress enacted a network neutrality mandate, it might prevent network owners from using private networks to work around this inherent shortcoming of the Internet. This, in turn, would discourage the offering of services that consumers want but that are disfavored by the Internet's current architecture.

By enacting a network neutrality mandate, Congress also might complicate efforts to keep the Internet safe and reliable. As recent events have shown, the phenomenal growth of the Internet also has made it more crowded and vulnerable to security risks, such as viruses and spam. Companies hoping to recoup or expand their investment in broadband networks will be eager to help solve such problems by offering content and applications developers new services that work around the Internet's technical limitations, at least until broader refinements can be made to the global Internet ecosystem. Broadband providers may not be free to offer such services if Congress enacts a network neutrality mandate.

Thus, a network neutrality mandate likely would not improve and could worsen conditions currently faced by developers of content, applications and devices. That some content and applications companies vigorously lobby Congress to enact such a mandate may be explained best by "public choice" theory. Public choice predicts that companies will lobby the government for rules that help them in the marketplace, thereby saving them the trouble of achieving the same results through competition and negotiation. Companies supporting network neutrality may see their greatest advantage in having a rule that frees them from negotiating with broadband providers, but such a rule is not likely to make *consumers* better off. Broadband providers already face strong pressures to add as many customers as possible, both to keep customers from signing up with competitors and to recoup providers' significant investments in network infrastructure. The facts speak for themselves; there is no persuasive evidence that broadband providers systematically have prevented or discouraged consumers from using any legal content, applications or devices. As such, Congress can accord little weight to companies' pleas for help in avoiding commercial negotiations as irrelevant to the main goal of regulation: maximizing consumer welfare.

B. A Network Neutrality Mandate Likely Would Undermine Investment and Innovation in Broadband Networks

Most significantly, a network neutrality mandate would discourage investment and innovation in broadband networks.

1. Ambiguities regarding what "network neutrality" actually means would burden and delay new broadband services and networks.   Perhaps the simplest definition of "network neutrality" would be "nondiscrimination," i.e., a requirement that broadband network owners serve all potential customers equally. As I have suggested, this kind of mandate could preclude broadband providers from offering services that address the Internet's inherent reliability and security limitations and thereby make it more difficult to offer or purchase valuable new Internet services.

A naked nondiscrimination requirement also could hamstring efforts by content and applications providers to develop sustainable business models. It is only very recently that companies began to trade the "virtual" profits that inflated the Internet bubble for real profits, largely based on targeted Internet advertisements. I suspect that even some proponents of regulation in this area would not want Congress to bar broadband providers from agreeing to feature content or links on consumers' Internet "home pages" or, as some companies have done, agree to make Yahoo!, AOL or others preferred Internet service providers on their networks. But these arrangements, which seem to benefit consumers, are difficult to square with the concept of nondiscrimination.

Further, more sophisticated notions of network neutrality—notions that allow companies to improve reliability or security, or develop pro-competitive business models—are likely to be more ambiguous than nondiscrimination. This added ambiguity would invite costly litigation before the FCC or the courts as to what Congress meant when it enacted a particular network neutrality mandate. The challenge of writing nuanced network neutrality rules also could result in unanticipated consequences.

2. Enacting a network neutrality mandate would push consumers and the industry down a "slippery slope" towards more burdensome regulation. Fears that a network neutrality mandate would usher in subsequent regulation are not merely speculative; they are supported by the FCC's experience in regulating "enhanced" services and attachments to the narrowband, telephone network in its *Computer Inquiry* and *Part 68* proceedings.

The *Computer Inquiry* requirements were adopted over many years beginning in the 1970s and, at base, were designed to allow telephone companies to participate in the emerging data processing industry on the condition that they afford competing "enhanced" or information service providers (e.g., third-party voicemail providers) the same access to the transmission capability of the phone network. Phone companies had to file the terms and conditions of these "basic" services with tariff reviewers at the FCC, subject to regulation that the prices for these services be "just and reasonable." The *Computer Inquiry* spawned a vast maze of requirements so Byzantine that few attorneys at the FCC or elsewhere claimed to understand it fully. Many of the requirements were rejected in a series of court appeals.

Not surprisingly, the FCC last year honored Congress' demand that it eliminate barriers to broadband investment by affording DSL providers the flexibility to opt out of the *Computer Inquiry* requirements along with other aspects of "common carrier" regulation. Likewise, in 2000, the FCC eliminated 125 pages of Part 68 rules governing the attachment of devices to the telephone network, that time responding to Congress' mandate that the agency eliminate unnecessary, and thus burdensome, regulation.

The risk that a network neutrality mandate would lead to further regulation is illustrated more generally by the FCC's implementation of the provisions in the Telecommunications Act of 1996 intended to open local telephone networks to competition. As that experience suggests, mandates that one company share its network with competitors almost always lead competitors to call for more regulation regarding how that sharing is done, especially with respect to price. Brushing aside any incentives network owners have to carry as much traffic over their networks as possible (to spread heavy fixed costs as widely as possible), competitors' argument is that it does no good to mandate access to a network if its owner can request price or other terms that make the access uneconomical for competitors.

By analogy to the broadband context, it seems likely that any network neutrality mandate that Congress adopts (and that survives implementation and judicial review) will be met with calls for additional regulation of the price and other terms of this "neutral" access. This additional regulation would heighten the burden imposed by a network neutrality mandate itself, thereby further discouraging investment in broadband networks.

3. A network neutrality mandate would undermine broadband deployment by deterring providers from addressing Internet reliability and security concerns. I mentioned earlier the benefits of allowing broadband providers to develop services to address some of the Internet's inherent technical limitations. The flipside of the value that those services could offer content and applications developers (and, ultimately, consumers) is that such services create new revenue opportunities for network owners. These revenues then can be used to fund the network upgrades and expansions that are necessary to support wider availability of valuable, bandwidth-intensive services, such as video and telemedicine. A network neutrality mandate risks blocking this flow of money, thereby reducing consumer welfare.

In sum, the most significant likely effect of a network neutrality mandate would be to weaken investment and innovation in broadband networks when they have not yet reached their full potential. Also, it is worth noting that a network neutrality mandate that denied broadband providers the value of the billions of dollars they have invested in their networks could raise issues as to whether the mandate amounted to an unconstitutional "taking" of property. Taken together with the likelihood that such mandates (at best) will merely free content and applications developers from having to negotiate with broadband providers, this explains why Congress need not enact a network neutrality to promote consumer welfare at this time.

IV. The Market Power Alternative: A Superior Solution to Protecting Consumer Welfare

If Congress decides it must assume the risk of harm to which an across-the-board network neutrality mandate would subject the Internet ecosystem, it should consider alternatives that reserve such mandates for situations in which they are needed to remedy abuses of market power.

Arguments in favor of network neutrality rely largely on the assumption that broadband providers have market power that they will use to deny consumers the freedom to use the content, applications and devices of their choice. Leave aside, for the moment, broadband providers' incentives to maximize the value of their networks by keeping the floodgates of content and applications open. It is clear that a provider cannot extract "monopoly rents" (as opposed to market-constrained fees) *unless* the provider has market power. Thus, imposing network neutrality only where a broadband provider has abused market power should limit that remedy to situations in which the provider truly is harming consumer welfare.

There are likely multiple options for limiting network neutrality remedies to abuses of market power. One option would be for Congress to rely on traditional antitrust enforcement; for example, in the face of demonstrable evidence that it had abused market power, a broadband provider could avoid an antitrust suit by agreeing to "neutrality" remedies.

Alternatively, Congress could specify a competitive standard according to which the FCC could identify and remedy market power abuses. This tracks the approaches recently proposed by Senator DeMint in S.2113, and by the Progress & Freedom Foundation in our Digital Age Communications Act project. The Foundation developed its proposal in conjunction with dozens of legal, engineering and economic scholars and practitioners representing a range of viewpoints. Nonetheless, these scholars share a passion to updating regulation to comport with the evolving demands of digital technology.

However Congress crafts a "market power alternative" to network neutrality concerns, it should satisfy at least two prerequisites. *First,* the alternative should be *narrowly targeted* to specific instances of market power, in terms of both the geographic scope and behavioral requirements of the remedy.

Second, the alternative should incorporate a *rigorous competitive standard and evidentiary showing* to ensure that neutrality mandates are imposed only to remedy demonstrable cases of market power abuse. A competitive standard that fails to satisfy these prerequisites likewise will fail to avoid many of the potential risks to consumer welfare that "one-size-fits-all" network neutrality mandates pose.

V. Conclusion

The debate over whether to enact a "network neutrality" mandate is no mere regulatory squabble; it confronts Congress with momentous decisions that will affect generations of Americans. We know that all the components of the broadband Internet—from networks to applications, content and devices—are critical to maximizing consumer welfare. In order to further this central goal of communications regulation, I urge Congress to remain cautious about imposing network a neutrality mandate at this early stage in the development of the broadband Internet. Imposing "neutrality" where it is not necessary to remedy abuses of market power could be far more damaging than endorsing a "solution in search of a problem." Doing so could make a network neutrality mandate *itself* the problem.

POSTSCRIPT

Should the Internet Be Neutral?

In June 2006, the U.S. House of Representatives passed the Communications Opportunity, Promotion and Enhancement Act after deleting a provision that would have mandated network neutrality. As passed, the Act "would let the [Federal Communications Commission] investigate complaints about broadband providers blocking Internet content only after the fact." See Grant Gross, "House Rejects 'Net Neutrality,' Passes Telecom Reform Bill," *Network World* (June 12, 2006) (http://www.networkworld.com/). The Senate Committee on Commerce, Science and Transportation, which had held the hearings from which the readings above were drawn in February 2006, held additional hearings on June 13, 2006. On June 28, the committee rejected, in a tie vote, an amendment to the telecommunications bill that would have mandated network neutrality. The committee then sent the bill to the full Senate, where a similar amendment could be reintroduced. See Tom Abate, "Net Neutrality Amendment Dies: Telecommunications Bill Goes to Senate Without Provision Sought by Web Firms," *San Francisco Chronicle* (June 29, 2006). Some have credited the telecommunications industry's heavy investment in lobbyists and campaign contributions with the result to that point. See Lisa Caruso, "Outmanned, Outfoxed, Outspent," *National Journal* (August 12, 2006). Lauren Weinstein, "Ma Bell's Revenge: The Battle for Network Neutrality," *Communications of the ACM* (January 2007), says that "Much of the anti-neutrality argument is simple greed in action" and warns that "most Internet users simply don't realize how drastically and negatively they could be affected if anti-neutrality arguments hold sway. Getting true network neutrality back after it's been lost is likely to be effectively impossible. Except for the anti-neutrality camp itself, we'd all be worse off with a non-neutral Internet, and that's a risk we simply must not accept."

The 109th Congress came to an end before the Senate took up the bill, but the bill was reintroduced on January 9, 2007. Activists (e.g., http://www.savetheinternet.com/) are hoping the new Congress will be friendlier to the cause of net neutrality. There are some signs that the telecommunication industry, with that same thought in mind, may be just as happy to see the Communications Opportunity, Promotion and Enhancement Act tabled for the time being. See Carol Wilson, "Net Neutrality Not Going Away," *Telephony* (September 11, 2006).

The overall significance of the issue is discussed by Daniel Krauss, "Net Neutrality and How It Just Might Change Everything," *American Libraries* (September 2006), and Michael Baumann, "Net Neutrality: The Internet's World War," *Information Today* (September 2006). Clearly, the debate is not over. In fact, it has barely begun.

Internet References . . .

Worldwatch Institute

The Worldwatch Institute is dedicated to fostering the evolution of an environmentally sustainable society, one in which human needs are met in ways that do not threaten the health of the natural environment or the prospects of future generations.

http://www.worldwatch.org

Department of Energy

The U.S. Department of Energy provides information on nuclear power, hydrogen, and other energy sources, as well as such energy-related issues as global warming.

http://www.energy.gov

Global Warming

The Environmental Protection Agency maintains this site to summarize the current state of knowledge about global warming.

http://www.epa.gov/climatechange/index.html

Intergovernmental Panel on Climate Change

The Intergovernmental Panel on Climate Change (IPCC) was formed by the World Meteorological Organization (WMO) and the United Nations Environment Programme (UNEP) to assess any scientific, technical, and socioeconomic information that is relevant to the understanding of the risk of human-induced climate change.

http://www.ipcc.ch

National Renewable Energy Laboratory

The National Renewable Energy Laboratory (NREL) is the leading center for renewable energy research in the United States.

http://www.nrel.gov

Heritage Foundation

The Heritage Foundation is a think tank whose mission is to formulate and promote conservative public policies based on the principles of free enterprise, limited government, individual freedom, traditional American values, and a strong national defense.

http://www.heritage.org

The Environment

*A*s *the damage that human beings do to their environment in the course of obtaining food, wood, ore, fuel, and other resources has become clear, many people have grown concerned. Some of that concern is for the environment—the landscapes and living things with which humanity shares its world. Some of that concern is more for human welfare; it focuses on the ways in which environmental damage threatens human health or even human survival.*

Among the major environmental issues are those related to energy. By releasing vast amounts of carbon dioxide, fossil fuels threaten to change the world's climate. Potential solutions include greatly expanding the use of nuclear power and changing our automobile fuel from gasoline to hydrogen.

- Should Society Act Now to Halt Global Warming?

- Is It Time to Revive Nuclear Power?

- Will Hydrogen Replace Fossil Fuels for Cars?

ISSUE 4

Should Society Act Now to Halt Global Warming?

YES: Nicholas Stern, from *Stern Review: The Economics of Climate Change* (October 30, 2006)

NO: Bush Administration, from "Global Climate Change Policy Book" (February 2002)

ISSUE SUMMARY

YES: Nicholas Stern, head of the British Government Economics Service, reports that although taking steps now to limit future impacts of global warming would be very expensive, the economic and social impacts of not doing so will be much more expensive.

NO: The Bush administration's plan for dealing with global warming insists that short-term economic health must come before reducing emissions of greenhouse gases. It is more useful to reduce "greenhouse gas intensity" or emissions per dollar of economic activity than to reduce total emissions.

Scientists have known for more than a century that carbon dioxide and other "greenhouse gases" (including water vapor, methane, and chlorofluorocarbons) help prevent heat from escaping the earth's atmosphere. In fact, it is this "greenhouse effect" that keeps the earth warm enough to support life. Yet there can be too much of a good thing. Ever since the dawn of the industrial age, humans have been burning vast quantities of fossil fuels, releasing the carbon they contain as carbon dioxide. Because of this, some estimate that by the year 2050, the amount of carbon dioxide in the air will be double what it was in 1850. By 1982 an increase was apparent. Less than a decade later, many researchers were saying that the climate had already begun to warm. Now the scientific consensus is that "The global warming debate is now over—at least the science part of it" (Milton Clark, "Editorial: Taking Action on Global Warming," *Human and Ecological Risk Assessment*, vol. 12, no. 6, 2006).

The debate has been heated, but the data are now very clear. See Richard A. Kerr, "A Worrying Trend of Less Ice, Higher Seas," *Science* (March 24, 2006), and Jeffrey Kluger, "By Any Measure, Earth Is at the Tipping Point," *Time*

(April 3, 2006). In February 2007, the Intergovernmental Panel on Climate Change (IPCC) released the first portions of its fourth report, saying that global warming is now beyond doubt, the certainty that humans are to blame is greater than ninety percent, future warming is unlikely to be "inconsequential," and the full impact on human civilization may be much worse than anyone has said so far; see Richard A. Kerr, "Scientists Tell Policymakers We're All Warming the World," *Science* (February 9, 2007).

Global warming, says the UN Environment Programme, will do some $300 billion in damage each year to the world economy by 2050. In March 2001 President George W. Bush announced that the United States would not take steps to reduce greenhouse emissions—called for by the international treaty negotiated in 1997 in Kyoto, Japan—because such reductions would harm the American economy (the U.S. Senate has not ratified the Kyoto treaty). Since the IPCC had just released its third report saying that past forecasts were, in essence, too conservative, Bush's stance provoked immense outcry. Then Sir Nicholas Stern, head of the British Government Economics Service, reports that although taking steps now to limit future impacts of global warming would be very expensive, "the benefits of strong, early action considerably outweigh the costs. . . . Ignoring climate change will eventually damage economic growth. . . . Tackling climate change is the pro-growth strategy for the longer term, and it can be done in a way that does not cap the aspirations for growth of rich or poor countries. The earlier effective action is taken, the less costly it will be."

The Bush administration's plan for dealing with global warming insists that short-term economic health must come before reducing emissions of greenhouse gases. It is more useful to reduce "greenhouse gas intensity" or emissions per dollar of economic activity, which will not interfere with continued economic growth the way reducing total emissions would surely do. Unfortunately, if greenhouse gas intensity is reduced and the economy grows, total emissions may well increase dramatically.

YES

Nicholas Stern

Stern Review: The Economics of Climate Change, Executive Summary

The scientific evidence is now overwhelming: climate change presents very serious global risks, and it demands an urgent global response.

This independent Review was commissioned by the Chancellor of the Exchequer, reporting to both the Chancellor and to the Prime Minister, as a contribution to assessing the evidence and building understanding of the economics of climate change. . . .

The Review takes an international perspective. Climate change is global in its causes and consequences, and international collective action will be critical in driving an effective, efficient and equitable response on the scale required. This response will require deeper international co-operation in many areas—most notably in creating price signals and markets for carbon, spurring technology research, development and deployment, and promoting adaptation, particularly for developing countries.

Climate change presents a unique challenge for economics: it is the greatest and widest-ranging market failure ever seen. The economic analysis must therefore be global, deal with long time horizons, have the economics of risk and uncertainty at centre stage, and examine the possibility of major, non-marginal change. To meet these requirements, the Review draws on ideas and techniques from most of the important areas of economics, including many recent advances.

The Benefits of Strong, Early Action on Climate Change Outweigh the Costs

The effects of our actions now on future changes in the climate have long lead times. What we do now can have only a limited effect on the climate over the next 40 or 50 years. On the other hand what we do in the next 10 or 20 years can have a profound effect on the climate in the second half of this century and in the next.

No-one can predict the consequences of climate change with complete certainty; but we now know enough to understand the risks. Mitigation—taking strong action to reduce emissions—must be viewed as an investment, a cost incurred now and in the coming few decades to avoid the risks of very severe

From *Stern Review*, October 30, 2006, pp. i–xiv, xvi–xvii, xxv–xxvii. Copyright © 2006 by Crown Publishers, Inc. Reprinted by permission.

consequences in the future. If these investments are made wisely, the costs will be manageable, and there will be a wide range of opportunities for growth and development along the way. For this to work well, policy must promote sound market signals, overcome market failures and have equity and risk mitigation at its core. That essentially is the conceptual framework of this Review.

The Review considers the economic costs of the impacts of climate change, and the costs and benefits of action to reduce the emissions of greenhouse gases (GHGs) that cause it, in three different ways:

- Using disaggregated techniques, in other words considering the physical impacts of climate change on the economy, on human life and on the environment, and examining the resource costs of different technologies and strategies to reduce greenhouse gas emissions;
- Using economic models, including integrated assessment models that estimate the economic impacts of climate change, and macro-economic models that represent the costs and effects of the transition to low-carbon energy systems for the economy as a whole;
- Using comparisons of the current level and future trajectories of the 'social cost of carbon' (the cost of impacts associated with an additional unit of greenhouse gas emissions) with the marginal abatement cost (the costs associated with incremental reductions in units of emissions).

From all of these perspectives, the evidence gathered by the Review leads to a simple conclusion: the benefits of strong, early action considerably outweigh the costs.

The evidence shows that ignoring climate change will eventually damage economic growth. Our actions over the coming few decades could create risks of major disruption to economic and social activity, later in this century and in the next, on a scale similar to those associated with the great wars and the economic depression of the first half of the 20th century. And it will be difficult or impossible to reverse these changes. Tackling climate change is the pro-growth strategy for the longer term, and it can be done in a way that does not cap the aspirations for growth of rich or poor countries. The earlier effective action is taken, the less costly it will be.

At the same time, given that climate change is happening, measures to help people adapt to it are essential. And the less mitigation we do now, the greater the difficulty of continuing to adapt in the future.

❧

The Scientific Evidence Points to Increasing Risks of Serious, Irreversible Impacts from Climate Change Associated with Business-as-Usual (BAU) Paths for Emissions

The scientific evidence on the causes and future paths of climate change is strengthening all the time. In particular, scientists are now able to attach probabilities to the temperature outcomes and impacts on the natural environment associated with different levels of stabilisation of greenhouse gases in the atmosphere. Scientists also now understand much more about the potential for dynamic feedbacks that have, in previous times of climate change, strongly amplified the underlying physical processes.

The stocks of greenhouse gases in the atmosphere (including carbon dioxide, methane, nitrous oxides and a number of gases that arise from industrial processes) are rising, as a result of human activity. . . .

The current level or stock of greenhouse gases in the atmosphere is equivalent to around 430 parts per million (ppm) CO_2, compared with only 280ppm before the Industrial Revolution. These concentrations have already caused the world to warm by more than half a degree Celsius and will lead to at least a further half degree warming over the next few decades, because of the inertia in the climate system.

Even if the annual flow of emissions did not increase beyond today's rate, the stock of greenhouse gases in the atmosphere would reach double pre-industrial levels by 2050—that is 550ppm CO_2-equivalent—and would continue growing thereafter. But the annual flow of emissions is accelerating, as fast-growing economies invest in high-carbon infrastructure and as demand for energy and transport increases around the world. The level of 550ppm CO_2-equivalent could be reached as early as 2035. At this level there is at least a 77% chance—and perhaps up to a 99% chance, depending on the climate model used—of a global average temperature rise exceeding 2°C.

Under a BAU scenario, the stock of greenhouse gases could more than treble by the end of the century, giving at least a 50% risk of exceeding 5°C global average temperature change during the following decades. This would take humans into unknown territory. An illustration of the scale of such an increase is that we are now only around 5°C warmer than in the last ice age.

Such changes would transform the physical geography of the world. A radical change in the physical geography of the world must have powerful implications for the human geography—where people live, and how they live their lives. . . .

Climate Change Threatens the Basic Elements of Life for People Around the World—Access to Water, Food Production, Health, and Use of Land and the Environment

. . . On current trends, average global temperatures will rise by 2–3°C within the next fifty years or so. The Earth will be committed to several degrees more warming if emissions continue to grow.

Warming will have many severe impacts, often mediated through water:

- Melting glaciers will initially increase flood risk and then strongly reduce water supplies, eventually threatening one-sixth of the world's

population, predominantly in the Indian sub-continent, parts of China, and the Andes in South America.
- Declining crop yields, especially in Africa, could leave hundreds of millions without the ability to produce or purchase sufficient food. At mid to high latitudes, crop yields may increase for moderate temperature rises (2–3°C), but then decline with greater amounts of warming. At 4°C and above, global food production is likely to be seriously affected.
- In higher latitudes, cold-related deaths will decrease. But climate change will increase worldwide deaths from malnutrition and heat stress. Vector-borne diseases such as malaria and dengue fever could become more widespread if effective control measures are not in place.
- Rising sea levels will result in tens to hundreds of millions more people flooded each year with warming of 3 or 4°C. There will be serious risks and increasing pressures for coastal protection in South East Asia (Bangladesh and Vietnam), small islands in the Caribbean and the Pacific, and large coastal cities, such as Tokyo, New York, Cairo and London. According to one estimate, by the middle of the century, 200 million people may become permanently displaced due to rising sea levels, heavier floods, and more intense droughts.
- Ecosystems will be particularly vulnerable to climate change, with around 15–40% of species potentially facing extinction after only 2°C of warming. And ocean acidification, a direct result of rising carbon dioxide levels, will have major effects on marine ecosystems, with possible adverse consequences on fish stocks.

The Damages from Climate Change Will Accelerate as the World Gets Warmer

Higher temperatures will increase the chance of triggering abrupt and large-scale changes.

- Warming may induce sudden shifts in regional weather patterns such as the monsoon rains in South Asia or the El Niño phenomenon—changes that would have severe consequences for water availability and flooding in tropical regions and threaten the livelihoods of millions of people.
- A number of studies suggest that the Amazon rainforest could be vulnerable to climate change, with models projecting significant drying in this region. One model, for example, finds that the Amazon rainforest could be significantly, and possibly irrevocably, damaged by a warming of 2–3°C.
- The melting or collapse of ice sheets would eventually threaten land which today is home to 1 in every 20 people.

While there is much to learn about these risks, the temperatures that may result from unabated climate change will take the world outside the range of human experience. This points to the possibility of very damaging consequences.

The Impacts of Climate Change Are not Evenly Distributed—the Poorest Countries and People Will Suffer Earliest and Most. And If and When the Damages Appear It Will Be Too Late to Reverse the Process. Thus We Are Forced to Look a Long Way Ahead

Climate change is a grave threat to the developing world and a major obstacle to continued poverty reduction across its many dimensions. First, developing regions are at a geographic disadvantage: they are already warmer, on average, than developed regions, and they also suffer from high rainfall variability. As a result, further warming will bring poor countries high costs and few benefits. Second, developing countries—in particular the poorest—are heavily dependent on agriculture, the most climate-sensitive of all economic sectors, and suffer from inadequate health provision and low-quality public services. Third, their low incomes and vulnerabilities make adaptation to climate change particularly difficult.

Because of these vulnerabilities, climate change is likely to reduce further already low incomes and increase illness and death rates in developing countries. Falling farm incomes will increase poverty and reduce the ability of households to invest in a better future, forcing them to use up meagre savings just to survive. At a national level, climate change will cut revenues and raise spending needs, worsening public finances.

Many developing countries are already struggling to cope with their current climate. Climatic shocks cause setbacks to economic and social development in developing countries today even with temperature increases of less than 1°C. The impacts of unabated climate change—that is, increases of 3 or 4°C and upwards—will be to increase the risks and costs of these events very powerfully.

Impacts on this scale could spill over national borders, exacerbating the damage further. Rising sea levels and other climate-driven changes could drive millions of people to migrate: more than a fifth of Bangladesh could be under water with a 1m rise in sea levels, which is a possibility by the end of the century. Climate-related shocks have sparked violent conflict in the past, and conflict is a serious risk in areas such as West Africa, the Nile Basin and Central Asia.

Climate Change May Initially Have Small Positive Effects for a Few Developed Countries, But Is Likely to Be Very Damaging for the Much Higher Temperature Increases Expected by Mid- to Late-Century under BAU Scenarios

In higher latitude regions, such as Canada, Russia and Scandinavia, climate change may lead to net benefits for temperature increases of 2 or 3°C, through higher agricultural yields, lower winter mortality, lower heating requirements, and a possible boost to tourism. But these regions will also experience the most rapid rates of warming, damaging infrastructure, human health, local livelihoods and biodiversity.

Developed countries in lower latitudes will be more vulnerable—for example, water availability and crop yields in southern Europe are expected to decline by 20% with a 2°C increase in global temperatures. Regions where water is already scarce will face serious difficulties and growing costs.

The increased costs of damage from extreme weather (storms, hurricanes, typhoons, floods, droughts, and heat waves) counteract some early benefits of climate change and will increase rapidly at higher temperatures. Based on simple extrapolations, costs of extreme weather alone could reach 0.5–1% of world GDP per annum by the middle of the century, and will keep rising if the world continues to warm.

- A 5 or 10% increase in hurricane wind speed, linked to rising sea temperatures, is predicted approximately to double annual damage costs, in the USA.
- In the UK, annual flood losses alone could increase from 0.1% of GDP today to 0.2–0.4% of GDP once the increase in global average temperatures reaches 3 or 4°C.
- Heat waves like that experienced in 2003 in Europe, when 35,000 people died and agricultural losses reached $15 billion, will be commonplace by the middle of the century.

At higher temperatures, developed economies face a growing risk of large-scale shocks—for example, the rising costs of extreme weather events could affect global financial markets through higher and more volatile costs of insurance.

Integrated Assessment Models Provide a Tool for Estimating the Total Impact on the Economy; Our Estimates Suggest That This Is Likely to Be Higher Than Previously Suggested

. . . Formal modelling of the overall impact of climate change in monetary terms is a formidable challenge, and the limitations to modelling the world over two centuries or more demand great caution in interpreting results. However, as we have explained, the lags from action to effect are very long and the quantitative analysis needed to inform action will depend on such long-range modelling exercises. The monetary impacts of climate change are now expected to be more serious than many earlier studies suggested, not least because those studies tended to exclude some of the most uncertain but potentially most damaging impacts. Thanks to recent advances in the science, it is now possible to examine these risks more directly, using probabilities.

Most formal modelling in the past has used as a starting point a scenario of 2–3°C warming. In this temperature range, the cost of climate change could be equivalent to a permanent loss of around 0–3% in global world output compared with what could have been achieved in a world without climate change. Developing countries will suffer even higher costs.

However, those earlier models were too optimistic about warming: more recent evidence indicates that temperature changes resulting from BAU trends in emissions may exceed 2-3°C by the end of this century. This increases the likelihood of a wider range of impacts than previously considered. Many of these impacts, such as abrupt and large-scale climate change, are more difficult to quantify. With 5-6°C warming—which is a real possibility for the next century—existing models that include the risk of abrupt and large-scale climate change estimate an average 5–10% loss in global GDP, with poor countries suffering costs in excess of 10% of GDP. Further, there is some evidence of small but significant risks of temperature rises even above this range. Such temperature increases would take us into territory unknown to human experience and involve radical changes in the world around us. . . .

[W]e estimate the total cost over the next two centuries of climate change associated under BAU emissions involves impacts and risks that are equivalent to an average reduction in global per-capita consumption of at least 5%, now and forever. While this cost estimate is already strikingly high, it also leaves out much that is important.

The cost of BAU would increase still further, were the model systematically to take account of three important factors:

- First, including direct impacts on the environment and human health (sometimes called 'non-market' impacts) increases our estimate of the total cost of climate change on this path from 5% to 11% of global per-capita consumption. There are difficult analytical and ethical issues of measurement here. The methods used in this model are fairly conservative in the value they assign to these impacts.
- Second, some recent scientific evidence indicates that the climate system may be more responsive to greenhouse-gas emissions than previously thought, for example because of the existence of amplifying feedbacks such as the release of methane and weakening of carbon sinks. Our estimates, based on modelling a limited increase in this responsiveness, indicate that the potential scale of the climate response could increase the cost of climate change on the BAU path from 5% to 7% of global consumption, or from 11% to 14% if the non-market impacts described above are included.
- Third, a disproportionate share of the climate-change burden falls on poor regions of the world. If we weight this unequal burden appropriately, the estimated global cost of climate change at 5-6°C warming could be more than one-quarter higher than without such weights.

Putting these additional factors together would increase the total cost of BAU climate change to the equivalent of around a 20% reduction in consumption per head, now and into the future.

In summary, analyses that take into account the full ranges of both impacts and possible outcomes—that is, that employ the basic economics of risk—suggest that BAU climate change will reduce welfare by an amount equivalent to a reduction in consumption per head of between 5 and 20%. Taking account of the increasing scientific evidence of greater risks, of aversion to the possibilities of catastrophe, and of a broader approach to the consequences than implied by narrow output measures, the appropriate estimate is likely to be in the upper part of this range. . . .

Emissions Have Been, and Continue to Be, Driven by Economic Growth; yet Stabilisation of Greenhouse-Gas Concentrations in the Atmosphere Is Feasible and Consistent with Continued Growth

CO_2 emissions per head have been strongly correlated with GDP per head. As a result, since 1850, North America and Europe have produced around 70% of all the CO_2 emissions due to energy production, while developing countries have accounted for less than one quarter. Most future emissions growth will come from today's developing countries, because of their more rapid population and GDP growth and their increasing share of energy-intensive industries.

Yet despite the historical pattern and the BAU projections, the world does not need to choose between averting climate change and promoting growth and development. Changes in energy technologies and the structure of economies have reduced the responsiveness of emissions to income growth, particularly in some of the richest countries. With strong, deliberate policy choices, it is possible to 'decarbonise' both developed and developing economies on the scale required for climate stabilisation, while maintaining economic growth in both.

Stabilisation—at whatever level—requires that annual emissions be brought down to the level that balances the Earth's natural capacity to remove greenhouse gases from the atmosphere. The longer emissions remain above this level, the higher the final stabilisation level. In the long term, annual global emissions will need to be reduced to below 5 $GtCO_2$-equivalent, the level that the earth can absorb without adding to the concentration of GHGs in the atmosphere. This is more than 80% below the absolute level of current annual emissions. . . .

Stabilising at or below 550ppm CO_2-equivalent would require global emissions to peak in the next 10–20 years, and then fall at a rate of at least 1–3% per year. . . . By 2050, global emissions would need to be around 25% below current levels. These cuts will have to be made in the context of a world economy in 2050 that may be 3–4 times larger than today—so emissions per unit of GDP would need to be just one quarter of current levels by 2050.

To stabilise at 450ppm CO_2-equivalent, without overshooting, global emissions would need to peak in the next 10 years and then fall at more than 5% per year, reaching 70% below current levels by 2050. . . .

Achieving These Deep Cuts in Emissions Will Have a Cost. The Review Estimates the Annual Costs of Stabilisation at 500–550ppm CO$_2$-Equivalent to Be around 1% of GDP by 2050—a Level That Is Significant but Manageable

Reversing the historical trend in emissions growth, and achieving cuts of 25% or more against today's levels is a major challenge. Costs will be incurred as the world shifts from a high-carbon to a low-carbon trajectory. But there will also be business opportunities as the markets for low-carbon, high-efficiency goods and services expand.

Greenhouse-gas emissions can be cut in four ways. Costs will differ considerably depending on which combination of these methods is used, and in which sector:

- Reducing demand for emissions-intensive goods and services
- Increased efficiency, which can save both money and emissions
- Action on non-energy emissions, such as avoiding deforestation
- Switching to lower-carbon technologies for power, heat and transport

Estimating the costs of these changes can be done in two ways. One is to look at the resource costs of measures, including the introduction of low-carbon technologies and changes in land use, compared with the costs of the BAU alternative. This provides an upper bound on costs, as it does not take account of opportunities to respond involving reductions in demand for high-carbon goods and services.

The second is to use macroeconomic models to explore the system-wide effects of the transition to a low-carbon energy economy. These can be useful in tracking the dynamic interactions of different factors over time, including the response of economies to changes in prices. But they can be complex, with their results affected by a whole range of assumptions.

On the basis of these two methods, central estimate is that stabilisation of greenhouse gases at levels of 500–550ppm CO$_2$-equivalent will cost, on average, around 1% of annual global GDP by 2050. This is significant, but is fully consistent with continued growth and development, in contrast with unabated climate change, which will eventually pose significant threats to growth.

Resource Cost Estimates Suggest That an Upper Bound for the Expected Annual Cost of Emissions Reductions Consistent with a Trajectory Leading to Stabilisation at 550ppm CO$_2$-Equivalent Is Likely to Be around 1% of GDP by 2050

This Review has considered in detail the potential for, and costs of, technologies and measures to cut emissions across different sectors. As with the impacts of climate change, this is subject to important uncertainties. These include the difficulties of estimating the costs of technologies several decades into the future, as well as the way in which fossil-fuel prices evolve in the future. It is also hard to know how people will respond to price changes.

The precise evolution of the mitigation effort, and the composition across sectors of emissions reductions, will therefore depend on all these factors. But it is possible to make a central projection of costs across a portfolio of likely options, subject to a range.

The technical potential for efficiency improvements to reduce emissions and costs is substantial. Over the past century, efficiency in energy supply improved ten-fold or more in developed countries, and the possibilities for further gains are far from being exhausted. Studies by the International Energy Agency show that, by 2050, energy efficiency has the potential to be the biggest single source of emissions savings in the energy sector. This would have both environmental and economic benefits: energy-efficiency measures cut waste and often save money.

Non-energy emissions make up one-third of total greenhouse-gas emissions; action here will make an important contribution. A substantial body of evidence suggests that action to prevent further deforestation would be relatively cheap compared with other types of mitigation, if the right policies and institutional structures are put in place.

Large-scale uptake of a range of clean power, heat, and transport technologies is required for radical emission cuts in the medium to long term. The power sector around the world will have to be at least 60%, and perhaps as much as 75%, decarbonised by 2050 to stabilise at or below 550ppm CO_2-equivalent. Deep cuts in the transport sector are likely to be more difficult in the shorter term, but will ultimately be needed. While many of the technologies to achieve this already exist, the priority is to bring down their costs so that they are competitive with fossil-fuel alternatives under a carbon-pricing policy regime.

A portfolio of technologies will be required to stabilise emissions. It is highly unlikely that any single technology will deliver all the necessary emission savings, because all technologies are subject to constraints of some kind, and because of the wide range of activities and sectors that generate greenhouse-gas emissions. It is also uncertain which technologies will turn out to be cheapest. Hence a portfolio will be required for low-cost abatement.

The shift to a low-carbon global economy will take place against the background of an abundant supply of fossil fuels. That is to say, the stocks of hydrocarbons that are profitable to extract (under current policies) are more than enough to take the world to levels of greenhouse-gas concentrations well beyond 750ppm CO_2-equivalent, with very dangerous consequences. Indeed, under BAU, energy users are likely to switch towards more carbon-intensive coal and oil shales, increasing rates of emissions growth.

Even with very strong expansion of the use of renewable energy and other low-carbon energy sources, hydrocarbons may still make over half of global energy supply in 2050. Extensive carbon capture and storage would allow this continued use of fossil fuels without damage to the atmosphere, and also guard against the danger of strong climate-change policy being undermined at some stage by falls in fossil-fuel prices.

Estimates based on the likely costs of these methods of emissions reduction show that the annual costs of stabilising at around 550ppm CO_2-equivalent are likely to be around 1% of global GDP by 2050, with a range from −1% (net gains) to +3.5% of GDP. . . .

Reducing the Expected Adverse Impacts of Climate Change Is Therefore Both Highly Desirable and Feasible

This conclusion follows from a comparison of . . . estimates of the costs of mitigation with the high costs of inaction. . . .

Preliminary calculations adopting the approach to valuation taken in this Review suggest that the social cost of carbon today, if we remain on a BAU trajectory, is of the order of $85 per tonne of CO_2—higher than typical numbers in the literature, largely because we treat risk explicitly and incorporate recent evidence on the risks, but nevertheless well within the range of published estimates. This number is well above marginal abatement costs in many sectors. Comparing the social costs of carbon on a BAU trajectory and on a path towards stabilisation at 550ppm CO_2-equivalent, we estimate the excess of benefits over costs, in net present value terms, from implementing strong mitigation policies this year, shifting the world onto the better path: the net benefits would be of the order of $2.5 trillion. This figure will increase over time. This is not an estimate of net benefits occurring in this year, but a measure of the benefits that could flow from actions taken this year; many of the costs and benefits would be in the medium to long term. . . .

Greater International Co-operation to Accelerate Technological Innovation and Diffusion Will Reduce the Costs of Mitigation

The private sector is the major driver of innovation and the diffusion of technologies around the world. But governments can help to promote international collaboration to overcome barriers in this area, including through formal arrangements and through arrangements that promote public-private co-operation such as the Asia Pacific Partnership. Technology co-operation enables the sharing of risks, rewards and progress of technology development and enables co-ordination of priorities. . . .

Curbing Deforestation Is a Highly Cost-Effective Way of Reducing Greenhouse Gas Emissions

Emissions from deforestation are very significant—they are estimated to represent more than 18% of global emissions, a share greater than is produced by the global transport sector.

Action to preserve the remaining areas of natural forest is needed urgently. Large-scale pilot schemes are required to explore effective approaches to combining national action and international support.

Policies on deforestation should be shaped and led by the nation where the particular forest stands. But those countries should receive strong help from the international community, which benefits from their actions to reduce deforestation. At a national level, defining property rights to forest-land, and determining the rights and responsibilities of landowners, communities and loggers, is key to effective forest management. This should involve local communities, respect informal rights and social structures, work with development goals and reinforce the process of protecting the forests.

Research carried out for this report indicates that the opportunity cost of forest protection in 8 countries responsible for 70 per cent of emissions from land use could be around $5 billion per annum initially, although over time marginal costs would rise.

Compensation from the international community should take account of the opportunity costs of alternative uses of the land, the costs of administering and enforcing protection, and the challenges of managing the political transition as established interests are displaced.

Carbon markets could play an important role in providing such incentives in the longer term. But there are short-term risks of destabilising the crucial process of strengthening existing strong carbon markets if deforestation is integrated without agreements that strongly increase demand for emissions reductions. These agreements must be based on an understanding of the scale of transfers likely to be involved.

Adaptation Efforts in Developing Countries Must Be Accelerated and Supported, Including through International Development Assistance

The poorest developing countries will be hit earliest and hardest by climate change, even though they have contributed little to causing the problem. Their low incomes make it difficult to finance adaptation. The international community has an obligation to support them in adapting to climate change. Without such support there is a serious risk that development progress will be undermined. . . .

Strong and early mitigation has a key role to play in limiting the long-run costs of adaptation. Without this, the costs of adaptation will rise dramatically.

Building and Sustaining Collective Action Is Now an Urgent Challenge

The key building blocks for any collective action include developing a shared understanding of the long-term goals for climate policy, building effective institutions for co-operation, and demonstrating leadership and working to build trust with others.

Without a clear perspective on the long-term goals for stabilisation of greenhouse gas concentrations in the atmosphere, it is unlikely that action will be sufficient to meet the objective.

Action must include mitigation, innovation and adaptation. There are many opportunities to start now, including where there are immediate benefits and where large-scale pilot programmes will generate valuable experience. And we have already begun to create the institutions to underpin co-operation.

The challenge is to broaden and deepen participation across all the relevant dimensions of action—including co-operation to create carbon prices and markets, to accelerate innovation and deployment of low-carbon technologies, to reverse emissions from land-use change and to help poor countries adapt to the worst impacts of climate change.

There Is Still Time to Avoid the Worst Impacts of Climate Change if Strong Collective Action Starts Now

This Review has focused on the economics of risk and uncertainty, using a wide range of economic tools to tackle the challenges of a global problem which has profound long-term implications. Much more work is required, by scientists and economists, to tackle the analytical challenges and resolve some of the uncertainties across a broad front. But it is already very clear that the economic risks of inaction in the face of climate change are very severe.

There are ways to reduce the risks of climate change. With the right incentives, the private sector will respond and can deliver solutions. The stabilisation of greenhouse gas concentrations in the atmosphere is feasible, at significant but manageable costs.

The policy tools exist to create the incentives required to change investment patterns and move the global economy onto a low-carbon path. This must go hand-in-hand with increased action to adapt to the impacts of the climate change that can no longer be avoided.

Above all, reducing the risks of climate change requires collective action. It requires co-operation between countries, through international frameworks that support the achievement of shared goals. It requires a partnership between the public and private sector, working with civil society and with individuals. It is still possible to avoid the worst impacts of climate change; but it requires strong and urgent collective action. Delay would be costly and dangerous.

Global Climate Change Policy Book

Executive Summary

"Addressing global climate change will require a sustained effort, over many generations. My approach recognizes that sustained economic growth is the solution, not the problem—because a nation that grows its economy is a nation that can afford investments in efficiency, new technologies, and a cleaner environment."

—President George W. Bush

The President announced a new approach to the challenge of global climate change. This approach is designed to harness the power of markets and technological innovation. It holds the promise of a new partnership with the developing world. And it recognizes that climate change is a complex, long-term challenge that will require a sustained effort over many generations. As the President has said, "The policy challenge is to act in a serious and sensible way, given the limits of our knowledge. While scientific uncertainties remain, we can begin now to address the factors that contribute to climate change."

While investments today in science will increase our understanding of this challenge, our investments in advanced energy and sequestration technologies will provide the breakthroughs we need to dramatically reduce our emissions in the longer term. In the near term, we will vigorously pursue emissions reductions even in the absence of complete knowledge. Our approach recognizes that sustained economic growth is an essential part of the solution, not the problem. Economic growth will make possible the needed investment in research, development, and deployment of advanced technologies. This strategy is one that should offer developing countries the incentive and means to join with us in tackling this challenge together. Significantly, the President's plan will:

- **Reduce the Greenhouse Gas Intensity of the U.S. Economy by 18 Percent in the Next Ten Years.** Greenhouse gas intensity measures the ratio of greenhouse gas (GHG) emissions to economic output. This new approach focuses on reducing the growth of GHG emissions, while sustaining the economic growth needed to finance investment in new, clean energy technologies. It sets America on a path to slow the growth of greenhouse gas emissions, and—as the science justifies—to stop and then reverse that growth:

- In efficiency terms, the 183 metric tons of emissions per million dollars GDP that we emit today will be lowered to 151 metric tons per million dollars GDP in 2012.
- Existing trends and efforts in technology improvement will play a significant role. Beyond that, the President's commitment will achieve 100 million metric tons of reduced emissions in 2012 alone, with more than 500 million metric tons in cumulative savings over the entire decade.
- This goal is comparable to the average progress that nations participating in the Kyoto Protocol are required to achieve.

- **Substantially Improve the Emission Reduction Registry.** The President directed the Secretary of Energy, in consultation with the Secretary of Commerce, the Secretary of Agriculture, and the Administrator of the Environmental Protection Agency, to propose improvements to the current voluntary emission reduction registration program under section 1605(b) of the 1992 Energy Policy Act within 120 days. These improvements will enhance measurement accuracy, reliability and verifiability, working with and taking into account emerging domestic and international approaches.

- **Protect and Provide Transferable Credits for Emissions Reduction.** The President directed the Secretary of Energy to recommend reforms to ensure that businesses and individuals that register reductions are not penalized under a future climate policy, and to give transferable credits to companies that can show real emissions reductions.

- **Review Progress Toward Goal and Take Additional Action if Necessary.** If, in 2012, we find that we are not on track toward meeting our goal, and sound science justifies further policy action, the United States will respond with additional measures that may include a broad, market-based program as well as additional incentives and voluntary measures designed to accelerate technology development and deployment.

- **Increase Funding for America's Commitment to Climate Change.** The President's FY '03 budget seeks $4.5 billion in total climate spending—an increase of $700 million. This commitment is unmatched in the world, and is particularly notable given America's focus on international and homeland security and domestic economic issues in the President's FY '03 budget proposal.

- **Take Action on the Science and Technology Review.** The Secretary of Commerce and Secretary of Energy have completed their review of the federal government's science and technology research portfolios and recommended a path forward. As a result of their review, the President has established a new management structure to advance and coordinate climate change science and technology research.
  - The President has established a Cabinet-level Committee on Climate Change Science and Technology Integration to oversee this effort. The Secretary of Commerce and Secretary of Energy will lead the

effort, in close coordination with the President's Science Advisor. The research effort will continue to be coordinated through the National Science and Technology Council in accordance with the Global Change Research Act of 1990.

- The President's FY '03 budget proposal dedicates $1.7 billion to fund basic scientific research on climate change and $1.3 billion to fund research on advanced energy and sequestration technologies.
- This includes $80 million in new funding dedicated to implementation of the Climate Change Research Initiative (CCRI) and the National Climate Change Technology Initiative (NCCTI) announced last June. This funding will be used to address major gaps in our current understanding of the natural carbon cycle and the role of black soot emissions in climate change. It will also be used to promote the development of the most promising "breakthrough" technologies for clean energy generation and carbon sequestration.
- **Implement a Comprehensive Range of New and Expanded Domestic Policies, Including:**
  - *Tax Incentives for Renewable Energy, Cogeneration, and New Technology.* The President's FY '03 budget seeks $555 million in clean energy tax incentives, as the first part of a $4.6 billion commitment over the next five years ($7.1 billion over the next 10 years). These tax credits will spur investments in renewable energy (solar, wind, and biomass), hybrid and fuel cell vehicles, cogeneration, and landfill gas conversion. Consistent with the National Energy Policy, the President has directed the Secretary of the Treasury to work with Congress to extend and expand the production tax credit for electricity generation from wind and biomass, to develop a new residential solar energy tax credit, and to encourage cogeneration projects through investment tax credits.
  - *Business Challenges.* The President has challenged American businesses to make specific commitments to improving the greenhouse gas intensity of their operations and to reduce emissions. Recent agreements with the semi-conductor and aluminum industries and industries that emit methane already have significantly reduced emissions of some of the most potent greenhouse gases. We will build upon these successes with new agreements, producing greater reductions.
  - *Transportation Programs.* The Administration is promoting the development of fuel-efficient motor vehicles and trucks, researching options for producing cleaner fuels, and implementing programs to improve energy efficiency. The President is committed to expanding federal research partnerships with industry, providing market-based incentives and updating current regulatory programs that advance our progress in this important area. This commitment includes expanding fuel cell research, in particular through the "FreedomCAR" initiative. The President's FY '03 budget seeks more than $3 billion in tax credits over 11 years for consumers to purchase fuel cell and hybrid vehicles. The Secretary of Transportation has asked the Congressional leadership to work with him on legislation that would authorize the Department of Transportation to reform the Corporate Average Fuel Economy (CAFE) program, fully considering the recent National

Academy Sciences report, so that we can safely improve fuel economy for cars and trucks.

- *Carbon Sequestration.* The President's FY '03 budget requests over $3 billion—a $1 billion increase above the baseline—as the first part of a ten year (2002–2011) commitment to implement and improve the conservation title of the Farm Bill, which will significantly enhance the natural storage of carbon. The President also directed the Secretary of Agriculture to provide recommendations for further, targeted incentives aimed at forest and agricultural sequestration of greenhouse gases. The President further directed the Secretary of Agriculture, in consultation with the Environmental Protection Agency and the Department of Energy, to develop accounting rules and guidelines for crediting sequestration projects, taking into account emerging domestic and international approaches.

- **Promote New and Expanded International Policies to Complement Our Domestic Program.** The President's approach seeks to expand cooperation internationally to meet the challenge of climate change, including:

  - *Investing $25 Million in Climate Observation Systems in Developing Countries.* In response to the National Academy of Sciences' recommendation for better observation systems, the President has allocated $25 million and challenged other developed nations to match the U.S. commitment.

  - *Tripling Funding for "Debt-for-Nature" Forest Conservation Programs.* Building upon recent Tropical Forest Conservation Act (TFCA) agreements with Belize, El Salvador, and Bangladesh, the President's FY '03 budget request of $40 million to fund "debt for nature" agreements with developing countries nearly triples funding for this successful program. Under TFCA, developing countries agree to protect their tropical forests from logging, avoiding emissions and preserving the substantial carbon sequestration services they provide. The President also announced a new agreement with the Government of Thailand, which will preserve important mangrove forest in Northeastern Thailand in exchange for debt relief worth $11.4 million.

  - *Fully Funding the Global Environmental Facility.* The Administration's FY '03 budget request of $178 million for the GEF is more than $77 million above this year's funding and includes a substantial $70 million payment for arrears incurred during the prior administration. The GEF is the primary international institution for transferring energy and sequestration technologies to the developing world under the United Nations Framework Convention on Climate Change (UNFCCC).

    - *Dedicating Significant Funds to the United States Agency for International Development (USAID).* The President's FY '03 budget requests $155 million in funding for USAID climate change programs. USAID serves as a critical vehicle for transferring American energy and sequestration technologies to developing countries to promote sustainable development and minimize their GHG emissions growth.

- *Pursue Joint Research with Japan.* The U.S. and Japan continue their High-Level Consultations on climate change issues. Later this month, a team of U.S. experts will meet with their Japanese counterparts to discuss specific projects within the various areas of climate science and technology, to identify the highest priorities for collaborative research.
- *Pursue Joint Research with Italy.* Following up on a pledge of President Bush and Prime Minister Berlusconi to undertake joint research on climate change, the U.S. and Italy convened a Joint Climate Change Research Meeting in January 2002. The delegations for the two countries identified more than 20 joint climate change research activities for immediate implementation, including global and regional modeling.
- *Pursue Joint Research with Central America.* The United States and Central American Heads of Government signed the Central American-United States of America Joint Accord (CONCAUSA) on December 10, 1994. The original agreement covered cooperation under action plans in four major areas: conservation of biodiversity, sound use of energy, environmental legislation, and sustainable economic development. On June 7, 2001, the United States and its Central American partners signed an expanded and renewed CONCAUSA Declaration, adding disaster relief and climate change as new areas for cooperation. The new CONCAUSA Declaration calls for intensified cooperative efforts to address climate change through scientific research, estimating and monitoring greenhouse gases, investing in forestry conservation, enhancing energy efficiency, and utilizing new environmental technologies.

National Goal

The President set a national goal to reduce the greenhouse gas intensity of the U.S. economy by 18 percent over the next ten years. Rather than pitting economic growth against the environment, the President has established an approach that promises real progress on climate change by tapping the power of sustained economic growth.

- **The President's Yardstick—Greenhouse Gas Intensity—Is a Better Way to Measure Progress Without Hurting Growth.** A goal expressed in terms of declining greenhouse gas intensity, measuring greenhouse gas emissions relative to economic activity, quantifies our effort to reduce emissions through conservation, adoption of cleaner, more efficient, and emission-reducing technologies, and sequestration. At the same time, an intensity goal accommodates economic growth.
- **Reducing Greenhouse Gas Intensity by 18 Percent Over the Next Ten Years Is Ambitious but Achievable.** The United States will reduce the 183 metric tons of emissions per million dollars GDP that we emit today to 151 metric tons per million dollars GDP in 2012. We expect existing trends and efforts in technology improvement to play a significant role. Beyond that, our commitment will achieve 100 million metric tons of reduced emissions in 2012 alone, with more than 500 million metric tons in cumulative savings over the entire decade.

- **Focusing on Greenhouse Gas Intensity Sets America on a Path to Slow the Growth of Greenhouse Gas Emissions, and—as the Science Justifies—to Stop and Then Reverse That Growth.** As we learn more about the science of climate change and develop new technologies to mitigate emissions, this annual decline can be accelerated. When the annual decline in intensity equals the economic growth rate (currently, about 3% per year), emission growth will have stopped. When the annual decline in intensity exceeds the economic growth rate, emission growth will reverse. Reversing emission growth will eventually stabilize atmospheric concentrations as emissions decline.

- **As We Advance Science and Develop Technology to Substantially Reduce Greenhouse Gas Emissions in the Long Term, We Do Not Want to Risk Harming the Economy in the Short Term.** Over the past 20 years, greenhouse gas emissions have risen with economic growth, as our economy benefited from inexpensive, fossil-fuel based—and greenhouse gas emitting—energy. While new technologies promise to break this emission-economy link, a rapid reduction in emissions would be costly and threaten economic growth. Sustained economic growth is essential for any long-term solution: Prosperity is what allows us to dedicate more resources to solving environmental problems. History shows that wealthier societies demand—and can afford—more environmental protection.

- **The Intensity Based Approach Promotes Near-Term Opportunities to Conserve Fossil Fuel Use, Recover Methane, and Sequester Carbon.** Until we develop and adopt breakthrough technologies that provide safe and reliable energy to fuel our economy without emitting greenhouse gases, we need to promote more rapid adoption of existing, improved energy efficiency and renewable resources that provide cost-effective opportunities to reduce emissions. Profitable methane recovery from landfills, coal mines and gas pipelines offers another opportunity—estimated by the EPA at about 30 million tons of carbon equivalent emissions. Finally, carbon sequestration in soils and forests can provide tens of millions of tons of emission reductions at very low costs.

- **The Intensity Based Approach Advances a Serious, but Measured Mitigation Response.** The President recognizes America's responsibility to reduce emissions. At the same time, any long-term solution—one that stabilizes atmospheric concentrations of greenhouse gases at safe levels—will require the development and deployment of new technologies that are not yet cost-effective. The President's policy balances the desire for immediate reductions with the need to protect the economy and to take advantage of developing science and technology.

The President's Goal Is Ambitious and Responsible

- **Reducing Greenhouse Gas Intensity by 18 Percent Over the Next Ten Years Is Comparable to the Average Progress that Nations Participating in the Kyoto Protocol Are Required to Achieve.** Our goal translates into a 4.5 percent reduction beyond forecasts of the progress that America is expected to make based on existing programs and private activity. Forecasts of the average reductions required by nations implementing the Kyoto Protocol range from zero to 7 percent.

- **While Producing Results Similar to What the Kyoto Protocol Participants Are Required to Achieve on Average, the President's Approach Protects the Economy and Develops Institutions for a Long-Term Solution.** The focus on greenhouse gas intensity separates the goal of reducing emissions from the potential economic harm associated with a rigid emission cap. By measuring greenhouse gas emissions relative to economic activity, we have a solid yardstick against which we can measure progress as we pursue a range of programs to reduce emissions. As we develop technologies to produce more goods with fewer greenhouse gas emissions, this yardstick does not penalize economic growth.
- **Greenhouse Gas Intensity Is a More Practical Way to Discuss Goals with Developing Countries.** The close connection between economic growth, energy use and greenhouse gas emissions implies that fixed appropriate emission limits are hard to identify when economic growth is uncertain and carbon-free, breakthrough energy technologies are not yet in place. Such targets are also hard to identify for developing countries where the future rate of emissions is even more uncertain. Given its neutrality with regard to economic growth, greenhouse gas intensity solves or substantially reduces many of these problems.

Enhanced National Registry for Voluntary Emissions Reductions

The Administration will improve the current federal GHG Reduction and Sequestration Registry that recognizes greenhouse gas reductions by non-governmental organizations, businesses, farmers, and the federal, state and local governments. Registry participants and the public will have a high level of confidence in the reductions recognized by this Registry, through capture and sequestration projects, mitigation projects that increase energy efficiency and/or switch fuels, and process changes to reduce emissions of potent greenhouse gases, such as methane. An enhanced registry will promote the identification and expansion of innovative and effective ways to reduce greenhouse gases. The enhanced registry will encourage participation by removing the risk that these actions will be penalized—or inaction rewarded—by future climate policy.

- **Improve the Quality of the Current Program.** A registry is a tool for companies to publicly record their progress in reducing emissions, providing public recognition of a company's accomplishments, and a record of mitigation efforts for future policy design. This tool goes hand-in-hand with voluntary business challenges, described below, by providing a standardized, credible vehicle for reporting and recognizing progress.
  - Although businesses can already register emission reductions under section 1605(b) of the 1995 Energy Policy Act, participation has been limited.
  - The President directed the Secretary of Energy, in consultation with the Secretary of Commerce, Secretary of Agriculture, and the Administrator of the Environmental Protection Agency, to propose improvements to the current voluntary emissions reduction registration program within 120 days.

- These improvements will enhance measurement accuracy, reliability and verifiability, working with and taking into account emerging domestic and international approaches.
- **Protect and Provide Transferable Credits for Emissions Reduction.** The President directed the Secretary of Energy to recommend reforms to ensure that businesses and individuals that register reductions are not penalized under a future climate policy, and to give transferable credits to companies that can show real emissions reductions. These protections will encourage businesses and individuals to pursue innovative strategies to reduce or sequester greenhouse gas emissions, without the risk that future climate policy will disadvantage them.
- **Background on Current Registry Program.** The Energy Policy Act of 1992 directed the Department of Energy (with EIA as the implementing agency) to develop a program to document voluntary actions that reduce emissions of greenhouse gases or remove greenhouse gases from the atmosphere.
  - Under the Energy Policy Act, EIA was directed to issue "procedures for the accurate reporting of information on annual reductions of greenhouse gas emissions and carbon fixation achieved through any measures, including fuel switching, forest management practices, tree planting, use of renewable energy, manufacture or use of vehicles with reduced greenhouse gas emissions, appliance efficiency, methane recovery, cogeneration, chlorofluorocarbon capture and replacement, and power plant heat rate improvement."
  - In 1999, 207 companies and other organizations, representing 24 different industries or services, reported on 1,722 projects that achieved 226 million metric tons of carbon dioxide equivalent reductions—equal to 3.4 percent of national emissions. Participating companies included Clairol, AT&T, Dow Chemical, Johnson & Johnson, IBM, Motorola, Pharmacia, Upjohn, Sunoco, Southern, General Motors and DuPont.
  - EIA released a February 2002 report demonstrating that this program continues to expand. In 2000, 222 companies had undertaken 1,882 projects to reduce or sequester greenhouse gases. These achieved 269 million metric tons of carbon dioxide equivalent reductions—equal to 3.9 percent of national emissions.
  - A number of proposals to reform the existing registry—or create a new registry—have appeared in energy and/or climate policy bills introduced in the past year. The Administration will fully explore the extent to which the existing authority under the Energy Policy Act is adequate to achieve these reforms.

Progress Check in 2012

The domestic programs proposed by the President allow consumers and businesses to make flexible decisions about emission reductions rather than mandating particular control options or rigid targets. If, however, by 2012, our progress is not sufficient, and sound science justifies further action, the United States will respond with additional measures that may include a broad, market-based program, as well as additional incentives and voluntary measures designed to accelerate technology development and deployment.

POSTSCRIPT

Should Society Act Now to Halt Global Warming?

The United Nations Conference on Environment and Development in Rio de Janeiro, Brazil, took place in 1992. High on the agenda was the problem of global warming, but despite widespread concern and calls for reductions in carbon dioxide releases, the United States refused to consider rigid deadlines or set quotas. The uncertainties seemed too great, and some thought the economic costs of cutting back on carbon dioxide might be greater than the costs of letting the climate warm.

The nations that signed the UN Framework Convention on Climate Change in Rio de Janeiro in 1992 met again in Kyoto, Japan, in December 1997 to set carbon emissions limits for the industrial nations. The United States agreed to reduce its annual greenhouse gas emissions 7 percent below the 1990 level between 2008 and 2012 but still has not ratified the Kyoto treaty. In November 1998 they met in Buenos Aires, Argentina, to work out practical details (see Christopher Flavin, "Last Tango in Buenos Aires," *World Watch* [November/December 1998]). Unfortunately, developing countries, where carbon emissions are growing most rapidly, face few restrictions, and political opposition in developed nations—especially in the United States—remains strong. Ross Gelbspan, in "Rx for a Planetary Fever," *American Prospect* (May 8, 2000), blames much of that opposition on "big oil and big coal [which] have relentlessly obstructed the best-faith efforts of government negotiators." Fred Pearce, "State of Denial," *New Scientist* (November 4, 2006), finds similar motives for resistance to recognizing and coping with the problem. At the most recent meeting of the nations that signed the Kyoto Protocol, held in Nairobi, Kenya, in November 2006, Kofi Annan, Secretary-General of the UN, said that the facts are so clear that skeptics about global warming are "out of step, out of arguments, and out of time." In January 2007, the Union of Concerned Scientists released "Smoke, Mirrors & Hot Air: How ExxonMobil Uses Big Tobacco's Tactics to 'Manufacture Uncertainty' on Climate Change" (http://www.ucsusa.org/news/press_release/ExxonMobil-GlobalWarming-tobacco.html). ExxonMobil, says the UCS, has given $16 million to researchers and "front organizations" to raise "doubts about even the most indisputable scientific evidence" and has "used its access to the Bush administration to block federal policies and shape government communications on global warming."

In June 2002 the U.S. Environmental Protection Agency (EPA) issued its *U.S. Climate Action Report—2002* (available at http://www.epa.gov/globalwarming/publications/car/index.html) to the United Nations. In it, the EPA admits for the first time that global warming is real and that human activities are most likely to blame. President George W. Bush immediately dismissed the report as "put out by the bureaucracy" and said he still opposes the Kyoto Protocol. He insists more research is necessary before we can even begin to plan a proper response. Unfortunately, the latest studies warn that the consequences of global warming may be severe. See, for instance, Richard A. Kerr, "Climate Modelers See Scorching Future as a Real Possibility," *Science* (January 28, 2005), and *Meeting the Climate Challenge: Recommendations of the International Climate Change Taskforce* (January 2005) (http://www.americanprogress.org/atf/cf/%7BE9245FE4-9A2B-43C7-A521-5D6FF2E06E03%7D/CLIMAT-ECHALLENGE.PDF), which warns that the world may already be on the verge of irreversible disaster, including "widespread agricultural failure, water shortages and major droughts, increased disease, sea-level rise and the death of forests."

James Lovelock, creator of the Gaia metaphor for the living Earth beloved by many environmental activists, warns in *The Revenge of Gaia: Earth's Climate in Crisis and the Fate of Humanity* (Basic Books, 2006) that global warming may prove catastrophic. The 2007 report of the Intergovernmental Panel on Climate Change (IPCC) strengthens these statements to the point that it is no longer possible to argue credibly that humanity need not worry about global warming; the Summary for Policymakers can be downloaded at http://www.ipcc.ch/SPM2feb07.pdf.

In June 2006, the National Academy of Sciences reported that the Earth is now warmer than it has been in the last 400 years, and perhaps in the last 1,000 (*Surface Temperature Reconstructions for the Last 2,000 Years*, National Academies Press, 2006). Concerns have been raised about the risks to coastal populations from rising seas and changes in storm patterns; see John Young, "Black Water Rising," *World Watch* (September/October 2006). States and environmental groups have brought before the U.S. Supreme Court a case demanding that the U.S. Environmental Protection Agency regulate carbon dioxide as a threat to public health; see Elizabeth McGowan, "High Court Hears Climate Case," *Waste News* (December 4, 2006).

Potential solutions include capturing carbon dioxide and storing it deep underground; see Robert H. Socolow, "Can We Bury Global Warming?" *Scientific American* (July 2005). "It's Not Too Late," a special report published by *Technology Review* (July/August 2006), discusses energy technologies that could be put into use today to forestall the worst; fossil fuels will continue to be used, but alternatives include nuclear power, ethanol, and solar energy. On a more grandiose scale, Paul Crutzen (who won the Nobel Prize for his work on ozone depletion), wrote in "Albedo Enhancement by Stratospheric Sulfur Injections: A Contribution to Resolve a Policy Dilemma?" *Climatic Change* (August 2006), that it may prove possible to reflect solar heat with clouds of what is in essence industrial pollution. Jerome Pearson, et al., suggest putting "An artificial planetary ring about the Earth, composed of passive particles or controlled spacecraft with parasols," at a cost of $125–500 billion, for a similar purpose in "Earth Rings for Planetary Environmental Control," *Acta Astronautica* (January 2006).

ISSUE 5

Is It Time to Revive Nuclear Power?

YES: Michael J. Wallace, from Testimony before the United States Senate Committee on Energy & Natural Resources, Hearing on the Department of Energy's Nuclear Power 2010 Program (April 26, 2005)

NO: Karen Charman, from "Brave Nuclear World," *World Watch* (July/August 2006)

ISSUE SUMMARY

YES: Michael J. Wallace argues that because the benefits of nuclear power include energy supply and price stability, air pollution control, and greenhouse gas reduction, new nuclear power plant construction—with federal support—is essential.

NO: Karen Charman argues that nuclear power's drawbacks and the promise of clean, lower-cost, less dangerous alternatives greatly weaken the case for nuclear power.

T he technology of releasing for human use the energy that holds together the atom did not get off to an auspicious start. Its first significant application was military, and the deaths associated with the Hiroshima and Nagasaki explosions have ever since tainted the technology with negative associations. It did not help that for the ensuing half-century, millions of people grew up under the threat of nuclear armageddon. But almost from the beginning, nuclear physicists and engineers wanted to put nuclear energy to more peaceful uses, largely in the form of power plants. Touted in the 1950s as an astoundingly cheap source of electricity, nuclear power soon proved to be more expensive than conventional sources, largely because safety concerns caused delays in the approval process and prompted elaborate built-in precautions. Safety measures have worked well when needed—Three Mile Island, often cited as a horrific example of what can go wrong, released very little radioactive material to the environment. The Chernobyl disaster occurred when safety measures were ignored. In both cases, human error was more to blame than the technology itself. The related issue of nuclear waste has also raised fears and proved to add expense to the technology.

It is clear that two factors—fear and expense—impede the wide adoption of nuclear power. If both could somehow be alleviated, it might become possible to gain the benefits of the technology. Among those benefits are that nuclear power does not burn oil, coal, or any other fuel, does not emit air pollution and thus contribute to smog and haze, does not depend on foreign sources of fuel and thus weaken national independence, and does not emit carbon dioxide. Avoiding the use of fossil fuels is an important benefit; see Robert L. Hirsch, Roger H. Bezdek, and Robert M. Wendling, "Peaking Oil Production: Sooner Rather than Later?" *Issues in Science and Technology* (Spring 2005). But avoiding carbon dioxide emissions may be more important at a time when society is concerned about global warming, and this is the benefit that prompted James Lovelock, creator of the Gaia Hypothesis and hero to environmentalists everywhere, to say, "If we had nuclear power we wouldn't be in this mess now, and whose fault was it? It was [the anti-nuclear environmentalists]." See his autobiography, *Homage to Gaia: The Life of an Independent Scientist* (Oxford University Press, 2001). Others have also seen this point. The OECD's Nuclear Energy Agency ("Nuclear Power and Climate Change," [Paris, France, 1998, http://www.nea.fr/html/ndd/climate/climate.pdf]) found that a greatly expanded deployment of nuclear power to combat global warming was both technically and economically feasible. Robert C. Morris published *The Environmental Case for Nuclear Power: Economic, Medical, and Political Considerations* (Paragon House) in 2000. "The time seems right to reconsider the future of nuclear power," say James A. Lake, Ralph G. Bennett, and John F. Kotek in "Next-Generation Nuclear Power," *Scientific American* (January 2002). Stewart Brand, long a leading environmentalist, predicts in "Environmental Heresies," *Technology Review* (May 2005), that nuclear power will soon be seen as the "green" energy technology. David Talbot, "Nuclear Powers Up," *Technology Review* (September 2005), notes that "While the waste problem remains unsolved, current trends favor a nuclear renaissance. Energy needs are growing. Conventional energy sources will eventually dry up. The atmosphere is getting dirtier." Peter Schwartz and Spencer Reiss, "Nuclear Now!" *Wired* (February 2005), argue that nuclear power is the one practical answer to global warming and coming shortages of fossil fuels.

In the following selections, Michael J. Wallace, executive vice president of a major energy company, argues that because the benefits of nuclear power include energy supply and price stability, air pollution control, and greenhouse gas reduction, new nuclear power plant construction is essential, and there is a clear place for federal support. Karen Charman argues that nuclear power's drawbacks—risk, expense, and waste—and the promise of clean, lower-cost, less dangerous alternatives greatly weaken the case for nuclear power.

YES

Michael J. Wallace

Nuclear Power 2010 Program

. . . Constellation Energy, a Fortune 200 company based in Baltimore, is the nation's leading competitive supplier of electricity to large and industrial customers and the nation's largest wholesale power seller. Constellation Energy also manages fuels and energy services on behalf of energy intensive industries and utilities. The company delivers electricity and natural gas through the Baltimore Gas and Electric Company (BGE), its regulated utility in Maryland. We are the owners of 107 generating units at 35 different locations in 11 states, totaling approximately 12,500 megawatts of generation capacity. In 2004, the combined revenues of the integrated energy company totaled more that $12.5 billion and we are the fastest growing Fortune 500 Company over the past two years.

Our portfolio based on electricity produced is approximately 50 percent nuclear, 35 percent coal-fired, 7 percent gas-fired and 5 percent renewables. We own and operate the Calvert Cliffs nuclear plant in Maryland, and the Nine Mile Point and Ginna nuclear stations in New York State.

Constellation is part of the NuStart consortium that is preparing an application to the NRC for a license that would allow us to build and operate a new nuclear plant. Additionally, in December 2004, we submitted a proposal to the Department of Energy (DOE) for studies that could lead to an application to the Nuclear Regulatory Commission for an Early Site Permit as part of the Nuclear Power 2010 program. So, as you can tell, we have a vested interest in the continued success of Nuclear Power 2010, and we're bullish on the future of nuclear power.

Although I am here testifying today on behalf of Constellation, this testimony is supported by our trade association, the Nuclear Energy Institute (NEI).

My statement this morning will address four major issues:

1. The strategic value of our 103 operating nuclear power plants, and the compelling need to build new nuclear plants to preserve our nation's energy security, meet our environmental goals, and sustain our economic growth.
2. The critical importance of the Department of Energy's Nuclear Power 2010 program as a platform from which to launch the next generation of nuclear power plants in the United States.

United States Senate Committee on Energy & Natural Resources Hearing on the Department of Energy's Nuclear Power 2010 Program, April 26, 2005.

3. The need to recognize that the Nuclear Power 2010 program does not address all of the challenges facing companies interested in building new nuclear power plants, and that additional joint investment initiatives by the federal government and the private sector will be necessary.

4. The urgent need for comprehensive energy legislation that squarely addresses the critical need for additional investment in our electricity and energy infrastructure, including advanced nuclear and coal-fired generating capacity, electric and natural gas transmission, and other areas. Construction of the next nuclear power plants in the United States will require some form of investment stimulus, but I know I speak for the entire electric sector when I say that the need for investment stimulus extends well beyond nuclear power. This sector is starved for investment capital, and new federal government policy initiatives are necessary to reverse that trend and place our economy and our future on a sound foundation.

The Strategic Value of Nuclear Power and the Need for New Nuclear Power Plants

The United States has 103 reactors operating today. Nuclear power represented 20 percent of U.S. electricity supply 10 years ago, and it represents 20 percent of our electricity supply today, even though we have six fewer reactors than a decade ago and even though total U.S. electricity supply has increased by 25 percent in the period.

Nuclear power has maintained its market share thanks to dramatic improvements in reliability, safety, productivity and management of our nuclear plants, which today operate, on average, at 90 percent capacity factors, year in and year out. Improved productivity at our nuclear plants satisfied 20 percent of the growth in electricity demand over the last decade.

Due, in part, to excellent plant performance, we've seen steady growth in public support for nuclear energy. The industry has monitored public opinion closely since the early 1980s and two key trends are clear: First, public favorability to nuclear energy has never been higher; and second, the spread between those who support the use of nuclear energy and those opposed is widening steadily: 80 percent of Americans think nuclear power is important for our energy future and 67 percent favor the use of nuclear energy; 71 percent favor keeping the option to build more nuclear power plants. Six in 10 Americans agree that "we should definitely build more nuclear power plants in the future." Sixty-two percent said it would be acceptable to build new plants next to a nuclear power plant already operating.

The operating nuclear plants are such valuable electric generating assets that virtually all companies are planning to renew the operating licenses for these plants, as allowed by law and Nuclear Regulatory Commission regulations, and operate for an additional 20 years beyond their initial 40-year license terms. Sixty-eight U.S. reactors have now renewed their licenses, filed their formal applications, or indicated to the Nuclear Regulatory Commission that they intend to do so. The remaining 35 reactors have not yet declared because most of them are not yet old enough to do so. We believe that virtually all U.S.

nuclear plants will renew their licenses and operate for an additional 20 years. At Constellation, we are proud that our Calvert Cliffs station was the first U.S. nuclear plant to renew its license. At the time, the license renewal process was a novel concept. Today, thanks to efficient management of the process by the Nuclear Regulatory Commission, it is a stable and predictable licensing action. Ten years from now, we hope and believe that the issuance of combined construction/operating licenses for new nuclear plants—a novel concept today— will be similarly efficient and predictable.

Although it has not yet started to build new nuclear plants, the industry continues to achieve small but steady increases in generating capability— either through power uprates or the restart of shutdown nuclear capacity. The Tennessee Valley Authority is restarting Unit 1 at its Browns Ferry site in northern Alabama. This is a very complex project—fully as challenging as building a new nuclear plant—and it is on schedule and within budget at the midpoint of the project.

However, despite the impressive gains in reliability and output, there are obviously limits to how much capacity we can derive from our existing nuclear power plants. The time has come to create the business conditions under which we can build new nuclear power plants in the United States. We believe there are compelling public policy reasons for new nuclear generating capacity.

First, new nuclear power plants will continue to contribute to the fuel and technology diversity that is the core strength of the U.S. electric supply system. This diversity is at risk because today's business environment and market conditions in the electric sector make investment in large, new capital-intensive technologies difficult, particularly the advanced nuclear power plants and advanced coal-fired power plants best suited to supply baseload electricity. More than 90 percent of all new electric generating capacity added over the past five years is fueled with natural gas. Natural gas has many desirable characteristics and should be part of our fuel mix, but over-reliance on any one fuel source leaves consumers vulnerable to price spikes and supply disruptions.

Second, new nuclear power plants provide future price stability that is not available from electric generating plants fueled with natural gas. Intense volatility in natural gas prices over the last several years is likely to continue, thanks partly to unsustainable demand for natural gas from the electric sector, and subjects the U.S. economy to potential damage. Although nuclear plants are capital-intensive to build, the operating costs of nuclear power plants are stable and can dampen volatility of consumer costs in the electricity market.

Third, new nuclear plants will reduce the price and supply volatility of natural gas, thereby relieving cost pressures on other users of natural gas that have no alternative fuel source.

And finally, new nuclear power plants will play a strategic role in meeting U.S. clean air goals and the nation's goal of reducing greenhouse gas emissions. New nuclear power plants produce electricity that otherwise would be supplied by oil-, gas- or coal-fired generating capacity, and thus avoid the emissions associated with that fossil-fueled capacity.

In summary, nuclear energy represents a unique value proposition: new nuclear power plants would provide large volumes of electricity—cleanly, reliably, safely and affordably. They would provide future price stability and serve as a hedge against price and supply volatility. New nuclear plants also have valuable environmental attributes. These characteristics demonstrate why new nuclear plant construction is such an imperative in the United States.

The Critical Value of the Nuclear Power 2010 Program

As I said earlier, the Department of Energy's Nuclear Power 2010 program is an essential foundation in the joint government/industry partnership to build new nuclear power plants. This committee and, in particular, you, Mr. Chairman, deserve great credit for your leadership in ensuring adequate funding for this program in the 2005 Fiscal Year.

Nuclear Power 2010 is designed to demonstrate the various components of the new licensing system for nuclear power plants, including the process of obtaining early site permits (ESPs) and combined construction/operating licenses (COLs), sharing the cost of the detailed design and engineering work necessary to prepare COLs, and resolving generic licensing issues. This work is an essential risk-management exercise because it allows industry and the NRC staff to identify and resolve scores of technical and regulatory issues that must be settled before companies can undertake high-risk, capital-intensive construction projects like new nuclear plant construction.

The Nuclear Power 2010 program is the springboard that launched a tangible and visible industry commitment to new plant construction. The industry's commitment to Nuclear Power 2010 includes a planned investment of $650 million over the next several years on design, engineering, and licensing work, which will create a business foundation for decisions to build. Three companies have applications for early site permits under review at NRC. In addition to these three, Constellation and possibly one other company are also considering ESP applications. The industry is developing at least three applications for construction/operating licenses; the first will be filed in 2007, the second and third in 2008.

As you know, the administration has proposed $56 million for the Nuclear Power 2010 program in the 2006 fiscal year. The $56 million funding proposed for 2006 is sufficient for the ESP and COL demonstration projects already underway. It is not adequate, however, to cover more recent expressions of interest from Constellation and others, and additional resources will be needed to ensure this program is viable into the future.

It is also important to recognize that Nuclear Power 2010 is a multi-year undertaking. Certainty of future funding and program stability are a big concern for industry. However, our biggest frustration with the Nuclear Power 2010 program involves the time it has taken the DOE to award the grants. In the case of NuStart, we submitted our application in April 2004 and we were not notified that we received the grant until November 2004. As for Constellation's ESP application, we submitted it almost four months ago and have yet to hear from DOE.

To support the ESP and COL demonstration projects currently underway and future projects, we anticipate that the Department of Energy will need to significantly increase funding for Nuclear Power 2010 over FY 2006 levels.

The process of developing the first COL applications, certifying new designs and completing NRC review of the first ESP and COL applications will take some time. We are looking for ways to accelerate that process, and the Congress may be able to help there—by ensuring sufficient funding for Nuclear Power 2010 and even accelerating that funding; and by providing NRC sufficient resources to ensure that the commission has adequate manpower to conduct licensing reviews and meet aggressive but realistic schedules.

The Nuclear Power 2010 Program Does Not Address All the Challenges Facing New Nuclear Plant Construction

The Department of Energy's Nuclear Power 2010 program is a necessary, but not sufficient, step toward new nuclear plant construction. We must address other challenges as well.

Our industry is not yet at the point where we can announce specific decisions to build. We are not yet at the point where we can take a $1.5 billion to $2 billion investment decision to our boards of directors. We do not have fully certified designs that are competitive, for example. We do not know the licensing process will work as intended: That is why we are working systematically through the ESP and COL processes. We must identify and contain the risks to make sure that nothing untoward occurs after we start building. We cannot make a $1.5–$2 billion investment decision and end up spending twice that because the licensing process failed us.

The industry believes federal investment is necessary and appropriate to offset some of the risks I've mentioned. We recommend that the federal government's investment include the incentives identified by the Secretary of Energy Advisory Board's Nuclear Energy Task Force in its recent report. That investment stimulus includes:

1. secured loans and loan guarantees;
2. transferable investment tax credits that can be taken as money is expended during construction;
3. transferable production tax credits;
4. accelerated depreciation.

This portfolio of incentives is necessary because it's clear that no single financial incentive is appropriate for all companies, because of differences in company-specific business attributes or differences in the marketplace— namely, whether the markets they serve are open to competition or are in a regulated rate structure.

The next nuclear plants might be built as unregulated merchant plants, or as regulated rate-base projects. The next nuclear plants could be built by single entities, or by consortia of companies. Business environment and project structure have a major impact on which financial incentives work best. Some companies prefer tax-related incentives. Others expect that construction loans or loan guarantees will enable them to finance the next nuclear plants.

It is important to preserve both approaches. We must maintain as much flexibility as possible.

It's important to understand why federal investment stimulus and investment protection is necessary and appropriate.

Federal investment stimulus is necessary to offset the higher first-time costs associated with the first few nuclear plants built.

Federal investment protection is necessary to manage and contain the one type of risk that we cannot manage, and that's the risk of some kind of regulatory failure (including court challenges) that delays construction or commercial operation.

The new licensing process codified in the 1992 Energy Policy Act is conceptually sound. It allows for public participation in the process at the time when that participation is most effective—before designs and sites are approved and construction begins. The new process is designed to remove the uncertainties inherent in the Part 50 process that was used to license the nuclear plants operating today. In principle, the new licensing process is intended to reduce the risk of delay in construction and commercial operation and thus the risk of unanticipated cost increases. The goal is to provide certainty before companies begin construction and place significant investment at risk.

In practice, until the process is demonstrated, the industry and the financial community cannot be assured that licensing will proceed in a disciplined manner, without unfounded intervention and delay. Only the successful licensing and commissioning of several new nuclear plants (such as proposed by the NuStart and Dominion-led consortia) can demonstrate that the licensing issues discussed above have been adequately resolved. Industry and investor concern over these potential regulatory impediments may require techniques like the standby default coverage and standby interest coverage contained in S. 887, introduced by Senators Hagel, Craig and others.

Let me also be clear on two other important issues:

1. The industry is not seeking a totally risk-free business environment. It is seeking government assistance in containing those risks that are beyond the private sector's control. The goal is to ensure that the level of risk associated with the next nuclear plants built in the U.S. generally approaches what the electric industry would consider normal commercial risks. The industry is fully prepared to accept construction management risks and operational risks that are properly within the private sector's control.

2. The industry's financing challenges apply largely to the first few plants in any series of new nuclear reactors. As capital costs decline to the "nth-of-a-kind" range, as investors gain confidence that the licensing process operates as intended and does not represent a source of unpredictable risk, follow-on plants can be financed more conventionally, without the support necessary for the first few projects. What is needed [is] limited federal investment in a limited

number of new plants for a limited period of time to overcome the financial and economic hurdles facing the first few plants built.

In summary, we believe the industry and the federal government should work together to finance the first-of-a-kind design and engineering work and to develop an integrated package of financial incentives to stimulate construction of new nuclear power plants. Any such package must address a number of factors, including the licensing/regulatory risks; the investment risks; and the other business issues that make it difficult for companies to undertake capital-intensive projects. Such a cooperative industry/government financing program is a necessary and appropriate investment in U.S. energy security.

I hope this Committee can find a place for this type of investment stimulus in the comprehensive energy legislation now being developed

In addition, I would be remiss if I did not thank the Chairman for his support for three additional programs/provisions that will assist in the construction of new nuclear power plants in the United States:

1. Sustained progress with the Yucca Mountain project is essential. This includes the funding necessary to maintain the schedule, ensure timely filing of the license application, and access to the full receipts of the Nuclear Waste Fund.
2. Renewal of the Price-Anderson Act, which provides the framework for the industry's self-funded liability insurance. I am pleased to note that this is included in the recently House-passed energy bill.
3. Updated tax treatment of decommissioning funds that would provide comparable treatment for unregulated merchant generating companies and regulated companies. This provision, included in the energy tax legislation passed recently by the House, would allow all companies to establish qualified decommissioning funds and ensure that annual contributions to those funds are treated appropriately as a deductible business expense.

The U.S. electricity business and our nation are paying the price today for our inability to strike an appropriate balance between what was expedient and easy in the short-term, and what was prudent and more difficult in the long-term. We are paying the price today for 10 to 15 years of neglect of longer-term imperatives and the oversupply of base-load generation in the 1990s.

The United States faces a critical need for investment in energy infrastructure, including the capital-intensive, long-lead-time advanced nuclear and coal-fired power plants that represent the backbone of the U.S. electricity supply system.

While some may not realize it, the United States faces an imminent energy crisis today.

Electric power sales represent three to four percent of our gross domestic product. But the other 96 to 97 percent of our $11-trillion-a-year economy depends on that three to four percent. We cannot afford to gamble with something as fundamental as energy supply, and the biggest problem we face with nuclear energy is not having enough of it.

Brave Nuclear World?

This year marks the 20th anniversary of the world's most notorious nuclear disaster. At 1:23 a.m. on April 26, 1986, the Number Four reactor at the Chornobyl* nuclear plant in northern Ukraine exploded and burned uncontrolled for 10 days, releasing over 100 times more radiation into the atmosphere than the Hiroshima and Nagasaki bombs combined. At least 19 million hectares were heavily contaminated in Belarus, Ukraine, and Russia. Prevailing winds and rain sent radioactive fallout over much of Europe, and it was measured as far away as Alaska. Approximately 7 million people lived in the contaminated zones in the former Soviet Union at the time of the accident (over 5 million still do). More than 350,000 were evacuated, and 2,000 villages were demolished. Radioactive foodstuffs from Belarus and Ukraine continue to show up in the markets of Moscow, and farmers on 375 properties in Wales, Scotland, and England still must grapple with restrictions due to radioactive contamination from Chornobyl.

The operating crew and the 600 men in the plant's fire service who first responded to the disaster received the highest doses of radiation, between 0.7 and 13 Sieverts (Sv). According to chernobyl.info, a United Nations Internet-based information clearinghouse, this is 700 to 13,000 times more radiation in just a few hours than the maximum dose of 1 millisievert that the European Union says people living near a nuclear power plant should be exposed to in one year. Thirty-one of those first on the scene died within three months. A total of 800,000 "liquidators"—mainly military conscripts from all over the former Soviet Union—were involved in the clean-up until 1989, and government agencies in Belarus, Ukraine, and Russia have reported that 25,000 have since died.

By any measure, Chornobyl was a horrific catastrophe and has become the icon of nuclear power's satanic side. Yet controversy has dogged the environmental and health impacts of Chornobyl from the beginning. The Soviet leadership first hoped nobody would notice the accident and then did their best to conceal and minimize the damage. As a result, a full and accurate assessment of the consequences has proved impossible. Historian and Chornobyl expert David

---

*In this article we use the Ukrainian spelling of "Chornobyl." The word may appear as "Chernobyl" in the formal names of organizations.

Marples wrote that authorities in the former Soviet Union classified all medical information related to the accident while denying that illnesses among cleanup workers resulted from their radiation exposure. Independent researchers have had difficulty locating significant numbers of evacuees and those who worked on the cleanup, and they have had to piece together their conclusions from interviews with medical providers, citizens, officials in the contaminated areas, others involved, and those cleanup workers they could find.

In September 2005, a report on the health impacts of Chornobyl by the UN Chernobyl Forum (seven UN agencies plus the World Bank and officials from Belarus, Ukraine, and Russia) said only 50 deaths could be attributed to Chornobyl and ultimately 4,000 will die as a result of the accident. The Chernobyl Forum report acknowledges that nine children died from thyroid cancer and that 4,000 children contracted the disease, but puts the survival rate at 99 percent. It denies any link with fertility problems and says that the most significant health problems are due to poverty, lifestyle (e.g., smoking, poor diet), and emotional problems, especially among evacuees. Marples notes that the overall assessment of the Chernobyl Forum is "a reassuring message."

The reality on the ground offers a different picture. In Gomel, a city of 700,000 in Belarus less than 80 kilometers from the destroyed reactor and one of the most severely contaminated areas, the documentary film *Chernobyl Heart* reports the incidence of thyroid cancer is 10,000 times higher than before the accident and by 1990 had increased 30-fold throughout Belarus, which received most of the radioactive fallout. Chernobyl.info states that congenital birth defects in Gomel have jumped 250 percent since the accident, and infant mortality is 300 percent higher than in the rest of Europe. A doctor interviewed in *Chernobyl Heart* says just 15 to 20 percent of the babies born at the Gomel Maternity Hospital are healthy. Chernobyl Children's Project International executive director Adi Roche says it's impossible to prove that Chornobyl caused the problems: "All we can say is the defects are increasing, the illnesses are increasing, the genetic damage is increasing." Referring to a facility for abandoned children, she adds, "places like this didn't exist before Chornobyl, so it speaks for itself." Marples, who has made numerous trips to the Chornobyl region over the past 20 years, reports the health crisis in Belarus today is so serious that there are open discussions of a "demographic doomsday."

The long-lived nature of the radionuclides and the fact that they are migrating through the contaminated regions' ecosystems into the groundwater and food chain further complicate the task of predicting the full impact of the disaster. But as the global campaign to build new reactors gains momentum, it bears asking whether a Chornobyl could happen elsewhere.

It Can't Happen Here

Nobody wants any more Chornobyls. The question is, can that outcome be ensured without phasing out nuclear power altogether? The Nuclear Energy Institute (NEI), the trade association and lobbying arm of the American nuclear power industry, says a Chornobyl-type accident is highly unlikely in the United States because of "key differences in U.S. reactor design, regulation, and emergency preparedness." Safety is assured, NEI says, by the strategy of "defense in depth," which relies on a combination of multiple, redundant, independently operating safety systems; physical barriers such as the steel reactor vessel and the typically three- to four-foot steel-reinforced concrete containment dome that would stop radiation from escaping; ongoing preventive and corrective maintenance; ongoing training of technical staff; and extensive government oversight. A key argument for nuclear power these days is the claim that nuclear reactors are safe and reliable.

The U.S. nuclear fleet has substantially increased its "capacity factor" (for a given period, the output of a generating unit as a percentage of total possible output if run at full power) since 1980. However, David Lochbaum, director of the Nuclear Safety Project at the Union of Concerned Scientists (UCS), points out that since the Three Mile Island accident in central Pennsylvania in 1979, 45 reactors (out of 104 operating U.S. units) have been shut down longer than one year to restore safety margins. A nuclear engineer by training, Lochbaum left the industry after 17 years when he and a co-worker were unable to get their employer or the Nuclear Regulatory Commission (NRC) to address safety issues at the Susquehanna plant in northeastern Pennsylvania. (The problem at that plant and others across the country was corrected after they testified before Congress.) For the last 10 years Lochbaum has been at UCS monitoring the safety of the nation's nuclear power plants and raising concerns with the NRC. He does not share the industry's confidence in the safety of the current fleet.

Nuclear power plants are incredibly complex systems that perform a relatively simple task: heating water to create steam that spins a turbine and generates electricity. Lochbaum explains that nuclear plant safety problems tend to follow a bathtub curve; the greatest number come at the beginning of a reactor's life, then after a few years when the plant is "broken in" and staff are familiar with its specific needs, problems drop and level off until the plant begins to age.

Most of the current U.S. fleet is either in or entering its twilight years, and since the late 1990s the NRC has allowed reactors to increase the amount of electricity they generate by up to 20 percent, which exceeds what the plants were designed to handle. Such "power uprates" push greater volumes of cooling water through the plant, causing more wear and tear on pipes and other equipment. The agency has also granted 20-year license extensions to 39 reactors, and most of the rest are expected to apply before their initial 40-year licenses expire. At the same time, Lochbaum says, the NRC is cutting back on the amount and frequency of safety tests and inspections. Tests that were carried out quarterly are now performed annually, and once-annual tests are now done when reactors are shut down for refueling, about every two years.

The NRC maintains that it is providing adequate oversight to keep the public safe and prevent serious reactor accidents. Gary Holahan, an official in the NRC's Office of Nuclear Reactor Regulation, explains that extended power uprates, which raise the power output of a reactor between 7 and 20 percent, require modifications to the plant that involve upgrading or replacing equipment like high pressure turbines, pumps, motors, main generators, and transformers. Before a power uprate is granted, he says, the NRC must make a finding that it complies with federal regulations and that there's "a reasonable assurance" that the health and safety of the public will not be endangered.

Lochbaum says the NRC's handling of the large power uprates illustrates the problems with its oversight. In an issue brief entitled "Snap, Crackle, & Pop: The BWR Power Uprate Experiment," he says the Quad Cities Unit 2 reactor in Illinois "literally began shaking itself apart at the higher power level" after operating for nearly 30 years at its originally licensed power level. After the uprate was approved, the steam dryer developed a 2.7 meter crack, and the component was replaced in May 2005. In early April of this year, he says Quad Cities staff found a 1.5 meter crack in the new steam dryer, and they still don't know exactly what is causing the problem. After the problem was first reported, manufacturer General Electric (GE) surveyed 15 of its other boiling water reactors around the world that had been granted 20-percent power uprates and reported problems—all vibration related—in 13.

Despite objections from the Vermont Public Service Board and one of its own commissioners, the NRC recently granted a 20-percent power uprate to the 33-year-old Vermont Yankee reactor. Stuart Richards, deputy director of the NRC's Division of Inspection, says the commission approved the power uprate after a first-time pilot engineering inspection that included an 11,000-manhour technical review failed to find any significant safety issues. "It's not the age of the plant but the physical condition of the components and how well the facility maintains the plant" that is important, he says. In addition, the power is being increased in NRC-monitored stages. But none of this reassures Lochbaum, who points out that this single-unit plant was badly maintained for much of its operating life, making it an especially poor candidate for a practice known to stress reactors. Applications for extended power uprates at six reactors are pending, and the NRC expects nine more through 2011.

The NRC says it is doing a smarter job of regulating the industry today by pinpointing areas likely to need more attention. "The agency and the industry as a whole over the last 10 to 15 years have developed better and better tools to determine what is risk-significant and what is less risk-significant," Richards explains. "So in some cases where in the past we have required more maintenance or surveillance, now those requirements are less stringent, because the components have been demonstrated to be less significant." In other cases, he says, performing too much maintenance can be detrimental, because the components are needed to do their job, and they can be tested "to the point where it causes them to have degradation."

Lochbaum says the flaw in that logic is well illustrated by a near miss at the Davis-Besse plant in Ohio. In 2002 it was discovered that boric acid escaping from the reactor for several years had eaten a 15-centimeter hole in the reactor vessel's steel lid, leaving a thin layer of stainless steel bulging outward from the pressure. Boric acid had been observed on the vessel head in 1996, 1998, and again in 2000, and NRC staff drafted an order in November 2001 to shut Davis-Besse down for a safety inspection. NRC nevertheless allowed the reactor to continue operating until February 2002, when plant workers almost accidentally found the hole. If the reactor head had burst, the reactor would likely have melted down.

Lochbaum and former NRC commissioner Peter Bradford say the Davis-Besse incident and numerous others indicate that the agency seems to be more interested in the short-term economic interest of the nuclear industry than in carrying out its mission to protect public health and safety. Bradford points to an internal NRC survey in 2002 revealing that nearly half of all NRC employees thought they would be retaliated against if they raised safety concerns, and that of those who did report problems, one-third said they suffered harassment as a result. Several critics say the safety culture of the commission changed after Senator Pete Domenici—perhaps the nuclear industry's biggest champion in Congress—told the NRC chairman in 1998 that he would cut the agency's budget by a third if it didn't reverse its "adversarial attitude" toward the industry.

Given the regulatory environment and an aging fleet of reactors, Lochbaum fears that another serious accident is inevitable. He uses the analogy of a slot machine, but instead of oranges, bananas, and cherries, the winning combination is an initiating event, like a broken pipe or a fire; equipment failure; and human error. "As the plants get older, we're starting to see the wheels come up more often, which suggests it's only a matter of time before all three come up at once," he says.

Nuclear proponents claim the new advanced designs are much safer. Unlike current plants with their multiple back-up systems, the new "passive safety" designs, such as Westinghouse's AP1000 pressurized water reactor (PWR) and GE's ABWR (Advanced Boiling Water Reactor) and ESBWR (Economic Simplified Boiling Water Reactor), rely on gravity rather than an army of pumps to push the water up into the reactor vessel and through the cooling system. Because the systems are smaller, there are fewer components to break.

Physicist Ed Lyman, a colleague of Lochbaum's at UCS who has been studying the new designs, is skeptical of the safety claims of the passive designs. He explains that slashing costs, particularly of piping and the enormously expensive steel-reinforced rebar concrete, motivated the new LWR designs, not safety. It was thought that if the power output of the reactors was lower, a gravity-driven system could dump water into the reactor core without the need for forced circulation and its miles of pipes and accompanying equipment.

Numerous tests of the gravity-driven water system for the AP600, the smaller predecessor to the AP 1000, showed the system worked, and NRC certified the design. However, the current trend in reactors is for larger units with higher output. The cost of the AP600 wasn't low enough to offset the loss in generation capacity, so none sold. The AP600 then morphed into the AP1000. GE's new "passive safety" designs followed a similar trajectory beginning with a 600-megawatt design, the SBWR (Simplified Boiling Water Reactor). The company's next design, the ABWR, was 1,350 megawatts, and its ESBWR is 1,560.

The NRC recently certified the AP1000. Lyman is concerned the agency is relying on computer modeling rather than experimental data to demonstrate that gravity-driven cooling will work in these much larger designs. He's also troubled that the containment structures of the new PWRs are less robust than those in the current fleet. NRC's Gary Holahan acknowledges that the agency relied on the tests from the AP600 and computer modeling for the AP 1000, but says that after extensive review by the commission's technical staff and the Advisory Committee on Reactor Safeguards, it determined that additional testing was not necessary. Nor does the NRC have any concerns about the thickness of the AP1000's containment dome compared to those of existing PWRs.

Increasing numbers of nuclear proponents and news reports are describing new reactor designs, such as the pebble bed modular reactor, as "accident-proof" or "fail-safe"—so safe, in fact, that the pebble bed doesn't need (or have) a containment structure. Lyman disagrees. The pebble bed is moderated by helium instead of water and uses uranium fuel pellets encased in silicon carbide, ceramic material, and graphite. He says experiments conducted at the AVR demonstration reactor in Germany, the first one ever built, have shown that the models underestimated how hot the pellets could get. The pellets degrade quickly upon reaching the critical temperature, which could lead to a large release of radiation. "So, they just don't have the predictive capacity or the understanding of how these reactors or the fuel technology work to say it's meltdown-proof," he says.

Going to Waste

In the light-water reactors that make up the majority of the world's reactor fleet, uranium fuel is loaded into the reactor, then bombarded by neutrons to trigger the nuclear fission chain reaction. After awhile all of the fissionable material in the uranium fuel is used up, or "spent." But the neutron bombardment makes the fuel two-and-a-half million times more radioactive, according to Marvin Resnikoff, a nuclear physicist with Radioactive Waste Management Associates in New York. By 2035, American nuclear power plants will have created an estimated 105,000 metric tons of spent fuel that is so deadly it must be completely isolated from the environment for tens or even hundreds of thousands of years. A Nevada state agency report put the toxicity in perspective: even after 10 years out of the reactor, an unshielded spent fuel assembly would emit enough radiation to kill somebody standing a meter away from it in less than three minutes.

No country has yet successfully dealt with its high-level nuclear waste from the first generation of reactors, let alone made plans for the added waste from a vast expansion of nuclear power. Most agree that deep geologic burial is the safest and cheapest disposal method, and countries are in various stages of picking and developing their sites. Steve Frishman of the Nevada Agency for Nuclear Projects thinks the Finns are furthest along, having chosen a permanent repository at a crystalline bedrock site at Olkiluoto that already hosts two operating reactors and one under construction. The site has been tested extensively to ensure it will effectively isolate the waste 420–520 meters down. The repository is expected to open in 2020.

The Swedes also plan to construct their repository in a deep underground granite site, though they have not yet picked the final location. They will encapsulate the spent nuclear fuel in copper canisters surrounded by bentonite clay, which swells up and makes its own watertight seal when exposed to water. Frishman says that's an extra precaution, because while they will probably find some water 500 meters underground where they plan to put the canisters, the water there is not oxygenated and would probably not corrode the canisters even if it did come in contact with them. The Swedish approach is enormously expensive, but they say results, not costs, are guiding their decisions.

These approaches seem reasonably cautious and thus offer some hope that the waste problem—which must be solved no matter what happens to nuclear power—might not be intractable. The U.S. approach, however, is less reassuring. Politics, rather than science-determined suitability, led the U.S. Department of Energy (DOE) to Yucca Mountain, a ridge of volcanic tuff on the edge of the U.S. Nuclear Test Site in the Nevada desert about 145 kilometers northwest of Las Vegas. Nevada was designated by default in an amendment (later tagged as the "Screw Nevada Bill") to the 1982 Nuclear Waste Policy Act that prohibited DOE from considering any sites in granite.

Aside from being located in the third most seismically active region in the country, Yucca Mountain is so porous that after just 50 years isotopes from atmospheric atom bomb tests have already seeped down into the underlying aquifer. But since the mountain was designated as the nation's only repository site, Frishman says DOE has been trying to engineer its way around the problems, and when it can't do that, change the rules. The latest attempt is legislation proposed by the Bush administration that among other things would raise the repository's current legal limit of 70,000 metric tons of high-level waste, remove the nuclear waste fund (money collected over the years from ratepayers by nuclear utilities to build a repository) from federal budgetary oversight, and exempt metals in the underground metal containers from regulation, leaving chromium, molybdenum, and zinc free to contaminate the area's groundwater.

On the basis of the geological instability of the site, Nevada is aggressively fighting the repository. In 2004 a federal court ruled that an Environmental Protection Agency (EPA) health standard that applied for the first 10,000 years was inadequate because the National Academy of Sciences determined that peak doses would likely occur at least 200,000 years after the waste was placed in the site. NRC therefore could not license the site. EPA has since proposed another health standard, which appears to ignore the court ruling by allowing radiation exposure to residents of the nearby Amargossa Valley to jump from a mean of 15 millirems per year for the first 10,000 years to a median value of 350 millirems per year subsequently.

Ultimately, Frishman does not believe Yucca Mountain can meet any real health-based standard. Furthermore, he points out, whatever standard is finally adopted is irrelevant once a licensing decision is made and the waste is placed in the repository: "The site is the standard."

Reprocessing

The nuclear power industry did not expect Nevada's legal challenges to be so successful, and U.S. nuclear proponents have begun to think beyond Yucca Mountain. They maintain that the development of fast breeder reactors, which create nuclear fuel by producing more fissile material than they consume, along with reprocessing the spent fuel (separating out the still-usable plutonium and uranium) will reduce the volume of waste and negate the need for geologic disposal.

Since it was originally assumed that reprocessing would be part of the nuclear fuel cycle, commercial reactors were not designed to house all of the waste they would create during their operational lives. Three commercial reprocessing facilities were built in the United States, though only one, at West Valley in western New York state, ever operated. After six years of troubled operation marked by accidents, mishandling of high-level wastes, and contamination of nearby waterways, it was shut down in 1972. In 1977 the Carter administration banned reprocessing due to concerns about nuclear weapons proliferation after India stunned the world by testing its first atomic bomb, which was made with plutonium from its reprocessing facility. According to UCS, approximately 240 metric tons of separated plutonium—enough for 40,000 nuclear weapons—was in storage worldwide as of the end of 2003. Reprocessing the U.S. spent fuel inventory would add more than 500 metric tons.

France, Britain, Russia, India, and Japan currently reprocess spent fuel, and the Bush administration is pushing to revive reprocessing in the United States. It has allocated $130 million to begin developing an "integrated spent fuel cycle," and recently announced another $250 million, primarily to develop UREX+, a technology said to address proliferation concerns by leaving the separated plutonium too radioactive for potential thieves to handle. In addition, the U.S. Congress has directed the administration to prepare a plan by 2007 to pick a technology to reprocess all of the spent fuel from commercial nuclear reactors and start building an engineering-scale demonstration plant.

UCS's Ed Lyman says it is "a myth" that reprocessing spent nuclear fuel reduces the volume of nuclear waste: "All reprocessing does is take spent fuel that's compact, and it spreads—smears—it out into dozens of different places." Current reprocessing technology uses nitric acid to dissolve the fuel assemblies and separate out plutonium and uranium. But it also leaves behind numerous extremely radioactive fission products as well as high-level liquid waste that is typically solidified in glass. In the process, a lot of radioactive gas is discharged into the environment, and there is additional liquid waste that's too expensive to isolate, he says: "So, that's just dumped into the ocean—that's the practice in France and the U.K."

Matthew Bunn, acting director of Harvard University's Project on Managing the Atom, has laid out a number of additional arguments against reprocessing. First, reprocessing spent fuel doesn't negate the need for or reduce the space required in a permanent repository, because a repository's size is determined by the heat output of the waste, not its volume. Second, reprocessing would substantially increase the cost of managing nuclear waste and wouldn't make sense economically unless uranium topped US$360 per kilogram, a price he says is not likely for several decades, if ever. Third, in this new era of heightened violence and terrorism, the proliferation risks—which would not be addressed by the new reprocessing technologies—take on even greater urgency. Fourth, reprocessing is also a dangerous technology with a track record of terrible accidents, including the world's worst pre-Chornobyl nuclear accident (a 1957 explosion at a reprocessing plant near Khystym in Russia) and other incidents in Russia and Japan as recently as the 1990s. Fifth, the new "advanced" reprocessing technologies, UREX+ and pyroprocessing, are complex, expensive, in their infancy, and unlikely to yield substantial improvements over existing reprocessing methods. Finally, Bunn argues, the Bush administration's rush to embrace reprocessing spent nuclear fuel is premature and unnecessary, since the spent fuel can remain in dry casks at nuclear power plants for decades while better solutions are sought.

Solution in Search of Problem

In the end, the case for nuclear power hinges on an evaluation of its costs and benefits compared with those of the alternatives. Many observers expect a growing ecological, social, and economic crisis unless we figure out how to retard and ultimately reverse climate change by weaning ourselves off increasingly scarce, expensive, and conflict-ridden fossil fuels. Nuclear power, until recently a pariah due to its enormous cost and demonstrated potential for serious accidents, is now touted as an indispensable solution. Nuclear power's dark side—its environmental legacy, high cost, and danger of accidents and the spread of atomic weapons—is currently downplayed. No energy system is without costs, but alternatives that avoid these particularly grave drawbacks do exist.

Space limitations preclude a comprehensive review of the alternatives, but their prospects have never been brighter. For instance, a 2005 report by the New Economics Foundation (NEF) says a broad mix of renewable energy sources that includes micro, small-, medium- and large-scale technologies applied flexibly could "more than meet all our needs." Besides solar and wind power, the mix includes tidal, wave, small-scale hydro, geothermal, biomass, and landfill gas. Rather than relying exclusively on large baseload suppliers of electricity like nuclear plants, or single sources of renewable energy that are not always available, the foundation says the key is setting up an extensive, diverse, and decentralized network of power sources, which would also be much less susceptible to widespread power outages. The total capital cost of setting up such a system has not been calculated and would vary greatly depending on whether it was implemented all at once or incrementally, building on transition technologies. According to the NEF report, a nuclear-generated kilowatthour of electricity—factoring in construction and operating costs but not waste management, insurance against accidents, or preventing nuclear weapons proliferation—costs up to 15.6 U.S. cents, significantly higher than other sources.

Governments and markets are beginning to recognize the potential of renewable energy and its use is growing rapidly. According to Worldwatch Institute's *Renewables 2005,* global investment in renewable energy in 2004 was about US$30 billion. The report points out that renewable sources generated 20 percent of the amount of electricity produced by the world's 443 operating nuclear reactors in 2004. Renewables now account for 20–25 percent of global power sector investment, and the Organisation for Economic Co-operation and

Development predicts that over the next 30 years one-third of the investment in new power sources in OECD countries will be for renewable energy.

Alternative energy guru Amory Lovins says the investment in alternatives is currently "an order of magnitude" greater than that now being spent on building new nuclear plants. Lovins has been preaching lower-cost alternatives, including energy conservation, for more than three decades, and the realization of his vision of sustainable, renewable energy is perhaps closer than ever. He argues that the current moves to re-embrace nuclear power are a huge step backwards, and that contrary to claims that we need to consider all options to deal with global warming, nuclear power would actually hinder the effort because of the high cost and the long time it would take to get enough carbon-displacing nuclear plants up and running. "In practice, keeping nuclear power alive means diverting private and public investment from the cheaper market winners—cogeneration, renewables, and efficiency—to the costly market loser. Its higher cost than competitors, per unit of net CO_2 displaced, means that every dollar invested in nuclear expansion will *worsen* climate change," he writes in his 2005 paper "Nuclear Power: Economics and Climate-Protection Potential."

[D]oubling the world's current nuclear energy output would reduce global carbon emissions by just one-seventh of the amount required to avoid the worst impacts of global warming. Researchers at the Massachusetts Institute of Technology point out that achieving even this inadequate result would require siting a permanent repository the size of Yucca Mountain every three to four years to deal with the additional waste—an enormous and expensive challenge. Given nuclear power's drawbacks, and the growth and promise of clean, lower cost, less dangerous alternatives, the case for nuclear power wobbles badly. Stripped of the pretext that nuclear power is the answer to climate change, the case essentially collapses.

POSTSCRIPT

Is It Time to Revive Nuclear Power?

Robert Evans, "Nuclear Power: Back in the Game," *Power Engineering* (October 2005), reports that a number of power companies are considering new nuclear power plants. See also Eliot Marshall, "Is the Friendly Atom Poised for a Comeback?" and Daniel Clery, "Nuclear Industry Dares to Dream of a New Dawn," *Science* (August 19, 2005). Nuclear momentum is growing, says Charles Petit, "Nuclear Power: Risking a Comeback," *National Geographic* (April 2006), thanks in part to new technologies. Karen Charman, "Brave Nuclear World?" (Part I) *World Watch* (May/June 2006), objects that producing nuclear fuel uses huge amounts of electricity derived from fossil fuels, so going nuclear can hardly prevent all releases of carbon dioxide (although using electricity derived from nuclear power would reduce the problem). She also notes that "Although no comprehensive and integrated study comparing the collateral and external costs of energy sources globally has been done, all currently available energy sources have them. . . . Burning coal—the single largest source of air pollution in the U.S.—causes global warming, acid rain, soot, smog, and other toxic air emissions and generates waste ash, sludge, and toxic chemicals. Landscapes and ecosystems are completely destroyed by mountaintop removal mining, while underground mining imposes high fatality, injury, and sickness rates. Even wind energy kills birds, can be noisy, and, some people complain, blights landscapes."

Michael J. Wallace tells us that there are 103 nuclear reactors operating in the United States today. Stephen Ansolabehere, et al., "The Future of Nuclear Power," *An Interdisciplinary MIT Study* (MIT, 2003), note that in 2000 there were 352 in the developed world as a whole, and a mere 15 in developing nations, and that even a very large increase in the number of nuclear power plants—to 1,000 to 1,500—will not stop all releases of carbon dioxide. In fact, if carbon emissions double by 2050 as expected, from 6,500 to 13,000 million metric tons per year, the 1,800 million metric tons not emitted because of nuclear power will seem relatively insignificant. Nevertheless, say John M. Deutch and Ernest J. Moniz, "The Nuclear Option," *Scientific American* (September 2006), such a cut in carbon emissions would be "significant." Christine Laurent, in "Beating Global Warming with Nuclear Power?" *UNESCO Courier* (February 2001), notes that "For several years, the nuclear energy industry has attempted to cloak itself in different ecological robes. Its credo: nuclear energy is a formidable asset in battle against global warming because it emits very small amounts of greenhouse gases. This stance, first presented in the late 1980s when the extent of the phenomenon was still the subject of controversy, is now at the heart of policy debates over how to avoid droughts, downpours and floods." Laurent adds that it makes more sense to focus on reducing carbon emissions by reducing energy consumption.

The debate over the future of nuclear power is likely to remain vigorous for some time to come. But as Richard A. Meserve says in a *Science* editorial ("Global Warming and Nuclear Power," *Science* [January 23, 2004]), "For those who are serious about confronting global warming, nuclear power should be seen as part of the solution. Although it is unlikely that many environmental groups will become enthusiastic proponents of nuclear power, the harsh reality is that any serious program to address global warming cannot afford to jettison any technology prematurely. . . . The stakes are large, and the scientific and educational community should seek to ensure that the public understands the critical link between nuclear power and climate change." Paul Lorenzini, "A Second Look at Nuclear Power," *Issues in Science and Technology* (Spring 2005), argues that the goal must be energy "sufficiency for the foreseeable future with minimal environmental impact." Nuclear power can be part of the answer, but making it happen requires that we shed ideological biases. "It means ceasing to deceive ourselves about what might be possible."

Alvin M. Weinberg, former director of the Oak Ridge National Laboratory, notes in "New Life for Nuclear Power," *Issues in Science and Technology* (Summer 2003), that to make a serious dent in carbon emissions would require perhaps four times as many reactors as suggested in the MIT study. The accompanying safety and security problems would be challenging. If the challenges can be met, says John J. Taylor, retired vice president for nuclear power at the Electric Power Research Institute, in "The Nuclear Power Bargain," *Issues in Science and Technology* (Spring 2004), there are a great many potential benefits. Are new reactor technologies needed? Richard K. Lester, "New Nukes," *Issues in Science and Technology* (Summer 2006), says that better centralized waste storage is what is needed, at least in the short term.

Environmental groups such as Friends of the Earth are adamantly opposed, saying "Those who back nuclear over renewables and increased energy efficiency completely fail to acknowledge the deadly radioactive legacy nuclear power has created and continues to create" ("Nuclear Power Revival Plan Slammed," Press Release, April 18, 2004, http://www.foe-scotland.org.uk/press/pr20040408.html).

ISSUE 6

Will Hydrogen Replace Fossil Fuels for Cars?

YES: **David L. Bodde,** from "Fueling the Future: The Road to the Hydrogen Economy," Statement Presented to the Committee on Science, Subcommittee on Research and Subcommittee on Energy, U.S. House of Representatives (July 20, 2005)

NO: **Michael Behar,** from "Warning: The Hydrogen Economy May Be More Distant Than It Appears," *Popular Science* (January 2005)

ISSUE SUMMARY

YES: Professor David L. Bodde argues that there is no question whether hydrogen can satisfy the nation's energy needs. The real issue is how to handle the transition from the current energy system to the hydrogen system.

NO: Michael Behar argues that the public has been misled about the prospects of the "hydrogen economy." We must overcome major technological, financial, and political obstacles before hydrogen can be a viable alternative to fossil fuels.

The 1973 "oil crisis" heightened awareness that the world—even if it was not yet running out of oil—was extraordinarily dependent on that fossil fuel (and therefore on supplier nations) for transportation, home heating, and electricity generation. Since the supply of oil and other fossil fuels was clearly finite, some people worried that there would come a time when demand could not be satisfied, and our dependence would leave us helpless. At the same time, we became acutely aware of the many unfortunate side effects of fossil fuels, notably air pollution.

The 1970s saw the modern environmental movement gain momentum. The first Earth Day was in 1970. Numerous government steps were taken to deal with air pollution, water pollution, and other environmental problems. In response to the oil crisis, a great deal of public money went into developing alternative energy supplies. The emphasis was on "renewable" energy, meaning conservation, wind, solar, and fuels such as hydrogen gas (which, when burned with pure oxygen, produces only water vapor as exhaust). However, when the crisis passed and oil supplies were once more ample (albeit it did cost more to fill a gasoline tank), most public funding for alternative-energy research and demonstration projects vanished. What work continued was at the hands of a few enthusiasts and those corporations that saw future opportunities. In 2001, the Worldwatch Institute published Seth Dunn's *Hydrogen Futures: Toward a Sustainable Energy System.* In 2002, MIT Press published Peter Hoffman's *Tomorrow's Energy: Hydrogen, Fuel Cells, and the Prospects for a Cleaner Planet.* Jeremy Ritkin, "Hydrogen: Empowering the People," *The Nation* (December 23, 2002), argues that hydrogen holds the potential both to replace fossil fuels and to reshape society. On the corporate side, fossil fuel companies have long been major investors in alternative energy systems.

What drives the continuing interest in hydrogen and other alternative or renewable energy systems is the continuing problems associated with fossil fuels (and the discovery of new problems such as global warming), concern about dependence and potential political instability, rising oil and gasoline prices, and the growing realization that the availability of petroleum will peak in the near future. See Colin J. Campbell, "Depletion and Denial: The Final Years of Oil," *USA Today Magazine* (November 2000), Charles C. Mann, "Getting Over Oil," *Technology Review* (January–February 2002), Robert L. Hirsch, Roger H. Bezdek, and Robert M. Wendling, "Peaking Oil Production: Sooner Rather than Later?" *Issues in Science and Technology* (Spring 2005), and *"The Peak Oil Forum,"* *World Watch* (January-February 2006).

Will that interest come to anything? There are, after all, a number of other ways to meet the need. Coal can be converted into oil and gasoline (though the air pollution and global warming problems remain). Cars can be made more efficient (and mileage efficiency is much greater than it was in the 1970s despite the popularity of SUVs). Cars can be designed to use natural gas or battery power; "hybrid" cars use combinations of gasoline and electricity and are proving more popular every year. See Brendan I. Koerner, "Rise of the Green Machine," *Wired* (April 2005).

The hydrogen enthusiasts remain. In the selections that follow, Clemson University professor David L. Bodde argues that there is no question whether hydrogen can satisfy the nation's energy needs. The real issue is how to handle the transition from the current energy system to the hydrogen system. He recommends research, education, and support for entrepreneurs. Michael Behar argues that the public has been misled about the prospects of the "hydrogen economy." It will come, but first we must overcome major technological, financial, and political obstacles.

YES

David L. Bodde

Fueling the Future: The Road to the Hydrogen Economy

Thank you, ladies and gentlemen, for this opportunity to discuss the *Road to the Hydrogen Economy*, a road I believe we must travel if we are to ensure a world well supplied with clean, affordable energy derived from secure sources. I will speak to this from the perspective of motor vehicle transportation and address the questions posed by the Committee within the framework of three basic ideas.

First, research policy should view the hydrogen transition as a marketplace competition. For the next several decades, three rival infrastructures will compete for a share of the world auto market: (a) the current internal combustion engine and associated fuels infrastructure; (b) the hybrid electric vehicles, now emerging on the market; and (c) the hydrogen fueled vehicles, now in early demonstration. We can judge policy alternatives and applied research investments by their ability to accelerate the shift in market share among these competing infrastructures.

Second, and in parallel with the marketplace transition, fundamental research should focus on sustaining the hydrogen economy into the far future. Key issues include: (a) storing hydrogen on-board vehicles at near-atmospheric pressure; (b) sequestering the carbon-dioxide effluent from manufacturing hydrogen from coal; (c) sharply reducing the cost of hydrogen produced from non-coal resources, especially nuclear, photobiological, photoelectrochemical, and thin-film solar processes; (d) improving the performance and cost of fuel cells; and (e) storing electricity on-board vehicles in batteries that provide both high energy performance and high power performance at reasonable cost.

And third, the results of this research must be brought swiftly and effectively to the marketplace. This requires economic policies that encourage technology-based innovation, both by independent entrepreneurs and those operating from the platform of established companies. Clemson University, through its International Center for Automotive Research and its Arthur M. Spiro Center for Entrepreneurial Leadership, intends to become a major contributor to this goal.

In what follows, I will set out my reasoning and the evidence that supports these three basic ideas.

From Committee on Research and Subcommittee on Energy, U. S. House of Representatives, July 20, 2005.

The Hydrogen Transition:
A Marketplace Competition

Much thinking about the hydrogen economy concerns "what" issues, visionary descriptions of a national fuels infrastructure that would deliver a substantial fraction of goods and services with hydrogen as the energy carrier. And yet, past visions of energy futures, however desirable they might have seemed at the time, have not delivered sustained action, either from a public or private perspective. The national experience with nuclear power, synthetic fuels, and renewable energy demonstrates this well.

The difficulty arises from insufficient attention to the transition between the present and the desired future—the balance between forces that lock the energy economy in stasis and the entrepreneurial forces that could accelerate it toward a more beneficial condition.

In effect, the present competes against the future, and the pace and direction of any transition will be governed by the outcome. Viewing the transition to a hydrogen economy through the lens of a competitive transition can bring a set of "how" questions to the national policy debate—questions of how policy can rebalance the competitive forces so that change prevails in the marketplace.

A Model of the Competitive Transition

The competitive battle will be fought over a half century among three competing infrastructures:[1]

- The internal combustion engine (ICE), either in a spark-ignition or compression-ignition form, and its attendant motor fuels supply chain;
- The hybrid electric vehicle (HEV), now entering the market, which achieves superior efficiency by supplementing an internal combustion engine with an electric drive system and which uses the current supply chain for motor fuels; and,
- The hydrogen fuel cell vehicle (HFCV), which requires radically distinct technologies for the vehicle, for fuel-production, and for fuel distribution.

Figure 1 shows one scenario, based on the most optimistic assumptions, of how market share could shift among the contending infrastructures (NRC 2004). Several aspects of this scenario bear special mention. First, note the extended time required for meaningful change: these are long-lived assets built around large, sunk investments. They cannot be quickly changed under the best of circumstances. Second, the road to the hydrogen economy runs smoothest through the hybrid electric vehicle. The HEV offers immediate gains in fuel economy and advances technologies that will eventually prove useful for hydrogen fuel cell vehicles, especially battery and electric system management technologies. Although this scenario shows significant market penetration for the HEV, its success cannot be assured. The HEV might remain a niche product, despite its current popularity if consumers conclude that the

Figure 1

Competition for Market Share

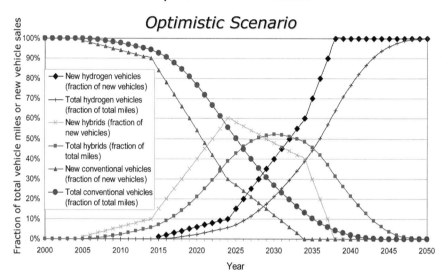

• *Complete replacement of ICE and HEV vehicles with fuel cell vehicles in 2050*

Source: NRC 2004

value of the fuel savings does not compensate for the additional cost of the HEV. Or, its gains in efficiency might be directed toward vehicle size and acceleration rather than fuel economy. Either circumstance would make an early hydrogen transition even more desirable.

Any transition to a HFCV fleet, however, will require overcoming a key marketplace barrier that is unique to hydrogen—widely available supplies of fuel. And to this we now turn.

The Chicken and the Egg[2]

Most analyses suggest that large-scale production plants in a mature hydrogen economy can manufacture fuel at a cost that competes well with gasoline at current prices (NRC 2004). However, investors will not build these plants and their supporting distribution infrastructure in the absence of large-scale demand. And, the demand for hydrogen will not be forthcoming unless potential purchasers of hydrogen vehicles can be assured widely available sources of fuel. Variants of this "chicken and egg" problem have limited the market penetration of other fuels, such as methanol and ethanol blends (M85 and E85) and compressed natural gas. This issue—the simultaneous development of the supply side and demand sides of the market—raises one of the highest barriers to a hydrogen transition.

Distributed Hydrogen Production for the Transition

To resolve this problem, a committee of the National Academy of Sciences (NRC 2004) recommended an emphasis on distributed production of hydrogen.

Figure 2

A Supply Chain Infrastructure

Delivered H₂ Costs of Alternative Technologies

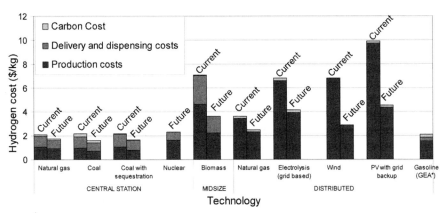

* GEA = Gasoline Efficiency Adjusted – scaled to hybrid vehicle efficiency

Source: NRC 2004

In this model, the hydrogen fuel would be manufactured at dispensing stations conveniently located for consumers. Once the demand for hydrogen fuel grew sufficiently, then larger manufacturing plants and logistic systems could be built to achieve scale economies. However, distributed production of hydrogen offers two salient challenges.

The first challenge is cost. Figure 2, shows the delivered cost of molecular hydrogen for a variety of production technologies. The "distributed" technologies, to the right in Figure 2, offer hydrogen at a cost between 2 and 5 times the cost of the large-scale, "central station" technologies, on the left in Figure 2. Technological advances can mitigate, but not remove entirely, this cost disadvantage.

The second challenge concerns the environment. Carbon capture and sequestration do not appear practical in distributed production. During the opening stage of a hydrogen transition, we might simply have to accept some carbon releases in order to achieve the later benefits.

Research to Accelerate a Transition by Distributed Hydrogen Production

A study panel convened by the National Academy of Sciences (NAS) recently recommended several research thrusts that could accelerate distributed production for a transition to hydrogen (NRC 2004). These include:

- Development of hydrogen fueling "appliance" that can be manufactured economically and used in service stations reliably and safely by relatively unskilled persons—station attendants and consumers.

- Development of an integrated, standard fueling facility that includes the above appliance as well as generation and storage equipment capable of meeting the sharply varying demands of a 24-hour business cycle.
- Advanced technologies for hydrogen production from electrolysis, essentially a fuel cell operated in reverse, to include enabling operation from intermittent energy sources, such as wind.
- Research on breakthrough technologies for small-scale reformers to produce hydrogen from fossil feedstocks.

The Department of Energy has adopted the NAS recommendations and modified its programs accordingly. It remains too early to judge progress, but in any case these technologies should receive continued emphasis as the desired transition to hydrogen nears. However, progress in research is notoriously difficult to forecast accurately. This suggests consideration be given to interim strategies that would work on the demand side of the marketplace, either to subsidize the cost of distributed hydrogen production while demand builds or to raise the cost of the competition, gasoline and diesel fuels. Such actions would relieve the research program of the entire burden for enabling the transition.

Fundamental Research to Sustain a Hydrogen Economy

At the same time that the marketplace transition advances, several high-payoff (but also high-risk) research campaigns should be waged. These include:

- Storing hydrogen on-board vehicles at near-atmospheric pressure;
- Sequestering the carbon-dioxide effluent from manufacturing hydrogen from coal;
- Sharply reducing the cost of hydrogen produced from non-coal resources, especially nuclear, photobiological, photoelectrochemical, and thin-film solar processes;
- Improving the performance and cost of fuel cells; and,
- Storing electricity on-board vehicles in batteries that provide both high energy performance and high power performance at reasonable cost.

On-Vehicle Hydrogen Storage

The most important long-term research challenge is to provide a more effective means of storing hydrogen on vehicles than the compressed gas or cryogenic liquid now in use. In my judgment, failure to achieve this comes closer to a complete "show-stopper" than any other possibility. I believe this true for two reasons: hydrogen leakage as the vehicle fleet ages, and cost.

With regard to leakage, high pressure systems currently store molecular hydrogen on demonstration vehicles safely and effectively. But these are new and specially-built, and trained professionals operate and maintain. What can we expect of production run vehicles that receive the casual maintenance afforded most cars? A glance at the oil-stained pavement of any parking lot offers evidence of the leakage of heavy fluids stored in the current ICE fleet at atmospheric pressure. As high pressure systems containing the lightest element in the universe age, we might find even greater difficulties with containment. With regard to cost, the energy losses from liquefaction and even compression severely penalize the use of hydrogen fuel, especially when manufactured at distributed stations.

The NAS Committee, cited earlier (NRC 2004), strongly supported an increased emphasis on game-changing approaches to on-vehicle hydrogen storage. One alternative could come from novel approaches to generating the hydrogen on board the vehicle.[3] Chemical hydrides, for example, might offer some promise here, such as the sodium borohydride system demonstrated by Daimler-Chrysler.

Carbon Sequestration

Domestic coal resources within the United States hold the potential to relieve the security burdens arising from oil dependence—but only if the environmental consequences of their use can be overcome. Further, as shown in Figure 2, coal offers the lowest cost pathway to a hydrogen-based energy economy, once the transient conditions have passed. Thus, the conditions under which this resource can be used should be established as soon as possible. The prevailing assumption holds that the carbon effluent from hydrogen manufacturing can be stored as a gas (carbon dioxide, or CO_2) in deep underground formations. Yet how long it must be contained and what leakage rates can be tolerated remain unresolved issues (Socolow 2005). Within the Department of Energy, the carbon sequestration program is managed separately from hydrogen and vehicles programs. The NAS committee recommended closer coordination between the two as well as an ongoing emphasis on carbon capture and sequestration (NRC 2004).

Producing Hydrogen Without Coal

Manufacturing hydrogen from non-fossil resources stands as an important hedge against future constraints on production from coal, or even from natural gas. And under any circumstance, the hydrogen economy will be more robust if served by production from a variety of domestic sources.

The non-fossil resource most immediately available is nuclear. Hydrogen could be produced with no CO_2 emissions by using nuclear heat and electricity in the high-temperature electrolysis of steam. Here the technology issues include the durability of the electrode and electrolyte materials, the effects of high pressure, and the scale-up of the electrolysis cell. Alternatively, a variety of thermochemical reactions could produce hydrogen with great efficiency. Here the needed research concerns higher operating temperatures (700°C to 1000°C) for the nuclear heat as well as research into the chemical cycles themselves. In both cases, the safety issues that might arise from coupling the nuclear island with a hydrogen production plant bear examination (NRC 2004).

In addition, hydrogen production from renewable sources should be emphasized, especially that avoiding the inefficiencies of the conventional chain of conversions: (1) from primary energy into electricity; (2) from electricity to hydrogen; (3) from hydrogen to electricity on-board the vehicle; (4) from electricity to mobility, which is what the customer wanted in the first place. Novel approaches to using renewable energy, such as photobiological or photoelectrochemical, should be supported strongly (NRC 2004).

Improved Fuel Cells

The cost and performance of fuel cells must improve significantly for hydrogen to achieve its full potential. To be sure, molecular hydrogen can be burned in specially designed internal combustion engines. But doing so foregoes the efficiency gains obtainable from the fuel cell, and becomes a costly and (from an energy perspective) inefficient process. The NAS Committee thought the fuel cell essential for a hydrogen economy to be worth the effort required to put it in place. They recommended an emphasis on long-term, breakthrough research that would dramatically improve cost, durability, cycling capacity, and useful life.

Improved Batteries

The battery is as important to a hydrogen vehicle as to a hybrid because it serves as the central energy management device. For example, the energy regained from regenerative braking must be stored in a battery for later reuse. Though energy storage governs the overall operating characteristics of the battery, a high rate of energy release (power) can enable the electric motor to assist the HEV in acceleration and relieve the requirements for fuel cells to immediately match their power output with the needs of the vehicle. Thus, advanced battery research becomes a key enabler for the hydrogen economy and might also expand the scope of the HEV.

Entrepreneurship for the Hydrogen Economy

For the results of DoE research to gain traction in a competitive economy, entrepreneurs and corporate innovators must succeed in bringing hydrogen-related innovations to the marketplace. In many cases, independent entrepreneurs provide the path-breaking innovations that lead to radical improvements in performance, while established companies provide continuous, accumulating improvement. The federal government, in partnership with states and universities, can become an important enabler of both pathways to a hydrogen economy.

Federal Policies Promoting Entrepreneurship

From the federal perspective, several policies could be considered to build an entrepreneurial climate on the "supply" side of the market. These include:

- Special tax consideration for investors in new ventures offering products relevant to fuel savings. The intent would be to increase the amount of venture capital available to startup companies.
- Commercialization programs might enable more entrepreneurs to bring their nascent technologies up to investment grade. For example, an enhanced and focused *Small Business Innovation Research* (SBIR) program might increase the number of participating entrepreneurs participating in fuel-relevant markets. A portion of the *Advanced Technology Program* (ATP) could be focused in like manner.
- Outreach from the National Laboratories to entrepreneurs might be improved. Some laboratories, the National Renewable Energy Laboratory (NREL) for example, offer small, but effective programs. But more systematic outreach, not to business in general, but to entrepreneurial business, would also increase the supply of market-ready innovations.

On the demand side, any policy that increases consumer incentives to purchase fuel efficient vehicles will provide an incentive for ongoing innovation—provided that the policy is perceived as permanent. Entrepreneurs and innovators respond primarily to opportunity; but that opportunity must be durable for the 10 year cycle required to establish a new, high-growth company.

States and Universities as Agents of Innovation/Entrepreneurship

Innovation/entrepreneurship is a contact sport, and that contact occurs most frequently and most intensely within the context of specific laboratories and specific relationships. I will use Clemson's International Center for Automotive Research (ICAR) to illustrate this principle. Most fundamentally, the ICAR is a partnership among the State of South Carolina, major auto makers,[4] and their Tier I, Tier II, and Tier III suppliers. The inclusion of these suppliers will be essential for the success of ICAR or any similar research venture. This is because innovation in the auto industry has evolved toward a global, networked process, much as it has in other industries like microelectronics. The "supply chain" is more accurately described as a network, and network innovation will replace the linear model.

For these reasons, the ICAR, when fully established, will serve as a channel for research and innovation to flow into the entire cluster of auto-related companies in the Southeast United States. We anticipate drawing together and integrating the best technology from a variety of sources:

- Research performed at Clemson University and at the ICAR itself;
- Research performed at the Savannah River National Laboratory and the University of South Carolina; and,
- Relevant science and technology anywhere in the world.

Beyond research, the ICAR will include two other components of a complete innovation package: education, and entrepreneur support. With regard to education, the Master of Science and PhD degrees offered through the ICAR will emphasize the integration of new technology into vehicle design, viewing the auto and its manufacturing plant as an integrated system. In addition, courses on entrepreneurship and innovation, offered through Clemson's Arthur M. Spiro Center for Entrepreneurial Leadership, will equip students with the skills to become effective agents of change within the specific context of the global motor vehicle industry.

With regard to entrepreneur support, the ICAR will host a state-sponsored innovation center to nurture startup companies that originate in the Southeast auto cluster and to draw others from around the world into that cluster. In addition, the ICAR innovation center will welcome teams from established companies seeking the commercial development of their technologies. The State of South Carolina has provided significant support through four recent legislative initiatives. The Research University Infrastructure and the Research Centers of Economic Excellence Acts build the capabilities of the state's universities; and the Venture Capital Act and Innovation Centers Act provide support for entrepreneurs.

None of these elements can suffice by itself; but taken together they combine to offer a package of technology, education, and innovation that can serve the hydrogen transition extraordinarily well.

A Concluding Observation

Revolutionary technological change of the kind contemplated here is rarely predictable and never containable. Every new technology from the computer to the airplane to the automobile carries with it a chain of social and economic consequences that reach far beyond the technology itself. Some of these consequences turn out to be benign; some pose challenges that must be overcome by future generations; but none have proven foreseeable.

For example, a hydrogen transition might bring prolonged prosperity or economic decline to the electric utility industry depending upon which path innovation takes. A pathway that leads through plug-hybrids to home appliances that manufacture hydrogen by electrolysis would reinforce the current utility business model. A pathway in which hydrogen fuel cell vehicles serve as generators for home electric energy would undermine that model. The same holds true for the coal industry. A future in which carbon sequestration succeeds will affect coal far differently from one in which it cannot be accomplished.

The only certainty is that the energy economy will be vastly different from that which we know today. It will have to be.

Notes

1. Another concept, the battery electric vehicle (BEV), offers an all-electric drivetrain with all on-board energy stored in batteries, which would be recharged from stationary sources when the vehicle is not in operation. I have not included this among the competitors because battery technology has not advanced rapidly enough for it to compete in highway markets. In contrast, BEV have proven quite successful in the personal transportation niche.

2. Alternatively framed: "Which comes first, the vehicle or the fuel?"
3. I do not include on-board reforming of fossil feedstocks, like gasoline, among these. These systems offer little gain beyond that achievable with the HEV, and most industrial proponents appear to have abandoned the idea.
4. BMW was the founding OEM and most significant supporter of the ICAR.

References

Socolow, Robert H. "Can We Bury Global Warming?" *Scientific American,* July 2005, pp. 49–55.

Sperling, Daniel and James D. Cannon, *The Hydrogen Transition*, Elsevier Academic Press, 2004.

U.S. National Research Council, *The Hydrogen Economy: Opportunities, Costs, Barriers, and R&D Needs*, The National Academies Press, 2004.

Michael Behar  **NO**

Warning: The Hydrogen Economy May Be More Distant Than It Appears

In the presidential campaign of 2004, Bush and Kerry managed to find one piece of common ground: Both spoke glowingly of a future powered by fuel cells. Hydrogen would free us from our dependence on fossil fuels and would dramatically curb emissions of air pollutants, including carbon dioxide, the gas chiefly blamed for global warming. The entire worldwide energy market would evolve into a "hydrogen economy" based on clean, abundant power. Auto manufacturers and environmentalists alike happily rode the bandwagon, pointing to hydrogen as the next big thing in U.S. energy policy. Yet the truth is that we aren't much closer to a commercially viable hydrogen-powered car than we are to cold fusion or a cure for cancer. This hardly surprises engineers, fuel cell manufacturers and policymakers, who have known all along that the technology has been hyped, perhaps to its detriment, and that the public has been misled about what Howard Coffman . . . describes as the "undeniable realities of the hydrogen economy." These experts are confident that the hydrogen economy will arrive—someday. But first, they say, we have to overcome daunting technological, financial and political roadblocks. Herewith, our checklist of misconceptions and doubts about hydrogen and the exalted fuel cell.

1. Hydrogen Is an Abundant Fuel

True, hydrogen is the most common element in the universe; it's so plentiful that the sun consumes 600 million tons of it every second. But unlike oil, vast reservoirs of hydrogen don't exist here on Earth. Instead, hydrogen atoms are bound up in molecules with other elements, and we must expend energy to extract the hydrogen so it can be used in fuel cells. We'll never get more energy out of hydrogen than we put into it.

"Hydrogen is a currency, not a primary energy source," explains Geoffrey Ballard, the father of the modern-day fuel cell and co-founder of Ballard Power Systems, the world's leading fuel-cell developer. "It's a means of getting energy from where you created it to where you need it."

2. Hydrogen Fuel Cells Will End
Global Warming

Unlike internal combustion engines, hydrogen fuel cells do not emit carbon dioxide. But extracting hydrogen from natural gas, today's primary source, does. And wresting hydrogen from water through electrolysis takes tremendous amounts of energy. If that energy comes from power plants burning fossil fuels, the end product may be clean hydrogen, but the process used to obtain it is still dirty.

Once hydrogen is extracted, it must be compressed and transported, presumably by machinery and vehicles that in the early stages of a hydrogen economy will be running on fossil fuels. The result: even more CO_2. In fact, driving a fuel cell car with hydrogen extracted from natural gas or water could produce a net increase of CO_2 in the atmosphere. "People say that hydrogen cars would be pollution-free," observes University of Calgary engineering professor David Keith. "Light-bulbs are pollution-free, but power plants are not."

In the short term, nuclear power may be the easiest way to produce hydrogen without pumping more carbon dioxide into the atmosphere. Electricity from a nuclear plant would electrolyze water—splitting H_2O into hydrogen and oxygen. Ballard champions the idea, calling nuclear power "extremely important, unless we see some other major breakthrough that none of us has envisioned."

Critics counter that nuclear power creates long-term waste problems and isn't economically competitive. An exhaustive industry analysis entitled "The Future of Nuclear Power," written last year by 10 professors from the Massachusetts Institute of Technology and Harvard University, concludes that "hydrogen produced by electrolysis of water depends on low-cost nuclear power." As long as electricity from nuclear power costs more than electricity from other sources, using that energy to make hydrogen doesn't add up.

3. The Hydrogen Economy Can
Run on Renewable Energy

Perform electrolysis with renewable energy, such as solar or wind power, and you eliminate the pollution issues associated with fossil fuels and nuclear power. Trouble is, renewable sources can provide only a small fraction of the energy that will be required for a full-fledged hydrogen economy.

From 1998 to 2003, the generating capacity of wind power increased 28 percent in the U.S. to 6,374 megawatts, enough for roughly 1.6 million homes. The wind industry expects to meet 6 percent of the country's electricity needs by 2020. But economist Andrew Oswald of the University of Warwick in England calculates that converting every vehicle in the U.S. to hydrogen power would require the electricity output of a million wind turbines—enough to cover half of California. Solar panels would likewise require huge swaths of land.

Water is another limiting factor for hydrogen production, especially in the sunny regions most suitable for solar power. According to a study done by the World Resources Institute, a Washington, D.C.-based nonprofit organization, fueling a hydrogen economy with electrolysis would require 4.2 trillion gallons of water annually—roughly the amount that flows over Niagara Falls every three months. Overall, U.S. water consumption would increase by about 10 percent.

4. Hydrogen Gas Leaks Are Nothing to Worry About

Hydrogen gas is odorless and colorless, and it burns almost invisibly. A tiny fire may go undetected at a leaky fuel pump until your pant leg goes up in flames. And it doesn't take much to set compressed hydrogen gas alight. "A cellphone or a lightning storm puts out enough static discharge to ignite hydrogen," claims Joseph Romm, author of *The Hype about Hydrogen: Fact and Fiction in the Race to Save the Climate* and founder of the Center for Energy and Climate Solutions in Arlington, Virginia.

A fender bender is unlikely to spark an explosion, because carbon-fiber-reinforced hydrogen tanks are virtually indestructible. But that doesn't eliminate the danger of leaks elsewhere in what will eventually be a huge network of refineries, pipelines and fueling stations. "The obvious pitfall is that hydrogen is a gas, and most of our existing petrochemical sources are liquids," says Robert Uhrig, professor emeritus of nuclear engineering at the University of Tennessee and former vice president of Florida Power & Light. "The infrastructure required to support high-pressure gas or cryogenic liquid hydrogen is much more complicated. Hydrogen is one of those things that people have great difficulty confining. It tends to go through the finest of holes."

To calculate the effects a leaky infrastructure might have on our atmosphere, a team of researchers from the California Institute of Technology and the Jet Propulsion Laboratory in Pasadena, California, looked at statistics for accidental industrial hydrogen and natural gas leakage—estimated at 10 to 20 percent of total volume—and then predicted how much leakage might occur in an economy in which everything runs on hydrogen. Result: The amount of hydrogen in the atmosphere would be four to eight times as high as it is today.

The Caltech study "grossly overstated" hydrogen leakage, says Assistant Secretary David Garman of the Department of Energy's Office of Energy Efficiency and Renewable Energy. But whatever its volume, hydrogen added to the atmosphere will combine with oxygen to form water vapor, creating noctilucent clouds—those high, wispy tendrils you see at dawn and dusk. The increased cloud cover could accelerate global warming.

5. Cars Are the Natural First Application For Hydrogen Fuel Cells

"An economically sane, cost-effective attack on the climate problem wouldn't start with cars," David Keith says. Cars and light trucks contribute roughly 20 percent of the carbon dioxide emitted in the U.S., while power plants burning fossil fuels are responsible for more than 40 percent of CO_2 emissions. Fuel cells designed for vehicles must cope with harsh conditions and severe limitations on size and weight.

A better solution to global warming might be to hold off building hydrogen cars, and instead harness fuel cells to generate electricity for homes and businesses. Plug Power, UTC, FuelCell Energy and Ballard Power Systems already market stationary fuel-cell generators. Plug Power alone has 161 systems in the U.S., including the first fuel-cell-powered McDonald's. Collectively, however, the four companies have a peak generating capacity of about 69 megawatts, less than 0.01 percent of the total 944,000 megawatts of U.S. generating capacity.

6. The U.S. Is Committed to Hydrogen, Pouring Billions Into R&D

Consider this: President George W. Bush promised to spend $1.2 billion on hydrogen. Yet he allotted $1.5 billion to promote "healthy marriages." The monthly tab for the war in Iraq is $3.9 billion—a total of $121 billion through last September. In 2004 the Department of Energy spent more on nuclear and fossil fuel research than on hydrogen.

The federal government's FreedomCAR program, which funds hydrogen R&D in conjunction with the big three American carmakers, requires that the companies demonstrate a hydrogen-powered car by 2008—but not that they sell one.

"If you are serious about [hydrogen], you have to commit a whole lot more money," contends Guenter Conzelmann, deputy director of the Center for Energy, Environmental and Economic Systems Analysis at Argonne National Laboratory near Chicago. Conzelmann develops computer models to help the energy industry make predictions about the cost of implementing new technology. His estimate for building a hydrogen economy: more than $500 billion, and that's if 60 percent of Americans continue to drive cars with internal combustion engines.

Shell, ExxonMobil and other oil companies are unwilling to invest in production, distribution, fueling facilities and storage if there are just a handful of hydrogen cars on the road. Nor will automakers foot the bill and churn out thousands of hydrogen cars if drivers have nowhere to fill them up. Peter Devlin, head of the Department of Energy's hydrogen-production research group, says, "Our industry partners have told us that unless a fourth to a third of all refueling stations in the U.S. offer hydrogen, they won't be willing to take a chance on fuel cells."

To create hydrogen fueling stations, California governor Arnold Schwarzenegger, who drives a Hummer, has championed the Hydrogen Highway Project. His plan is to erect 150 to 200 stations—at a cost of at least $500,000 each—along the state's major highways by the end of the decade. So that's one state. Now what about the other 100,775 filling stations in the rest of the U.S.? Retrofitting just 25 percent of those with hydrogen fueling systems would cost more than $13 billion.

7. If Iceland Can Do It, So Can We

Iceland's first hydrogen fueling station is already operating on the outskirts of Reykjavík. The hydrogen, which powers a small fleet of fuel cell buses, is produced onsite from electrolyzed tap water. Meanwhile the recently formed Icelandic New Energy—a consortium that includes automakers, Royal Dutch/Shell and the Icelandic power company Norsk Hydro—is planning to convert the rest of the island nation to a hydrogen system.

Impressive, yes. But 72 percent of Iceland's electricity comes from geothermal and hydroelectric power. With so much readily available clean energy, Iceland can electrolyze water with electricity directly from the national power grid. This type of setup is impossible in the U.S., where only about 15 percent of grid electricity comes from geothermal and hydroelectric sources, while 71 percent is generated by burning fossil fuels.

Another issue is the sheer scale of the system. It could take as few as 16 hydrogen fueling stations to enable Icelanders to drive fuel cell cars anywhere in the country. At close to 90 times the size of Iceland, the U.S. would require a minimum of 1,440 fueling stations. This assumes that stations would be strategically placed to collectively cover the entire U.S. with no overlap and that everyone knows where to find the pumps.

8. Mass Production Will Make Hydrogen Cars Affordable

Simply mass-producing fuel cell cars won't necessarily slash costs. According to Patrick Davis, the former leader of the Department of Energy's fuel cell research team, "If you project today's fuel cell technologies into high-volume production—about 500,000 vehicles a year—the cost is still up to six times too high."

Raj Choudhury, operations manager for the General Motors fuel cell program, claims that GM will have a commercial fuel cell vehicle ready by 2010. Others are doubtful. Ballard says that first there needs to be a "fundamental engineering rethink" of the proton exchange membrane (PEM) fuel cell, the type being developed for automobiles, which still cannot compete with the industry standard for internal combustion engines—a life span of 15 years, or about 170,000 driving miles. Because of membrane deterioration, today's PEM fuel cells typically fail during their first 2,000 hours of operation.

Ballard insists that his original PEM design was merely a prototype. "Ten years ago I said it was the height of engineering arrogance to think that the architecture and geometry we chose to demonstrate the fuel cell in automobiles would be the best architecture and geometry for a commercial automobile," he remarks. "Very few people paid attention to that statement. The truth is that the present geometry isn't getting the price down to where it is commercial. It isn't even entering into the envelope that will allow economies of scale to drive the price down."

In the short term, conventional gasoline-burning vehicles will be replaced by gas-electric hybrids, or by vehicles that burn clean diesel, natural gas, methanol or ethanol. Only later will hydrogen cars make sense, economically and environmentally. "Most analysts think it will take several decades for hydrogen to make a large impact, assuming hydrogen technologies reach their goals," notes Joan Ogden, an associate professor of environmental science and policy at the University of California at Davis and one of the world's leading researchers of hydrogen energy.

9. Fuel Cell Cars Can Drive Hundreds of Miles on a Single Tank of Hydrogen

A gallon of gasoline contains about 2,600 times the energy of a gallon of hydrogen. If engineers want hydrogen cars to travel at least 300 miles between fill-ups—the automotive-industry benchmark—they'll have to compress hydrogen gas to extremely high pressures: up to 10,000 pounds per square inch.

Even at that pressure, cars would need huge fuel tanks. "High-pressure hydrogen would take up four times the volume of gasoline," says JoAnn Milliken, chief engineer of the Department of Energy's Office of Hydrogen, Fuel Cells and Infrastructure Technologies.

Liquid hydrogen works a bit better. GM's liquid-fueled HydroGen3 goes 250 miles on a tank roughly double the size of that in a standard sedan. But the car must be driven every day to keep the liquid hydrogen chilled to –253 degrees Celsius—just 20 degrees above absolute zero and well below the surface temperature of Pluto—or it boils off. "If your car sits at the airport for a week, you'll have an empty tank when you get back," Milliken says.

10. If Not Hydrogen, Then *What*?

The near-future prospects for a hydrogen economy are dim, concludes *The Hydrogen Economy: Opportunities, Costs, Barriers, and R&D Needs,* a major government-sponsored study published last February by the National Research Council. Representatives from ExxonMobil, Ford, DuPont, the Natural Resources Defense Council and other stakeholders contributed to the report, which urges lawmakers to legislate tougher tailpipe-emission standards and to earmark additional R&D funding for renewable energy and alternative fuels. It foresees "major hurdles on the path to achieving the vision of the hydrogen economy" and recommends that the Department of Energy "keep a balanced portfolio of R&D efforts and continue to explore supply-and-demand alternatives that do not depend on hydrogen."

Of course, for each instance where the study points out how hydrogen falls short, there are scores of advocates armed with data to show how it can succeed. Physicist Amory Lovins, who heads the Rocky Mountain Institute, a think tank in Colorado, fastidiously rebuts the most common critiques of hydrogen with an armada of facts and figures in his widely circulated white paper "Twenty Hydrogen Myths." But although he's a booster of hydrogen, Lovins is notably pragmatic. "A lot of silly things have been written both for and against hydrogen," he says. "Some sense of reality is lacking on both sides." He believes that whether the hydrogen economy arrives at the end of this decade or closer to midcentury, interim technologies will play a signal role in the transition.

The most promising of these technologies is the gas-electric hybrid vehicle, which uses both an internal combustion engine and an electric motor, switching seamlessly between the two to optimize gas mileage and engine efficiency. U.S. sales of hybrid cars have been growing steadily, and the 2005 model year saw the arrival of the first hybrid SUVs—the Ford Escape, Toyota Highlander and Lexus RX400h.

Researchers sponsored by the FreedomCAR program are also investigating ultralight materials—plastics, fiberglass, titanium, magnesium, carbon fiber—and developing lighter engines made from aluminum and ceramic materials. These new materials could help reduce vehicle power demands, bridging the cost gap between fossil fuels and fuel cells.

Most experts agree that there is no silver bullet. Instead the key is developing a portfolio of energy-efficient technologies that can help liberate us from fossil fuels and ease global warming. "If we had a wider and more diverse set of energy sources, we'd be more robust, more stable," says Jonathan Pershing, director of the Climate, Energy and Pollution Program at the World Resources Institute. "The more legs your chair rests on, the less likely it is to tip over."

Waiting for hydrogen to save us isn't an option. "If we fail to act during this decade to reduce greenhouse gas emissions, historians will condemn us," Romm writes in *The Hype about Hydrogen.* "And they will most likely be living in a world with a much hotter and harsher climate than ours, one that has undergone an irreversible change for the worse."

POSTSCRIPT

Will Hydrogen Replace Fossil Fuels for Cars?

Hydrogen as a fuel offers definite benefits. As Joan M. Ogden notes in "Hydrogen: The Fuel of the Future?" *Physics Today* (April 2002), the technology is available and compared to the alternatives, it "offers the greatest potential environmental and energy-supply benefits." To put hydrogen to use, however, will require massive investments in facilities for generating, storing, and transporting the gas, as well as manufacturing hydrogen-burning engines and fuel cells. Currently, large amounts of hydrogen can easily be generated by "reforming" natural gas or other hydrocarbons. Hydrolysis— splitting hydrogen from water molecules with electricity—is also possible, and in the future this may use electricity from renewable sources such as wind or from nuclear power. The basic technologies are available right now. See Thammy Evans, Peter Light, and Ty Cashman, "Hydrogen—A Little PR," *Whole Earth* (Winter 2001). Daniel Sperling notes in "Updating Automotive Research," *Issues in Science and Technology* (Spring 2002), that "Fuel cells and hydrogen show huge promise. They may indeed prove to be the Holy Grail, eventually taking vehicles out of the environmental equation," but making that happen will require research, government assistance in building a hydrogen distribution system, and incentives for both industry and car buyers. First steps along these lines are already visible in a few places; see Bill Keenan, "Hydrogen: Waiting for the Revolution," *Across the Board* (May/June 2004), and Annie Birdsong, "California Drives the Future of the Automobile," *World Watch* (March/April 2005). M. Z. Jacobson, W. G. Colella, and D. M. Golden, "Cleaning the Air and Improving Health with Hydrogen Fuel-Cell Vehicles," *Science* (June 24, 2005), conclude that if all onroad vehicles are replaced with fuel-cell vehicles using hydrogen generated by wind power, air pollution and human health impacts will both be reduced and overall costs will be less than for gasoline.

Joan Ogden, "High Hopes for Hydrogen," *Scientific American* (September 2006), agrees that the potential is great but stresses that the transition to a hydrogen future will take decades. Henry Payne and Diane Katz, "Gas and Gasbags . . . or, the Open Road and Its Enemies," *National Review* (March 25, 2002), contend that a major obstacle to hydrogen is market mechanisms that will keep fossil fuels in use for years to come, local hydrogen production is unlikely, and adequate supplies will require that society invest heavily in nuclear power. Jim Motavalli, "Hijacking Hydrogen," *E Magazine* (January–February 2003), worries that the fossil fuel and nuclear industries will dominate the hydrogen future. The former wish to use "reforming" to generate hydrogen from coal, and the latter see hydrolysis as creating demand for nuclear power.

Nuclear power, he says, is particularly favored by the U.S. government's 2001 National Energy Policy. Freyr Sverrisson, "Missing in Action: Iceland's Hydrogen Economy," *World Watch* (November/December 2006), notes that the demand of industry for electricity has shifted plans to develop hydrogen to the development of hydroelectric dams instead.

In January 2003, and again on Earth Day 2006, President George W. Bush proposed $1.2 billion in funding for making hydrogen-powered cars an on-the-road reality. Gregg Easterbrook, "Why Bush's H-Car Is Just Hot Air," *New Republic* (February 24, 2003), thinks it would make much more sense to address fuel-economy standards; Bush should "leave futurism to the futurists." Peter Schwartz and Doug Randall, "How Hydrogen Can Save America," *Wired* (April 2003), commend Bush's proposal but say the proposed funding is not enough. We need, they say, "an Apollo-scale commitment to hydrogen power. The fate of the republic depends on it." Toward that end, they list five steps essential to making the hydrogen future real.

1. Develop fuel tanks that can store hydrogen safely and in adequate quantity.
2. Encourage mass production of fuel cell vehicles.
3. Convert the fueling infrastructure to hydrogen.
4. Increase hydrogen production.
5. Mount a PR campaign.

The difficulty of the task is underlined by Robert F. Service in "The Hydrogen Backlash," *Science* (August 13, 2004) (the lead article in a special section titled "Toward a Hydrogen Economy"), and again by Jeff Wise, "The Truth about Hydrogen," *Popular Mechanics* (November 2006). The difficulty will be eased if cheap, efficient ways to generate hydrogen are developed; fortunately, progress is being made; see David Talbot, "Cheap Hydrogen Fuel," *Technology Review* (online at http://www.technologyreview.com/BizTech/16523/) (March 9, 2006).

But are fossil fuels as scarce as industry critics and hydrogen enthusiasts say? They are certainly finite, but it has become apparent that not all fossil fuels are included in most accountings of available supply. A major omission is methane hydrate, a form of natural gas locked into cage-like arrangements of water molecules and found as masses of white ice-like material on the seabed. There appear to be vast quantities of methane hydrate on the bottom of the world's seas. If they can be recovered—and there are major difficulties in doing so—they may provide huge amounts of additional fossil fuels. Once liberated, their methane may be burned directly or "reformed" to generate hydrogen, making the nuclear approach less necessary. However, the methane still poses global warming risks. Indeed, if methane hydrate deposits ever gave up their methane naturally, they could change world climate abruptly (just such releases may have been responsible for past global climate warmings). See Erwin Suess, Gerhard Bohrmann, Jens Greinert, and Erwin Lausch, "Flammable Ice," *Scientific American* (November 1999).

Internet References . . .

Facing the Future: People and the Planet

Facing the Future strives to educate people about critical global issues, including population growth, poverty, overconsumption, and environmental destruction.

http://www.facingthefuture.org/

Cell Phones and Cancer

At this site, John E. Moulder, professor of radiation oncology, radiology, and pharmacology/toxicology at the Medical College of Wisconsin, answers frequently asked questions about the relationship between cell phones and cancer. The site also links to two related FAQ sites—the relationship between power lines and cancer, and the relationship between static electromagnetic fields and cancer.

http://www.mcw.edu/gcrc/cop/
cell-phone-health-FAQ/toc.html

Malaria Foundation International

The Malaria Foundation International seeks "to facilitate the development and implementation of solutions to the health, economic and social problems caused by malaria."

http://www.malaria.org/

The Foresight Nanotech Institute

The Foresight Nanotech Institute works closely with governments, environmental groups, the policy community, professional associations, and civic sector organizations to improve education on and public policy on nanotechnology.

http://www.foresight.org/

SCOPE Forum

SCOPE designs and tests web-based environments for on-line, knowledge-building communities centered around current scientific controversies.

http://scope.educ.washington.edu/gmfood/

National Institute of Environmental Health Sciences

The National Institute of Environmental Health Sciences studies the health risks of numerous environmental factors, many of which are associated with the use of technology.

http://www.niehs.nih.gov

Human Health and Welfare

*M*any people are concerned about new technological and scientific discoveries because they fear their potential impacts on human health and welfare. In the past, fears have been expressed concerning nuclear bombs and power plants, irradiated food, the internal combustion engine, medications such as thalidomide and diethylstilberstrol, vaccines, pesticides and other chemicals, and more. Not too long ago, people worried that the population explosion would harm both the environment and human well-being. Today the trend appears to be toward a population "implosion," and human well-being remains of concern. On the technology front, people worry about the possible health risks of cell phones, nanotechnology, and genetically modified foods, among other things. It is worth stressing that risks may be real (as they are with insecticides such as DDT), but there may be a trade-off for genuine health benefits.*

• Do Falling Birth Rates Pose a Threat to Human Welfare?

• Is There Sufficient Scientific Research to Conclude that Cell Phones Cause Cancer?

• Should DDT Be Banned Worldwide?

• Should Potential Risks Slow the Development of Nanotechnology?

• Are Genetically Modified Foods Safe to Eat?

ISSUE 7

Do Falling Birth Rates Pose a Threat to Human Welfare?

YES: Michael Meyer, from "Birth Dearth," *Newsweek* (September 27, 2004)

NO: David Nicholson-Lord, from "The Fewer the Better," *New Statesman* (November 8, 2004)

ISSUE SUMMARY

YES: Michael Meyer argues that when world population begins to decline after about 2050, economies will no longer continue to grow, government benefits will decline, young people will have to support an elderly population, and despite some environmental benefits, quality of life will suffer.

NO: David Nicholson-Lord argues that the economic problems of population decline all have straightforward solutions. A less-crowded world will not suffer from the environmental ills attendant on over-crowding and will, overall, be a roomier, gentler, less materialistic place to live, with cleaner air and water.

In 1798 the British economist Thomas Malthus published his *Essay on the Principle of Population.* In it, he pointed with alarm at the way the human population grew geometrically (a hockey-stick curve of increase) and at how agricultural productivity grew only arithmetically (a straight-line increase). It was obvious, he said, that the population must inevitably outstrip its food supply and experience famine. Contrary to the conventional wisdom of the time, population growth was not necessarily a good thing. Indeed, it led inexorably to catastrophe. For many years, Malthus was something of a laughingstock. The doom he forecast kept receding into the future as new lands were opened to agriculture, new agricultural technologies appeared, new ways of preserving food limited the waste of spoilage, and the birth rate dropped in the industrialized nations (the "demographic transition"). The food supply kept ahead of population growth and seemed likely—to most observers—to continue to do so. Malthus's ideas were dismissed as irrelevant fantasies.

Yet overall population kept growing. In Malthus's time, there were about 1 billion human beings on Earth. By 1950—when Warren S. Thompson worried that civilization would be endangered by the rapid growth of Asian and Latin American populations during the next five decades (see "Population," *Scientific American* [February 1950])—there were a little over 2.5 billion. In 1999 the tally passed 6 billion. By 2025 it will be over 8 billion. Statistics like these, which are presented in *World Resources 2005—The Wealth of the Poor: Managing Ecosystems to Fight Poverty* (World Resources Institute, 2005) (http://www.wri.org/biodiv/pubs_description.cfm?pid=4073), published in collaboration with the United Nations Development Programme, the United Nations Environment Programme, and the World Bank, are positively frightening. The Worldwatch Institute's yearly *State of the World* reports (W. W. Norton) are no less so. By 2050 the UN expects the world population to be about 9 billion (see *World Population Prospects: The 2004 Revision Population Database*; http://esa.un.org/unpp/; United Nations, 2005). While global agricultural production has also increased, it has not kept up with rising demand, and—because of the loss of topsoil to erosion, the exhaustion of aquifers for irrigation water, and the high price of energy for making fertilizer (among other things)—the prospect of improvement seems exceedingly slim to many observers.

Two centuries never saw Malthus' forecasts of doom come to pass. Population continued to grow, and environmentalists pointed with alarm at a great many problems that resulted from human use of the world's resources (air and water pollution, erosion, loss of soil fertility and ground water, loss of species, and a great deal more). "Cornucopian" economists such as the late Julian Simon, insisted that the more people there are on Earth, the more people there are to solve problems and that humans can find ways around all possible resource shortages. See Simon's essay, "Life on Earth Is Getting Better, Not Worse," *The Futurist* (August 1983).

Was Malthus wrong? Both environmental scientists and many economists now say that if population continues to grow, problems are inevitable. But earlier predictions of a world population of 10 or 12 billion by 2050 are no longer looking very likely. The UN's population statistics show a slowing of growth, to be followed by an actual decline in population.

Some people worry that such a decline will not be good for human welfare. Michael Meyer argues that a shrinking population will mean that the economic growth that has meant constantly increasing standards of living must come to an end, government programs (from war to benefits for the poor and elderly) will no longer be affordable, a shrinking number of young people will have to support a growing elderly population, and despite some environmental benefits, quality of life will suffer. David Nicholson-Lord argues that the economic problems of population decline all have straightforward solutions. A less crowded world will not suffer from the environmental ills attendant on overcrowding and will, overall, be a roomier, gentler, less materialistic place to live, with cleaner air and water.

YES

Michael Meyer

Birth Dearth

Everyone knows there are too many people in the world. Whether we live in Lahore or Los Angeles, Shanghai or Sao Paulo, our lives are daily proof. We endure traffic gridlock, urban sprawl and environmental depredation. The evening news brings variations on Ramallah or Darfur—images of Third World famine, poverty, pestilence, war, global competition for jobs and increasingly scarce natural resources.

Just last week the United Nations warned that many of the world's cities are becoming hopelessly overcrowded. Lagos alone will grow from 6.5 million people in 1995 to 16 million by 2015, a miasma of slums and decay where a fifth of all children will die before they are 5. At a conference in London, the U.N. Population Fund weighed in with a similarly bleak report: unless something dramatically changes, the world's 50 poorest countries will triple in size by 2050, to 1.7 billion people.

Yet this is not the full story. To the contrary, in fact. Across the globe, people are having fewer and fewer children. Fertility rates have dropped by half since 1972, from six children per woman to 2.9. And demographers say they're still falling, faster than ever. The world's population will continue to grow—from today's 6.4 billion to around 9 billion in 2050. But after that, it will go sharply into decline. Indeed, a phenomenon that we're destined to learn much more about—depopulation—has already begun in a number of countries. Welcome to the New Demography. It will change everything about our world, from the absolute size and power of nations to global economic growth to the quality of our lives.

This revolutionary transformation will be led not so much by developed nations as by the developing ones. Most of us are familiar with demographic trends in Europe, where birthrates have been declining for years. To reproduce itself, a society's women must each bear 2.1 children. Europe's fertility rates fall far short of that, according to the 2002 U.N. population report. France and Ireland, at 1.8, top Europe's childbearing charts. Italy and Spain, at 1.2, bring up the rear. In between are countries such as Germany, whose fertility rate of 1.4 is exactly Europe's average. What does that mean? If the U.N. figures are right, Germany could shed nearly a fifth of its 82.5 million people over the next 40 years—roughly the equivalent of all of east Germany, a loss of population not seen in Europe since the Thirty Years' War.

And so it is across the Continent. Bulgaria will shrink by 38 percent, Romania by 27 percent, Estonia by 25 percent. "Parts of Eastern Europe, already sparsely populated, will just empty out," predicts Reiner Klingholz, director of the Berlin Institute for Population and Development. Russia is already losing close to 750,000 people yearly. (President Vladimir Putin calls it a "national crisis.") So is Western Europe, and that figure could grow to as much as 3 million a year by midcentury, if not more.

The surprise is how closely the less-developed world is following the same trajectory. In Asia it's well known that Japan will soon tip into population loss, if it hasn't already. With a fertility rate of 1.3 children per woman, the country stands to shed a quarter of its 127 million people over the next four decades, according to U.N. projections. But while the graying of Japan (average age: 42.3 years) has long been a staple of news headlines, what to make of China, whose fertility rate has declined from 5.8 in 1970 to 1.8 today, according to the U.N.? Chinese census data put the figure even lower, at 1.3. Coupled with increasing life spans, that means China's population will age as quickly in one generation as Europe's has over the past 100 years, reports the Center for Strategic and International Studies in Washington. With an expected median age of 44 in 2015, China will be older on average than the United States. By 2019 or soon after, its population will peak at 1.5 billion, then enter a steep decline. By midcentury, China could well lose 20 to 30 percent of its population every generation.

The picture is similar elsewhere in Asia, where birthrates are declining even in the absence of such stringent birth-control programs as China's. Indeed, it's happening despite often generous official incentives to procreate. The industrialized nations of Singapore, Hong Kong, Taiwan and South Korea all report subreplacement fertility, says Nicholas Eberstadt, a demographer at the American Enterprise Institute in Washington. To this list can be added Thailand, Burma, Australia and Sri Lanka, along with Cuba and many Caribbean nations, as well as Uruguay and Brazil. Mexico is aging so rapidly that within several decades it will not only stop growing but will have an older population than that of the United States. So much for the cliche of those Mexican youths swarming across the Rio Grande? "If these figures are accurate," says Eberstadt, "just about half of the world's population lives in subreplacement countries."

There are notable exceptions. In Europe, Albania and the outlier province of Kosovo are reproducing energetically. So are pockets of Asia: Mongolia, Pakistan and the Philippines. The United Nations projects that the Middle East will double in population over the next 20 years, growing from 326 million today to 649 million by 2050. Saudi Arabia has one of the highest fertility rates in the world, 5.7, after Palestinian territories at 5.9 and Yemen at 7.2. Yet there are surprises here, too. Tunisia has tipped below replacement. Lebanon and Iran are at the threshold. And though overall the region's population continues to grow, the increase is due mainly to lower infant mortality; fertility rates themselves are falling faster than in developed countries, indicating that over the coming decades the Middle East will age far more rapidly than other regions of the world. Birthrates in Africa remain high, and despite the AIDS epidemic its population is projected to keep growing. So is that of the United States.

We'll return to American exceptionalism, and what that might portend. But first, let's explore the causes of the birth dearth, as outlined in a pair of new books on the subject. "Never in the last 650 years, since the time of the Black Plague, have birth and fertility rates fallen so far, so fast, so low, for so long, in so many places," writes the sociologist Ben Wattenberg in "Fewer: How the New Demography of Depopulation Will Shape Our Future." Why? Wattenberg suggests that a variety of once independent trends have conjoined to produce a demographic tsunami. As the United Nations reported last week, people everywhere are leaving the countryside and moving to cities, which will be home to more than half the world's people by 2007. Once there, having a child becomes a cost rather than an asset. From 1970 to 2000, Nigeria's urban population climbed from 14 to 44 percent. South Korea went from 28 to 84 percent. So-called megacities, from Lagos to Mexico City, have exploded seemingly overnight. Birthrates have fallen in inverse correlation.

Other factors are at work. Increasing female literacy and enrollment in schools have tended to decrease fertility, as have divorce, abortion and the worldwide trend toward later marriage. Contraceptive use has risen dramatically over the past decade; according to U.N. data, 62 percent of married or "in union" women of reproductive age are now using some form of nonnatural birth control. In countries such as India, now the capital of global HIV, disease has become a factor. In Russia, the culprits include alcoholism, poor public health and industrial pollution that has whacked male sperm counts. Wealth discourages childbearing, as seen long ago in Europe and now in Asia. As Wattenberg puts it, "Capitalism is the best contraception."

The potential consequences of the population implosion are enormous. Consider the global economy, as Phillip Longman describes it in another recent book, "The Empty Cradle: How Falling Birthrates Threaten World Prosperity and What to Do About It." A population expert at the New America Foundation in Washington, he sees danger for global prosperity. Whether it's real estate or consumer spending, economic growth and population have always been closely linked. "There are people who cling to the hope that you can have a vibrant economy without a growing population, but mainstream economists are pessimistic," says Longman. You have only to look at Japan or Europe for a whiff of what the future might bring, he adds. In Italy, demographers forecast a 40 percent decline in the working-age population over the next four decades—accompanied by a commensurate drop in growth across the Continent, according to the European Commission. What happens when Europe's cohort of baby boomers begins to retire around 2020? Recent strikes and demonstrations in Germany, Italy, France and Austria over the most modest pension reforms are only the beginning of what promises to become a major sociological battle between Europe's older and younger generations.

That will be only a skirmish compared with the conflict brewing in China. There market reforms have removed the cradle-to-grave benefits of the planned economy, while the Communist Party hasn't constructed an adequate social safety net to take their place. Less than one quarter of the population is covered by retirement pensions, according to CSIS. That puts the burden of elder care almost entirely on what is now a generation of only children. The one-child policy has led to the so-called 4-2-1 problem, in which each child will be potentially responsible for caring for two parents and four grandparents.

Incomes in China aren't rising fast enough to offset this burden. In some rural villages, so many young people have fled to the cities that there may be nobody left to look after the elders. And the aging population could soon start to dull China's competitive edge, which depends on a seemingly endless supply of cheap labor. After 2015, this labor pool will begin to dry up, says economist Hu Angang. China will have little choice but to adopt a very Western-sounding solution, he says: it will have to raise the education level of its work force and make it more productive. Whether it can is an open question. Either way, this much is certain: among Asia's emerging economic powers, China will be the first to grow old before it gets rich.

Equally deep dislocations are becoming apparent in Japan. Akihiko Matsutani, an economist and author of a recent best seller, "The Economy of a Shrinking Population," predicts that by 2009 Japan's economy will enter an era of "negative growth." By 2030, national income will have shrunk by 15 percent. Speculating about the future is always dicey, but economists pose troubling questions. Take the legendarily high savings that have long buoyed the Japanese economy and financed borrowing worldwide, especially by the United States. As an aging Japan draws down those assets in retirement, will U.S. and global interest rates rise? At home, will Japanese businesses find themselves competing for increasingly scarce investment capital? And just what will they be investing in, as the country's consumers grow older, and demand for the latest in hot new products cools off? What of the effect on national infrastructure? With less tax revenue in state coffers, Matsutani predicts, governments will increasingly be forced to skimp on or delay repairs to the nation's roads, bridges, rail lines and the like. "Life will become less convenient," he says. Spanking-clean Tokyo might come to look more like New York City in the 1970s, when many urban dwellers decamped for the suburbs (taking their taxes with them) and city fathers could no longer afford the municipal upkeep. Can Japanese cope? "They will have to," says Matsutani. "There's no alternative."

Demographic change magnifies all of a country's problems, social as well as economic. An overburdened welfare state? Aging makes it collapse. Tensions over immigration? Differing birthrates intensify anxieties, just as the need for imported labor rises—perhaps the critical issue for the Europe of tomorrow. A poor education system, with too many kids left behind? Better fix it, because a shrinking work force requires higher productivity and greater flexibility, reflected in a new need for continuing job training, career switches and the health care needed to keep workers working into old age.

In an ideal world, perhaps, the growing gulf between the world's wealthy but shrinking countries and its poor, growing ones would create an opportunity. Labor would flow from the overpopulated, resource-poor south to the depopulating north, where jobs would continue to be plentiful. Capital and remittance income from the rich nations would flow along the reverse path, benefiting all. Will it happen? Perhaps, but that presupposes considerable labor mobility. Considering the resistance Europeans display toward large-scale immigration from North Africa, or Japan's almost zero-immigration policy, it's hard to be optimistic. Yes, attitudes are changing. Only a decade ago, for instance, Europeans also spoke of zero immigration. Today they recognize the need and, in bits and pieces, are beginning to plan for it. But will it happen on the scale required?

A more probable scenario may be an intensification of existing tensions between peoples determined to preserve their beleaguered national identities on the one hand, and immigrant groups on the other seeking to escape overcrowding and lack of opportunity at home. For countries such as the Philippines—still growing, and whose educated work force looks likely to break out of low-status jobs as nannies and gardeners and move up the global professional ladder—this may be less of a problem. It will be vastly more serious for the tens of millions of Arab youths who make up a majority of the population in the Middle East and North Africa, at least half of whom are unemployed.

America is the wild card in this global equation. While Europe and much of Asia shrinks, the United States' indigenous population looks likely to stay relatively constant, with fertility rates hovering almost precisely at replacement levels. Add in heavy immigration, and you quickly see that America is the only modern nation that will continue to grow. Over the next 45 years the United States will gain 100 million people, Wattenberg estimates, while Europe loses roughly as many.

This does not mean that Americans will escape the coming demographic whammy. They, too, face the problems of an aging work force and its burdens. (The cost of Medicare and Social Security will rise from 4.3 percent of GDP in 2000 to 11.5 percent in 2030 and 21 percent in 2050, according to the Congressional Budget Office.) They, too, face the prospect of increasing ethnic tensions, as a flat white population and a dwindling black one become gradually smaller minorities in a growing multicultural sea. And in our interdependent era, the troubles of America's major trading partners—Europe and Japan—will quickly become its own. To cite one example, what becomes of the vaunted "China market," invested in so heavily by U.S. companies, if by 2050 China loses an estimated 35 percent of its workers and the aged consume an ever-greater share of income?

America's demographic "unipolarity" has profound security implications as well. Washington worries about terrorism and failing states. Yet the chaos of today's fragmented world is likely to prove small in comparison to what could come. For U.S. leaders, Longman in "The Empty Cradle" sketches an unsettling prospect. Though the United States may have few military competitors, the technologies by which it projects geopolitical power—from laser-guided missiles and stealth bombers to a huge military infrastructure—may gradually become too expensive for a country facing massively rising social entitlements in an era of slowing global economic growth. If the war on terrorism turns out to be the "generational struggle" that national-security adviser Condoleezza Rice says it is, Longman concludes, then the United States might have difficulty paying for it.

None of this is writ, of course. Enlightened governments could help hold the line. France and the Netherlands have instituted family-friendly policies that help women combine work and motherhood, ranging from tax credits for kids to subsidized day care. Scandinavian countries have kept birthrates up with generous provisions for parental leave, health care and part-time employment. Still, similar programs offered by the shrinking city-state of Singapore—including a state-run dating service—have done little to reverse the birth dearth. Remember, too, that such prognoses have been wrong in the past. At the cusp of the postwar baby boom, demographers predicted a sharp fall in fertility and a global birth dearth. Yet even if this generation of seers turns out to be right, as seems likely, not all is bad. Environmentally, a smaller world is almost certainly a better world, whether in terms of cleaner air or, say, the return of wolves and rare flora to abandoned stretches of the East German countryside. And while people are living longer, they are also living healthier—at least in the developed world. That means they can (and probably should) work more years before retirement.

Yes, a younger generation will have to shoulder the burden of paying for their elders. But there will be compensations. As populations shrink, says economist Matsutani, national incomes may drop—but not necessarily per capita incomes. And in this realm of uncertainty, one mundane thing is probably sure: real-estate prices will fall. That will hurt seniors whose nest eggs are tied up in their homes, but it will be a boon to youngsters of the future. Who knows? Maybe the added space and cheap living will inspire them to, well, do whatever it takes to make more babies. Thus the cycle of life will restore its balance. . . .

David Nicholson-Lord  **NO**

The Fewer the Better

This is a story of two Britains and two futures. In the first Britain, the work culture dominates; the talk is of economic growth and dynamism and competing with the rest of the world. Labour is young, cheap and biddable, and driven by the urge to "succeed"—to make it in material and career terms, with the consumer goods and lifestyles to match. In the cities of this 24/7 society, population densities rise: so do crime, violence and antisocial behaviour. Outside the cities, urbanisation spreads, along with noise, congestion, the creep of human clutter and development. Unspoilt places are increasingly hard to find. Pollution gets steadily worse.

The second Britain is a quieter place. The age profile is older, the values less strident and materialistic. People work longer—they are not pensioned off in their fifties—but they save more and spend less, at least on ephemera and gadgets. They drink much less, too, and don't get involved in fights. Work is important but so are hobbies, family and community life. Cities are more spacious, roads emptier, the countryside more rural. The air and water are cleaner and there is hope of getting the weather back to normal because the planet is no longer warming so rapidly.

Which future would we prefer? The first—let us call it "UK plc"—with its economic engine revving at full speed? Or the second, where quality of life matters more: not so much a plc as a community enterprise, with the emphasis on community rather than enterprise? Most people would plump for the second. Yet we seem to be heading for the first.

What we do not admit is that the difference between the two futures is largely one of human numbers. Population is a subject we don't like to mention. In September Michael Howard, the Conservative leader, pointed out that, over the next 30 years, Britain's population would grow by 5.6 million—an increase of nearly 10 percent on the current 59 million. Immigration, running at an average net inflow of 158,000 a year in the past five years, accounts for 85 percent of this increase. Because population is forecast to rise, the government plans an extra 3.8 million houses in England over the next 20 years. But that plan is based on net immigration of 65,000 a year. If it continues at 158,000 a year, we will need 4.85 million new homes.

Howard went on to quote, with approval, the conclusions of the government's Community Cohesion Panel, which said in July that people "need sufficient time to come to terms with and accommodate incoming groups, regardless of their ethnic origin. The 'pace of change' . . . is simply too great . . . at present."

Alarmist? Electioneering? Playing the race card? In so far as these parts of Howard's speech were reported at all, that was how the left-liberal media interpreted them. Yet his figures understate the contribution of immigration to housing forecasts, because they ignore the changes in fertility and household formation resulting from a younger population. According to the Optimum Population Trust, a continuation of the 2001–2003 growth rate of 0.4 percent would result in a UK population of 71 million in 2050 and 100 million by the end of the century.

The implications of this bear examination. Given a population of "only" 65–66 million by mid-century, for example, we would need an extra nine or ten million houses by 2050—more than twice the numbers Howard was talking about, and an increase of nearly 50 percent on the current English housing stock. Should this worry us? Clearly many people think so; the government's housing plans have been a source of controversy ever since they were published. Examine this controversy in greater depth, and you will find a developing awareness of what ecologists call "carrying capacity": the balance (or lack of it) between a physical environment and the numbers it can support.

About all this, the environmental lobby is now silent. The last time such issues were deemed fit for public debate was in 1973, when a government population panel said Britain must accept "that its population cannot go on increasing indefinitely." The progressive-minded believe, on the one hand, in liberal multiculturalism and, on the other, in sustainability. They cannot resolve the conflict. The field has thus been abandoned to the political right.

The demographic facts are undeniable, however. Before the start of the current immigration surge in the 1990s, Britain's population, like that of many other developed countries, was heading for decline—as early as 2013, according to some forecasts. British women are having 1.7 children each, on average, above Germany (1.4) and Japan (1.3) but below the replacement level of 2.1. If this had been allowed to continue, with no immigration, we would be down to 30 million by 2120.

What would it be like to live in a country where population halved in the space of three or four generations? Environmentally, the case for population decline is unanswerable—less pollution, less strain on natural systems, greater national self-sufficiency, a reduction in fossil-fuel emissions, the freeing up of land for other species and higher-order human uses, such as wilderness. Psychologically, what the economist Fred Hirsch called "positional goods"—a view, an unspoilt beach, a piece of heritage—would be freer of the crowds and queues that now, for most people, mar them. Applied to social and economic life, this might reduce the awful sense of competitiveness that is a relatively recent feature of cultural life, for jobs, places at school or university, or entry to prized social institutions or niches.

Given the close association between crowding, densities, congestion and stress, and the greater distances available between people, we would also probably see less casual public aggression: less of the "rage" that emerged in the late 1980s. And, because young people are more likely to commit crimes, the ageing of society that would result from population decline would reinforce these trends. A Britain of 30 million people would almost certainly be a kindlier, more easygoing, more socially concerned place—exactly the sort of Britain that many readers of the *New Statesman* would like to see.

❧❦❧

Most of the argument so far, however, has focused on the perils of decline: economic and social stagnation, the decrease in the support ratio (of workers to pensioners), emerging labour shortages and so on. Given that all of these "problems" are either illusory, fantastical or soluble it is instructive to ask why they obsess us. Why were the Tories, for example, thinking until recently about encouraging people to have babies and why does the government still envisage no upper limit on immigration? There are two answers. First, population growth is such a feature of the past two centuries—although not of preceding ages—that it has become synonymous in our minds with progress. Second, economic growth is how politicians and economists measure national success. And having more people is the quickest and easiest way to boost gross domestic product.

Much is made, therefore, of the impact of immigration on economic growth. Yet the growth comes almost entirely from additions to the national headcount. The increased wealth per person may be as little as 0.1 percent a year, according to US research.

More important is what happens when "immigrants" become "natives." This is the central fallacy of the demographic "timebomb" argument. Immigrants eventually become pensioners, and pensioners keep living longer. The only way to preserve a support ratio regarded as optimal is thus to have permanently high levels of immigration—and a population permanently, indeed infinitely, growing. David Coleman, professor of demography at Oxford University, has calculated that to keep the support ratio between pensioners and those of working age at roughly current levels would require a UK population in 2100 of approximately 300 million and rising. He calls it "the incredible in pursuit of the implausible."

And what about the world as a whole? How are developing countries, presumably expected to provide the young immigrants to the UK and other western countries, supposed to support their own old people?

New figures from the US Population Reference Bureau suggest a world population of roughly 9.3 billion in 2050, against 6.4 billion now. Studies such as the WWF's *Living Planet Report* say that by that time, humanity's footprint will be up to 220 percent of the earth's biological capacity. We would need, in other words, another couple of planets to survive. But if we manage to control global population (and it looks increasingly likely that we can) numbers will start to decline, possibly around 2070. What is the world supposed to do then? Import extra-planetary aliens to maintain the support ratio?

Even within Britain, it is hard to make a case for labour shortages when unemployment is three times the number of vacancies and economic inactivity, notably among the over-fifties, is at an all-time high. It is also hard, morally

at least, to argue that we should deliberately cream off the skilled and educated workers of poorer countries—little different from people-trafficking,
according to a National Health Service overseas recruiter addressing this year's
Royal College of Nursing conference—or that we should bring people in
because there is nobody else to sweep our streets and clean our toilets.

⋅᠅⋅

The solutions to the "problems" of population decline, in fact, lie safely
within the range of realistic policy options. They include: people saving more
and consuming less; governments investing more in preventative health measures, to lengthen illness-free old age; better labour productivity; a higher
retirement age; drawing the economically inactive back into economic activity (with penalties for ageism); and restructuring hard-to-fill jobs to make
them more attractive. Population decline creates a (relative) shortage of workers and therefore shifts power from capital to labour and raises pay rates generally, as happened after the Black Death. Isn't the left supposed to be in
favour of such an outcome and against the use of immigrants to create a US-style
low-wage economy?

Yet the argument is not primarily about economics. Those who advocate
increases in immigration and population do so largely on the grounds that
they are good for GDP. They forget, as most economists do, that they are often
bad for the environment and society. Economic growth, after all, is ethically
undiscriminating: the wages earned from clearing up the effects of a car crash
or a pollution mishap count towards GDP in the same way as those earned
from making a loaf of bread. All over the world, Britain included, population
growth is generating an extraordinary range of negative effects, from climate
change and resource exhaustion to the destruction of species and habitats and
the poisoning of the biosphere. Deliberately boosting Britain's population,
either through large-scale net immigration or by telling people to have more
babies, will ultimately make it a much worse place to live in.

How big should Britain's population be? That depends which sums
you do—but some calculations from the Optimum Population Trust suggest
20 million or fewer.

Before you throw up your hands in disbelief at this idea, consider the view
of a liberal from another generation, John Stuart Mill, who in his *Principles of
Political Economy* (1848) acknowledged the economic potential for a "great
increase in population" but confessed he could see little reason for desiring it.
"The density of population necessary to enable mankind to obtain . . . all the
advantages both of co-operation and of social intercourse," he wrote, "has, in all
the most populous countries, been attained." In 1848, the world contained just
over a billion people and the population of Britain was 21 million.

POSTSCRIPT

Do Falling Birth Rates Pose a Threat to Human Welfare?

Resources and population come together in the concept of "carrying capacity," defined very simply as the size of the population that the environment can support, or "carry," indefinitely, through both good years and bad. It is not the size of the population that can prosper in good times alone, for such a large population must suffer catastrophically when droughts, floods, or blights arrive or the climate warms or cools. It is a long-term concept, where "long term" means not decades or generations, nor even centuries, but millennia or more. See Mark Nathan Cohen, "Carrying Capacity," *Free Inquiry* (August/September 2004).

What is Earth's carrying capacity for human beings? It is surely impossible to set a precise figure on the number of human beings the world can support for the long run. As Joel E. Cohen discusses in *How Many People Can the Earth Support?* (W. W. Norton, 1996), estimates of Earth's carrying capacity range from under a billion to over a trillion. The precise number depends on our choices of diet, standard of living, level of technology, willingness to share with others at home and abroad, and desire for an intact physical, chemical, and biological environment, as well as on whether or not our morality permits restraint in reproduction and our political or religious ideology permits educating and empowering women. The key, Cohen stresses, is human choice, and the choices are ones we must make within the next 50 years. Phoebe Hall, "Carrying Capacity," *E Magazine* (March/April 2003), notes that even countries with large land areas and small populations, such as Australia and Canada, can be overpopulated in terms of resource availability. The critical resource appears to be food supply; see Russell Hopfenberg, "Human Carrying Capacity Is Determined by Food Availability," *Population & Environment* (November 2003).

Andrew R. B. Ferguson, in "Perceiving the Population Bomb," *World Watch* (July/August 2001), sets the maximum sustainable human population at about 2 billion. Sandra Postel, in the Worldwatch Institute's *State of the World 1994* (W. W. Norton, 1994), says, "As a result of our population size, consumption patterns, and technology choices, we have surpassed the planet's carrying capacity. This is plainly evident by the extent to which we are damaging and depleting natural capital" (including land and water).

If population growth is now declining and world population will actually begin to decline during this century, there is clear hope. But the question of carrying capacity remains. Most estimates of carrying capacity put it at well below the current world population size, and it will take a long time for global population to fall far enough to reach such levels. We seem to be moving in the right direction, but it remains an open question whether our numbers will decline far enough soon enough (i.e., before environmental problems become critical). On the other hand, Jeroen Van den Bergh and Piet Rietveld, "Reconsidering the Limits to World Population: Meta-Analysis and Meta-Prediction," *Bioscience* (March 2004), set their best estimate of human global carrying capacity at 7.7 billion, which is distinctly reassuring.

How high a level will population actually reach? Fertility levels are definitely declining in many developed nations; see Alan Booth and Ann C. Crouter (eds.), *The New Population Problem: Why Families in Developed Countries Are Shrinking and What It Means* (Lawrence Erlbaum Associates, 2005). Does this mean an actual "birth dearth"? Not according to Doug Moss, "What Birth Dearth?" *E Magazine* (November–December 2006), who reminds us that there is still a large surplus of births—and therefore a growing population—in the less developed world. If we think globally, there is no shortage of people. Developed nations worried about falling fertility should not try to raise fertility levels but rather should increase immigration

ISSUE 8

Is There Sufficient Scientific Research to Conclude That Cell Phones Cause Cancer?

YES: George Carlo and Martin Schram, from *Cell Phones: Invisible Hazards in the Wireless Age: An Insider's Alarming Discoveries About Cancer and Genetic Damage* (Carroll & Graf, 2001)

NO: United Kingdom's National Radiation Protection Board, from *Mobile Phones and Health 2004: Report by the Board of NRPB* (Doc NRPB 15(5), 2004)

ISSUE SUMMARY

YES: Public health scientist George Carlo and journalist Martin Schram argue that there is a definite risk that the electromagnetic radiation generated by cell phone antennae can cause cancer and other health problems.

NO: The National Radiation Protection Board (now the Radiation Protection Division, http://www.hpa.org.uk/radiation/, of the United Kingdom's Health Protection Agency) argues that there is no clear indication of adverse health effects, including cancer, from the use of mobile phones, but precautions are nevertheless in order.

It seems inevitable that new technologies will alarm people. For example, in the late 1800s, when electricity was new, people feared the new wires that were strung overhead. See Joseph P. Sullivan, "Fearing Electricity: Overhead Wire Panic in New York City," *IEEE Technology and Society Magazine* (Fall 1995). More recently, electromagnetic fields (EMFs) have drawn attention. Now cell phones and other forms of wireless communications technology are the focus of controversy.

EMFs are emitted by any device that uses electricity. They weaken rapidly as one gets farther from the source, but they can be remarkably strong close to the source. Users of electric blankets (before the blankets were redesigned to minimize EMFs) and personal computers are thus subject to high exposures. Since EMF strength also depends on how much electricity is flowing through the source, people who live near power lines, especially high-tension, long-distance transmission lines, are also open to high EMF exposure.

Are EMFs dangerous? There have been numerous reports suggesting a link between EMF exposure and cancer, but inconsistency has been the curse of research in this area. In 1992 the Committee on Interagency Radiation Research and Policy Coordination, an arm of the White House's Office of Science and Technology Policy, released *Health Effects of Low Frequency Electric and Magnetic Fields,* a report that concluded, "There is no convincing [published] evidence . . . to support the contention that exposures to extremely low frequency electric and magnetic fields generated by sources such as household appliances, video terminals, and local powerlines are demonstrable health hazards." Jon Palfreman, in "Apocalypse Not," *Technology Review* (April 1996), summarized the controversy and the evidence against any connection between cancer and EMFs. And in "Residential Exposure to Magnetic Fields and Acute Lymphoblastic Leukemia in Children," *The New England Journal of Medicine* (July 3, 1997), Martha S. Linet et al. report that they failed to find any support for such a connection.

Since cell phones are electrical devices, they emit EMFs. But they—or their antennae—also emit electromagnetic radiation in the form of radio signals. And after a few cell phone users developed brain cancer and sued the phone makers, people began to worry. See Gordon Bass, "Is Your Cell Phone Killing You?" *PC Computing* (December 1999). Now more lawsuits are being filed, and the research reports are coming in. Professor John Moulder and his colleagues published a review of the evidence in "Cell Phones and Cancer: What Is the Evidence for a Connection?" *Radiation Research* (May 1999). In it, they concluded, "Overall, the existing evidence for a causal relationship between RF radiation from cell phones and cancer is found to be weak to nonexistent." Tamar Nordenberg, "Cell Phones and Brain Cancer: No Clear Connection," *FDA Consumer* (November–December 2000), reported no real signs that cell phones caused cancer but noted that the evidence was sufficient to justify continuing research.

In the following selections, George Carlo and Martin Schram argue that there is a definite risk that the electromagnetic radiation generated by cell phone antennae can cause cancer and other health problems. Furthermore, wireless Internet devices also emit such radiation and may pose similar risks. The National Radiation Protection Board (now the Radiation Protection Division of the United Kingdom's Health Protection Agency) argues that the widespread adoption of mobile phones has not been accompanied by any clear increase in adverse health effects, including cancer, but the technology is still young, there has not been enough time for epidemiological studies of users, especially in subgroups of users, and there have been some suggestive laboratory studies. There are no clear indications of risk, but precautions are nevertheless in order.

YES  George Carlo and Martin Schram

Cell Phones: Invisible Hazards in the Wireless Age

Follow-the-Science: Piecing Together the Cancer Puzzle

Scientific findings are like pieces of a puzzle. Individually, they may not seem to show anything clearly. But by trying to fit the pieces together, it is possible to see if they form a big, coherent picture.

In the puzzle of cell phone radiation research, the pieces of scientific evidence we have now do fit together. Although many pieces are still missing, those that are in place indicate a big picture of cancer and health risk. The picture is alarming, because even if the risk eventually proves to be small, it will still be real—and that means millions of people around the world will develop cancer or other health problems due to using mobile phones.

Even more alarming, however, is that many in the industry, who are paid by the industry—and some who are paid by the public to oversee and regulate the industry—have persisted in talking publicly as if they cannot see the picture that is taking shape even as they speak.

In the study of public health, there is a well-known template that researchers use to put together individual scientific findings—like the pieces of a puzzle—to see if they show evidence of a public-health hazard. This template, known as the Koch-Henle Postulates, is a means of determining whether the findings indicate a true cause-and-effect process, from biological plausibility to exposure and dose-response. The postulates are:

1. If there is a biological explanation for the association derived from separate experiments that is consistent with what is known about the development of the disease, then the association is more likely to be causal. Scientists term this *biological plausibility*.
2. If several studies of people are showing the same finding while employing different methods and different investigators, the association that is being seen is more likely to be cause and effect, or causal. Scientists term this *consistency*.
3. If it is clear that the exposure precedes the development of the disease, then the association is more likely to be causal. Scientists term this *temporality*.

4. If the increase in risk is significant—more than a doubling in the risk or an increase that is statistically significant—the association is more likely to be causal. Scientists term this *significance.*
5. If the more severe the level of exposure, the higher the risk for the disease or the biological effect that is being studied, the association is more likely to be causal. Scientists term this *dose-response upward.*
6. If the absence of exposure corresponds to the absence of the disease, the more likely the association is to be causal. Scientists term this *dose-response downward.*
7. If there are similar findings in human, animal, and *in vitro* studies— in other words, if the same conclusions can be drawn from all—the more likely the association that is seen is causal. Scientists term this *concordance.*

Researchers use the Koch-Henle Postulates as a checklist. The greater the number of postulates that are met, the greater the likelihood that a hazard exists. For some of the more commonly recognized carcinogens, it has taken decades for the hazards to be judged as valid. For example, in the case of cigarette smoking, it took two decades of study and more than 100 years of consumer use to gather enough information that could be judged against the Koch-Henle standards to demonstrate the need for the U.S. Surgeon General's warning label on cigarette packs.

In the case of cellular telephones, consumers are fortunate that the health-hazard picture can be seen much sooner than that. Each of the red-flag findings about cell phone radiation provides a vital piece of information that fits into the overall cancer puzzle. A number of the other earlier studies, which on their own were inconclusive or seemed uninterpretable, now appear to fit into the puzzle as well. They clarify a troubling picture of cancer and health risk that is just now becoming clear.

Here is how the scientific pieces fit into the larger cancer puzzle:

Human blood studies   These studies—by Drs. Ray Tice and Graham Hook, and most recently [corroborated by] Dr. Joseph Roti Roti—show genetic damage in the form of micronuclei in blood cells exposed to cell phone radiation. They provide evidence of the Koch-Henle postulate of *biological plausibility* for the development of the tumors following exposure to radio waves. Without some type of genetic damage, it is unlikely that radio waves would be able to cause cancer. Every direct mechanism that has been identified in the development of cancer involves genetic damage; the linkage is so strong that if an absence of genetic damage had been proven in these studies, scientists would have considered that to be reason enough to conclude that cancer is not caused by cell phones. (Indeed, that is what scientists were justified in saying prior to 1999.) Scientific literature has repeatedly confirmed that brain cancer is clearly linked to chromosome damage; brain tumors have consistently been shown to have a variety of chromosomal abnormalities. The studies by Tice, Hook, and Roti Roti consistently showed chromosomal damage in blood exposed to wireless phone radio waves.

Breakdown in the blood brain barrier   The findings of genetic damage by Tice, Hook, and Roti Roti now give new meaning and importance to Dr. Leif

Salford's 1994 studies that showed a breakdown in the blood brain barrier of rats when they were exposed to radio waves. The blood brain barrier findings now fit into the overall cancer picture by providing a two-step explanation for how cancer could be caused by cell phone radiation. (The blood brain barrier filters the blood by not allowing dangerous chemicals to reach sensitive brain tissue.)

Step One: A breakdown in the blood brain barrier filter would provide an avenue for chemical carcinogens in the bloodstream (from tobacco, pesticides, or air pollution, for example) to leak into the brain and reach sensitive brain tissue that would otherwise be protected. Those chemicals, upon reaching sensitive brain tissue, could break the DNA in the brain or cause other harm to reach those cells.

Step Two: While a number of studies showed that cell phone radiation by itself does not appear to break DNA, the micronuclei findings of Tice, Hook, and Roti Roti suggest that DNA repair mechanisms in brain cells could be impaired by mobile phone radiation. (One reason micronuclei occur is that there has been a breakdown in the cell's ability to repair itself.) If the brain cells become unable to repair themselves, the process of chemically induced carcinogenesis—the creation of tumors—could begin.

This is further evidence of the Koch-Henle postulate of *biological plausibility* for cell phone radiation involvement in the development of brain cancer.

Studies of tumors in people who use cell phones   There have been four studies of tumors in people who use cellular phones—Dr. Ken Rothman's study of deaths among cell phone users, Joshua Muscat's two studies of brain cancer and acoustic neuroma, and Dr. Lennart Hardell's study of brain tumors. All four epidemiological studies, done by different investigators who used different methods, show some evidence of an increased risk of tumors associated with the use of cellular phones. This is evidence of the Koch-Henle postulate of *consistency.*

All four epidemiological studies provide some assurance in the methods used by the investigators that the people studied had used cellular telephones before they were clinically diagnosed as having tumors. This is evidence of the Koch-Henle postulate of *temporality.*

All four epidemiological studies showed increases in risk of developing brain tumors. Muscat's study of cell phone users showed a doubling of the risk of developing neuro-epithelial tumors. (The result was statistically significant.) Hardell's study showed that among cell phone users, tumors were twice as likely to occur in areas of the brain at the side where the user normally held the phone. (This result was also statistically significant.) Rothman's study showed that users of handheld cell phones have more than twice the risk of dying from brain cancer than do car phone users—whose antennas are mounted on the body of the car, far removed from the users' heads. (That finding was not statistically significant.) Muscat's study of acoustic neuroma indicates that cell phone users have a 50-percent increase in risk of developing tumors of the auditory nerve. (This finding was statistically significant only when correlated with the years of cell phone usage by the patient.) These findings are evidence of the Koch-Henle postulate of *significance.*

Studies of cell phone radiation dosage and response   In Dr. Michael Repacholi's study of mice, the risk of lymphoma increased significantly with the number of months that mice were exposed to the radio waves.

In the work by Tice, Hook, and Roti Roti, the risks of genetic damage as measured by the formation of micronuclei increased as the amount of radiation increased.

In the three epidemiological studies—two by Muscat and one by Hardell—that were able to estimate radiation exposure to specific parts of the brain, the risk of tumors was greater in the areas of the brain near where the cell phone was held.

These findings are all evidence of the Koch-Henle postulate known as *dose-response upward*. (In cell phones, minutes of phone usage are not a reliable indication of dosage, because the distance of the telephone from a base station during the call and any physical barriers to the signal are the most important factors in the amount of radiation the phone antenna emits during the call.)

The Hardell epidemiological study showed that patients with tumors in areas of the brain that could not be reached by radiation from a cell phone antenna were likely not to have been cell phone users. Similarly, in Muscat's study, when all brain-tumor patients were included in his analysis—those with tumors that were outside the range of radiation from the cellular phone antenna and those whose tumors were within that range—there was no increase in the risk of brain cancer. This is evidence of the Koch-Henle postulate that is called *dose-response downward*—which simply means that if there is no chance that cell phone radiation dosage could have been received, chances are the tumor was caused by something else.

Agreement of findings from in vitro and in vivo studies   The test-tube studies by Tice and Hook; the mouse study by Repacholi; and the four epidemiological studies by Rothman, Muscat, and Hardell are all in agreement in that they suggest an increase in the risk of cancer among people who use mobile phones. This is evidence of the Koch-Henle postulate of *concordance*.

. . . And the Largest Piece of the Puzzle

As the officials of the government, officials of the industry, and just plain unofficial people try to fit together jigsaw pieces to see whether mobile phones indeed pose a cancer risk, the cancer experts themselves have provided what is by far the biggest and most revealing piece of the puzzle. Writing in the U.S. government's own *Journal of the National Cancer Institute*, and other prestigious professional publications, these experts have made it clear that, if there are findings that micronuclei develop in blood cells exposed to mobile phone radiation, that is in itself evidence of a cancer risk. The risk is so persuasive, the experts have written, that preventative treatment should be given in order to best protect those people whose levels of micronuclei have increased.

The Big Picture

The pieces of the cell phone puzzle do indeed fit together to form the beginnings of a picture that researchers, regulators, and mobile phone users can all see for themselves. Many pieces are still missing. But enough pieces are already in place to see that there are legitimate reasons to be concerned about the health of people who use wireless phones.

Most alarming to public health scientists should be the fact that all seven of the Koch-Henle postulates have been met within the first decade of widespread mobile phone usage.

The big picture is becoming disturbingly clear: There is a definite risk that the radiation plume that emanates from a cell phone antenna can cause cancer and other health problems. It is a risk that affects hundreds of millions of people around the world. It is a risk that must be seen and understood by all who use cell phones so they can take all the appropriate and available steps to protect themselves—and especially to protect young children whose skulls are still growing and who are the most vulnerable to the risks of radiation.

Safety First: Health Recommendations

As the big picture becomes clear and we see that radiation from mobile phones poses a real cancer and health risk, it also becomes clear that there are basic recommendations that now demand the urgent attention of all who use, make, research, or regulate cell phones.

Mobile telephones are a fact of life and a fixture in the lifestyles of more than half a billion people around the world. That only makes it all the more vital that we understand and follow the recommendations by which all who use mobile phones can minimize their health risk, and especially can protect our children. Here are some basic suggestions for mobile phone users, manufacturers, and science and medical researchers.

Recommendations for Consumers

To avoid radiation exposure and minimize health risks when using wireless phones:

1. The best advice is to keep the antenna away from your body by using a phone with a headset or earpiece. Another option is a phone with speakerphone capability.
2. If you must use your phone without a headset, be sure the antenna is fully extended during the phone's use. Radiation plumes are emitted mainly from the mid-length portion of the antenna; when the antenna is recessed inside the phone, the entire phone functions as the antenna—and the radiation is emitted from the entire phone into a much wider area of your head, jaw, and hand.
3. Children under the age of ten should not use wireless devices of any type; for children over the age of ten, pagers are preferable to wireless phones because pagers are not put up to the head and they can be used away from the body.
4. When the signal strength is low, do not use your phone. The reason: The lower the signal strength, the harder the instrument has to work to carry the call—and the greater the radiation that is emitted from the antenna.

5. Emerging studies, and common sense, make clear that handheld phones should not be used while driving a vehicle.

A Few Words of Caution for Consumers

The public is bombarded with waves of claims that are made at times by individuals who are well-meaning but not well-informed—and at other times by special interests who really want to sell a product. For example, there is no scientific basis for recommendations that have been made by some groups to limit phone use as a means of minimizing the risk of health effects. It is not possible to determine scientifically the difference in radiation exposure from one ten-minute call and ten one-minute calls. The total number of minutes is the same, but the pattern and amount of radiation could be very different. Also, the amount of radiation emitted by a mobile phone depends on the distance of the phone from a base station; the further the distance, the harder the phone has to work and the greater the radiation. Finally, the greatest amount of radiation emitted by a phone is during dialing and ringing. People who keep their phones on their belts or in their pockets should move the phones away from their bodies when the phones are ringing. (The amounts of radiation in a single call can vary by factors of ten to 100 depending on all of these variables.)

Consumers also need to be cautious about unverified claims that seem to have scientific backing. For example: The media recently carried an account published in Britain's *Which?* magazine that said a group called the Consumers' Association (with which the magazine is affiliated) had shown in tests that some cell phone headsets actually cause more radiation to go to the brain than the phones themselves. But the claim is unsubstantiated by any scientific evidence, and has been refuted by a number of studies by recognized researchers using established scientific methods. The only conclusion that can be drawn from existing scientific evidence is that headsets are the best option for mobile phone users to minimize exposure to wireless phone radiation.

Also, a number of devices on the market claim to eliminate the effects of antenna radiation and are being marketed as alternatives to using headsets or speakerphones. These products need to be tested to see if they will really protect consumers—a caution expressed by Great Britain's Stewart Commission. They recommended that their government set in place "a national system which enables independent testing of shielding devices and hands-free kits . . . which enable clear information to be given about the effectiveness of such devices. A kite mark or equivalent should be introduced to demonstrate conformity with the testing standard." In the United States, the FDA has been silent on the matter.

Recommendations for the Mobile Phone Industry

To enhance consumer protection:

1. Phones should be redesigned to minimize radiation exposure to consumers—antennas that extend out at an angle, away from the head, or that carry the radiation outward should be developed.

2. Headsets and other accessories that minimize radiation exposure should be redesigned so they are more durable and can be conveniently used.
3. Consumers should be given complete information about health risks and solutions through brochures, product inserts, and Internet postings so they can make their own decisions about how much of the risk inherent to mobile telephone use they wish to assume.
4. Emerging and advancing phone technologies need to be premarket tested for biological effects so dangerous products do not make it to the market.
5. Post-market surveillance is necessary for all phone users—surveys of analog and digital phone users to see if they experience any adverse health effects, and databases should be maintained where people can report any health effects they have experienced due to their phones.

Recommendations for Scientific, Medical, and Public Health Officials

To help consumers:

1. Science, medicine, and government must move immediately and aggressively with the goal of minimizing the impact of radio waves on adults, children, and pregnant women.
2. One federal agency must be designated as the lead agency for protecting people who use wireless communications devices, rather than having the responsibility remain undefined and shared among multiple agencies including the FDA, FCC, EPA, and others.
3. A genuine safety standard needs to be established to serve as the basis for future regulatory decisions. Since the specific absorption rate alone does not measure biological effects on humans, it does not serve the safety needs of consumers. . . .

Recommendations for Industry and Government Concerning the Wireless Internet

We need to recognize and learn from the mistakes we made when cellular phones were first introduced. The phones were sold to the public before there had been any premarket testing to determine whether they were safe or posed a potential health risk. Because the cell phones were not tested initially, by the time they were on the market, efforts to research the problem became intertwined with the forces of politics and profit. Consumer protection was not the highest priority.

As we enter the age of the wireless Internet, no one can say for sure whether or not the radio waves of these new wireless products will prove harmless or harmful. But this much is known: The concern about mobile phones focuses on the near-field radiation that extends in a 2-to-3-inch plume from an antenna, and the radiation from the many wireless laptop and hand-held computer products is just about the same. It would seem that these latter products should be safer because users don't hold their laptops and handheld computers against their heads. But no one has researched what the effect will be of a roomful of wireless products all being used simultaneously, with radio waves invisibly crisscrossing the space that is occupied by people. Will these passive occupants run a risk similar to nonsmokers in a room filled with smokers, who end up affected by passive smoke?

Thus, it is important that these new products must be formally testing under official regulatory control that includes specific premarket screening guidelines. There must also be post-market surveys of people who use the wireless Internet to see if health problems emerge that were not found in the premarket testing.

**United Kingdom's National
Radiation Protection Board**

Mobile Phones and Health 2004

Executive Summary

Background

1. There are currently about 50 million mobile phones in use in the UK compared with around 25 million in 2000 and 4.5 million in 1995. These are supported by about 40,000 base stations in the UK network. The majority of these base stations operate under the Global System for Mobile Communications (GSM).

2. In less than ten years since the first GSM network was commercially launched as the second generation of mobile phones, it has become the world's leading and fastest growing telecommunications system. It is in use by more than one-sixth of the world's population and it has been estimated that at the end of January 2004 there were 1 billion GSM subscribers across more than 200 countries. The growth of GSM continues unabated with more than 160 million new customers in the last 12 months.

3. The revolution in communications continues world-wide. The third generation of mobile phones, 3G, is now being marketed in the UK and in many other countries and it is to be expected that further developments will become available in due course. In addition, there are many other telecommunications and related systems in use, all of which result in exposure of the population to radiofrequency (RF) fields.

4. The UK government has given strong encouragement to the development of mobile phone technology. Operators have been given support for the installation of the cellular networks and government has seen this as an important area for UK-based firms to establish themselves as world leaders. There have also been extensive developments in security-related equipment that utilise radiocommunications systems.

Public Health Concerns

5. The extensive use of mobile phones suggests that users do not in general judge them to present a significant health hazard. Rather they have welcomed the technology and brought it into use in their everyday lives. Nevertheless, since their introduction, there have

From *DOC NRPB* 15(5) 1-116(2004), 2004, pp. #1–25, 31–37, 40–44, 55–32, 64–66, 69–71, 84–89.

been persisting concerns about the possible impact of mobile phone technologies on health.

6. This was appreciated by the UK government, which in 1999 took the early initiative of setting up the Independent Expert Group on Mobile Phones (IEGMP) to review the situation. Its report, *Mobile Phones and Health* (the Stewart Report), was published in May 2000. It stated:

"The balance of evidence to date suggests that exposures to RF radiation below NRPB and ICNIRP (International Commission on Non-Ionizing Radiation Protection) guidelines do not cause adverse health effects to the general population."

"There is now scientific evidence, however, which suggests that there may be biological effects occurring at exposures below these guidelines."

"We conclude therefore that it is not possible at present to say that exposure to RF radiation, even at levels below national guidelines, is totally without potential adverse health effects, and that the gaps in knowledge are sufficient to justify a precautionary approach."

"We recommend that a precautionary approach to the use of mobile phone technologies be adopted until much more detailed and scientifically robust information on any health effects becomes available."

7. The Board notes that a central recommendation in the Stewart Report was that a precautionary approach to the use of mobile phone technologies be adopted until much more detailed and scientifically robust information on any health effects becomes available.

8. The Stewart Report was welcomed by government, the general public and by industry. Various subsequent reports from across the world have supported the main thrust of its general conclusions.

9. Since then, the widespread development in the use of mobile phones world-wide has not been accompanied by associated, clearly established increases in adverse health effects. Within the UK, there is a lack of hard information showing that the mobile phone systems in use are damaging to health. It is important to emphasise this crucial point.

10. Nevertheless, the following issues have to be taken into consideration.

11. First, the widespread use of mobile phone technologies is still fairly recent and technologies are continuing to develop at a pace which is outstripping analyses of any potential impact on health (see paragraphs 55–57, 84 and 85).

12. Second, there are data which suggest that RF fields can interfere with biological systems.

13. Third, because the use of mobile phone technologies is a fairly recent phenomenon, it has not yet been possible to carry out necessary long-term epidemiological studies and evaluate the findings. However, an increase in the risk of acoustic neuromas has recently been reported in people in Sweden with more than ten years' use of mobile phones. This study has been able to obtain long-term follow-up data and highlights the need for extended follow-up studies on phone users, as has been noted in a number of reviews. Epidemiological studies, because of a lack of sensitivity, may miss any effects

in small subsets of the general populations studied. This is a reason why the Board welcomes the large international cohort study proposed for support by the Mobile Telecommunications and Health Research (MTHR) programme (see paragraph 89). A recent German study has also suggested concerns.

14. Fourth, a recent paper has suggested possible effects on brain function resulting from the use of 3G phones, although the study has some limitations and needs replication. The Stewart Report had previously identified the need for research on brain function.

15. Fifth, populations are not homogeneous and people can vary in their susceptibility to environmental and other challenges. There are well-established examples in the literature of the genetic predisposition of some groups that could influence sensitivity to disease. This remains an outstanding issue in relation to RF exposure and one on which more information is needed. A number of people also report symptoms they ascribe to electromagnetic hypersensitivity arising from exposure to a range of electromagnetic fields (EMFs) encountered in everyday life. There is concern by an increasing number of individuals, although relatively small in relation to the total UK population, that they are adversely affected by exposure to RF fields from mobile phones (see also paragraphs 58–64).

16. Sixth, IEGMP considered that children might be more vulnerable to any effects arising from the use of mobile phones because of their developing nervous system, the greater absorption of energy in the tissues of the head and a longer lifetime of exposure. Data on the impact on children have not yet been forthcoming. The potential for undertaking studies to examine any possible effects on children, however, are limited for ethical reasons.

17. Seventh, there are ongoing concerns in the UK about the use of Terrestrial Trunked Radio (TETRA) by the police and the nature of the signals emitted as well as about exposures to RF from other telecommunications technologies.

18. Eighth, there remain particular concerns in the UK about the impact of base stations on health, including well-being. Despite current evidence which shows that exposures of individuals are likely to be only a small fraction of those from phones, they may impact adversely on well-being. The large numbers of additional base stations which will be necessary to effectively roll out the 3G and other new networks are likely to exacerbate the potential impact. People can also be concerned about effects on property values when base stations are built near their homes.

19. The Board believes that the main conclusions reached in the Stewart Report in 2000 still apply today and that a precautionary approach to the use of mobile phone technologies should continue to be adopted.

Progress Made in Addressing Public Health Concerns

20. The recommendation in the Stewart Report to adopt a precautionary approach was immediately accepted by government. It also endorsed many of the other recommendations in the Report.

21. The Stewart Report made a number of other recommendations that were designed to provide more information about the operation of mobile phones and base stations and to address public concerns about this technology. This sought to allow individuals, local communities and local authorities to make informed choices about how the technology should be developed.

22. The responses to the recommendations in the Stewart Report are reviewed in the report by the Board and issues where further progress is needed have been identified. The key findings are summarised below.

Tightening of Exposure Guidelines

23. A recommendation in the Stewart Report was that, as a precautionary approach, the ICNIRP guidelines for public exposure be adopted for use in the UK for mobile phone frequencies. It was felt that this would bring the UK into line with other countries in the European Union. These guidelines have now been adopted by government for application across the UK and provide for a five-fold reduction in exposure guidelines for members of the public compared with the recommended values for people whose work brings them into contact with sources of RF fields.

24. The Board welcomes the introduction by government of tighter exposure guidelines for the general public.

Base Stations

25. A wide variety of types of base stations make up the UK network. Macrocells provide the main framework of the system. Where there are areas of high demand, as in busy streets and shopping areas, microcells are used to infill the network and help to prevent 'lost' calls. Picocells may be installed in buildings or other enclosed areas to improve signal strength and to infill the network in areas of high demand for calls. . . .

31. The Board recommends that monitoring of potential exposures from 3G base stations should be concomitant with the rollout of the network.

Mobile Phones and SAR Values

32. In September 2001 the European Committee for Electrical Standardisation (CENELEC) published a standard testing procedure for the measurement of specific energy absorption rate (SAR) from mobile phones. Information on all phones marketed in the UK, using this standard testing procedure, is now available.

33. However, it is still difficult for people to readily and easily acquire the necessary information so that comparisons of different phones can be made.

34. The Board welcomes the provision of information on the SAR from phones by all manufacturers using a standard testing procedure. This is an important contribution to providing information to the

public about the potential for exposure and informs consumer choice. It recommends that comparative information on the SAR from phones is readily available to the consumer. The inclusion of comparative data on the SAR from phones in its promotional literature by at least one retailer is a welcome development. The public also need to be able to understand the merits and limitations of published SAR values.

Planning Guidance on Base Station Locations

35. IEGMP was concerned that anxiety about the presence of local base stations and resulting exposure to RF fields could affect peoples' health, including well-being. IEGMP also heard at open meetings that information about base station developments was frequently not provided to the local community.

36. A number of recommendations were made in the Stewart Report to improve the transparency of the local planning process and to improve the planning procedure. A specific recommendation was that permitted development rights for the erection of masts under 15 m should be revoked and that the siting of all new base stations should be subject to the normal planning process.

37. Following publication of the Stewart Report reviews of the planning process were put in place throughout the UK. Revised guidance that was issued aimed to provide for more discussions between operators and local authorities on the development of all proposals for telecommunications equipment and to minimise visual intrusion. . . .

40. The Board notes that whilst there has been a plethora of documents about planning issues for base stations, public concerns have not abated.

41. The Board supports the government view that whilst planning is necessarily a local issue, the assessment of evidence related to possible health concerns associated with exposures to RF fields from base stations is best dealt with nationally.

42. Accepting that, the Board believes that it is timely for there to be set in place a much clearer and more readily understandable template of protocols and procedures to be followed by local authorities and phone operators across the UK. It is clear that at present the application of guidance is very variable and that the extent to which the underpinning facts are presented can also be variable. It recommends that there should be an independent review of the extent to which implementation of good practice guidelines by operators and local authorities is being carried out.

43. The Board considers that it is important that 'best practice' in relation to network development operates consistently across the country and that how planning applications are dealt with should be an open and transparent process.

44. The Board welcomes the ODPM *Code of Best Practice on Mobile Phone Network Development*, that incorporates the 'ten commitments on best siting practice'. . . .

Developing Technologies

55. A variety of additional technologies are now being progressively developed and implemented in the field of telecommunications. New technologies include third-generation (3G) mobile telephony, wireless local area networks (WLANs), Bluetooth and ultra-wideband (UWB) technology, and radio-frequency identification (RFID) devices.

56. The Board considers that it is important to understand the signal characteristics and field strengths arising from new telecommunications systems and related technologies, to assess the RF exposure of people, and to understand the potential biological effects on the human body.

57. The Board also believes it important to ensure that the exposure of people from all new and existing systems complies with ICNIRP guidelines.

Sensitive Groups

58. Populations as a whole are not genetically homogeneous and people can vary in their susceptibility to environmental hazards. There could also be a dependency on age. The issue of individual sensitivity remains an outstanding one in relation to RF exposure and one on which more information is needed.

59. IEGMP considered that children might be more vulnerable to any effects arising from the use of mobile phones. The potential for undertaking studies to examine any possible effects on children are, however, limited for ethical reasons. It was recommended in the Stewart Report that the use of mobile phones by children should be minimised and this was supported by the Departments of Health. Text messaging has considerable advantages as the phone is in use for only a short time, when the phone transmits the message, compared with voice communication.

60. The Board concludes that, in the absence of new scientific evidence, the recommendation in the Stewart Report on limiting the use of mobile phones by children remains appropriate as a precautionary measure.

61. The Board also welcomes an initiative by the World Health Organization in its EMF programme to focus attention on research relevant to the potential sensitivity of children.

62. Additionally, there is concern by an increasing number of individuals, although relatively small in relation to the total UK population, that they are adversely affected by exposure either to EMFs in general or specifically to RF fields from mobile phones. A European Commission group of experts termed the syndrome 'electromagnetic hypersensitivity'. Similar concerns have been raised in the past in relation to exposure to agricultural chemicals and other materials. . . .

64. The Board considers that the issue of electromagnetic hypersensitivity needs to be carefully examined in the UK. It supports the strengthening of work designed to understand the reasons for the reported electromagnetic hypersensitivity of some members of the public.

Occupational Exposure

65. Levels of exposure to RF fields can be higher through occupational exposure than for members of the public and sometimes approach guideline levels.

66. The Board welcomes the establishment of a register of occupationally exposed people at the Institute of Occupational Health, Birmingham. This should facilitate the determination of whether, occupationally, there are health effects from exposure to RF fields not observed in the general public. . . .

Mobile Phones and Driving

69. The Stewart Report demonstrated that there is good experimental evidence that the use of mobile phones whilst driving has a detrimental effect on drivers' responsiveness. This translates into a substantial increased risk of an accident. The evidence suggested that the negative effects of phone use while driving were similar whether the phone was hand-held or hands-free.

70. The Board welcomes the intention of government to increase the penalty for the offence of using a hand-held mobile phone while driving by making it endorsable with three penalty points and an increased fine of £60.

71. The Board notes that the UK legislation on the use of phones in motor vehicles, making it illegal to use any hand-held phone, is tailored to the practicality of enforcement. The evidence remains, however, that the use of mobile phones in moving vehicles, both hand-held and hands-free, can significantly increase the risk of an accident. . . .

Health-Related Research

84. Outstanding health-related concerns can be addressed by epidemiological (human health) studies, experimental investigations with animals, and the use of cell-based techniques. Dosimetric studies are important for understanding the exposure of people from various sources and human volunteer studies can investigate short-term interactions of RF fields, for example, with brain function. In the area of telecommunications, however, technological change is rapid and it is a challenge to carry out comprehensive research and to determine the possibility of any health effects.

85. Research into any health effects of exposure to RF fields is still in a developmental phase. There are analogies with work on the consequences of exposure to EMFs from power lines. In the early 1980s, the epidemiological studies on exposure to extremely low frequency (ELF) EMFs lacked methods to directly assess exposure of individuals and instead surrogates for exposure were frequently used. Subsequently portable measurement equipment became available in the late 1980s/early 1990s and the quality of studies providing exposure-response information, for both occupational and domestic exposures, rapidly improved. Studies on RF exposure were in a similar position in the 1990s to those on ELF EMFs in the early 1980s. In

recent years, however, considerable effort has gone into developing RF-related studies that combine high quality dosimetry with well-designed studies in experimental biology and epidemiology. Inevitably it will be some time before the present generation of studies comes to fruition. The MTHR programme in the UK has been at the forefront of this advance in RF-related research.

86. The MTHR programme was launched in February 2001 with an initial budget of £7.36 million funded by government and industry on a 50 : 50 basis. To date around 30 projects have been funded through MTHR with additional support from the Home Office, the Department of Trade and Industry, and industry. It presently has a budget of £8.8 million, all of which has now been allocated to the ongoing research programme. The RF-related research in the UK is complementary to further research being carried out world-wide, much of it co-ordinated through the WHO EMF programme.

87. The Board considers that the MTHR programme, which was first announced in December 2000, has set the standard for independent, high quality, health-related research on RF exposure.

88. The Board further recommends that government and industry should provide support for a continuation of the programme.

89. The Board particularly supports the need for further research, in the following areas:

   (a) an international cohort study of mobile phone users aimed at pooling and sharing experimental design, findings and expertise internationally,
   (b) an expanded programme of research on TETRA signals and biological effects,
   (c) effects of RF exposure on children,
   (d) investigation of public concerns about mobile phone technology,
   (e) electromagnetic hypersensitivity and its possible impact on health, including well-being, associated with mobile phone technology,
   (f) studies of RF effects on direct and established measures of human brain function and investigations of possible mechanisms involved,
   (g) complementary dosimetry studies focused on ascertaining the exposure of people to RF fields.

In developing the MTHR and other research programmes, care needs to be taken to prevent unnecessary duplication of studies whilst at the same time seeking to replicate significant findings.

POSTSCRIPT

Is There Sufficient Scientific Research to Conclude That Cell Phones Cause Cancer?

Is the cell phone cancer scare nothing more than media hype, as Sid Deutsch called the EMF cancer scare in "Electromagnetic Field Cancer Scares," *Skeptical Inquirer* (Winter 1994)? Or do cell phones pose a genuine hazard? L. Hardell, et al., reported in "Cellular and Cordless Telephones and the Risk for Brain Tumours," *European Journal of Cancer Prevention* (August 2002), that long-term users of older, analog phones were more likely to suffer brain tumors. U.S. District Judge Catherine Blake, presiding over the most famous phone-cancer lawsuit, was not swayed. She declared that the claimant had provided "no sufficiently reliable and relevant scientific evidence" and said she intended to dismiss the case (Mark Parascandola, "Judge Rejects Cancer Data in Maryland Cell Phone Suit," *Science*, October 11, 2002). Robert Clark, "Clean Bill of Health for Cell Phones," *America's Network* (April 1, 2004), reports that "A survey by the Danish Institute of Cancer Epidemiology . . . says there is no short-term danger of developing brain tumors." A Swedish study found no breast cancer link to electromagnetic fields; see Janet Raloff, "Study Can't Tie EMFs to Cancer," *Science News* (February 26, 2005), and U. M. Forssen, et al., "Occupational Magnetic Fields and Female Breast Cancer: A Case-Control Study using Swedish Population Registers and New Exposure Data," *American Journal of Epidemiology* (vol. 161, no. 3, 2005). In early 2006, three European studies reported an increased risk of some kinds of brain tumors in people who had used cell phones for more than ten years; see, for example, Joachim Schuz, et al., "Cellular Phones, Cordless Phones, and the Risks of Glioma and Meningioma," *American Journal of Epidemiology* (March 2006). In September, a Danish study reported that cell phone users suffer no more risk that nonusers; see Joachim Schuz, "Cellular Telephone Use and Cancer Risk: Update of a Nationwide Danish Cohort," *Journal of the National Cancer Institute* (December 6, 2006). If there are any effects, they do not seem to be large and, say Reetta Nylund and Darius Leszczynski, "Mobile Phone Radiation Causes Changes in Gene and Protein Expression in Human Endothelial Cell Lines and the Response Seems to Be Genome- and Proteome-Dependent," *Proteomics* (September 2006), they may depend upon differences in the genes possessed by those exposed.

Skeptics insist that the threat is real. However, if it is real, this is not yet clear beyond a doubt. Unfortunately, society cannot always wait for certainty. In connection with EMFs, Gordon L. Hester, in "Electric and Magnetic Fields: Managing an Uncertain Risk," *Environment* (January/February 1992), asserts that just the possibility of a health hazard is sufficient to justify more research into the problem. The guiding principle, says Hester, is " 'prudent avoidance,' which was originally intended to mean that people should avoid fields 'when this can be done with modest amounts of money and trouble.' " The same guideline surely applies to cell phone radiation.

Is it possible to prove that cell phones do *not* cause cancer? Unfortunately, no, because small, sporadic effects might not be detected even in massive studies. Thus, for some people, the jury will forever be out.

What should society do in the face of weak, uncertain, and even contradictory data? Can we afford to conclude that there is no hazard? Or must we ban or redesign a useful technology with no justification other than our fear that there might be a real hazard? Many scientists and politicians argue that even if there is no genuine medical risk, there is a genuine impact in terms of public anxiety. See Gary Stix, "Closing the Book," *Scientific American* (March 1998). It is therefore appropriate, they say, to fund further research and to take whatever relatively inexpensive steps to minimize exposure are possible. Failure to do so increases public anxiety and distrust of government and science.

Some of those "relatively inexpensive steps" are pretty simple. As Carlo and Schram note, they include repositioning cell phone antennae and using headsets. As Tamar Nordenberg, "Cell Phones and Brain Cancer: No Clear Connection," *FDA Consumer* (November–December 2000), says, quoting Professor John Moulder, using a cell phone while driving is much more hazardous even than using a conventional high-radiation cell phone. By 2003, cell phones were being broadly indicted as hazards on the highway. The basic problem is that using a cell phone increases the mental workload on the driver, according to Roland Matthews, Stephen Legg, and Samuel Charlton, "The Effect of Cell Phone Type on Drivers' Subjective Workload During Concurrent Driving and Conversing," *Accident Analysis & Prevention* (July, 2003); they too recommend using a hands-free phone. As a result of such studies, several states have already banned handheld phones while driving, with initial good effect; see Anne T. McCartt, Elisa R. Braver, and Lori L. Geary, "Drivers' Use of Handheld Cell Phones Before and After New York State's Cell Phone Law," *Preventive Medicine* (May 2003). Unfortunately, the initial good results have not lasted. See "Motorists' Cell Phone Use Rising: NHTSA," *Safety & Health* (May 2005).

ISSUE 9

Should DDT Be Banned Worldwide?

YES: Anne Platt McGinn, from "Malaria, Mosquitoes, and DDT," *World Watch* (May/June 2002)

NO: Donald R. Roberts, from Statement before U.S. Senate Committee on Environment & Public Works, Hearing on the Role of Science in Environmental Policy-Making (September 28, 2005)

ISSUE SUMMARY

YES: Anne Platt McGinn, a senior researcher at the Worldwatch Institute, argues that although DDT is still used to fight malaria, there are other, more effective and less environmentally harmful methods. She maintains that DDT should be banned or reserved for emergency use.

NO: Donald R. Roberts argues that the scientific evidence regarding the environmental hazards of DDT has been seriously misrepresented by anti-pesticide activists. The hazards of malaria are much greater and, properly used, DDT can prevent them and save lives.

The story of DDT is a crucial element in the story of how science and technology interact with society. The chemical was first synthesized in 1874. Its insecticidal properties were first noticed by Paul Mueller, and it was very quickly realized that this implied the chemical could save human lives. It had long been known that in wars, more soldiers died because of disease than because of enemy fire. During World War I, some 5 million lives were lost to typhus, a disease carried by body lice. DDT was first deployed during World War II to halt a typhus epidemic in Naples, Italy. Dramatic success soon meant that DDT was used routinely as a dust for soldiers and civilians. During and after the war, it was also successfully deployed against the mosquitoes that carry malaria and other diseases. In the United States, cases of malaria fell from 120,000 in 1934 to 72 in 1960. Yellow fever cases dropped from 100,000 in 1878 to none. In 1948, Mueller received the Nobel Prize for Medicine and Physiology because DDT had saved so many civilian lives. Roger Bate, director of Africa Fighting Malaria, argues in "A Case of the DDTs," *National Review* (May 14, 2001), that DDT remains the cheapest and most effective way to combat malaria and that it should remain available for use.

DDT was by no means the first pesticide. But its predecessors were such things as arsenic, strychnine, cyanide, copper sulfate, and nicotine, all of which had such marked toxicity to humans that they gave rise to a host of murder mysteries such as the play "Arsenic and Old Lace." DDT was not only more effective as an insecticide; it was also less hazardous to users (not to mention potential murder victims). It is thus not surprising that DDT was seen as a beneficial substance, and was soon applied routinely to agricultural crops and used to control mosquito populations in American suburbs ("Rachel Carson's Silent Spring," a PBS American Experience video, includes footage of children at a picnic being engulfed in a cloud of DDT). However, insects quickly became resistant to the insecticide (in any population of insects, some will be more resistant than others; when the insecticide kills the more vulnerable members of the population, the resistant ones are left to breed and multiply; this is an example of natural selection). In *Silent Spring* (1961), Rachel Carson documented that DDT was concentrated in the food chain and affected the reproduction of predators such as hawks and eagles. In 1972, the U.S. Environmental Protection Agency banned almost all DDT uses (it could still be used to protect public health). Other developed countries soon banned it as well, but developing nations, especially in the tropics, saw it as an essential tool for fighting diseases such as malaria.

DDT is by no means the only pesticide or organic toxin with environmental effects. On May 24, 2001, the United States joined 90 other nations in signing the Stockholm Convention on Persistent Organic Pollutants (POPs). This treaty aims to eliminate from use the entire class of chemicals to which DDT belongs, beginning with the "dirty dozen," pesticides DDT, aldrin, dieldrin, endrin, chlordane, heptachlor, mirex, toxaphene, and the industrial chemicals polychlorinated biphenyls (PCBs), hexachlorobenzene (HCB), dioxins, and furans. Since then, 59 countries, not including the United States and the European Union, have formally ratified the treaty, which took effect in May 2004. Fiona Proffitt, "U.N. Convention Targets Dirty Dozen Chemicals," *Science* (May 21, 2004), notes that "About 25 countries will be allowed to continue using DDT against malaria-spreading mosquitoes until a viable alternative is found."

In the following selections, Worldwatch researcher Anne Platt McGinn grants that malaria remains a serious problem in the developing nations of the tropics, especially in Africa. DDT is still used to fight malaria in these nations, but because of resistance, it is far less effective than it used to be and environmental effects are serious concerns. She argues that alternative measures such as mosquito nets impregnated with pyrethrin insecticides are more effective and less environmentally harmful. DDT should be banned or reserved for emergency use. In the second selection, Professor Donald R. Roberts argues that the scientific evidence regarding the environmental hazards of DDT has been seriously misrepresented by anti-pesticide activists. The hazards of malaria are much greater and, properly used, DDT can prevent them and save lives. Efforts to prevent the use of DDT have produced a "global humanitarian disaster."

YES

Anne Platt McGinn

Malaria, Mosquitoes, and DDT

This year, like every other year within the past couple of decades, uncountable trillions of mosquitoes will inject malaria parasites into human blood streams billions of times. Some 300 to 500 million full-blown cases of malaria will result, and between 1 and 3 million people will die, most of them pregnant women and children. That's the official figure, anyway, but it's likely to be a substantial underestimate, since most malaria deaths are not formally registered, and many are likely to have escaped the estimators. Very roughly, the malaria death toll rivals that of AIDS, which now kills about 3 million people annually.

But unlike AIDS, malaria is a low-priority killer. Despite the deaths, and the fact that roughly 2.5 billion people (40 percent of the world's population) are at risk of contracting the disease, malaria is a relatively low public health priority on the international scene. Malaria rarely makes the news. And international funding for malaria research currently comes to a mere $150 million annually. Just by way of comparison, that's only about 5 percent of the $2.8 billion that the U.S. government alone is considering for AIDS research in fiscal year 2003.

The low priority assigned to malaria would be at least easier to understand, though no less mistaken, if the threat were static. Unfortunately it is not. It is true that the geographic range of the disease has contracted substantially since the mid-20th century, but over the past couple of decades, malaria has been gathering strength. Virtually all areas where the disease is endemic have seen drug-resistant strains of the parasites emerge—a development that is almost certainly boosting death rates. In countries as various as Armenia, Afghanistan, and Sierra Leone, the lack or deterioration of basic infrastructure has created a wealth of new breeding sites for the mosquitoes that spread the disease. The rapidly expanding slums of many tropical cities also lack such infrastructure; poor sanitation and crowding have primed these places as well for outbreaks—even though malaria has up to now been regarded as predominantly a rural disease.

What has current policy to offer in the face of these threats? The medical arsenal is limited; there are only about a dozen antimalarial drugs commonly in use, and there is significant malaria resistance to most of them. In the absence of a reliable way to kill the parasites, policy has tended to focus on killing the mosquitoes that bear them. And that has led to an abundant use

From Anne Platt McGinn, "Malaria, Mosquitoes, and DDT," *World Watch*, vol. 15, no. 3 (May/June 2002). Copyright © 2002 by The Worldwatch Institute. Reprinted by permission. http://www.worldwatch.org.

of synthetic pesticides, including one of the oldest and most dangerous: dichlorodiphenyl trichloroethane, or DDT.

DDT is no longer used or manufactured in most of the world, but because it does not break down readily, it is still one of the most commonly detected pesticides in the milk of nursing mothers. DDT is also one of the "dirty dozen" chemicals included in the 2001 Stockholm Convention on Persistent Organic Pollutants [POPs]. The signatories to the "POPs Treaty" essentially agreed to ban all uses of DDT except as a last resort against disease-bearing mosquitoes. Unfortunately, however, DDT is still a routine option in 19 countries, most of them in Africa. (Only 11 of these countries have thus far signed the treaty.) Among the signatory countries, 31—slightly fewer than one-third—have given notice that they are reserving the right to use DDT against malaria. On the face of it, such use may seem unavoidable, but there are good reasons for thinking that progress against the disease is compatible with *reductions* in DDT use.

⋅❀⋅

Malaria is caused by four protozoan parasite species in the genus *Plasmodium.* These parasites are spread exclusively by certain mosquitoes in the genus *Anopheles.* An infection begins when a parasite-laden female mosquito settles onto someone's skin and pierces a capillary to take her blood meal. The parasite, in a form called the *sporozoite,* moves with the mosquito's saliva into the human bloodstream. About 10 percent of the mosquito's lode of sporozoites is likely to be injected during a meal, leaving plenty for the next bite. Unless the victim has some immunity to malaria—normally as a result of previous exposure—most sporozoites are likely to evade the body's immune system and make their way to the liver, a process that takes less than an hour. There they invade the liver cells and multiply asexually for about two weeks. By this time, the original several dozen sporozoites have become millions of *merozoites*—the form the parasite takes when it emerges from the liver and moves back into the blood to invade the body's red blood cells. Within the red blood cells, the merozoites go through another cycle of asexual reproduction, after which the cells burst and release millions of additional merozoites, which invade yet more red blood cells. The high fever and chills associated with malaria are the result of this stage, which tends to occur in pulses. If enough red blood cells are destroyed in one of these pulses, the result is convulsions, difficulty in breathing, coma, and death.

As the parasite multiplies inside the red blood cells, it produces not just more merozoites, but also *gametocytes,* which are capable of sexual reproduction. This occurs when the parasite moves back into the mosquitoes; even as they inject sporozoites, biting mosquitoes may ingest gametocytes if they are feeding on a person who is already infected. The gametocytes reproduce in the insect's gut and the resulting eggs move into the gut cells. Eventually, more sporozoites emerge from the gut and penetrate the mosquito's salivary glands, where they await a chance to enter another human bloodstream, to begin the cycle again.

Of the roughly 380 mosquito species in the genus *Anopheles,* about 60 are able to transmit malaria to people. These malaria vectors are widespread throughout the tropics and warm temperate zones, and they are very efficient at spreading the disease. Malaria is highly contagious, as is apparent from a measurement that epidemiologists call the "basic reproduction number," or BRN. The BRN indicates, on average, how many new cases a single infected person is likely to cause. For example, among the nonvectored diseases (those in which the pathogen travels directly from person to person without an intermediary like a mosquito), measles is one of the most contagious. The BRN for measles is 12 to 14, meaning that someone with measles is likely to infect 12 to 14 other people. (Luckily, there's an inherent limit in this process: as a pathogen spreads through any particular area, it will encounter fewer and fewer susceptible people who aren't already sick, and the outbreak will eventually subside.) HIV/AIDS is on the other end of the scale: it's deadly, but it burns through a population slowly. Its BRN is just above 1, the minimum necessary for the pathogen's survival. With malaria, the BRN varies considerably, depending on such factors as which mosquito species are present in an area and what the temperatures are. (Warmer is worse, since the parasites mature more quickly.) But malaria can have a BRN in excess of 100: over an adult life that may last about a week, a single, malaria-laden mosquito could conceivably infect more than 100 people.

Seven Years, Seven Months

"Malaria" comes from the Italian "mal'aria." For centuries, European physicians had attributed the disease to "bad air." Apart from a tradition of associating bad air with swamps—a useful prejudice, given the amount of mosquito habitat in swamps—early medicine was largely ineffective against the disease. It wasn't until 1897 that the British physician Ronald Ross proved that mosquitoes carry malaria.

The practical implications of Ross's discovery did not go unnoticed. For example, the U.S. administration of Theodore Roosevelt recognized malaria and yellow fever (another mosquito-vectored disease) as perhaps the most serious obstacles to the construction of the Panama Canal. This was hardly a surprising conclusion, since the earlier and unsuccessful French attempt to build the canal—an effort that predated Ross's discovery—is thought to have lost between 10,000 and 20,000 workers to disease. So the American workers draped their water supplies and living quarters with mosquito netting, attempted to fill in or drain swamps, installed sewers, poured oil into standing water, and conducted mosquito-swatting campaigns. And it worked: the incidence of malaria declined. In 1906, 80 percent of the workers had the disease; by 1913, a year before the Canal was completed, only 7 percent did. Malaria could be suppressed, it seemed, with a great deal of mosquito netting, and by eliminating as much mosquito habitat as possible. But the labor involved in that effort could be enormous.

That is why DDT proved so appealing. In 1939, the Swiss chemist Paul Müller discovered that this chemical was a potent pesticide. DDT was first used during World War II, as a delousing agent. Later on, areas in southern Europe, North Africa, and Asia were fogged with DDT, to clear malaria-laden mosquitoes from the paths of invading Allied troops. DDT was cheap and it seemed to be harmless to anything other than insects. It was also long-lasting: most other insecticides lost their potency in a few days, but in the early years of its use, the effects of a single dose of DDT could last for up to six months. In 1948, Müller won a Nobel Prize for his work and DDT was hailed as a chemical miracle.

A decade later, DDT had inspired another kind of war—a general assault on malaria. The "Global Malaria Eradication Program," launched in 1955, became one of the first major undertakings of the newly created World Health Organization [WHO]. Some 65 nations enlisted in the cause. Funding for DDT factories was donated to poor countries and production of the insecticide climbed.

The malaria eradication strategy was not to kill every single mosquito, but to suppress their populations and shorten the lifespans of any survivors, so that the parasite would not have time to develop within them. If the mosquitoes could be kept down long enough, the parasites would eventually disappear from the human population. In any particular area, the process was expected to take three years—time enough for all infected people either to recover or die. After that, a resurgence of mosquitoes would be merely an annoyance, rather than a threat. And initially, the strategy seemed to be working. It proved especially effective on islands—relatively small areas insulated from reinfestation. Taiwan, Jamaica, and Sardinia were soon declared malaria-free and have remained so to this day. By 1961, arguably the year at which the program had peak momentum, malaria had been eliminated or dramatically reduced in 37 countries.

One year later, Rachel Carson published *Silent Spring,* her landmark study of the ecological damage caused by the widespread use of DDT and other pesticides. Like other organochlorine pesticides, DDT bioaccumulates. It's fat soluble, so when an animal ingests it—by browsing contaminated vegetation, for example—the chemical tends to concentrate in its fat, instead of being excreted. When another animal eats that animal, it is likely to absorb the prey's burden of DDT. This process leads to an increasing concentration of DDT in the higher links of the food chain. And since DDT has a high chronic toxicity—that is, long-term exposure is likely to cause various physiological abnormalities—this bioaccumulation has profound implications for both ecological and human health.

With the miseries of malaria in full view, the managers of the eradication campaign didn't worry much about the toxicity of DDT, but they were greatly concerned about another aspect of the pesticide's effects: resistance. Continual exposure to an insecticide tends to "breed" insect populations that are at least partially immune to the poison. Resistance to DDT had been reported as early as 1946. The campaign managers knew that in mosquitoes, regular exposure to DDT tended to produce widespread resistance in four to seven years. Since it took three years to clear malaria from a human population, that didn't leave a lot of leeway for the eradication effort. As it turned out, the logistics simply couldn't be made to work in large, heavily infested areas with high human populations, poor housing and roads, and generally minimal infrastructure. In 1969, the campaign was abandoned. Today, DDT resistance is widespread in *Anopheles,* as is resistance to many more recent pesticides.

Undoubtedly, the campaign saved millions of lives, and it did clear malaria from some areas. But its broadest legacy has been of much more dubious value. It engendered the idea of DDT as a first resort against mosquitoes and it established the unstable dynamic of DDT resistance in *Anopheles* populations. In mosquitoes, the genetic mechanism that confers resistance to DDT does not usually come at any great competitive "cost"—that is, when no DDT is being sprayed, the resistant mosquitoes may do just about as well as nonresistant mosquitoes. So once a population acquires resistance, the trait is not likely to disappear even if DDT isn't used for years. If DDT is reapplied to such a population, widespread resistance will reappear very rapidly. The rule of thumb among entomologists is that you may get seven years of resistance-free use the first time around, but you only get about seven months the second time. Even that limited respite, however, is enough to make the chemical an attractive option as an emergency measure—or to keep it in the arsenals of bureaucracies committed to its use.

Malaria Taxes

In December 2000, the POPs Treaty negotiators convened in Johannesburg, South Africa, even though, by an unfortunate coincidence, South Africa had suffered a potentially embarrassing setback earlier that year in its own POPs policies. In 1996, South Africa had switched its mosquito control programs from DDT to a less persistent group of pesticides known as pyrethroids. The move seemed solid and supportable at the time, since years of DDT use had greatly reduced *Anopheles* populations and largely eliminated one of the most troublesome local vectors, the appropriately named *A. funestus* ("funestus" means deadly). South Africa seemed to have beaten the DDT habit: the chemical had been used to achieve a worthwhile objective; it had then been discarded. And the plan worked—until a year before the POPs summit, when malaria infections rose to 61,000 cases, a level not seen in decades. *A. funestus* reappeared as well, in KwaZulu-Natal, and in a form resistant to pyrethroids. In early 2000, DDT was reintroduced, in an indoor spraying program. (This is now a standard way of using DDT for mosquito control; the pesticide is usually applied only to walls, where mosquitoes alight to rest.) By the middle of the year, the number of infections had dropped by half.

Initially, the spraying program was criticized, but what reasonable alternative was there? This is said to be the African predicament, and yet the South African situation is hardly representative of sub-Saharan Africa as a whole.

Malaria is considered endemic in 105 countries throughout the tropics and warm temperate zones, but by far the worst region for the disease is sub-Saharan Africa. The deadliest of the four parasite species, *Plasmodium falciparum,* is widespread throughout this region, as is one of the world's most effective malaria vectors, *Anopheles gambiae.* Nearly half the population of sub-Saharan Africa is at risk of infection, and in much of eastern and central Africa, and pockets of west Africa, it would be difficult to find anyone who has not been exposed to the parasites. Some 90 percent of the world's malaria infections and deaths occur in sub-Saharan Africa, and the disease now accounts for 30 percent of African childhood mortality. It is true that malaria is a grave problem in many parts of the world, but the African experience is misery on a very different order of magnitude. The average Tanzanian suffers more infective bites each *night* than the average Thai or Vietnamese does in a year.

As a broad social burden, malaria is thought to cost Africa between $3 billion and $12 billion annually. According to one economic analysis, if the disease had been eradicated in 1965, Africa's GDP would now be 35 percent higher than it currently is. Africa was also the gaping hole in the global eradication program: the WHO planners thought there was little they could do on the continent and limited efforts to Ethiopia, Zimbabwe, and South Africa, where eradication was thought to be feasible.

But even though the campaign largely passed Africa by, DDT has not. Many African countries have used DDT for mosquito control in indoor spraying programs, but the primary use of DDT on the continent has been as an agricultural insecticide. Consequently, in parts of west Africa especially, DDT resistance is now widespread in *A. gambiae*. But even if *A. gambiae* were not resistant, a full-bore campaign to suppress it would probably accomplish little, because this mosquito is so efficient at transmitting malaria. Unlike most *Anopheles* species, *A. gambiae* specializes in human blood, so even a small population would keep the disease in circulation. One way to get a sense for this problem is to consider the "transmission index"—the threshold number of mosquito bites necessary to perpetuate the disease. In Africa, the index overall is 1 bite per person per month. That's all that's necessary to keep malaria in circulation. In India, by comparison, the TI is 10 bites per person per month.

And yet Africa is not a lost cause—it's simply that the key to progress does not lie in the general suppression of mosquito populations. Instead of spraying, the most promising African programs rely primarily on "bednets"—mosquito netting that is treated with an insecticide, usually a pyrethroid, and that is suspended over a person's bed. Bednets can't eliminate malaria, but they can "deflect" much of the burden. Because *Anopheles* species generally feed in the evening and at night, a bednet can radically reduce the number of infective bites a person receives. Such a person would probably still be infected from time to time, but would usually be able to lead a normal life.

In effect, therefore, bednets can substantially reduce the disease. Trials in the use of bednets for children have shown a decline in malaria-induced mortality by 25 to 40 percent. Infection levels and the incidence of severe anemia also declined. In Kenya, a recent study has shown that pregnant women who use bednets tend to give birth to healthier babies. In parts of Chad, Mali, Burkina Faso, and Senegal, bednets are becoming standard household items. In the tiny west African nation of The Gambia, somewhere between 50 and 80 percent of the population has bednets.

Bednets are hardly a panacea. They have to be used properly and retreated with insecticide occasionally. And there is still the problem of insecticide resistance, although the nets themselves are hardly likely to be the main cause of it. (Pyrethroids are used extensively in agriculture as well.) Nevertheless, bednets can help transform malaria from a chronic disaster to a manageable public health problem—something a healthcare system can cope with.

So it's unfortunate that in much of central and southern Africa, the nets are a rarity. It's even more unfortunate that, in 28 African countries, they're taxed or subject to import tariffs. Most of the people in these countries would have trouble paying for a net even without the tax. This problem was addressed in the May 2000 "Abuja Declaration," a summit agreement on infectious diseases signed by 44 African countries. The Declaration included a pledge to do away with "malaria taxes." At last count, 13 countries have actually acted on the pledge, although in some cases only by reducing rather than eliminating the taxes. Since the Declaration was signed, an estimated 2 to 5 million Africans have died from malaria.

This failure to follow through with the Abuja Declaration casts the interest in DDT in a rather poor light. Of the 31 POPs treaty signatories that have reserved the right to use DDT, 21 are in Africa. Of those 21, 10 are apparently still taxing or imposing tariffs on bednets. (Among the African countries that have *not* signed the POPs treaty, some are almost certainly both using DDT and taxing bednets, but the exact number is difficult to ascertain because the status of DDT use is not always clear.) It is true that a case can be made for the use of DDT in situations like the one in South Africa in 1999—an infrequent flare-up in a context that lends itself to control. But the routine use of DDT against malaria is an exercise in toxic futility, especially when it's pursued at the expense of a superior and far more benign technology.

Learning to Live with the Mosquitoes

A group of French researchers recently announced some very encouraging results for a new anti-malarial drug known as G25. The drug was given to infected aotus monkeys, and it appears to have cleared the parasites from their systems. Although extensive testing will be necessary before it is known whether the drug can be safely given to people, these results have raised the hope of a cure for the disease.

Of course, it would be wonderful if G25, or some other new drug, lives up to that promise. But even in the absence of a cure, there are opportunities for progress that may one day make the current incidence of malaria look like some dark age horror. Many of these opportunities have been incorporated into an initiative that began in 1998, called the Roll Back Malaria (RBM) campaign, a collaborative effort between WHO, the World Bank, UNICEF, and the UNDP [United Nations Development Programme]. In contrast to the earlier WHO eradication program, RBM grew out of joint efforts between WHO and various African governments specifically to address African malaria. RBM focuses on household- and community-level intervention and it emphasizes apparently modest changes that could yield major progress. Below are four "operating principles" that are, in one way or another, implicit in RBM or likely to reinforce its progress.

1. Do away with all taxes and tariffs on bednets, on pesticides intended for treating bednets, and on antimalarial drugs. Failure to act on this front certainly undercuts claims for the necessity of DDT; it may also undercut claims for antimalaria foreign aid.

2. Emphasize appropriate technologies. Where, for example, the need for mud to replaster walls is creating lots of pothole sized cavities near houses—cavities that fill with water and then with mosquito larvae—it makes more sense to help people improve their housing maintenance than it does to set up a program for squirting pesticide into every pothole. To be "appropriate," a technology has to be both affordable and culturally acceptable. Improving home maintenance should pass this test; so should bednets. And of course there are many other possibilities. In Kenya, for example, a research institution called the International Center for Insect Physiology and Ecology has identified at least a dozen native east African plants that repel *Anopheles gambiae* in lab tests. Some of these plants could be important additions to household gardens.

3. Use existing networks whenever possible, instead of building new ones. In Tanzania, for example, an established healthcare program (UNICEF's Integrated Management of Childhood Illness Program) now dispenses antimalarial drugs—and instruction on how to use them. The UNICEF program was already operating, so it was simple and cheap to add the malaria component. Reported instances of severe malaria and anemia in infants have declined, apparently as a result. In Zambia, the government is planning to use health and prenatal clinics as the network for a coupon system that subsidizes bednets for the poor. Qualifying patients would pick up coupons at the clinics and redeem them at stores for the nets.

4. Assume that sound policy will involve action on many fronts. Malaria is not just a health problem—it's a social problem, an economic problem, an environmental problem, an agricultural problem, an urban planning problem. Health officials alone cannot possibly just make it go away. When the disease flares up, there is a strong and understandable temptation to strap on the spray equipment and douse the mosquitoes. But if this approach actually worked, we wouldn't be in this situation today. Arguably the biggest opportunity for progress against the disease lies, not in our capacity for chemical innovation, but in our capacity for *organizational innovation*—in our ability to build an awareness of the threat across a broad range of policy activities. For example, when government officials are considering loans to irrigation projects, they should be asking: has the potential for malaria been addressed? When foreign donors are designing antipoverty programs, they should be asking: do people need bednets? Routine inquiries of this sort could go a vast distance to reducing the disease.

Where is the DDT in all of this? There isn't any, and that's the point. We now have half a century of evidence that routine use of DDT simply will not prevail against the mosquitoes. Most countries have already absorbed this lesson, and banned the chemical or relegated it to emergency only status.

Now the RBM campaign and associated efforts are showing that the frequency and intensity of those emergencies can be reduced through systematic attention to the chronic aspects of the disease. There is less and less justification for DDT, and the futility of using it as a matter of routine is becoming increasingly apparent: in order to control a disease, why should we poison our soils, our waters, and ourselves?

Donald R. Roberts

Statement before the U.S. Senate Committee on Environment & Public Works, Hearing on the Role of Science in Environmental Policy-Making

Thank you, Chairman Inhofe, and distinguished members of the Committee on Environment and Public Works, for the opportunity to present my views on the misuse of science in public policy. My testimony focuses on misrepresentations of science during decades of environmental campaigning against DDT.

Before discussing how and why DDT science has been misrepresented, you first must understand why this misrepresentation has not helped, but rather harmed, millions of people every year all over the world. Specifically you need to understand why the misrepresentation of DDT science has been and continues to be deadly. By way of explanation, I will tell you something of my experience.

I conducted malaria research in the Amazon Basin in the 1970s. My Brazilian colleague—who is now the Secretary of Health for Amazonas State—and I worked out of Manaus, the capitol of Amazonas State. From Manaus we traveled two days to a study site where we had sufficient numbers of cases for epidemiological studies. There were no cases in Manaus, or anywhere near Manaus. For years before my time there and for years thereafter, there were essentially no cases of malaria in Manaus. However, in the late 1980s, environmentalists and international guidelines forced Brazilians to reduce and then stop spraying small amounts of DDT inside houses for malaria control. As a result, in 2002 and 2003 there were over 100,000 malaria cases in Manaus alone.

Brazil does not stand as the single example of this phenomenon. A similar pattern of declining use of DDT and reemerging malaria occurs in other countries as well, Peru for example. Similar resurgences of malaria have occurred in rural communities, villages, towns, cities, and countries around the world. As illustrated by the return of malaria in Russia, South Korea, urban areas of the Amazon Basin, and increasing frequencies of outbreaks in the United States, our malaria problems are growing worse. Today there are 1 to 2 million malaria deaths each year and hundreds of millions of cases. The poorest of the

U.S. Senate Committee on Environment & Public Works Hearing on the Role of Science in Environmental Policy-Making, September 28, 2005.

world's people are at greatest risk. Of these, children and pregnant women are the ones most likely to die.

We have long known about DDT's effectiveness in curbing insect-borne disease. Othmar Zeidler, a German chemistry student, first synthesized DDT in 1874. Over sixty years later in Switzerland, Paul Müller discovered the insecticidal property of DDT. Allied forces used DDT during WWII, and the new insecticide gained fame in 1943 by successfully stopping an epidemic of typhus in Naples, an unprecedented achievement. By the end of the war, British, Italian, and American scientists had also demonstrated the effectiveness of DDT in controlling malaria-carrying mosquitoes. DDT's proven efficacy against insect-borne diseases, diseases that had long reigned unchecked throughout the world, won Müller the Nobel Prize for Medicine in 1948. After WWII, the United States conducted a National Malaria Eradication Program, commencing operations on July 1, 1947. The spraying of DDT on internal walls of rural homes in malaria endemic counties was a key component of the program. By the end of 1949, the program had sprayed over 4,650,000 houses. This spraying broke the cycle of malaria transmission, and in 1949 the United States was declared free of malaria as a significant public health problem. Other countries had already adopted DDT to eradicate or control malaria, because wherever malaria control programs sprayed DDT on house walls, the malaria rates dropped precipitously. The effectiveness of DDT stimulated some countries to create, for the first time, a national malaria control program. Countries with pre-existing programs expanded them to accommodate the spraying of houses in rural areas with DDT. Those program expansions highlight what DDT offered then, and still offers now, to the malaria endemic countries. As a 1945 U.S. Public Health Service manual explained about the control of malaria: "Drainage and larviciding are the methods of choice in towns of 2,500 or more people. But malaria is a rural disease. Heretofore there has been no economically feasible method of carrying malaria control to the individual tenant farmer or sharecropper. Now, for the first time, a method is available–the application of DDT residual spray to walls and ceilings of homes." Health workers in the United States were not the only ones to recognize the particular value of DDT. The head of malaria control in Brazil characterized the changes that DDT offered in the following statement: "Until 1945–1946, preventive methods employed against malaria in Brazil, as in the rest of the world, were generally directed against the aquatic phases of the vectors (draining, larvicides, destruction of bromeliads, etc. . . . .). These methods, however, were only applied in the principal cities of each state and the only measure available for rural populations exposed to malaria was free distribution of specific drugs."

DDT was a new, effective, and exciting weapon in the battle against malaria. It was cheap, easy to apply, long-lasting once sprayed on house walls, and safe for humans. Wherever and whenever malaria control programs sprayed it on house walls, they achieved rapid and large reductions in malaria rates. Just as there was a rush to quickly make use of DDT to control disease, there was also a rush to judge how DDT actually functioned to control malaria. That rush to judgment turned out to be a disaster. At the heart of the debate–to the extent there was a debate–was a broadly accepted model that established a mathematical framework for using DDT to kill mosquitoes and eradicate malaria. Instead of studying real data to see how DDT actually worked in controlling malaria, some scientists settled upon what they thought was a logical conclusion: DDT worked solely by killing mosquitoes. This conclusion was based on their belief in the model. Scientists who showed that DDT did not function by killing mosquitoes were ignored. Broad acceptance of the mathematical model led to strong convictions about DDT's toxic actions. Since they were convinced that DDT worked only by killing mosquitoes, malaria control specialists became very alarmed when a mosquito was reported to be resistant to DDT's toxic actions. As a result of concern about DDT resistance, officials decided to make rapid use of DDT before problems of resistance could eliminate their option to use DDT to eradicate malaria. This decision led to creation of the global malaria eradication program. The active years of the global malaria eradication program were from 1959 to 1969. Before, during, and after the many years of this program, malaria workers and researchers carried out their responsibilities to conduct studies and report their research. Through those studies, they commonly found that DDT was functioning in ways other than by killing mosquitoes. In essence, they found that DDT was functioning through mechanisms of repellency and irritancy. Eventually, as people forgot early observations of DDT's repellent actions, some erroneously interpreted new findings of repellent actions as the mosquitoes' adaptation to avoid DDT toxicity, even coining a term, "behavioral resistance," to explain what they saw. This new term accommodated their view that toxicity was DDT's primary mode of action and categorized behavioral responses of mosquitoes as mere adaptations to toxic affects. However this interpretation depended upon a highly selective use of scientific data. The truth is that toxicity is not DDT's primary mode of action when sprayed on house walls. Throughout the history of DDT use in malaria control programs there has always been clear and persuasive data that DDT functioned primarily as a spatial repellent. Today we know that there is no insecticide recommended for malaria control that rivals, much less equals, DDT's spatial repellent actions, or that is as long-acting, as cheap, as easy to apply, as safe for human exposure, or as efficacious in the control of malaria as DDT. . . . The 30 years of data from control programs of the Americas plotted . . . illustrate just how effective DDT is in malaria control. The period 1960s through 1979 displays a pattern of malaria controlled through house spraying. In 1979 the World Health Organization (WHO) changed its strategy for malaria control, switching emphasis from spraying houses to case detection and treatment. In other words, the WHO changed emphasis from malaria prevention to malaria treatment. Countries complied with WHO guidelines and started to dismantle their spray programs over the next several years. . . .

I find it amazing that many who oppose the use of DDT describe its earlier use as a failure. Our own citizens who suffered under the burden of malaria, especially in the rural south, would hardly describe it thus.

Malaria was a serious problem in the United States and for some localities, such as Dunklin County, Missouri, it was a very serious problem indeed. For four counties in Missouri, the average malaria mortality from 1910 to 1914 was

168.8 per 100,000 population. For Dunklin County, it was 296.7 per 100,000, a rate almost equal to malaria deaths in Venezuela and actually greater than the mortality rate for Freetown, Sierra Leone. Other localities in other states were equally as malarious. Growing wealth and improved living conditions were gradually reducing malaria rates, but cases resurged during WWII. The advent of DDT, however, quickly eradicated malaria from the United States.

DDT routed malaria from many other countries as well. The Europeans who were freed of malaria would hardly describe its use as a failure. After DDT was introduced to malaria control in Sri Lanka (then Ceylon), the number of malaria cases fell from 2.8 million in 1946 to just 110 in 1961. Similar spectacular decreases in malaria cases and deaths were seen in all the regions that began to use DDT. The newly formed Republic of China (Taiwan) adopted DDT use in malaria control shortly after World War II. In 1945 there were over 1 million cases of malaria on the island. By 1969 there were only 9 cases and shortly thereafter the disease was eradicated from the island and remains so to this day. Some countries were less fortunate. South Korea used DDT to eradicate malaria, but without house spray programs, malaria has returned across the demilitarized zone with North Korea. As DDT was eliminated and control programs reduced, malaria has returned to other countries such as Russia and Argentina. Small outbreaks of malaria are even beginning to appear more frequently in the United States.

These observations have been offered in testimony to document first that there were fundamental misunderstandings about how DDT functioned to exert control over malaria. Second, that regardless of systematic misunderstandings on the part of those who had influence over malaria control strategies and policies, there was an enduring understanding that DDT was the most cost-effective compound yet discovered for protecting poor rural populations from insect-borne diseases like malaria, dengue, yellow fever, and leishmaniasis. I want to emphasize that misunderstanding the mode of DDT action did not lead to the wholesale abandonment of DDT. It took an entirely new dimension in the misuse of science to bring us to the current humanitarian disaster represented by DDT elimination.

The misuse of science to which I refer has found fullest expression in the collection of movements within the environmental movement that seek to stop production and use of specific man-made chemicals. Operatives within these movements employ particular strategies to achieve their objectives. By characterizing and understanding the strategies these operatives use, we can identify their impact in the scientific literature or in the popular press.

The first strategy is to develop and then distribute as widely as possible a broad list of claims of chemical harm. This is a sound strategy because individual scientists can seldom rebut the scientific foundations of multiple and diverse claims. Scientists generally develop expertise in a single, narrow field and are disinclined to engage issues beyond their area of expertise. Even if an authoritative rebuttal of one claim occurs, the other claims still progress. A broad list of claims also allows operatives to tailor platforms for constituencies, advancing one set of claims with one constituency and a different combination for another. Clever though this technique is, a list of multiple claims of harm is hardly sufficient to achieve the objective of a ban. The second strategy then is to mount an argument that the chemical is not needed and propose that alternative chemicals or methods can be used instead. The third strategy is to predict that grave harm will occur if the chemical continues to be used.

The success of Rachel Carson's *Silent Spring* serves as a model for this tricky triad. In *Silent Spring*, Rachel Carson used all three strategies on her primary target, DDT. She described a very large list of potential adverse effects of insecticides, DDT in particular. She argued that insecticides were not really needed and that the use of insecticides produces insects that are insecticide resistant, which only exacerbates the insect control problems. She predicted scary scenarios of severe harm with continued use of DDT and other insecticides. Many have written rebuttals to Rachel Carson and others who have, without scientific justification, broadcast long lists of potential harms of insecticides. . . .

[T]ime and science have discredited most of Carson's claims. Rachel Carson's descriptions of inappropriate uses of insecticides that harmed wildlife are more plausible. However, harm from an inappropriate use does not meet the requirements of anti-pesticide activists. They can hardly lobby for eliminating a chemical because someone used it wrongly. No, success requires that even the proper use of an insecticide will cause a large and systematic adverse effect. However, the proper uses of DDT yield no large and systematic adverse effects. Absent such adverse actions, the activists must then rely on claims about insidious effects, particularly insidious effects that scientists will find difficult to prove one way or the other and that activists can use to predict a future catastrophe.

Rachel Carson relied heavily on possible insidious chemical actions to alarm and frighten the public. Many of those who joined her campaign to ban DDT and other insecticides made extensive use of claims of insidious effects. These claims were amplified by the popular press and became part of the public perception about modern uses of chemicals. For example, four well-publicized claims about DDT were:

1. DDT will cause the obliteration of higher trophic levels. If not obliterated, populations will undergo reproductive failure. Authors of this claim speculated that, even if the use of DDT were stopped, systematic and ongoing obliterations would still occur.
2. DDT causes the death of algae. This report led to speculations that use of DDT could result in global depletion of oxygen.
3. DDT pushed the Bermuda petrel to the verge of extinction and that full extinction might happen by 1978.
4. DDT was a cause of premature births in California sea lions.

Science magazine, the most prestigious science journal in the United States, published these and other phantasmagorical allegations and/or predictions of DDT harm. Nonetheless, history has shown that each and every one of these claims and predictions were false.

1. The obliteration of higher trophic levels did not occur; no species became extinct; and levels of DDT in all living organisms declined

precipitously after DDT was de-listed for use in agriculture. How could the prediction have been so wrong? Perhaps it was so wrong because the paper touting this view used a predictive model based on an assumption of no DDT degradation. This was a startling assertion even at the time as *Science* and other journals had previously published papers that showed DDT was ubiquitously degraded in the environment and in living creatures. It was even more startling that *Science* published a paper that flew so comprehensively in the face of previous data and analysis.

2. DDT's action against algae reportedly occurred at concentrations of 500 parts per billion. But DDT cannot reach concentrations in water higher than about 1.2 parts per billion, the saturation point of DDT in water.

3. Data on the Bermuda petrel did not show a cause-and-effect relationship between low numbers of birds and DDT concentrations. DDT had no affect on population numbers, for populations increased before DDT was de-listed for use in agriculture and after DDT was delisted as well.

4. Data gathered in subsequent years showed that "despite relatively high concentrations [of DDT], no evidence that population growth or the health of individual California sea lions have been compromised. The population has increased throughout the century, including the period when DDT was being manufactured, used, and its wastes discharged off southern California."

If time and science have refuted all these catastrophic predictions, why do many scientists and the public not know these predictions were false? In part, we do not know the predictions were false because the refutations of such claims rarely appear in the literature.

When scientists hear the kinds of claims described above, they initiate research to confirm or refute the claims. After Charles Wurster published his claim that DDT kills algae and impacts photosynthesis, I initiated research on planktonic algae to quantify DDT's effects. From 1968–1969, I spent a year of honest and demanding research effort to discover that not enough DDT would even go into solution for a measurable adverse effect on planktonic algae. In essence, I conducted a confirmatory study that failed to confirm an expected result. I had negative data, and journals rarely accept negative data for publication. My year was practically wasted. Without a doubt, hundreds of other scientists around the world have conducted similar studies and obtained negative results, and they too were unable to publish their experimental findings. Much in the environmental science literature during the last 20–30 years indicates that an enormous research effort went into proving specific insidious effects of DDT and other insecticides. Sadly, the true magnitude of such efforts will never be known because while the positive results of research find their way into the scientific literature, the negative results rarely do. Research on insidious actions that produce negative results all too often ends up only in laboratory and field notebooks and is forgotten. For this reason, I place considerable weight on a published confirmatory study that fails to confirm an expected result.

The use of the tricky triad continues. A . . . recent paper . . . published in *The Lancet* illustrates the triad's modern application. Two scientists at the National Institute of Environmental Health Sciences, Walter Rogan and Aimin Chen, wrote this paper, entitled "Health risks and benefits of bis(4-chlorophenyl)-1,1,1-trichloroethane (DDT)." It is interesting to see how this single paper spins all three strategies that gained prominence in Rachel Carson's *Silent Spring*.

The journal *Emerging Infectious Diseases* had already published a slim version of this paper, which international colleagues and I promptly rebutted. The authors then filled in some parts, added to the claims of harm, and republished the paper in the British journal, *The Lancet*. To get the paper accepted by editors, the authors described studies that support (positive results) as well as studies that do not support (negative results) each claim. Complying with strategy number 1 of the triad, Rogan and Chen produce a long list of possible harms, including the charge that DDT causes cancer in nonhuman primates. The literature reference for Rogan and Chen's claim that DDT causes cancer in nonhuman primates was a paper by Takayama et al. Takayama and coauthors actually concluded from their research on the carcinogenic effect of DDT in nonhuman primates that "the two cases involving malignant tumors of different types are inconclusive with respect to a carcinogenic effect of DDT in nonhuman primates." Clearly, the people who made the link of DDT with cancer were not the scientists who actually conducted the research.

The authors enacted strategy number two of the triad by conducting a superficial review of the role of DDT in malaria control with the goal of discrediting DDT's value in modern malaria control programs. The authors admitted that DDT had been very effective in the past, but then argued that malaria control programs no longer needed it and should use alternative methods of control. Their use of the second strategy reveals, in my opinion, the greatest danger of granting authority to anti-pesticide activists and their writings. As *The Lancet* paper reveals, the NIEHS scientists assert great authority over the topic of DDT, yet they assume no responsibility for the harm that might result from their erroneous conclusions. After many malaria control specialists have expressed the necessity for DDT in malaria control, it is possible for Rogan and Chen to conclude that DDT is not necessary in malaria control only if they have no sense of responsibility for levels of disease and death that will occur if DDT is not used.

Rogan and Chen also employ the third strategy of environmentalism. Their list of potential harms caused by DDT includes toxic effects, neurobehavior effects, cancers, decrements in various facets of reproductive health, decrements in infant and child development, and immunology and DNA damage. After providing balanced coverage of diverse claims of harm, the authors had no option but to conclude they could not prove that DDT caused harm. However, they then promptly negated this honest conclusion by asserting that if DDT is used for malaria control, then great harm might occur. So, in an amazing turn, they conclude they cannot prove DDT causes harm, but still predict severe harm if it is used.

Rogan and Chen end their paper with a call for more research. One could conclude that the intent of the whole paper is merely to lobby for research to better define DDT harm, and what's the harm in that? Surely increasing knowledge is a fine goal. However, if you look at the specific issue of the relative need for research, you will see that the harm of this technique is great. Millions of children and pregnant women die from malaria every year, and the disease sickens hundreds of millions more. This is an indisputable fact: impoverished people engage in real life and death struggles every day with malaria. This also is a fact: not one death or illness can be attributed to an environmental exposure to DDT. Yet, a National Library of Medicine literature search on DDT reveals over 1,300 published papers from the year 2000 to the present, almost all in the environmental literature and many on potential adverse effects of DDT. A search on malaria and DDT reveals only 159 papers. DDT is a spatial repellent and hardly an insecticide at all, but a search on DDT and repellents will reveal only 7 papers. Is this not an egregiously disproportionate research emphasis on non-sources of harm compared to the enormous harm of malaria? Does not this inequity contribute to the continued suffering of those who struggle with malaria? Is it possibly even more than an inequity? Is it not an active wrong?

Public health officials and scientists should not be silent about enormous investments into the research of theoretical risks while millions die of preventable diseases. We should seriously consider our motivations in apportioning research money as we do. Consider this: the U.S. used DDT to eradicate malaria. After malaria disappeared as an endemic disease in the United States, we became richer. We built better and more enclosed houses. We screened our windows and doors. We air conditioned our homes. We also developed an immense arsenal of mosquito control tools and chemicals. Today, when we have a risk of mosquito borne disease, we can bring this arsenal to bear and quickly eliminate risks. And, as illustrated by aerial spray missions in the aftermath of hurricane Katrina, we can afford to do so. Yet, our modern and very expensive chemicals are not what protect us from introductions of the old diseases. Our arsenal responds to the threat; it does not prevent the appearance of old diseases in our midst. What protects us is our enclosed, screened, air-conditioned housing, the physical representation of our wealth. Our wealth is the factor that stops dengue at the border with Mexico, not our arsenal of new chemicals. Stopping mosquitoes from entering and biting us inside our homes is critical in the prevention of malaria and many other insect-borne diseases. This is what DDT does for poor people in poor countries. It stops large proportions of mosquitoes from entering houses. It is, in fact, a form of chemical screening, and until these people can afford physical screening or it is provided for them, this is the only kind of screening they have.

DDT is a protective tool that has been taken away from countries around the world, mostly due to governments acceding to the whims of the anti-pesticide wing of environmentalism, but it is not only the anti-pesticide wing that lobbies against DDT. The activists have a sympathetic lobbying ally in the pesticide industry. As evidence of insecticide industry working to stop countries from using DDT, I am attaching an email message dated 23rd September and authored by a Bayer official. . . . The Bayer official states

"[I speak] Not only as the responsible manager for the vector control business in Bayer, being the market leader in vector control and pointing out by that we know what we are talking about and have decades of experiences in the evolution of this very particular market. [but] Also as one of the private sector representatives in the RBM Partnership Board and being confronted with that discussion about DDT in the various WHO, RBM et al circles. So you can take it as a view from the field, from the operational commercial level—but our companies [sic] point of view. I know that all of my colleagues from other primary manufacturers and internationally operating companies are sharing my view."

The official goes on to say that

"DDT use is for us a commercial threat (which is clear, but it is not that dramatical because of limited use), it is mainly a public image threat."

However the most damning part of this message was the statement that

"we fully support EU to ban imports of agricultural products coming from countries using DDT"

[There is] . . . clear evidence of international and developed country pressures to stop poor countries from using DDT to control malaria. This message also shows the complicity of the insecticide industry in those internationally orchestrated efforts.

Pressures to eliminate spray programs, and DDT in particular, are wrong. I say this not based on some projection of what might theoretically happen in the future according to some model, or some projection of theoretical harms, I say this based firmly on what has already occurred. The track record of the anti-pesticide lobby is well documented, the pressures on developing countries to abandon their spray programs are well documented, and the struggles of developing countries to maintain their programs or restart their uses of DDT for malaria control are well documented. The tragic results of pressures against the use of DDT, in terms of increasing disease and death, are quantified and well documented. How long will scientists, public health officials, the voting public, and the politicians who lead us continue policies, regulations and funding that have led us to the current state of a global humanitarian disaster? How long will support continue for policies and programs that favor phantoms over facts?

POSTSCRIPT

Should DDT Be Banned Worldwide?

Professor Roberts is not alone in his disapproval of the efforts to halt the use of DDT. Angela Logomasini comes close to accusing environmentalists of condemning DDT more on the basis of politics or ideology than of science in "Chemical Warfare: Ideological Environmentalism's Quixotic Campaign Against Synthetic Chemicals," in Ronald Bailey, ed., *Global Warming and Other Eco-Myths: How the Environmental Movement Uses False Science to Scare Us to Death* (Prima Publishing, 2002). Her admission that public health demands have softened some environmentalists' resistance to the use of DDT points to a basic truth about environmental debates. Over and over again, they come down to what we should do first: Should we meet human needs whether or not species die and air and water are contaminated? Or should we protect species, air, water, and other aspects of the environment even if some human needs must go unmet? Even if those human needs are the lives of children? This opposition is very clear in the debate over DDT. The human needs are clear, for insect-borne diseases have killed and continue to kill a great many people. Yet the environmental needs are also clear; the title of Rachel Carson's *Silent Spring* says it all. The question is one of choosing priorities and balancing risks. See John Danley, "Balancing Risks: Mosquitoes, Malaria, Morality, and DDT" (*Business & Society Review [1974]*, Spring 2002). It is worth noting that John Beard, "DDT and Human Health," *Science of the Total Environment* (February 2006), finds the evidence for the ill effects of DDT more convincing and says that it is still too early to say it does not contribute to human disease.

Malaria can be treated with drugs, but the parasite has developed resistance to standard medications such as chloroquine. A new medication based on a Chinese plant extract (from Artemisia, or sweet wormwood or Qinghao) has shown promise but is in far too short supply; see Martin Enserink, "Source of New Hope Against Malaria in Short Supply," *Science* (January 7, 2005). Mosquitoes can be controlled in various ways: Swamps can be drained (which carries its own environmental price), and other breeding opportunities can be eliminated. Fish can be introduced to eat mosquito larvae. Bednets can keep the mosquitoes away from people. But these (and other) alternatives do not mean that there does not remain a place for chemical pesticides. In "Pesticides and Public Health: Integrated Methods of Mosquito Management," *Emerging Infectious Diseases* (January–February 2001), Robert I. Rose, an arthropod biotechnologist with the Animal and Plant Health Inspection Service of the U.S. Department of Agriculture, says, "Pesticides have a role in public health as part of sustainable integrated mosquito management. Other components of such management include surveillance, source reduction or prevention, biological control, repellents, traps, and pesticide-resistance management." "The most effective programs today rely on a range of tools," says Anne Platt McGinn in "Combating Malaria," *State of the World 2003* (W. W. Norton, 2003).

Today some countries see DDT as essential. See Tina Rosenberg, "What the World Needs Now Is DDT," *New York Times Magazine* (April 11, 2004). However, when the World Health Organization (WHO) endorsed the use of DDT to fight malaria, there was immediate outcry; see Allan Schapira, "DDT: A Polluted Debate in Malaria Control," *Lancet* (December 16, 2006).

It has proven difficult to find effective, affordable drugs against malaria; see Ann M. Thayer, "Fighting Malaria," *Chemical and Engineering News* (October 24, 2005), and Claire Panosian Dunavan, "Tackling Malaria," *Scientific American* (December 2005). A great deal of effort has gone into developing vaccines against malaria, but the parasite has demonstrated a persistent talent for evading all attempts to arm the immune system against it. See Z. H. Reed, M. Friede, and M. P. Kieny, "Malaria Vaccine Development: Progress and Challenges," *Current Molecular Medicine* (March 2006). A newer approach is to develop genetically engineered (transgenic) mosquitoes that either cannot support the malaria parasite or cannot infect humans with it; see George K. Christophides, "Transgenic Mosquitoes and Malarial Transmission," *Cellular Microbiology* (March 2005). On the other hand, Nicholas J. White, "Malaria—Time to Act," *New England Journal of Medicine* (November 9, 2006), argues that rather than wait for a perfect solution, we should recognize that present tools—including DDT—are effective enough now that there is no excuse to avoid using them.

It is worth stressing that malaria is only one of several mosquito-borne diseases that pose threats to public health. Two others are yellow fever and dengue. A new arrival in the United States is West Nile virus, which mosquitoes can transfer from birds to humans. However, West Nile virus is far less fatal than malaria, yellow fever, or dengue fever. Pesticides are already being used in the United States to kill the mosquitoes that carry West Nile virus, and health effects are being seen; see Grace Ziem, "Pesticide Spraying and Health Effects," *Environmental Health Perspectives* (March 2005). Fortunately, a vaccine is in development. See Dwight G. Smith, "A New Disease in the New World," *The World & I* (February 2002), and Michelle Mueller, "The Buzz on West Nile Virus," *Current Health 2* (April/May 2002). But "West Nile Virus Still a Threat," says *Clinical Infectious Diseases* (April 15, 2006).

It is also worth stressing that global warming (see Issue 4) means climate changes that may increase the geographic range of disease-carrying mosquitoes. Many climate researchers are concerned that malaria, yellow fever, and other now mostly tropical and subtropical diseases may return to temperate-zone nations and even spread into areas where they have never been known. See Atul A. Khasnis and Mary D. Nettleman, "Global Warming and Infectious Disease," *Archives of Medical Research* (November 2005).

ISSUE 10

Should Potential Risks Slow the Development of Nanotechnology?

YES: John Balbus et al., from "Getting Nanotechnology Right the First Time," *Issues in Science and Technology* (Summer 2005)

NO: Mike Treder, from "Molecular Nanotech: Benefits and Risks," *The Futurist* (January–February 2004)

ISSUE SUMMARY

YES: John Balbus, Richard Denison, Karen Florini, and Scott Walsh of Environmental Defense in Washington, D.C., argue that much more needs to be done to assess risks to health and the environment before nanotechnology-based products are put on the market.

NO: Mike Treder, executive director of the Center for Responsible Nanotechnology, argues that the task at hand is to realize the benefits of nanotechnology while averting the dangers but that attempts to control all risks may lead to abusive restrictions and wind up exacerbating the hazards.

$\mathbf{T}$he concept of nanotechnology dates back to 1959, when the late physicist Richard Feynman discussed in an American Physical Society talk ("There's Plenty of Room at the Bottom," *Engineering and Science* [February 1960]) the possibility of building machines the size of viruses. As described by K. Eric Drexler in his 1986 book *Engines of Creation*, such machines would be able to manipulate and position single atoms and molecules. For a time, enthusiasts talked of the devices as self-reproducing robots that needed only suitable programming to manufacture practically anything from dirt, air, and water, or to disassemble anything into its component atoms. Consumer goods—from steaks to cars—would be essentially free! Furthermore, nanomachines would repair wounds, destroy cancer, and scrub the cholesterol from our arteries. It sounded like magic, and it stirred debate over the possibility that out-of-control nanobeasts might turn everything into grey goo. Bill Joy, "Why the Future Doesn't Need Us," *Wired* (April 2000), argues that the hazards of nanotechnology, robotics, and genetic engineering are so serious that they threaten to make humans an endangered species; research into these areas should be halted immediately. However, Ken Donaldson and Vicki Stone, "Nanoscience Fact versus Fiction," *Communications of the ACM* (November 2004), say that the grey goo scenario "is a scientific fantasy, more in the tradition of *King Kong* than the realms of scientific plausibility."

Enthusiasts such as the Foresight Institute (founded by Eric Drexler) remain optimistic. The National Heart, Lung, and Blood Institute published a report in 2003 (Denis B. Buxton, et al., "Recommendations of the National Heart, Lung, and Blood Institute Nanotechnology Working Group," *Circulation*, vol. 108, pp. 2737–2742) that called the medical prospects encouraging and called for increased research effort and funding. On February 15, 2006, Mark E. Davis, professor of chemical engineering at California Institute of Technology, told the Senate Committee on Commerce, Science, and Transportation that "The benefits of treating human disease with nanoparticle therapeutics far exceed the potential safety risks." Chuck Lenatti, in "Nanotech's First Blockbusters?" *Technology Review* (March 2004), reports that the effort to learn how to make tiny things is having some practical payoffs already. No one is building tiny robots of any kind, but some companies are making tiny components (such as "nanowires") from which they hope to build marketable photovoltaic cells, LEDs, flexible circuitry, electronic devices, and so on. See, for instance, "Nanotechnology, Fuel Cells, and the Future," *Global Environmental Change Report* (June 2005).

How long will it take to go from the first primitive nanomachines able to build very simple things to the tiny robots that can make or unmake virtually anything? Most people have thought that if the step is possible at all, it will take decades. But in summer 2003, the Center for Responsible Nanotechnology concluded that instead it could be a matter of weeks, because even simple nanomanufacturing, combined with computer-aided design and manufacturing techniques, would enable extraordinarily rapid progress. This prospect, despite admittedly enticing potential benefits, alarms some people. So far, however, nanotechnology is reaching the market in the much more limited form of "nanomaterials" containing nano-sized particles whose toxicity and other potential ill effects are largely unknown. John Balbus, Richard Denison, Karen Florini, and Scott Walsh of Environmental Defense in Washington, D.C., argue that much more needs to be done to assess risks to health and the environment before nanotechnology-based products are put on the market. "With the right mix of increased risk research, improved regulatory oversight, self-initiated corporate standards, and inclusive stakeholder engagement, we have the opportunity to nanotechnology right the first time." Mike Treder, executive director of the Center for Responsible Nanotechnology, argues that the task at hand is to realize the benefits of nanotechnology while averting the dangers but that attempts to control all risks may lead to abusive restrictions and wind up exacerbating the hazards.

YES

John Balbus et al.

Getting Nanotechnology Right the First Time

Nanotechnology—the design and manipulation of materials at the molecular and atomic scale—has great potential to deliver environmental as well as other benefits. The novel properties that emerge as materials reach the nanoscale (changes in surface chemistry, reactivity, electrical conductivity, and other properties) open the door to innovations in cleaner energy production, energy efficiency, water treatment, environmental remediation, and "lightweighting" of materials, among other applications, that provide direct environmental improvements.

At the same time, these novel properties may pose new risks to workers, consumers, the public, and the environment. The few data now available give cause for concern: Some nanomaterials appear to have the potential to damage skin, brain, and lung tissue, to be mobile or persistent in the environment, or to kill microorganisms (potentially including ones that constitute the base of the food web). This trickle of data only highlights how little is known about the environmental and health effects of engineered nanomaterials. . . .

As illustrated by the problems caused by asbestos, chlorofluorocarbons, DDT, leaded gasoline, PCBs, and numerous other substances, the fact that a product is useful does not ensure that it is benign to health or the environment. And if the danger becomes known after the product is widely used, the consequences can go beyond human suffering and environmental harm to include lengthy regulatory battles, costly cleanup efforts, expensive litigation quagmires, and painful public-relations debacles. So far, rapid development and commercial introduction of nanomaterials in varied applications are outpacing efforts to understand their implications, let alone ensure their safety. Fortunately, nanotechnology development and commercialization are still at an early stage, so it is not too late to begin managing this process wisely.

Nanotechnology offers an important opportunity to apply the lessons from prior mistakes by identifying risks up front, taking the necessary steps to address them, and meaningfully engaging stakeholders to help shape this technology's trajectory. There is an opportunity to get nanotechnology right the first time.

Reason for Concern

Nanoparticles can be naturally occurring or generated as byproducts of chemical reactions such as combustion. But attention now is focusing on the large number of engineered nanomaterials—fullerenes (also known as buckyballs), carbon nanotubes, quantum dots, and nanoscale metal oxides, among others—that are beginning to reach the market in growing quantities and in a wide variety of applications.

Studies performed to date are inadequate to provide a full picture of the risks of these engineered nanomaterials and leave open even more questions about other variants and types of engineered nanomaterials. Even so, they offer reason for concern. Studies have demonstrated that some nanomaterials can be mobile or persist in the environment and can be toxic to animals as diverse as fish and rats. A recent Rice University study of buckyballs found that although individual buckyballs do not dissolve well in water, they have a tendency to form aggregates that are both very water-soluble and bacterio-cidal, a property that raises strong concerns about ecosystem impacts, because bacteria constitute the bottom of the food chain in many ecosystems. In addition, nanoparticles are deposited throughout the respiratory tract when inhaled. Some of the particles settle in the nasal passages, where they have been shown to be taken up by the olfactory nerves and carried past the blood-brain barrier directly into brain cells. Nanoparticles in the 30- to 50-nanometer range have been shown to penetrate deeply into the lungs, where they readily cross through lung tissue and enter the systemic circulation. This potential for rapid and widespread distribution within the body offers promise of a new array of diagnostic and therapeutic applications for these substances, but it also heightens the importance of having a full understanding of their toxicity.

A variety of nanomaterials have the capacity to cause tissue and cellular damage by causing oxidative stress (the same type of damage that people take antioxidant pills to protect against). Buckyballs caused oxidative damage to brain and liver cells in a study in largemouth bass; other nanoparticles have also been shown to cause oxidative stress in skin cells and in the liver. Most research has used prototypical or "plain" nanoparticles, such as uncoated buckyballs and carbon nanotubes. The few studies that have looked at the effects of variations and coatings have shown that these changes modify the toxicity of the original particle, further complicating the picture and raising the question of how these coatings may degrade over time within the body or in the environment. Oxidative stress may also be part of the mechanism behind the damage to lung tissue that has been observed in several studies of carbon nanotubes. Carbon nanotubes instilled into the lungs of rats and mice have caused unusual localized immune lesions (granulomas) within 30 days, and a separate aspiration study noted this effect as well as dose-dependent lung fibrosis throughout the lung tissue. These and other studies suggest that some nanomaterials can evade the lung's normal clearance and defense mechanisms.

Although the doses and methods of administration used in these studies may not perfectly mirror likely exposure scenarios, these studies strongly suggest the potential for some nanomaterials to pose significant risks.

Urgent Need for Action

These initial studies highlight how little is known about the health and environmental effects of engineered nanomaterials. Thousands of tons of nanomaterials are already being produced each year, and hundreds of products incorporating nanomaterials are reportedly already on the market. The global market for nanotechnology products is expected to reach at least $1 trillion over the next decade. Given the length of time it will take to develop an adequate understanding of the potential risks posed by a wide variety of nanomaterials and to apply this knowledge to inform appropriate regulation, it is imperative to take action now.

Both the public and private sector's best interests are served by an investment to identify and manage potential risks from nanomaterials now, rather than waiting until problems arise and then struggling to remediate or otherwise cope with them. History demonstrates that embracing a technology without a careful assessment and control of its risks can be extremely costly from both human and financial perspectives. The failure to sufficiently consider the adverse effects of using lead in paint, plumbing, and gasoline has resulted in widespread health problems that continue to this day and burden us with extremely high cleanup costs. Asbestos is another example where enormous sums of money are being spent by private companies for remediation, litigation, and compensation, even beyond that spent by the public sector to alleviate harm to human health and the environment. Standard & Poor's has estimated that the total cost of liability for asbestos-related losses could reach $200 billion.

The risks at issue here are not only those related to health and the environment but also risks to the very success of this promising set of technologies. If the public is not convinced that nanomaterials are being developed in a way that identifies and minimizes negative consequences to human health and the environment, a backlash could develop that delays, reduces, or even prevents the realization of many of the potential benefits of nanotechnology. As demonstrated with genetically modified organisms just a few years ago, rapid commercialization combined with a failure to address risks early on can lead to product bans and closed markets, resulting in that case in hundreds of millions of dollars in annual export losses for U.S. farmers and companies.

Timely implementation of the following four actions will allow for the most efficient and safest use of nanotechnology.

Increase risk research.   The U.S. government, as the largest single investor in nanotechnology R&D, needs to spend more to assess the health and environmental implications of nanotechnology and ensure that the critical research needed to identify potential risks is done, and done expeditiously. Of the roughly $1 billion that the federal government spends annually on nanotechnology, spending for environmental and health implications research accounted for only $8.5 million (less than 1 percent) in fiscal year (FY) 2004 and is proposed to increase to only $38.5 million (less than 4 percent) for FY 2006.

Environmental Defense has called on the U.S. government to increase federal funding for nanomaterial risk research under the National Nanotechnology

Initiative (NNI) to at least $100 million annually for the next several years. Although an annual expenditure of $100 million is a significant increase over current levels, it is still a small fraction of the overall federal budget for nano-technology development. Moreover, it is a modest investment compared to the potential benefits of risk avoidance and to the $1 trillion or more that nanotechnology is projected to provide to the world economy by 2015. Given the complexity of the task, the scope of the necessary research, and available benchmarks for comparison, $100 million per year is a reasonable lower-bound estimate of what is needed.

Broad agreement exists among stakeholders that addressing the potential risks of nanotechnology will be an unusually complex task. Nanotechnology is a potentially limitless collection of technologies and associated materials. The sheer diversity of potential materials and applications, which is a source of nanotechnology's enormous promise, also poses major challenges with respect to characterizing potential risks. Nanotechnology entails many funda-mentally different types of materials (and hundreds or thousands of potential variants of each); many novel properties that are potentially relevant to risk; many potential types of applications; and multiple sources and routes of exposure over the full life cycle of a given material or application.

Even before the research is done that will allow hazards and exposures to be evaluated in detail, a number of more fundamental needs must be addressed. At present, even a basic understanding of which specific properties determine nanomaterials' risk potential is lacking. Many of the methods, protocols, and tools needed to characterize nanomaterials or to detect and measure their pres-ence in a variety of settings, including the workplace environment, the human body, and environmental media, are still in a very early stage of development.

Nor is it clear the extent to which existing knowledge about conventional chemicals can be used to predict risks of nanomaterials. The defining charac-ter of nanotechnology—the emergence of novel properties when materials are reduced to or assembled at the nanoscale—carries with it the potential for novel risks and even novel mechanisms of toxicity that cannot be predicted from the properties and behavior of their bulk counterparts. Risk research is needed to understand nanomaterial characterization, biological and environmental fate and transport, and acute and chronic toxicity.

In each of these areas, existing testing and assessment methods and protocols need to be reexamined to determine the extent to which they can be modified to account for nanomaterials' novel characteristics or need to be supplemented with new methods. Similar challenges will arise with respect to methods and technologies for sampling, analysis and monitoring, all of which will be needed to detect nanomaterials and their transformation products in living systems and in various environmental media.

The view that significantly more money needs to be spent on nanotechnology risk research is further supported by experts' assessments, known testing costs associated with hazard characterization programs for conventional chemicals, and the research budgets for a roughly analogous risk-characterization effort, namely the Environmental Protection Agency's (EPA's) research on risks of airborne particulate matter (PM).

Experts' assessments.   Experts from a variety of fields have declared that the NNI's current funding for nanotechnology risk research needs to be significantly increased. Invited government, industry, and academic experts at a September 2004 workshop sponsored by the NNI called for at least a 10-fold increase in federal spending on nanotechnology risk-related research, relative to the approximately $10 million spent in fiscal year 2004. The United Kingdom's Royal Society and Royal Academy of Engineering called for the UK government to devote £5 million to £6 million ($9 million to $11 million) per year for 10 years just to do its part to develop the methodologies and instrumentation needed to set the stage for actual testing of nanomaterials. The chemical industry's "nanotechnology development roadmap," requested by the NNI, indicates that the assessment of hazards to human health and the environment will require a level of cumulative R&D investment that is among the highest of any assigned to the industry's priority research requirements. President Bush's science advisor John H. Marburger III noted that the current toxicity studies now under way through the NNI are "a drop in the bucket compared to what needs to be done."

Hazard endpoint testing costs.   Several estimates available from chemical hazard assessment programs can be used to provide at least a lower bound on the costs of testing a nanomaterial for hazardous properties. These costs are for the testing of a conventional chemical for an assortment of hazard endpoints of concern (toxicity plus environmental fate); notably, they do not include costs associated with assessing exposure, which is also needed to assess risk. Generating the Screening Information Data Set, a basic set of hazard information designed to screen chemicals only in order to set priorities for further scrutiny, is estimated to cost roughly $250,000 per chemical. Estimates for filling the more extensive data requirements applicable to high-volume chemicals under the European Union's proposed Registration, Evaluation, and Authorization of Chemicals program exceed $2 million per chemical. The test battery required to register a pesticide under U.S. law can reportedly cost as much as $10 million per pesticide.

EPA research budgets for risks of airborne PM.   In response to recommendations from the National Research Council, the EPA spent $40 million to $60 million annually for the first 6 years of a multiyear research program on risks posed by airborne PM. The scope of needed research on nanomaterials is considerably broader and thus likely to cost much more than for airborne PM. This is because airborne PM is a relatively well-studied mixture of chemicals to which exposure arises from a discrete (though highly diffuse) set of sources and through a single route: inhalation. In contrast, nanomaterials

- are composed of many entirely novel, often poorly characterized classes of materials
- will be applied and used in ways that will create the potential for release and exposure through many more pathways, including breathing, ingesting drinking water, and skin absorption

- may be present in wastes, water discharges, and a wide array of products
- may result in the exposure of consumers, as well as the general public and workers, through incorporation into products
- pose potential environmental as well as human health risks that need to be considered

Hence, regardless of the ultimate magnitude of risk identified, the research needed to assess the risks is likely to be considerably more involved and costly for nanomaterials than for airborne PM.

The President's Subcommittee on Nanoscale Science, Engineering and Technology already plays a role in coordinating and exchanging information on federal R&D spending for nanotechnology. That coordinating role needs to be enhanced to include the ability to shape and direct the overall federal risk research agenda across agencies to ensure that all critical needs are being addressed, as well as the responsibility and authority to ensure that individual agencies have sufficient resources to conduct the needed research in their areas. In light of the rapidity with which nanomaterials are reaching the market, this added authority is essential to ensure that the fight questions are asked and answered on a timely basis.

This is not to say that the U.S. government should be the sole, or even the principal, funder of nanomaterial risk research. Other governments are also spending heavily to promote nanotechnology R&D, and they too should allocate some portion of their spending to address nanotechnology risks. And although government risk research has a critical role to play in developing the infrastructure needed to characterize and assess the risks of nanomaterials, private industry should fund the majority of the research and testing on the products they are planning to bring to market. Clearly, all parties will benefit if governments and industry coordinate their research to avoid redundancy and optimize efficiency.

Improve regulatory policy.   Although the United States has many regulatory programs in place to address environmental and health risks, those programs are neither comprehensive in their design nor without flaws in their implementation. As a result, some substances can fall through regulatory cracks and go unregulated or underregulated, posing risks that are not discovered until adverse effects are widespread. There are signs that some nanomaterials may be poised to fall between those cracks. Consider a few examples:

- For many substances and products, there is little or no governmental review before they are marketed; regulation occurs only after a problem has arisen.
- Other programs are triggered only if a substance is considered "new." Yet at least some nanomaterial producers are apparently proceeding on the assumption that their products are not new despite their novel properties, and government agencies have not clarified the regulatory status of these materials. As a result, nanomaterials with novel properties are entering commerce without the scrutiny of potential health and environmental effects they warrant.

- Some programs for "new" substances have historically required very limited data to be submitted by producers, relying instead on extrapolation from information on existing chemicals, an approach that is highly questionable for nanomaterials, given how few hazard data now exist.
- Under many regulatory programs, coverage is triggered by mass-based thresholds or standards. Yet because of their high surface-area-to-mass ratios or other properties, nanomaterials often exhibit dramatically increased potency or other activity relative to their bulk counterparts, a distinction not reflected in existing mass-based measures.
- Some potential nanotechnology applications may fall through the cracks between the jurisdictions of multiple regulatory programs. For example, sunscreens using nanoparticles of titanium dioxide were reviewed by the Food and Drug Administration (FDA) for potential immediate health effects on consumers, but neither the FDA nor the EPA reviewed how titanium dioxide nanoparticles may affect aquatic ecosystems when these sunscreens wash off.

At this point, federal agencies need to vigorously use their existing statutory authorities to address potential nanomaterial risks as effectively as possible. Regrettably, there are few signs of action on this score. For example, the EPA has been conspicuously silent regarding the extent to which nanomaterials are "new" or "existing" chemical substances for purposes of the Toxic Substances Control Act, an important distinction because only new chemicals trigger pre-manufacture notification and review requirements. The EPA can and should clarify the principle that nanomaterials are new unless they demonstrably lack novel properties as compared to a conventional counterpart. Further, the EPA should clarify that nanomaterials do not automatically qualify for the exemptions from premanufacture notice provisions that are allowed for materials produced in low volumes or thought to result in low exposure, at least until appropriate nanomaterial-specific definitions of "low volume" and "low exposure" can be set. Likewise, before assuming that the existing exemption of polymers from the premanufacture notification program applies to nanomaterials, the EPA needs to determine whether nanomaterials meet the rationale for the exemption; namely, that the molecules are too large to be biologically available and that they degrade only into substances that have already been evaluated. The EPA should also state publicly that it is unlikely to approve the commercial manufacture of a nanomaterial in the absence of hazard and exposure data sufficient to characterize its potential risks.

As agencies apply their existing authorities (or fail to do so), the need for further steps may well become evident. A comprehensive and independent process that identifies deficiencies as well as steps to address them will be vital.

Develop corporate standards of care.   Even under the most optimistic scenario, it appears unlikely that federal agencies will put into place adequate provisions for nanomaterials quickly enough to address the materials now entering or poised to enter the market. Out of enlightened self-interest, industry must take the lead in evaluating and managing nanomaterial risks for the near term, working with other stakeholders to quickly establish and implement life cycle-based "standards of care" for nanomaterials.

These standards should include a framework and a process by which to identify and manage nanomaterials' risks across a product's full life cycle, taking into account worker safety, manufacturing releases and wastes, product use, and product disposal. Standards of care should also include and be responsive to feedback mechanisms, including environmental and health monitoring programs to check the accuracy of the assumptions about a material's risks and the effectiveness of risk management practices. Such standards should be developed and implemented in a transparent and accountable manner, including by publicly disclosing the assumptions, processes, and results of the risk identification and risk management systems.

Ideally, such standards of care would help provide a model for sensible regulatory policies as they emerge. This would assure the public that all companies, not just those who participate in voluntary programs, are taking the steps needed to safely manage nanomaterials. This would also set a level playing field for companies, so that responsible companies are not at a disadvantage relative to those that cut corners.

Engage a diverse range of stakeholders.   To date, neither government nor industry has sufficiently engaged the wide array of stakeholders—including labor groups, health organizations, consumer advocates, community groups, and environmental organizations—whose constituencies both stand to benefit from this technology and are most likely to bear any risks that arise. Government and industry need to engage these various stakeholders and consider their views in deciding how to develop and manage this promising technology in a way that maximizes its benefits and minimizes its risks.

All too often, "stakeholder involvement" translates in practice into either communicating the end result of a process to those who have been excluded (whether intentionally or by default) from participating in it, or seeking to "educate" the public in order to promote a technology and allay concerns that the technology's proponents believe to be unfounded. Engagement is not simply top-down communication. It means involving stakeholders from the outset in helping to identify expectations and concerns, and providing a role for them in helping to set priorities for research and action. And many of these stakeholders not only have a stake or interest in nanotechnology, they also have relevant perspective, experience, and expertise to offer.

Here again, there is an opportunity to get this fight the first time. The potential payoff in terms of reduced risks and increased market and public acceptance will almost certainly greatly exceed the investment necessary to draw these important voices into the discussion.

The rapid commercialization of nanotechnology, coupled with the potential risks from at least certain nanomaterials as demonstrated in initial studies, lend urgency to the need for government and industry to direct more of their investments in nanotechnology development toward identifying the potential risks and addressing them. Government and industry have done a great job so far in accentuating nanotechnology's potential up sides and in accelerating its development, but they have yet to come to terms with their equally critical roles in identifying and avoiding the down sides. A far better balance between these two roles must be struck if nanotechnology is to deliver on its promise without delivering unintended adverse consequences. With the right mix of increased risk research, improved regulatory oversight, self-initiated corporate standards, and inclusive stakeholder engagement, we have the opportunity to get nanotechnology right the first time.

Mike Treder

 **NO**

Molecular Nanotech: Benefits and Risks

The future shock of rapid change and technology run amok described by Alvin Toffler in his 1970 best seller has perhaps been less debilitating for most people than predicted, but even Toffler could not have envisioned the tidal wave of change that will hit us when *nanofactories* make the scene.

Imagine a world with billions of desktop-size, portable, nonpolluting, cheap machines that can manufacture almost anything—from clothing to furniture to electronics, and much more—in just a few hours. Today, such devices do not exist. But in the years ahead, this advanced form of nanotechnology could create the next Industrial Revolution—or the world's worst nightmare.

The technology described in this article is *molecular nanotechnology* (MNT). This is a big step beyond most of today's nanotech research, which deals with exploring and exploiting the properties of materials at the nanoscale. Industry has begun using the term *nanotechnology* to cover almost any technology significantly smaller than microtechnology, such as those involving nanoparticles or nanomaterials. This broad field will produce important and useful results, but their societal effects—both positive and negative—will be modest compared with later stages of the technology.

MNT, by contrast, is about constructing shapes, machines, and products at the atomic level—putting them together molecule by molecule. With parts only a few nanometers wide, it may become possible to build a supercomputer smaller than a grain of sand, a weapon smaller than a mosquito, or a self-contained nanofactory that sits on your kitchen counter.

"Picture an automated factory, full of conveyor belts, computers, and swinging robot arms," writes scientist and engineer K. Eric Drexler, who first brought nanotechnology to public attention with his 1986 book *Engines of Creation*. "Now imagine something like that factory, but a million times smaller and working a million times faster, with parts and workpieces of molecular size."

Unlike any machine ever built, the nanofactory will be assembled from the bottom up, constructed of specifically designed and placed molecules. Drexler says, "Nanotechnology isn't primarily about miniaturizing machines,

Originally published in the January/February 2004 issue of THE FUTURIST. Used with permission from the World Future Society, 7910 Woodmont Avenue, Suite 450, Bethesda, Maryland 20814. Telephone: 301/656-8274; Fax: 301/951-0394; http://www.wfs.org.

but about extending precise control of molecular structures to larger and larger scales. Nanotechnology is about making precise things *big*."

Virtually every previous technological improvement has been accomplished by making things smaller and more precise. But as the scales at which we work get smaller and smaller, we approach limits imposed by physics. The smallest unit of matter we can build with is the atom, or combinations of atoms known as molecules. The earthshaking insight of molecular nanotechnology is that, when we reach this scale, we can reverse direction and begin building *up*, making products by placing individual atoms and molecules exactly where we want them.

Ever since Richard Feynman enunciated MNT's basic concepts in 1959, and especially since Drexler began detailing its amazing possibilities in the 1980s, proposals for building products in various ways have been put forth. Some of these have been fanciful and many have been impractical. At this point, it appears that the idea of a nanofactory is the safest and most useful method of building general-purpose products by molecular manufacturing.

Inside a Nanofactory

The inner architecture of a nanofactory will be a stunning achievement, outside the realm of anything previously accomplished. Nanofactories will make use of a vast number of moving parts, each designed and precisely constructed to do a specific job. Some of these parts will be visible to the human eye. Most will be microscopic or even nanoscale, smaller than a human cell. An important feature of a nanofactory is that all of its parts will be fixed in place. This is significant because it greatly simplifies development of the device. Engineers won't have to figure out how to tell each little nanobot in a swarm where to go and how to get there, and none of the parts can get lost or go wild.

Perhaps the easiest way to envision the inner workings of a nanofactory is to picture a large city, with all the streets laid out on a grid. Imagine that in this city everyone works together to build gigantic products—ocean liners, for instance. To build something that big, you have to start with small parts and put them together. In this imaginary city, all the workers stand along the streets and pass the parts along to each other. The smallest parts are assembled on the narrowest side streets, and then handed up to the end of the block. Other small parts from other side streets are joined together to make medium-sized parts, which are joined together to make large parts. At the end, the largest parts converge in one place, where they are joined together to make the finished product. A nanofactory performs in this way, with multiple assembly lines operating simultaneously and steadily feeding into each other.

The first and hardest step in building a nanofactory is building an *assembler*, a tiny device that can combine individual molecules into useful shapes. An early plan for molecular manufacturing imagined lots of free-floating assemblers working together to build a single massive product, molecule by molecule. A more efficient approach is to fasten down the assemblers in orderly arrays of chemical fabricators, instruct each fabricator to create a tiny piece of the product, and then fasten the pieces together, passing them along to the next level within the nanofactory.

A human-scale nanofactory will consist of trillions of fabricators, and it could only be built by another nanofactory. But at the beginning, an assembler could build a very small nanofactory, with just a few fabricators. A smaller nanofactory could build a bigger one, and so on. According to the best estimates we have today, a fabricator could make its own mass in just a few hours. So a small nanofactory could make another one twice as big in just a few days—maybe less than a day. Do that about 60 times, and you have a tabletop model.

By the time the first working assembler is ready, the blueprint for a basic nanofactory may already be prepared. But until we have an assembler, we can't make a nanofactory.

Building an assembler is one of the ambitious research projects of Zyvex, a Texas firm that bills itself as "the first molecular nanotechnology company." Zyvex has gathered many leading minds in physics, chemistry, mechanical engineering, and computer programming to focus on the long-range goal of molecular assembler manufacturing technology. Along the way, the company has developed some of the world's most precise tools for manipulating and testing materials and structures at the nanoscale. Numerous other projects at research universities and in corporations around the world are contributing valuable knowledge to the field.

How far are we from having a working assembler? A 1999 media report on nanotech said, "Estimates vary. From five to 10 years, according to Zyvex, or from eight to 15 years, according to the research community."

And how long will it take from building a single assembler to having a fully functional nanofactory? The report continues, "After that, it could be decades before we'll be able to manufacture finished consumer goods." This reflects the common wisdom, but it's wrong. Very wrong.

The Center for Responsible Nanotechnology (CRN), a non-profit think tank co-founded by this author, published a detailed study in summer 2003 of the work required to progress from a single assembler to a full-fledged nanofactory that can create a wide variety of low-cost products. The startling conclusion of this report is that the span of time could be measured in weeks—probably less than two months. And what will the first nanofactory build? Another one, and another one.

Each nanofactory will be able to duplicate itself in as little as a few hours, or perhaps a half a week at most. Even using the most conservative estimate, in a couple of months you could have a million nanofactories, and a few months after that, a billion. Less than a year after the first basic assembler is completed, every household in the world conceivably could have its own nanofactory.

Creativity Unleashed

Before a tidal wave strikes, another dramatic event—usually an earthquake or major landslide—must occur to trigger it. The first generation of products to come out of nanofactories—inexpensive but high quality clothing, furniture, electronics, household appliances, bicycles, tools, building supplies, and more—may be like that: a powerful landslide of change, but only a portent of the gigantic wave that is to follow.

Most of these early products will probably be similar to what are current at the time nanofactories begin production. Because they are built by MNT, with every atom precisely placed, they will be better in every way—stronger, lighter, cheaper—but they still will be built on existing models.

The world-changing shock wave will hit when we realize that we no longer need be restricted to existing models—not when a supercomputer smaller than a grain of sand can be integrated into any product, and not when people everywhere—young, old, male, female, technical, nontechnical, practical, artistic, and whimsical—will have the opportunity to be designers.

MNT product design will be eased by CAD (computer-aided design) programs so simple that a child can do it—and that's no exaggeration. New product prototypes can be created, tested, and refined in a matter of hours instead of months and without the expense of traditional production facilities. No special expertise is needed beyond the skill for using CAD programs—only imagination, curiosity, and the desire to create.

Within months, conceivably, even the most up-to-date appliances, machines, communication media, and other electronics will be outmoded. Imagine embedding "smart" gadgetry into everything you own or might want to have. Demand for these new products will be intense. The cost of manufacturing them may be almost negligible.

To maximize the latent innovation potential in nanofactory proliferation, and to help prevent illicit, unwise, or malicious product design and manufacture, CRN recommends that designers work (and play) with modular *nanoblocks* of various compositions and purposes to create a wide variety of products, from consumer goods and educational tools to building supplies and even new modes of transportation. When combined with automated verification of design safety and protection of intellectual property, this should open up huge new areas for originality and improvement while maintaining safety and commercial viability.

Working with nanoblocks, designers can create to their hearts' content. The combination of user-friendly CAD and rapid prototyping will result in a spectacular synergy, enabling unprecedented levels of innovation and development. Among the many remarkable benefits accruing to humanity from nanofactory proliferation will be this unleashing of millions of eager new minds, allowed for the first time to freely explore and express their brilliant creative energy.

It becomes impossible to predict what might be devised then. The smart components and easy design systems of the nanotech revolution will rewrite the rules.

Benefits and Dangers

This all adds up to change that is sudden and shocking and could be extremely disruptive.

On the plus side, MNT could solve many of the world's problems. Simple products like plumbing, water filters, and mosquito nets—made cheaply on the spot—would greatly reduce the spread of infectious diseases. The efficient, cheap construction of strong and lightweight structures, electrical equipment, and power storage devices will allow the use of solar thermal power as a primary and abundant energy source.

Many areas of the world could not support a twentieth-century manufacturing infrastructure, with its attendant costs, difficulties, and environmental impacts, but MNT should be self-contained and clean. A single packing crate or suitcase could contain all the equipment required for a village-scale industrial revolution.

Computers and display devices will become stunningly inexpensive and could be made widely available. Much social unrest can be traced directly to material poverty, ill health, and ignorance. Nanofactories could greatly reduce these problems.

On the other hand, all this sudden change—the equivalent of a century's development packed into a few years—has the potential to disrupt many aspects of society and politics.

When a consumer purchases a manufactured product today, he is paying for its design, raw materials, the labor and capital of manufacturing, transportation, storage, marketing, and sales. Additional money—usually a fairly low percentage—goes to the owners of each of these businesses, and eventually to the employed workers. If nanofactories can produce a wide variety of products when and where they are wanted, most of this additional effort will become superfluous. This raises many questions about the nature of a post-MNT economy: Who will own the technology for molecular manufacturing? Will it be heavily restricted, or widely available? Will products become cheaper? Will major corporations disappear? Will new monopolies arise? Will most people retire—or be unemployed? What will it do to the gap between rich and poor?

It seems clear that molecular manufacturing could severely disrupt the present economic structure, greatly reducing the value of many material and human resources, including much of our current infrastructure. Despite utopian postcapitalist hopes, it is unclear whether a workable replacement system could appear in time to prevent the human consequences of massive job displacement.

MNT manufacturing will allow the cheap creation of incredibly powerful devices and products. Stronger materials will allow the creation of much larger machines, capable of excavating or otherwise destroying large areas of the planet at a greatly accelerated pace. It is too early to tell whether there will be economic incentive to do this. However, given the large number of activities and purposes that would damage the environment if taken to extremes, and the ease of taking them to extremes with molecular manufacturing, it seems likely that this problem is worth worrying about.

Some forms of damage can result from an aggregate of individual actions, each almost harmless by itself. For example, the extreme compactness of nanomanufactured machinery may lead to the use of very small products, which can easily turn into nanolitter that will be hard to clean up and may cause health problems. Collection of solar energy on a sufficiently large scale—by corporations, municipalities, and individuals—could modify the planet's albedo and directly affect the environment. In addition, if we are not careful, the flexibility and compactness of molecular manufacturing may allow the creation of free-floating, foraging self-replicators—a "gray goo" that could do serious damage to the biosphere by replicating out of control.

Molecular manufacturing raises the possibility of horrifically effective weapons. As an example, the smallest insect is about 200 microns; this creates a plausible size estimate for a nanotech-built antipersonnel weapon capable of seeking and injecting toxin into unprotected humans. The human lethal dose of botulism toxin is about 100 nanograms, or about 1/100 the volume of the weapon. As many as 50 billion toxin-carrying devices—theoretically enough to kill every human on earth—could be packed into a single suitcase. Guns of all sizes would be far more powerful, and their bullets could be self-guided. Aerospace hardware would be far lighter and offer higher performance; built with minimal or no metal, such craft would be much harder to spot on radar.

The awesome power of MNT may cause two or more competing nations to enter into an unstable arms race. Increased uncertainty of the capabilities of an adversary, less time to respond to an attack, and better targeted destruction of the enemy's resources during an attack all make nanotech arms races less stable than a nuclear arms race. Also, unless nanotech is tightly controlled on an international level, the number of nanotech nations in the world could be much higher than the number of nuclear nations, increasing the chance of a regional conflict expanding globally.

Criminals and terrorists with stronger, more powerful, and more compact devices could do serious damage to society. Chemical and biological weapons could become much deadlier and easier to conceal. Many other types of terrifying devices are possible, including several varieties of remote assassination weapons that would be difficult to detect or avoid. If such devices were available from a black market or a home factory, it would be nearly impossible to detect them before they were used; a random search capable of spotting them would be a clear violation of current human rights standards in most civilized countries.

Surveillance devices could be made microscopically small, low-priced, and very numerous—leading to questions of pervasive invasions of privacy, from illicit selling of sexual or other images to ubiquitous covert government or industrial spying. Attempts to control all these risks may lead to abusive restrictions, or create a black market that would be very risky and almost impossible to stop, because small nanofactories will be very easy to smuggle and fully dangerous.

Searching for Solutions

If you knew that in one year's time you would be forced to walk a tightrope without a net hundreds of feet above a rocky canyon, how soon would you begin practicing? The analogy applies to nanofactory technology. Because we know it is possible—maybe even probable—that everything we've reviewed here could happen within a decade, how soon should we start to prepare?

A report issued by the University of Toronto Joint Centre for Bioethics in February 2003 calls for serious consideration of the ethical, environmental, economic, legal, and social implications of nanotechnology. Report co-author Peter Singer says, "Open public discussion of the benefits and risks of this new technology is urgently needed."

There's no doubt that such discussion is warranted and urgent. But beyond talking about ethics, immediate research into the need, design, and building of an effective global administration structure is crucial. Unwise regulation is a serious hazard. Simple solutions won't work.

"A patchwork of extremist solutions to the wide-ranging risks of advanced nanotechnology is a grave danger," says Chris Phoenix, research director for the Center for Responsible Nanotechnology. "All areas of society stand to be affected by molecular manufacturing, and unless comprehensive international plans are developed, the multiplicity of cures could be worse than the disease. The threat of harm would almost certainly be increased, while many extraordinary benefits could go unrealized."

We have much to gain, and much to lose. The advantages promised by MNT are real, and they could be ours soon. Living conditions worldwide could be dramatically improved, and human suffering greatly diminished. But everything comes at a cost. The price for safe introduction of the miracles of nanofactory technology is thorough, conscientious preparation.

Several organizations are stepping up to this challenge. For example:

- The Foresight Institute has drafted a set of molecular nanotechnology guidelines for researchers and developers. These are mostly aimed at restricting the development of MNT to responsible parties and preventing the production of free-ranging self-replicating nanobots.
- The Millennium Project of the American Council for the United Nations University is exploring various scenarios for safe and socially conscious implementation of molecular manufacturing and other emerging technologies. These scenarios depict the world in 2050, based on various policy choices we might make between now and then.
- The Center for Responsible Nanotechnology is studying all the issues involved—political, economic, military, humanitarian, technological, and environmental—and developing well-grounded, complete, and workable proposals for effective administration and safe use of advanced nanotechnology. Current results of CRN's research lead to the conclusion that establishing a single international program to develop molecular manufacturing technology may be the safest course. The leading nations of the world would have to agree to join— or at least not to oppose—this effort, and a mechanism to detect and deter competing programs would have to be devised.

It will take all this and more. The brightest minds and clearest thinkers, the most energetic activists and committed organizers, the smartest scientists, most dedicated ethicists, and most creative social planners desperately will be needed.

Will it be easy to realize the benefits of nanofactory technology while averting the dangers? Of course it will not. Is it even possible? It had better be. Our future is very uncertain, and it's very near. Much nearer than we might have thought. Let's get started.

POSTSCRIPT

Should Potential Risks Slow the Development of Nanotechnology?

Nanotechnology sounds like the most wild-eyed of science-fiction dreams, and it has become a frequent guest-star in modern science fiction novels. But it seems reasonable to say that nanotechnology will not remain science fiction for very long. Nanotechnologists are not yet close to building the first nanofactories, but nanotechnology is gaining significant attention from government, industry, and investors. Its momentum is growing, as suggested by two recent book titles: Douglas Mulhall's *Our Molecular Future: How Nanotechnology, Robotics, Genetics and Artificial Intelligence Will Transform Our World* (Prometheus, 2002) and Mark A. Ratner's and Daniel Ratner's *Nanotechnology: A Gentle Introduction to the Next Big Idea* (Prentice Hall, 2002). The promise of the technology is so great that some are calling for increased government support. See Neal Lane and Thomas Kalil, "The National Nanotechnology Initiative: Present at the Creation," *Issues in Science and Technology* (Summer 2005), and George Allen, "The Economic Promise of Nanotechnology," *Issues in Science and Technology* (Summer 2005).

In December 2004, the European Commission published "Towards a European Strategy for Nanotechnology" (http://europa.eu.int/comm/research/industrial_technologies/pdf/nanotechnology_communication_en.pdf), which called for a number of steps designed both to stimulate the development of nanotechnology in Europe and to "integrate societal considerations into the R&D process at an early stage; address any potential public health, safety, environmental and consumer risks upfront by generating the data needed for risk assessment, integrating risk assessment into every step of the life cycle of nanotechnology-based products, and adapting existing methodologies and, as necessary, developing novel ones; [and] complement the above actions with appropriate cooperation and initiatives at international level."

In July 2004, the Royal Society and Royal Academy of Engineering published "Nanoscience and Nanotechnologies: Opportunities and Uncertainties," recommending tighter UK and European regulations and public dialog. In February 2005, the UK government published a lengthy response to the report (http://www.ost.gov.uk/policy/issues/nanotech_final.pdf) that agreed on the need for research and regulation but failed to promise additional money.

Anthony Seaton and Kenneth Donaldson, in "Nanoscience, Nanotoxicology, and the Need to Think Small," *Lancet* (March 12, 2005), comment on the potential health risks of nanomaterials. Rory O'Neill, "Dangers Come in Small Particles," *Hazards* (July–September 2004), warns that the industry holds the potential for "tomorrow's occupational health calamity." So far, the hazards of nanotechnology are largely speculative; see Gloria Gonzalez, "Nanotechnology

215

Risks Still Largely a Mystery," *Business Insurance* (November 13, 2006). Philip E. Ross, "Tiny Toxins?" *Technology Review* (May/June 2006), notes that the number of commercial products containing nanomaterials is growing rapidly, and some research is already finding worrisome signs of toxicity. There is growing awareness of the need for risk assessment (see Aimee Cunningham, "Particular Problems," *Science News* [May 6, 2006]) and considerable debate over how to set priorities and fund the necessary research (see Robert F. Service, "Priorities Needed for Nano-Risk Research and Development," *Science* [October 6, 2006]). In February 2007, the United Nations Environment Programme released its *Global Environment Outlook Year Book 2007* (http://www.unep.org/geo/yearbook/yb2007/), which called nanotechnology an "emerging challenge" and noted that it holds great promise but "more research is needed to identify environmental, health and socio-economic hazards."

People such as Bill Joy are sounding strong cautionary notes, but others, such as John Seely Brown and Paul Duguid, "A Response to Bill Joy and the Doom-and-Gloom Technofuturists," *The Industry Standard* (April 13, 2000), are more optimistic. Joy, say Brown and Duguid, far too blithely assumes that very large obstacles in the development of nanotechnology will be overcome in short order. He focuses on hype and oversimplifications (and indeed, the "grey goo" problem is no longer taken seriously at all). He also ignores the role of society, which has shown itself quite capable of controlling the development of technologies in the past. On the other hand, society may not have adequate information in time to make an informed decision on whether to let nanotechnology proceed, perhaps especially considering the speed with which nanotechnology is likely to develop after the first simple assemblers are built. Fariborz Ghadar and Heather Spindler, in "Nanotechnology: Small Revolution," *Industrial Management* (May/June 2005), note that "While scientists and the federal government recognize the potential benefits of nanotechnology and it will not be possible to say that all nanotech applications are safe or are dangerous, it will be important to listen and address public concerns. And although much more data will be available in 10 years that will facilitate the decision, society will be forced to make a decision before then in the absence of complete data. And the adoption of nanotechnologies will be a very diverse and complex problem."

ISSUE 11

Are Genetically Modified Foods Safe to Eat?

YES: **Henry I. Miller and Gregory Conko,** from "Scary Food," *Policy Review* (June/July 2006)

NO: **Jeffrey M. Smith,** from "Frankenstein Peas," *The Ecologist* (April 2006)

ISSUE SUMMARY

YES: Henry I. Miller and Gregory Conko of the Hoover Institution argue that genetically modified (GM) crops are safer for the consumer and better for the environment than non-GM crops.

NO: Jeffrey M. Smith argues that there are so many ways in which genetic modification may lead to health risks that it is impossible to claim "that GM crops are adequately tested, well-regulated, and safe."

In the early 1970s scientists first discovered that it was technically possible to move genes—biological material that determines a living organism's physical makeup—from one organism to another and thus (in principle) to give bacteria, plants, and animals new features and to correct genetic defects of the sort that cause many diseases, such as cystic fibrosis. Most researchers in molecular genetics were excited by the potentialities that suddenly seemed within their grasp. However, a few researchers—as well as many people outside the field—were disturbed by the idea; they thought that genetic mix-and-match games might spawn new diseases, weeds, and pests. Some people even argued that genetic engineering should be banned at the outset, before unforeseeable horrors were unleashed.

Researchers in support of genetic experimentation responded by declaring a moratorium on their own work until suitable safeguards could be devised. Once those safeguards were in place in the form of government regulations, work resumed. James D. Watson and John Tooze document the early years of this research in *The DNA Story: A Documentary History of Gene Cloning* (W. H. Freeman, 1981). For a shorter, more recent review of the story, see Bernard D. Davis, "Genetic Engineering: The Making of Monsters?" *The Public Interest* (Winter 1993).

By 1989 the technology had developed tremendously: researchers could obtain patents for mice with artificially added genes ("transgenic" mice); fire-fly genes had been added to tobacco plants to make them glow (faintly) in the dark; and growth hormone produced by genetically engineered bacteria was being used to grow low-fat pork and increase milk production by cows. Critics argued that genetic engineering was unnatural and violated the rights of both plants and animals to their "species integrity"; that expensive, high-tech, tinkered animals gave the competitive advantage to big agricultural corporations and drove small farmers out of business; and that putting human genes into animals, plants, or bacteria was downright offensive. See Betsy Hanson and Dorothy Nelkin, "Public Responses to Genetic Engineering," *Society* (November/December 1989).

Thoughts of tinkering with humans themselves have prompted such comments as the following from Richard Hayes, "In the Pipeline: Genetically Modified Humans?" *Multinational Monitor* (January/February 2000): "No one can be sure how the technology will evolve, but a techno-eugenic future appears ever more likely unless an organized citizenry demands such visions be consigned to science fiction dystopias."

Skepticism about the benefits remains, but agricultural genetic engineering has proceeded at a breakneck pace largely because, as Robert Shapiro, CEO of Monsanto Corporation, said in June 1998, it "represents a potentially sustainable solution to the issue of feeding people." Between 1996 and 1998 the area planted with genetically engineered crops jumped from 1.7 million hectares to 27.8 million hectares. Also, sales of genetically engineered crop products are expected to reach $25 billion by 2010. See Brian Halweil, "The Emperor's New Crops," *WorldWatch* (July/August 1999).

Many people are not reassured by such data. They see potential problems in nutrition, toxicity, allergies, and ecology. In protest, some people even destroy research labs and test plots of trees, strawberries, and corn. Other people lobby for stringent regulations and even outright bans on the basis of their fears, while others insist that regulation should be based on sound science. See Karen A. Goldman, "Bioengineered Food—Safety and Labeling," *Science* (October 20, 2000) and Henry I. Miller and Gregory Conko. See Martin Teitel and Kimberly A. Wilson, *Genetically Engineered Food: Changing the Nature of Nature* (Park Street Press, 2001), and Henry I. Miller and Gregory Conko, "Agricultural Biotechnology: Overregulated and Underappreciated," *Issues in Science and Technology* (Winter 2005).

In the following selections, Henry I. Miller and Gregory Conko of the Hoover Institution argue that genetically modified (GM) crops are safer for the consumer and better for the environment than non-GM crops. People have failed to embrace them because news coverage has been dominated by the out-landish claims and speculations of anti-technology activists. Jeffrey M. Smith argues that there are so many ways in which genetic modification may lead to health risks that it is impossible to claim "that GM crops are adequately tested, well-regulated, and safe." "Governments must immediately ban GM crops and start funding rigorous, thorough and independent safety assessments."

**Henry I. Miller and
Gregory Conko**

Scary Food

Like a scene from some Hollywood thriller, a team of U.S. Marshals stormed a warehouse in Irvington, New Jersey, last summer to intercept a shipment of evildoers from Pakistan. The reason you probably haven't heard about the raid is that the objective was not to seize Al Qaeda operatives or white slavers, but $80,000 worth of basmati rice contaminated with weevils, beetles, and insect larvae, making it unfit for human consumption. In regulation-speak, the food was "adulterated," because "it consists in whole or in part of any filthy, putrid, or decomposed substance, or if it is otherwise unfit for food."

Americans take food safety very seriously. Still, many consumers tend to ignore Mother Nature's contaminants while they worry unduly about high technology, such as the advanced technologies that farmers, plant breeders, and food processors use to make our food supply the most affordable, nutritious, varied, and safe in history.

For example, recombinant DNA technology—also known as food biotechnology, gene-splicing, or genetic modification (GM)—is often singled out by critics as posing a risk that new allergens, toxins, or other nasty substances will be introduced into the food supply. And, because of the mainstream media's "if it bleeds, it leads" approach, news coverage of food biotech is dominated by the outlandish claims and speculations of anti-technology activists. This has caused some food companies—including fastfood giant McDonald's and baby-food manufacturers Gerber and Heinz—to forgo superior (and even cost-saving) gene-spliced ingredients in favor of ones the public will find less threatening.

Scientists agree, however, that gene-spliced crops and foods are not only better for the natural environment than conventionally produced food crops, but also safer for consumers. Several varieties now on the market have been modified to resist insect predation and plant diseases, which makes the harvested crop much cleaner and safer. Ironically (and also surprisingly in these litigious times), in their eagerness to avoid biotechnology, some major food companies may knowingly be making their products less safe and wholesome for consumers. This places them in richly deserved legal jeopardy.

Don't Trust Mother Nature

Every year, scores of packaged food products are recalled from the American market due to the presence of all-natural contaminants like insect parts, toxic molds, bacteria, and viruses. Because farming takes place out-of-doors and in dirt, such contamination is a fact of life. Fortunately, modern technology has enabled farmers and food processors to minimize the threat from these contaminants.

The historical record of mass food poisoning in Europe offers a cautionary tale. From the ninth to the nineteenth centuries, Europe suffered a succession of epidemics caused by the contamination of rye with ergot, a poisonous fungus. Ergot contains the potent toxin ergotamine, the consumption of which induces hallucinations, bizarre behavior, and violent muscle twitching. These symptoms gave rise at various times to the belief that victims were possessed by evil spirits. Witch-hunting and persecution were commonplace—and the New World was not immune. One leading explanation for the notorious 1691–92 Salem witch trials also relates to ergot contamination. Three young girls suffered violent convulsions, incomprehensible speech, trance-like states, odd skin sensations, and delirious visions in which they supposedly saw the mark of the devil on certain women in the village. The girls lived in a swampy meadow area around Salem; rye was a major staple of their diet; and records indicate that the rye harvest at the time was complicated by rainy and humid conditions, exactly the situation in which ergot would thrive.

Worried villagers feared the girls were under a spell cast by demons, and the girls eventually named three women as witches. The subsequent panic led to the execution of as many as 20 innocent people. Until a University of California graduate student discovered this link, a reasonable explanation had defied historians. But the girls' symptoms are typical of ergot poisoning, and when the supply of infected grain ran out, the delusions and persecution likewise disappeared.

In the twenty-first century, modern technology, aggressive regulations, and a vigorous legal liability system in industrialized countries such as the United States are able to mitigate much of this sort of contamination. Occasionally, though, Americans will succumb to tainted food picked from the woods or a backyard garden. However, elsewhere in the world, particularly in less-developed countries, people are poisoned every day by fungal toxins that contaminate grain. The result is birth defects, cancer, organ failure, and premature death.

About a decade ago, Hispanic women in the Rio Grande Valley of Texas were found to be giving birth to an unusually large number of babies with crippling and lethal neural tube defects (NTDS) such as spina bifida, hydrocephalus, and anencephaly—at a rate approximately six times higher than the national average for non-Hispanic women. The cause remained a mystery until recent research revealed a link between NTDS and consumption of large amounts of unprocessed corn like that found in tortillas and other staples of the Latino diet.

The connection is obscure but fascinating. The culprit is fumonisin, a deadly mycotoxin, or fungal toxin, produced by the mold *Fusarium* and sometimes found in unprocessed corn. When insects attack corn, they open wounds in the plant that provide a perfect breeding ground for *Fusarium*. Once molds get a foothold, poor storage conditions also promote their postharvest growth on grain.

Fumonisin and some other mycotoxins are highly toxic, causing fatal diseases in livestock that eat infected corn and esophageal cancer in humans. Fumonisin also interferes with the cellular uptake of folic acid, a vitamin that is known to reduce the risk of NTDS in developing fetuses. Because fumonisin prevents the folic acid from being absorbed by cells, the toxin can, in effect, induce functional folic acid deficiency—and thereby cause NTDS—even when the diet contains what otherwise would be sufficient amounts of folic acid.

The epidemiological evidence was compelling. At the time that the babies of Hispanic women in the Rio Grande Valley experienced the high rate of neural tube defects, the fumonisin level in corn in that locale was two to three times higher than normal, and the affected women reported much higher dietary consumption of homemade tortillas than in women who were unaffected.

Acutely aware of the danger of mycotoxins, regulatory agencies such as the U.S. Food and Drug Administration and Britain's Food Safety Agency have established recommended maximum fumonisin levels in food and feed products made from corn. Although highly processed cornstarch and corn oil are unlikely to be contaminated with fumonisin, unprocessed corn or lightly processed corn (e.g., cornmeal) can have fumonisin levels that exceed recommended levels.

In 2003, the Food Safety Agency tested six organic cornmeal products and twenty conventional cornmeal products for fumonisin contamination. All six organic cornmeals had elevated levels—from nine to 40 times greater than the recommended levels for human health—and they were voluntarily withdrawn from grocery stores.

A Technical Fix

The conventional way to combat mycotoxins is simply to test unprocessed and processed grains and throw out those found to be contaminated—an approach that is both wasteful and dubious. But modern technology—specifically in the form of gene-splicing—is already attacking the fungal problem at its source. An excellent example is "Bt corn," crafted by splicing into commercial corn varieties a gene from the bacterium *Bacillus thuringiensis*. The "Bt" gene expresses a protein that is toxic to corn-boring insects but is perfectly harmless to birds, fish, and mammals, including humans.

As the Bt corn fends off insect pests, it also reduces the levels of the mold *Fusarium*, thereby reducing the levels of fumonisin. Thus, switching to the gene-spliced, insect-resistant corn for food processing lowers the levels of fumonisin—as well as the concentration of insect parts—likely to be found in the final product. Researchers at Iowa State University and the U.S. Department of Agriculture found that Bt corn reduces the level of fumonisin by as much as 80 percent compared to conventional corn.

Thus, on the basis of both theory and empirical knowledge, there should be potent incentives—legal, commercial, and ethical—to use such gene-spliced grains more widely. One would expect public and private sector advocates of public health to demand that such improved varieties be cultivated and used for food—not unlike requirements for drinking water to be chlorinated and fluoridated. Food producers who wish to offer the safest and best products to their customers—to say nothing of being offered the opportunity to advertise "New and Improved!"—should be competing to get gene-spliced products into the marketplace.

Alas, none of this has come to pass. Activists have mounted intractable opposition to food biotechnology in spite of demonstrated, significant benefits, including reduced use of chemical pesticides, less runoff of chemicals into waterways, greater use of farming practices that prevent soil erosion, higher profits for farmers, and less fungal contamination. Inexplicably, government oversight has also been an obstacle, by subjecting the testing and commercialization of gene-spliced crops to unscientific and draconian regulations that have vastly increased testing and development costs and limited the use and diffusion of food biotechnology.

The result is jeopardy for everyone involved in food production and consumption: Consumers are subjected to avoidable and often undetected health risks, and food producers have placed themselves in legal jeopardy. The first point is obvious, the latter less so, but as described first by Drew Kershen, professor of law at the University of Oklahoma, it makes a fascinating story: Agricultural processors and food companies may face at least two kinds of civil liability for their refusal to purchase and use fungus-resistant, gene-spliced plant varieties, as well as other superior products.

Food for Thought

In 1999 the Gerber foods company succumbed to activist pressure, announcing that its baby food products would no longer contain any gene-spliced ingredients. Indeed, Gerber went farther and promised it would attempt to shift to organic ingredients that are grown without synthetic pesticides or fertilizers. Because corn starch and corn sweeteners are often used in a range of foods, this could mean changing Gerber's entire product line.

But in its attempt to head off a potential public relations problem concerning the use of gene-spliced ingredients, Gerber has actually increased the health risk for its baby consumers—and, thereby, its legal liability. As noted above, not only is gene-spliced corn likely to have lower levels of fumonisin than conventional corn; organic corn is likely to have the highest levels, because it suffers greater insect predation due to less effective pest controls.

If a mother some day discovers that her "Gerber baby" has developed liver or esophageal cancer, she might have a legal case against Gerber. On the child's behalf, a plaintiff's lawyer can allege liability based on mycotoxin contamination in the baby food as the causal agent of the cancer. The contamination would be considered a *manufacturing defect* under product liability law because the baby food did not meet its intended product specifications or level of safety. According to Kershen, Gerber could be found liable "even though all possible care was exercised in the preparation and marketing of the product," simply because the contamination occurred.

The plaintiff's lawyer could also allege a *design defect* in the baby food, because Gerber knew of the existence of a less risky design—namely, the use of gene-spliced varieties that are less prone to *Fusarium* and fumonisin contamination—but deliberately chose not to use it. Instead, Gerber chose to use non-gene-spliced, organic food ingredients, knowing that the foreseeable risks of harm posed by them could have been reduced or avoided by adopting a reasonable alternative design—that is, by using gene-spliced Bt corn, which is known to have a lower risk of mycotoxin contamination.

Gerber might answer this design defect claim by contending that it was only responding to consumer demand, but that alone would not be persuasive. Product liability law subjects defenses in design defect cases to a risk-utility balancing in which consumer expectations are only one of several factors used to determine whether the product design (e.g., the use of only non-gene-spliced ingredients) is reasonably safe. A jury might conclude that whatever consumer demand there may be for non-biotech ingredients does not outweigh Gerber's failure to use a technology that is known to lower the health risks to consumers.

Even if Gerber was able to defend itself from the design defect claim, the company might still be liable because it failed to provide adequate instructions or warnings about the potential risks of non-gene-spliced ingredients. For example, Gerber could label its non-gene-spliced baby food with a statement such as: "This product does not contain gene-spliced ingredients. Consequently, this product has a very slight additional risk of mycotoxin contamination. Mycotoxins can cause serious diseases such as liver and esophageal cancer and birth defects."

Whatever the risk of toxic or carcinogenic fumonisin levels in non-biotech corn may be (probably low in industrialized countries, where food producers generally are cautious about such contamination), a more likely scenario is potential liability for an allergic reaction.

Six percent to 8 percent of children and 1 to 2 percent of adults are allergic to one or another food ingredient, and an estimated 150 Americans die each year from exposure to food allergens. Allergies to peanuts, soybeans, and wheat proteins, for example, are quite common and can be severe. Although only about 1 percent of the population is allergic to peanuts, some individuals are so highly sensitive that exposure causes anaphylactic shock, killing dozens of people every year in North America.

Protecting those with true food allergies is a daunting task. Farmers, food shippers and processors, wholesalers and retailers, and even restaurants must maintain meticulous records and labels and ensure against cross-contamination. Still, in a country where about a billion meals are eaten every day, missteps are inevitable. Dozens of processed food items must be recalled every year due to accidental contamination or inaccurate labeling.

Fortunately, biotechnology researchers are well along in the development of peanuts, soybeans, wheat, and other crops in which the genes coding for allergenic proteins have been silenced or removed. According to University of California, Berkeley, biochemist Bob Buchanan, hypoallergenic varieties of wheat could be ready for commercialization within the decade, and nuts soon thereafter. Once these products are commercially available, agricultural processors and food companies that refuse to use these safer food sources will open themselves to products-liability, design-defect lawsuits.

Property Damage and Personal Injury

Potato farming is a growth industry, primarily due to the vast consumption of french fries at fast-food restaurants. However, growing potatoes is not easy, because they are preyed upon by a wide range of voracious and difficult-to-control pests, such as the Colorado potato beetle, virus-spreading aphids, nematodes, potato blight, and others.

To combat these pests and diseases, potato growers use an assortment of fungicides (to control blight), insecticides (to kill aphids and the Colorado potato beetle), and fumigants (to control soil nematodes). Although some of these chemicals are quite hazardous to farm workers, forgoing them could jeopardize the sustainability and profitability of the entire potato industry. Standard application of synthetic pesticides enhances yields more than 50 percent over organic potato production, which prohibits most synthetic inputs.

Consider a specific example. Many growers use methamidophos, a toxic organophosphate nerve poison, for aphid control. Although methamidophos is an EPA-approved pesticide, the agency is currently reevaluating the use of organophosphates and could ultimately prohibit or greatly restrict the use of this entire class of pesticides. As an alternative to these chemicals, the Monsanto Company developed a potato that contains a gene from the bacterium *Bacillus thuringiensis* (Bt) to control the Colorado potato beetle and another gene to control the potato leaf roll virus spread by the aphids. Monsanto's NewLeaf potato is resistant to these two scourges of potato plants, which allowed growers who adopted it to reduce their use of chemical controls and increase yields.

Farmers who planted NewLeaf became convinced that it was the most environmentally sound and economically efficient way to grow potatoes. But after five years of excellent results it encountered an unexpected snag. Under pressure from anti-biotechnology organizations, McDonald's, Burger King, and other restaurant chains informed their potato suppliers that they would no longer accept gene-spliced potato varieties for their french fries. As a result, potato processors such as J.R. Simplot inserted a nonbiotech-potato clause into their farmer-processor contracts and informed farmers that they would no longer buy gene-spliced potatoes. In spite of its substantial environmental, occupational safety, and economic benefits, NewLeaf became a sort of contractual poison pill and is no longer grown commercially. Talk about market distortions.

Now, let us assume that a farmer who is required by contractual arrangement to plant nonbiotech potatoes sprays his potato crop with methamidophos (the organophosphate nerve poison) and that the pesticide drifts into a nearby stream and onto nearby farm laborers. Thousands of fish die in the stream, and the laborers report to hospital emergency rooms complaining of neurological symptoms.

This hypothetical scenario is, in fact, not at all far-fetched. Fish-kills attributed to pesticide runoff from potato fields are commonplace. In the potato-growing region of Prince Edward Island, Canada, for example, a dozen such incidents occurred in one 13-month period alone, between July 1999 and August 2000. According to the UN's Food and Agriculture Organization, "normal" use of the pesticides parathion and methamidophos is responsible for some 7,500 pesticide poisoning cases in China each year.

In our hypothetical scenario, the state environmental agency might bring an administrative action for civil damages to recover the cost of the fish-kill, and a plaintiff's lawyer could file a class-action suit on behalf of the farm laborers for personal injury damages.

Who's legally responsible? Several possible circumstances could enable the farmer's defense lawyer to shift culpability for the alleged damages to the contracting food processor and to the fast-food restaurants that are the ultimate purchasers of the potatoes. These circumstances include the farmer's having planted Bt potatoes in the recent past; his contractual obligation to the potato processor and its fast-food retail buyers to provide only nonbiotech varieties; and his demonstrated preference for planting gene-spliced, Bt potatoes, were it not for the contractual proscription. If these conditions could be proved, the lawyer defending the farmer could name the contracting processor and the fast-food restaurants as cross-defendants, claiming either contribution in tort law or indemnification in contract law for any damages legally imposed upon the farmer client.

The farmer's defense could be that those companies bear the ultimate responsibility for the damages because they compelled the farmer to engage in higher-risk production practices than he would otherwise have chosen. The companies chose to impose cultivation of a non-gene-spliced variety upon the farmer although they knew that in order to avoid severe losses in yield, he would need to use organophosphate pesticides. Thus, the defense could argue that the farmer should have a legal right to pass any damages (arising from contractually imposed production practices) back to the processor and the fast-food chains.

Why Biotech?

Companies that insist upon farmers' using production techniques that involve foreseeable harms to the environment and humans may be—we would argue, *should* be—legally accountable for that decision. If agricultural processors and food companies manage to avoid legal liability for their insistence on nonbiotech crops, they will be "guilty" at least of externalizing their environmental costs onto the farmers, the environment, and society at large.

Food biotechnology provides an effective—and cost-effective—way to prevent many of these injurious scenarios, but instead of being widely encouraged, it is being resisted by self-styled environmental activists and even government officials.

It should not fall to the courts to resolve and reconcile what are essentially scientific and moral issues. However, other components of society—industry, government, and "consumer advocacy" groups—have failed abjectly to fully exploit a superior, life-enhancing, and life-saving technology. Even the biotechnology trade associations have been unhelpful. All are guilty, in varying measures, of sacrificing the public interest to self-interest and of helping to perpetuate a gross public misconception—that food biotechnology is unproven, untested, and unregulated.

If consumers genuinely want a safer, more nutritious, and more varied food supply at a reasonable cost, they need to know where the real threats lie. They must also become better informed, demand public policy that makes sense, and deny fringe anti-technology activists permission to speak for consumers.

Jeffrey M. Smith  **NO**

Frankenstein Peas

In the mid 1990s, Australian scientists at the Commonwealth Scientific and Industrial Research Organization (CSIRO) started research into manufacturing a GM pea that would be resistant to the pea weevil—a small but voracious pest that was eating up to 30 percent of pea yields. Given that the Australian pea harvest is estimated to be worth AUS$100 million, defeating this pest was potentially worth millions.

What they hoped to achieve was a GM pea plant containing an anti-nutrient (alpha-amylase inhibitor) that interferes with the bugs' digestion, thereby starving them to death. The protein is produced from a gene normally found in kidney beans which, when fully cooked, is safe for humans.

The scientists at CSIRO spliced the gene into peas, figuring it would be safe there as well. Everything appeared to be on schedule for approval until the pea developer, TJ Higgins, asked scientists from the John Curtin School of Medical Research in Canberra to evaluate the peas to see if they might cause allergies.

They fed the mice GM peas, non-GM peas or kidney beans. After four weeks, the mice were subjected to a battery of tests. The researchers did not check for allergies *per se,* but used tests that can predict allergenicity.

They were surprised to discover that only the mice fed GM peas had an immune response to GM protein. In addition, they became more sensitive to other substances. For example, mice fed GM peas reacted to egg albumin, while those fed non-GM peas did not. Even GM peas that had been boiled for 20 minutes and were no longer effective at protecting against weevils still caused an immune response in mice. The findings suggested that both raw and cooked GM peas might cause allergic reactions in humans, as well as promote reactions to a wide range of other foods.

When the scientists confirmed that the GM peas created an immune response in mice, they were faced with a challenge. The gene in kidney beans produces a protein that is harmless. That same gene, when inserted into GM peas, produces a protein with the same amino acid sequence. But somehow, that 'same' protein in the GM peas was dangerous. Why?

This question intrigued lead pea researcher Simon Hogan and his team. He said their 'scientific, inquisitive nature' led them to look for subtle differences in the protein's structure. Their investigation went beyond just identifying the amino acids, which are the building blocks. Judy Carman, who has analyzed GM applications to Australia and New Zealand, says, 'If you knock down a house and then study the pile of bricks, it won't describe the house. Similarly, the amino acids don't reveal the structure, shape and unique characteristics of the protein.'

Scientists do know that when sugar chains become attached to proteins, this process, known as glycosylation, can turn a harmless protein into a dangerous allergen. Using a sensitive test (called MALDI-TOF), Hogan's team confirmed that the GM pea protein and the non-GM kidney protein had slightly different glycosylation patterns. They were surprised to see that a protein that is naturally created in kidney beans had been altered in such a closely related species as peas. They believe that this subtle difference may be why the GM pea protein created an immune response.

Implications for the Rest of GM Food

• **The world's strictest regulatory bodies only require that GM crops be evaluated for allergenicity by testing protein stability in test tubes and comparing amino acid sequences with known allergens. The peas could have passed these tests.** The first method is based on the fact that allergenic proteins often—but not always—break down slowly in the stomach and intestines. (If they were destroyed quickly, they might not be around long enough to solicit an allergic reaction.) Scientists, therefore, put the GM protein into a test tube with acid and digestive enzymes to see how quickly it breaks down. Companies can rig these type of studies, however, in order to break down their GM protein more quickly. In one of Monsanto's GM corn tests, for example, they used about 1,250 times the amount of enzymes and a much stronger acid, compared to recommendations by the FAO-WHO.

Even if done properly, the test tube does not accurately mimic what happens inside animal and human digestive tracts. In real life, for example, a protein can bind with other substances in the gut and be more stable and long-lasting. When *Bt*-toxin—the pesticidal protein created in GM corn and cotton—was evaluated using test tube studies, results suggested that it would break down quickly in digestion. When independent researchers fed *Bt*-toxin to mice, however, the animals developed abnormal and excessive cell growth in the lower part of their small intestines. In another experiment, mice produced a significant immune response. Thus, the *Bt* obviously survives long enough to create a reaction. These findings should have forced regulators to abandon the test tube in favor of animal studies. Moreover, they point out serious problems with *Bt* crops that might impact human health. Unfortunately, regulators have largely ignored these studies and continue to rely on test tube experiments and unproven assumptions.

The second method used to evaluate allergenicity is to search databases to see if the amino acid sequence of the GM protein is similar to known allergens. This method also offers no guarantees—not all allergenic sequences have been identified. Furthermore, according to the FAO-WHO criteria, GM soya, corn, and papaya fail this test—they have short sequences that are identical to known allergens. The crops were nonetheless approved.

What happened when the GM peas were evaluated by these two methods? According to their developer TJ Higgins, the results were 'borderline.' Those borderline results, however, are *better* than those of some GM crops already on the market. Thus, if scientists had not done the advanced animal testing and instead relied on the allergy studies that are normally used in safety assessments, the GM peas would most likely have been approved.

• **Evaluations of GM crops are based on the obsolete assumption that proteins will act the same across species.** The pea study revealed that when genes are passed between closely related species, subtle and unpredictable changes in the protein can make it dangerous—even deadly. Characteristics of proteins can vary between species and even between different cells in the same species. The genes put into approved GM foods, however, cross entire kingdoms. Bacterial genes are spliced into GM soybeans, corn, cotton and canola, and viral genes are inserted into papaya, zucchini and crook neck squash. How these crops will alter bacterial proteins is anyone's guess—unfortunately. According to David Schubert of The Salk Institute for Biological Studies, 'A toxin that is harmless to humans when made in bacteria could be modified by plant cells in many ways, some of which might be harmful.'

Schubert says, depending on where a protein is produced, molecular chains 'such as phosphate, sulfate, sugars, or lipids' can be attached to the protein and alter its function. In a 2002 article challenging the safety of GM foods, he warned, 'With our current state of knowledge . . . there is no way of predicting either the modifications or their biological effects.' The altered sugar chains in the GM peas provide an example of a dangerous modification that was almost missed.

In addition to attaching molecules, a protein's shape also determines its effect. According to cellular biologist Barry Commoner, 'The newly made protein, a strung-out ribbon of a molecule, must be folded up into a precisely organized . . . structure.' He points out that according to the old theory of genetics, the protein 'always folded itself up in the right way once its amino acid sequence had been determined. In the 1980s, however, it was discovered that some . . . proteins are, on their own, likely to become misfolded—and therefore remain biochemically inactive—unless they come in contact with a special type of 'chaperone' protein that properly folds them.'

For millions of years the chaperone folders have evolved along with the proteins they fold. What happens when a foreign bacterial protein comes in contact with a plant's chaperone folders? Will the protein be folded correctly? Prions, responsible for mad cow disease and the deadly Creutzfeld-Jacob disease in humans, are examples of misfolded proteins (unrelated to GM).

In GM plants, even the amino acid building blocks of the protein could be altered. Amino acids are built according to the genetic code, or sequence, in the gene. This sequence, however, can get mixed up when the gene is inserted into DNA. Genes spliced into soybeans and corn, for example, were mutated, fragmented or truncated, and several appeared to rearrange over time. The amino acids that they produce, therefore, may be quite different from those that were intended. But regulatory agencies do not require companies to check the gene and amino acid sequences to see if unpredicted changes have occurred. According to Bill Freese, a research analyst at Friends of the Earth, 'At present, the standard practice is to sequence just five to 25 amino acids', even if the protein has more than 600 in total. If the short sample matches what is expected, they *assume* that the rest are also fine. If they are wrong, however, a rearranged protein could be quite dangerous.

If a GM protein was mixed up, misfolded or had attached molecules, how would we know if it were dangerous? When evaluating medicines, scientists conduct long-term feeding trials on animals, followed by clinical trials on humans and then they monitor side-effects after the product is introduced. This is not done for GM foods. Instead, biotech companies often rely on an 'acute oral toxicity study', in which, according to Monsanto's website, a high dose of 'the additional protein is fed in its pure form to mice'. The mice are then observed over the next 14 days to see if there's a problem. (As its name implies, acute toxicity tests will not detect moderate or chronic problems that may manifest over time, only acute reactions to the additional protein.)

The additional protein referred to by Monsanto is the protein produced by their inserted gene. In Roundup Ready soybeans, for example, the inserted gene produces a protein that allows the soybean plant to survive applications of the company's Roundup herbicide. For the toxicity test, one might assume that researchers grind up soybeans and then isolate and extract this protein. While this certainly *can* be done, it is not what Monsanto and other biotech companies typically do. Instead, they insert their gene into bacteria and let the GM bacteria produce the protein. It's cheaper and easier to extract the protein from the bacteria, than it is to do so from the plant. Thus, they feed bacteria-derived protein to mice and *assume* that the protein will have the same structure and effect as the protein from GM plants. But as the pea study illustrates, the assumption is rubbish. That same protein, if produced in a plant, could have added molecules. It could be misfolded or have a different amino acid sequence. None of these potentially deadly changes would be picked up in a test that uses protein from bacteria. It's another way in which industry studies avoid finding problems. Although several regulatory agencies ask companies to use only bacteria-derived protein if they can demonstrate that it is equivalent to the GM plant protein, biotech companies consistently ignore this request. Now that the GM pea study demonstrates how proteins can be changed in subtle but dangerous ways—even between closely related species—it is essential that regulators end the use of surrogate proteins in safety assessments.

• **The methods used in most safety assessments to identify changes in the protein are inadequate.** In order to evaluate the difference between the GM protein in the peas and its natural counterpart in the beans, the Australians used the sensitive MOLDI-TOF test, which is almost never used in GM safety assessments. According to Doug Gurian-Sherman, a senior scientist at the Centre for Food Safety and formerly at the US Environmental Protection Agency, those subtle differences in glycosylation patterns found in the pea study 'would not be detected by the tests that are currently required by US regulatory agencies'. In fact, in the 1990s, when the GM peas were tested with an inferior 'gel test' method that is sometimes used in GM food assessments, Higgins didn't see any difference between the GM and non-GM proteins. The peas had passed this test.

• **Cooking GM food will not necessarily destroy allergens.** One argument used to defend the safety of the *Bt*-toxin is that cooked *Bt* no longer acts as a pesticide. Heat changes the shape—or denatures—the protein. Scientists have claimed that denatured GM proteins will also no longer cause allergies. The cooked GM pea was sufficiently denatured to no longer be effective as a pesticide. But industry assumptions notwithstanding, it was still able to create an immune response in the mice.

• **Even the GM pea study is not adequate.** While the pea research reveals serious loopholes in GM safety studies, it should not be held as a model of an adequate assessment. There is a long list of other potential side-effects in GM crops that remain untested for. For example, during the process of making a GM crop, the plant's natural genes can become scrambled, mutated, deleted or changed. These alterations may create additional toxins, allergens or anti-nutrients that are impossible to predict and difficult to detect. The GM pea study overlooked them entirely. The methodology failed to take into account the possibility that the peas' natural genes were disrupted when the kidney bean gene was inserted, causing a change in the plant's composition. This could have sensitized the mice in some way, making them more susceptible to an immune reaction. Earlier unpublished tests on the GM peas did show major unexpected changes in composition, including a doubling of a known allergen (trypsin inhibitor) and a four-fold increase in an anti-nutrient (a lectin).

Similarly, acute toxicity studies also miss these types of side effects. Even if the biotech industry used the protein from plants and not from bacteria, they only test the reaction to single isolated GM protein. There could be scores of other dangerous proteins created or elevated in GM crops that are never tested for.

• **Immune reactions to GM plants are common.** What is not unique about the pea study is that immune responses were associated with GM crops. This was true with experimental soybeans, experimental potatoes, and StarLink corn in various tests of *Bt*-toxin and with Monsanto's MON 863 corn. According to Arpad Pusztai, 'A consistent feature of all the studies done, published or unpublished, including MON 863, indicates major problems with changes in the immune status of animals fed on various GM crops/foods, the latest example of this coming from the GM pea research in Australia.' In addition, unpublished research suggests that Filipinos may have adversely reacted to *Bt* corn pollen from nearby fields, and recent medical reports in India claim that farm workers handling *Bt* cotton developed moderate to severe allergic reactions.

Immune systems react when they interpret something as foreign, different and offensive. But all GM foods, by definition, have something foreign and different. The pea study confirms that even small differences—which industry and regulators had chosen to ignore—may create big, life threatening problems. According to Judy Carman, an epidemiologist and the director of the Institute of Health and Environmental Research in Australia, 'If a GM food was introduced onto supermarket shelves and caused an immune reaction, it would be very difficult to find the culprit, particularly if it caused reactions to other, different foods, as this GM pea was found to do.'

So how did the GM industry defend a regulatory system that clings to outdated science and could have approved those dangerous peas if advanced test had not been conducted?

Tony Combes, Monsanto's UK director of corporate affairs, said, 'The CSIRO decision to halt research and destroy the GM pea that inflamed lung tissue in laboratory mice showed how the regulatory system was working exactly as intended.'

This carefully crafted PR spin appears logical only to those unfamiliar with GM safety assessments. In truth, very few people *are* familiar with exactly what goes on. Even many biotech researchers and crop developers make the assumption that companies will do what is necessary to protect the public. If they discover the truth, they are often shocked.

Higgins, the GM peas' crop developer, may be in for such a shock. He too claimed that his pea study 'shows that the regulatory system works.' His explanation reveals what he doesn't know. He said, 'I didn't feel that we were breaking particularly new ground . . . We were following basically the recommendations for a proper risk assessment and I feel it is typical of the kinds of assessments that have been done for other GM crops around the world. 'Pea researcher Simon Hogan said the same thing. But neither scientist could name a single GM food on the market that has had the same level of testing. Experts who have studied GM safety assessments submitted around the world know that there *are* none.

Arpad Pusztai, for example, who had co-authored a paper with Higgins on GM peas in the 1990s, has studied nearly every industry submission to regulators. In fact, he recently published an analysis of all peer-reviewed safety assessments. He says that the GM pea study, does, in fact, break new ground. Professor G.E. Seralini, who has officially reviewed all the submissions to Europe as well as all the commentaries on the submissions, wrote, 'To my knowledge, no GM plant on the market has undergone such detailed experiments to assess allergenicity.'

Likewise, Doug Gurian-Sherman and Bill Freese, both experts on submissions to US authorities, acknowledge that industry immune studies are considerably weaker than the pea study. Judy Carman, who has analyzed GM applications to Australia and New Zealand, concurs. In fact, Marc Rothenberg, who is a co-author of the current pea study and was also on an expert panel assessing the allergenicity of a GM corn variety (StarLink), said of the pea research, 'It was very unique. It was much more extensive and rigorous than what was previously done.'

This study is just the latest in a series of such wake up calls. Each year, key assumptions that were used as the basis for GM crop approvals are overturned. All expose the fact that GM food crops were rushed onto the market long before the science was ready.

There are currently seven such crops being produced for consumption: soya, corn, cottonseed, canola, Hawaiian papaya, zucchini, and crook neck squash. None have been evaluated like the GM peas. None have been tested through long-term feeding studies. Any one of them might be creating serious health problems in the population.

The claim that GM crops are adequately tested, well-regulated and safe is a dangerous façade. Governments must immediately ban GM crops and start funding rigorous, thorough and independent safety assessments of them.

POSTSCRIPT

Are Genetically Modified Foods Safe to Eat?

At first, most of the attention aimed at genetic engineering focused first on its use to modify bacteria and other organisms to generate drugs needed to fight human disease, and second on its potential to modify human genes and attack hereditary diseases at their roots. See Eric B. Kmiec, "Gene Therapy," *American Scientist* (May–June 1999).

Despite some successes, gene therapy has not yet become a multimillion-dollar industry. Pharmaceutical applications of genetic engineering have been much more successful. According to Brian Halweil, in "The Emperor's New Crops," *World Watch* (July/August 1999), so have agricultural applications. Halweil is skeptical, saying that genetically modified foods have potential benefits but that they may also have disastrous effects on natural ecosystems and—because high-tech agriculture is controlled by major corporations such as Monsanto—on less-developed societies. He argues that "ecological" agriculture (e.g., using organic fertilizers and natural enemies instead of pesticides) offers much more hope for the future. Similar arguments are made by those who demonstrate against genetically modified foods and lobby for stringent labeling requirements or for outright bans on planting and importing these crops. See Capulalpum, "Risking Corn, Risking Culture," *WorldWatch* (November–December 2002). Many protestors argue against GM technology in terms of the precautionary principle; see "GMOs and Precaution in EU Countries," *Outlook on Science Policy* (September 2005).

Many researchers see more hope in genetically modified foods. In July 2000, for example, the Royal Society of London, the U.S. National Academy of Sciences, the Brazilian Academy of Sciences, the Chinese Academy of Sciences, the Indian Academy of Sciences, the Mexican Academy of Sciences, and the Third World Academy of Sciences issued a joint report entitled "Transgenic Plants and World Agriculture" (available at http://www.royalsoc.ac. uk/document.asp?tip=1&id=1448). This report stresses that during the twenty-first century, both population and the need for food are going to increase dramatically, especially in developing nations. According to the report, "Foods can be produced through the use of GM [genetic modification] technology that are more nutritious, stable in storage and in principle, health promoting. . . . New public sector efforts are required for creating transgenic crops that benefit poor farmers in developing nations and improve their access to food. . . . Concerted, organised efforts must be undertaken to investigate the potential environmental effects, both positive and negative, of GM technologies [compared to those] from conventional agricultural technologies. . . . Public health regulatory systems need to be put in place in every country to identify and monitor any potential adverse human health effects."

The worries surrounding genetically modified foods and the scientific evidence to support them are summarized by Kathryn Brown, in "Seeds of Concern," and Karen Hopkin, in "The Risks on the Table," both in *Scientific American* (April 2001). In the same issue, Sasha Nemecek poses the question "Does the World Need GM Foods?" to two prominent figures in the debate: Robert B. Horsch, a Monsanto vice president and recipient of the 1998 National Medal of Technology for his work on modifying plant genes, who says yes, and Margaret Mellon, of the Union of Concerned Scientists, who says no, adding that much more work needs to be done on safety. Jeffrey M. Smith, *Seeds of Deception: Exposing Industry and Government Lies about the Safety of the Genetically Engineered Foods You're Eating* (Chelsea Green, 2003), argues that the dangers of GM foods have been deliberately concealed. Henry I. Miller and Gregory Conko, in *The Frankenfood Myth: How Protest and Politics Threaten the Biotech Revolution* (Praeger, 2004), address at length the fallacy that GM foods are especially risky. Harihara M. Mehendale, "Genetically Modified Foods: Why the Public Frenzy? Role of Mainstream News Media," *International Journal of Toxicology* (September 2004), blames "the role of the press in spreading misleading facts related to the technology." Walter F. Deal and Stephen L. Baird, in "Genetically Modified Foods: A Growing Need," *Technology Teacher* (April 2003), contend that GM foods "can help overcome the world's concern for feeding its ever-growing population." *The Economist* (May 6, 2006) notes in "Up from the Dead" that GM technology has now been accepted in more than 20 countries, with more than a billion acres planted to GM crops, and is growing rapidly. In addition, applications are broadening; some GM crops are "nutraceuticals" designed to confer health benefits in the form of additional nutrients and even vaccines.

Is the issue safety? Human welfare? Or economics? When genetically modified corn and other foods were offered as relief supplies to African nations threatened by famine, some accepted the aid. Others, pressured by European activists, turned it down. Robert L. Paarlberg discusses what the U.S. can do to counter resistance to GM foods in "Reinvigorating Genetically Modified Crops," *Issues in Science and Technology* (Spring 2003); he favors addressing the needs of developing countries.

And is the issue only genetically modified food? The July/August 2002 issue of *WorldWatch* magazine bore the overall title of "Beyond Cloning: The Risks of Rushing into Human Genetic Engineering." The editorial says that human genetic engineering poses "profound medical and social risks." Contributors object to it as unnatural, commercial, a violation of human integrity, potentially racist, and more. Francis Fukuyama, "In Defense of Nature, Human and Non-Human," says, "Anyone who feels strongly about defending non-human nature from technological manipulation should feel equally strongly about defending human nature as well. . . . Nature—both the natural environment around us, and our own—deserves an approach based on respect and stewardship, not domination and mastery."

Internet References . . .

National Aeronautics and Space Administration

At this site, you can find out the latest information on the International Space Shuttle, space exploration, and other space-related news.

http://www.nasa.gov

SETI Institute

The SETI Institute serves as a home for scientific research in the general field of life in the universe, with an emphasis on the search for extraterrestrial intelligence (SETI).

http://www.seti.org

SETI League

The SETI League, Inc., is dedicated to the electromagnetic (radio) search for extraterrestrial intelligence.

http://www.setileague.org

Close Approaches

NASAs Near Earth Object Program lists past and future close approaches to Earth.

http://neo.jpl.nasa.gov/ca/

Near Earth Objects

The Near Earth Object Dynamic Site (NEODyS) provides information on all near earth asteroids (NEAs). Each NEA has its own dynamically generated home page. Note the Risk Page, which presents information on the likelihood of impacts with Earth.

http://131.114.72.13/cgi-bin/neodys/neoibo

Space

*M*any interesting controversies arise in connection with technologies that are so new that they often sound more like science fiction than fact. Some examples are technologies that allow the exploration of outer space, the search for extraterrestrial intelligence, and genetic engineering. Such advances offer capabilities undreamed of in earlier ages, and they raise genuine, important questions about what it is to be a human being, the limits on human freedom in a technological age, and the place of humanity in the broader universe. They also raise questions of how we should respond: Should we accept the new devices and abilities offered by scientists and engineers? Or should we reject them? Should we use them to make human life safer and more secure? Or should we remain at the mercy of the heavens?

- Should We Expand Efforts to Find Near-Earth Objects?

- Will the Search for Extraterrestrial Life Ever Succeed?

- Is "Manned Space Travel" a Delusion?

ISSUE 12

Should We Expand Efforts to Find Near-Earth Objects?

YES: Joseph Burns, from *Statement (for the National Research Council) before House Committee on Science* (October 3, 2002)

NO: Edward Weiler, from *Statement before House Committee on Science* (October 3, 2002)

ISSUE SUMMARY

YES: Professor of engineering and astronomy Joseph Burns contests that the hazards posed to life on Earth by near-Earth objects (NEOs) are great enough to justify increased efforts to detect and catalog NEOs. Scientific benefits may also be expected.

NO: Edward Weiler asserts that NASA's present efforts to detect the larger and more hazardous NEOs are adequate. It is premature to expand the program.

Thomas Jefferson once said that he would rather think scientists were crazy than believe that rocks could fall from the sky. Since then, we have recognized that rocks do indeed fall from the sky. Most are quite small and do no more than make pretty streaks across the sky as they burn up in the atmosphere; they are known as meteors. Some—known as meteorites—are large enough to reach the ground and even to do damage. Every once in a while, the news reports one that crashed through a car or house roof, as indeed one did in January 2007 in New Jersey. Very rarely, a meteorite is big enough to make a crater in the Earth's surface, much like the ones that mark the face of the Moon. An example is Meteor Crater in Arizona, almost a mile across, created some 50,000 years ago by a meteorite 150 feet in diameter. (The Meteor Crater Web site, http://www.meteorcrater.com/, includes an animation of the impact.) A more impressive impact is the one that occurred 65 million years ago; the scar has been found at Chicxulub, Mexico: The results included the extinction of the dinosaurs (as well as a great many other species). Chicxulub-scale events are very rare; a hundred million years may pass between them. Meteor Crater–scale events may occur every thousand

238

years, releasing as much energy as a 100-megaton nuclear bomb and destroying an area the size of a city. And it has been calculated that a human being is more likely to die as the result of such an event than in an airplane crash.

It's not just Hollywood sci-fi, *Deep Impact* and *Armageddon*. Some people think we really should be worried. We should be doing our best to identify meteoroids (as they are called before they become meteors or meteorites) in space, plot their trajectories, tell when they are coming our way, and even develop ways of deflecting them before they cause enormous loss of life. In 1984, Thomas Gehrels, a University of Arizona astronomer, initiated the Spacewatch project, which aimed to identify space rocks that cross Earth's orbit. In the early 1990s, NASA workshops considered the hazards of these rocks. NASA now funds the international Spaceguard Survey, which finds about 25 new near-Earth Asteroids every month, and has identified more than 600 over 1 kilometer in diameter (1000 meters; 1.6 km equals 1 mile); none seem likely to strike Earth in the next century. See Peter Tyson, "Comet Busters," *Technology Review* (February/March 1995), Duncan Steel, *Target Earth: How Rogue Asteroids and Doomsday Comets Threaten our Planet* (Reader's Digest Association, 2000), David Morrison, "Target Earth," *Astronomy* (February 2002), and David Morrison, "Asteroid and Comet Impacts: The Ultimate Environmental Catastrophe," *Philosophical Transactions: Mathematical, Physical & Engineering Sciences* (August 2006). However, the news periodically issues alarming reports; in 2004, an asteroid 130 feet across looked for awhile like it would hit Earth in 2029 with the equivalent of a 10,000 megaton nuclear bomb, but improved data downgraded the warning to "near-miss"; see Govert Schilling, "The Sky Is Falling!" *Science Now* (February 7, 2005), and Guy Gugliotta, "Science's Doomsday Team vs. The Asteroids," *Washington Post* (April 9, 2005). Without the downgrade in the warning, we would have faced the serious question of whether we could devise effective methods for warding off disaster by 2029; see Russell L. Schweickart, Edward T. Lu, Piet Hut, and Clark R. Chapman, "The Asteroid Tugboat," *Scientific American* (November 2003).

Professor of engineering and astronomy Joseph Burns argues that the hazards posed to life on Earth by near-Earth objects (NEOs) are large. NEOs less than 300 meters (about 1,000 feet) in diameter can cause enormous numbers of deaths, and there is about a 1 percent chance of such a disaster in every century. Increased efforts to detect and catalog NEOs are justified. The same efforts would increase scientific knowledge of the solar system. Edward Weiler argues that only larger objects, over 1 kilometer in diameter, pose truly serious, global risks. NASA's present efforts have focused on those objects and are adequate. It is premature to expand the program before public discussion settles the question of where to set the cutoff point between NEOs "big enough" and "too small" to worry about.

YES

Joseph Burns

The Threat of Near-Earth Asteroids, October 2002

Statement of Joseph Burns (for the National Research Council)

. . . [T]he Astronomy and Astrophysics community has a long history of creating, through the National Research Council (NRC), decadal surveys of their field. These surveys lay out the community's research goals for the next decade, identify key questions that need to be answered, and propose new facilities with which to conduct this fundamental research.

In April 2001, NASA Associate Administrator for Space Science Edward Weiler asked the NRC to conduct a similar survey for planetary exploration. Our report, New Frontiers in the Solar System, is the result of that activity. The Solar System Exploration Survey was conducted by an ad hoc committee of the Space Studies Board (SSB), overseen by COMPLEX. This committee was comprised of some 50 scientists, drawn from a diverse set of institutions, research areas, and backgrounds; it also received input from more than 300 colleagues. The SSE Survey had four subpanels which focused on issues pertaining to different types of solar system bodies (Inner Planets, Giant Planets, Large Satellites, and Primitive Bodies) and received direct input from COMPLEX on Mars issues and from the Committee on the Origins and Evolution of Life on issues pertaining to Astrobiology.

New Frontiers in the Solar System (the Executive Summary is appended to this statement) recommends a scientific and exploration strategy for NASA's Office of Space Science that will both enable dramatic new discoveries in this decade and position the agency to continue to make such discoveries well into the future. Your invitation indicated that I should focus on the conclusions that the SSE Survey reached in the area of Near-Earth Objects (NEOs).

Near-Earth Objects

The SSE Survey's charge from NASA included a request to summarize the extent of our current understanding of the solar system. This task was delegated to the subpanels, which in the particular case of NEOs was handled by the Primitive Bodies Panel.

From a Statement before the House Committee on Science, October 3, 2002.

Scientifically, the history of impacts on the Earth is vital for understanding how the planet evolved and how life arose. For example, it has been suggested that a majority of the water on this planet was delivered by comet impacts. A better known example of the role of impacts is the Cretaceous-Tertiary event that led to global mass extinctions, including that of the dinosaurs. Another case is the 20 megaton (MT) equivalent-energy explosion that devastated 2000 square-kilometers of pine forest in the Siberian tundra in 1908. The SSE Survey identifies the exploration of the terrestrial space environment with regards to potential hazards as a new goal for the nation's solar system exploration enterprise.

Current surveys have identified an estimated 50 percent of NEOs that have a diameter of 1 kilometer or greater and approximately 10–15 percent of objects between 0.5 and 1 km. The vast majority of these latter objects have yet to be discovered, but a statistical analysis indicates a 1% probability of impact by a 300-m body in the next century. Such an object would deliver 1000 MT of energy, cause regional devastation, and (assuming an average of 10 people per square-kilometer on Earth) result in 100,000 fatalities. The damage caused by an impact near a city or into a coastal ocean would be orders of magnitude higher. As of a year ago, 340 objects larger than a kilometer had been catalogued as Potentially Hazardous Asteroids. In addition, the number of undiscovered comets with impact potential is large and unknown.

The Primitive Bodies panel went on to state: "Important scientific goals are associated with the NEO populations, including their origin, fragmentation and dynamical histories, and compositions and differentiation. These and other scientific issues are also vital to the mitigation of the impact hazard (emphasis added), as methods of deflection of objects potentially on course for an impact with Earth are explored. Information especially relevant to hazard mitigation includes knowledge of the internal structures of near-Earth asteroids and comets, their degree of fracture and the presence of large core pieces, the fractal dimensions of their structures, and their degree of cohesion or friction."

While almost all of the SSE Survey's recommendations involved NASA flight missions, the Primitive Bodies subpanel recommended that ground-based telescopes be used to do a majority of the study of NEOs, supplemented by airborne and orbital telescopes.

A survey for NEOs demands an exacting observational strategy. To locate NEOs as small as 300 m requires a survey down to 24th magnitude (16 million times fainter than the feeblest stars that are visible to the naked eye). If images are to be taken every 10 sec to allow the sky to be studied often, the necessary capability is almost 100 times better than that of existing survey telescopes. NEOs spend only a fraction of each orbit in Earth's neighborhood, where they are most easily seen. Repeated observations over a decade would be required to explore the full volume of space populated by these objects. Such a survey would identify several hundred NEOs per night and obtain astrometric (positional) measurements on the much larger (and growing) number of NEOs that it had already discovered. Precise astrometry is needed to determine the orbital parameters of the NEOs and to assign a hazard assessment to each object.

Astrometry at monthly intervals would ensure against losing track of these fast-moving objects in the months and years after discovery.

Large-Aperture Synoptic Survey Telescope   In its most recent decadal survey, the Astronomy and Astrophysics community selected the proposed Large-aperture Synoptic Survey Telescope (LSST) as their third major ground-based priority. In addition, our SSE Survey chose LSST to be its top-ranked ground-based facility. Telescopes like HST and Keck peer at selected, very localized regions of the sky or study individual sources with high sensitivity. However, another type of telescope is needed to survey the entire sky relatively quickly, so that periodic maps can be constructed that will reveal not only the positions of target sources, but their time variability as well. The Large-aperture Synoptic Survey Telescope is a 6.5-m-effective-diameter, very wide field (~3 deg) telescope that will produce a digital map of the visible sky every week. For this type of survey observation, the LSST will be a hundred times more powerful than the Keck telescopes, the world's largest at present. Not only will LSST carry out an optical survey of the sky far deeper than any previous survey, but also—just as importantly—it will also add the new dimension of time and thereby open up a new realm of discovery. By surveying the sky each month for over a decade, LSST would revolutionize our understanding of various topics in astronomy concerning objects whose brightnesses vary on time scales of days to years. NEOs, which drift across a largely unchanging sky, are easily identified. The LSST could locate 90 percent of all near-Earth objects down to 300 m in size, enable computations of their orbits, and permit assessment of their threat to Earth. In addition, this facility could be used to discover and track objects in the Kuiper Belt, a largely unexplored, primordial component of our solar system. It would discover and monitor a wide variety of variable objects, such as the optical afterglows of gamma-ray bursts. In addition, it would find approximately 100,000 supernovae per year, and be useful for many other cosmological observations.

The detectors of choice for the temporal monitoring tasks would be thinned charge-coupled devices (CCDs); the requisite extrapolation from existing systems should constitute only a small technological risk. An infrared capability of a comparably wide field would be considerably more challenging but could evolve as the second phase of the telescope's operation. Instrumentation for LSST would be an ideal way to involve independent observatories with this basically public facility.

NASA/NSF Cooperation

Historically, the National Science Foundation (NSF) has built and operated ground-based telescopes, whereas NASA has done the same for space-based observatories. Although the Astronomy and Astrophysics Survey was noncommittal on who should build the LSST, the SSE Survey included a recommendation that NASA share equally with NSF in the telescope's construction and operations costs.

Such an arrangement has precedent. The SSE Survey noted that "NASA continues to play a major role in supporting the use of Earth-based optical telescopes for planetary studies. It funds the complete operations of the IRTF (InfraRed Telescope Facility), a 3-m diameter telescope located on Hawaii's Mauna Kea. In return for access to 50 percent of the observing time for non-solar-system observations, the NSF supports the development of IRTF's instrumentation. This telescope has provided vital data in support of flight missions and will continue to do so. As another example, NASA currently buys one-sixth of the observing time on the privately operated Keck 10-m telescopes. This time was purchased to test interferometric techniques in support of future spaceflight missions such as SIM (Space Interferometry Mission) and TPF (Terrestrial Planet Finder)."

The solar system exploration community is concerned that the NSF is often unwilling to fund solar system research. This is particularly unfortunate given NSF's charter to support the best science and its leadership role in other aspects of ground-based astronomy.

The shared responsibility between NASA and the NSF that we recommend is also endorsed by the more general findings last year of the NRC's Committee on the Organization and Management of Research in Astronomy and Astrophysics (COMRAA), chaired by Norman Augustine. COMRAA's report recommended that NASA continue to "support critical ground-based facilities and scientifically enabling precursor and follow-up observations that are essential to the success of space missions." COMRAA also noted that in 1980 the NSF provided most of the research grants in astronomy and astrophysics, but today NASA is the major supporter of such research.

The roles of the agencies also affect the ability of scientists to conduct a census of Near-Earth Objects. The SSE Survey commented that:

> "interestingly enough, NASA has no systematic survey-capability to discover the population distribution of the solar-system bodies. To do this, NASA relies on research grants to individual observers who must gain access to their own facilities. The large NEOs are being efficiently discovered using small telescopes for which NASA provides instrumentation funding, but all the other solar system populations—e.g., comets, Centaurs, satellites of the outer planets, and Kuiper Belt Objects—are being characterized almost entirely using non-NASA facilities. This is a major deficiency . . ."

The construction of the LSST would provide a central, federally sponsored location for such research.

LSST Costs and Survey Below 300 Meters The costs of the LSST are projected by the 2001 Astronomy and Astrophysics Survey as being $83 million for capital construction and $42 million for data processing and distribution for 5 years of operation, for a total cost of $125 million. Routine operating costs, including a technical and support staff of 20 people, are estimated at approximately $3 million per year. The LSST will be able to routinely discover and characterize NEOs down to 300 m in diameter. Increasing the sensitivity of the survey to 100 m would mean increasing the sensitivity of the telescope by a factor of ten. This may represent a "beyond the state-of-the-art" challenge to telescope builders, and certainly a much larger telescope—3 times the LSST and probably 10 to 100 times the cost unless innovative designs are found. The number of discovered objects would correspondingly increase substantially; this large data set may challenge current capabilities.

Concluding Thoughts   By way of summary, let me place the LSST into the context of a robust scientific program. Systematically building an inventory of the Near-Earth Objects is crucial to an improved understanding of Earth's environment, especially to the prediction of future hazards posed to our species. It is also a necessary first step towards a rational program of NASA's exploration of these bodies with spacecraft: many of the most interesting targets may remain, as yet, undiscovered. The ability to create and play a "motion picture" of the night sky will also provide new insights in a wide variety of disciplines from cosmology to astrophysics to solar system exploration. A suitable analog might be the deepened knowledge that is obtained from dynamic movies of swirling clouds and weather patterns, as compared to an occasional static photo.

The immense volume of data from the LSST would provide a reservoir of information for numerous graduate students and researchers, as well as established scientists. Further, LSST will support flight missions—for example, identifying possible fly-by targets for a spacecraft mission to explore the Kuiper Belt. All in all, the SSE Survey committee believes that broad areas of planetary science, particularly NEO studies, would benefit very substantially from the construction of the LSST for a relatively small investment. . . .

The Threat of Near-Earth Asteroids, October 2002

Statement of Edward Weiler

NASA's NEO Program makes ground-based observations with the goal of identifying 90 percent of those NEOs that are 1 km or larger and characterizing a sample of them. This is a ten-year program, which began in 1998 and should be completed in 2008. (It should be noted that NASA had begun searching for NEOs many years before this program officially started.)

The threshold size for an asteroid striking the Earth to produce a global catastrophe is 1 km in diameter. NASA has an active program to detect such objects that could potentially strike the Earth and to identify their orbits. The best current estimates are that the total population of NEOs with diameters larger than 1 km is about 1000. The 1-km diameter limit for an NEO was set after extensive discussions within the scientific community to determine the size of an object that would likely threaten civilization. This community consensus is codified in the Spaceguard Report and in the Shoemaker Report. For comparison, the object that likely caused the extinction of the dinosaurs was in the 5–10 km range. The current survey of NEOs in that range is considered complete.

Status: NASA's NEO Search Program

As of the end of September, NASA has detected 619 NEOs with diameters larger than 1 km. We are currently discovering about 100 per year. At the present time, we have six groups which are funded by NASA's Near Earth Objects program to conduct this type of research. These groups, selected though peer review, have ten telescopes among them searching for NEOs. One of these groups just completed (and another one is about to complete) major upgrades to its facility; therefore, we expect this pace of discovery to continue, if not increase. In some cases, the search programs are not able to obtain the number of observations required to determine the orbit elements of certain objects to sufficient accuracy to fully characterize the orbital parameters. These objects require additional astrometric observations, commonly called "follow-up observations." We have also funded four investigations to obtain astrometric follow-up observations of those objects that cannot be easily followed by the primary search programs.

From a Statement before the House Committee on Science, October 3, 2002.

Now, how well are we doing? I am happy to report that we are doing quite well; in fact, we are even a bit ahead of schedule.

There have been various reports to the effect that NASA would not reach its metric—90 percent of all the NEOs with diameters larger than 1 km—until many years after the end of 2008. However, these analyses have been based on the performance of individual search efforts, and they have tended not to use the current performance of the NEO search effort as a whole. As with most things, experience increases proficiency; therefore, we expect the rate of detection to increase. Even if we were to stay at our current rate, however, we are more than halfway to our goal of 90 percent by the end of 2008.

That does not mean we will grow complacent; we intend to continue to vigorously pursue detection of NEOs. In fact, we anticipate even better results due to technological developments such as better detector arrays, migration of existing search efforts to larger telescopes, and additional telescopes dedicated to the search program. In short, we are working to achieve both our goal and our metric and expect to be successful at both. One unanticipated result of the NEO search will be a list of over 1,000 potential candidates for future space science missions.

NASA's Future Role with Respect to NEOs

Next I would like to turn to another question. What should NASA's role be in the future? NASA is a space agency. While we are proud of our success in implementing the Congress's direction to us with regard to the search for NEOs, we do not feel that we should play a role in any follow-on search and cataloging effort unless that effort needs to be specifically space-based in nature. There are other agencies with far more expertise in ground-based observations that would be more suitable candidates to lead that portion of a future NEO endeavor.

NASA does, however, continue to have a large role to play in the scientific space exploration of asteroids. The frequent access to space for small missions offered by NASA's Discovery Program has benefited the study of asteroids and comets as no other program to date. The first in-depth study of an NEO, Eros, was performed by the NEAR-Shoemaker mission. The body of data returned by NEAR-Shoemaker was so large, and the quality of the data so high, that NEAR's database will require years of analysis. Just this year, we initiated funding for the first 17 investigations of that data. NEAR-Shoemaker's exploration of Eros will be followed by detailed exploration of two other asteroids, Vesta and Ceres, by the upcoming DAWN mission, currently scheduled to launch in 2006. There is no reason to expect that science-driven exploration of the asteroids, and of course NEOs, will not continue through the Discovery program. We believe that the critical measurements required for developing potential mitigation efforts are substantially the same as those required to achieve the pure scientific goals identified for these objects. We must be able to understand and characterize these objects before any mitigation efforts are even considered.

In addition to NEAR and DAWN, NASA has several other missions dedicated to studying comets and asteroids, such as Deep Impact and Stardust.

Our total investment in understanding these bodies, both in the past and in our current FY 2003 budget run-out, is approximately $1.6 billion. That does not even take into account those spacecraft that have provided "bonus" information, such as Galileo, which found a moon orbiting asteroid Ida, and Deep Space 1, a technology demonstration mission that performed a close-up fly-by of comet Borelly. NASA deeply regrets not having the potential discoveries from the recently failed CONTOUR mission, which was to have studied Comets Encke and Schwassmann-Wachmann 3.

NASA's bold new technology initiatives, the In-Space Propulsion (ISP) Initiative and the Nuclear Systems Initiative (NSI), together offer new opportunities to enable capable new missions to NEOs early in the next decade. Improvements in solar-electric propulsion and development of solar sails are examples of new capabilities that might allow a spacecraft like NEAR-Shoemaker to visit many NEOs during a single mission rather than just one (and at the cost of a Discovery mission). If we are ever faced with the requirement to modify the motion of an NEO over time to ensure that the object will not come close to the Earth, nuclear propulsion may very well be the answer. The Nuclear Systems Initiative could address two elements in understanding the potential hazards of NEOs by: (1) providing technologies that could significantly increase our ability to identify and track NEOs, and (2) to possibly—in the future—provide sufficient power to move an Earth-intersecting object. The NSI could enable power and propulsion for an extended survey (in one mission) of multiple NEOs to determine their composition, which is a critical factor in understanding how to mitigate the risk of an Earth-intersecting object. In the future, the technologies under development by the NSI could provide us with the means to redirect the path of an Earth-intersecting asteroid, once we understand the orbital mechanics of these objects sufficiently to understand how to do this. These programs are being developed to serve a wide range of needs across NASA, but they will most certainly prove beneficial for space missions that help us to better understand and characterize NEOs.

What Should the Nation Be Doing beyond the Current Goal?

I feel that it is premature to consider an extension of our current national program to include a complete search for smaller-sized NEOs. There are several reasons for this belief. The first is that we need to have a better understanding of the true size of the population down to at least 100 m. How will we get the improved data we need on this population? We will obtain the necessary data from the existing NASA search effort for NEOs. The search program now finds about two NEOs with diameters less than 1 km for every large one (diameter greater than 1 km) that we find. In addition, we are supporting a search program which is optimized to detect smaller NEOs. We expect by the end of this decade to have a much better picture of the true size of the population, and hence, what will be required to detect all of them.

The second issue is how such a search could be most efficiently and cost-effectively implemented. Two groups that wish to build large survey systems have argued that the search goal should be extended to 300 m. NASA has at least two concerns with this proposition. First, we do not possess a non-advocate trade study to tell us how best to do such a search. For example, one issue to be addressed is whether it would be better to build one large 8-m class telescope or 2 4-m search telescopes. At these sizes, is a space-based system an option? Second, why 300m? The present limiting diameter of 1 km was the product of a broad public discussion. When we have another broad public discussion, the answer could be: "Leave the present limiting diameter as it stands." Or, perhaps the result of broad national debate on this issue would be: "Catalog the population down to 100 m." We at NASA don't know the answers to these questions, and we believe that further commitments to extend the search are simply premature at this point.

Within the Office of Space Science, the Solar System Exploration Division Director has appointed a small Science Definition Team (SDT) to consider the technical issues related to extending the search for NEOs to smaller sizes. The goal of the SDT is to evaluate what is technologically possible today. The scope of the SDT does not include consideration of any change to our present NEO search goal.

Conclusion

NASA has made impressive strides in achieving its goal of cataloging 90 percent of all Near-Earth Objects with diameters of more than 1 km and characterizing a sample of them. We are currently ahead of schedule with respect to having this effort completed in the 2008 time frame. While NASA certainly agrees that because these objects pose a potential threat to the Earth, they should be studied and understood, we respectfully defend our position that any expansion of NASA's current NEO effort is premature. Before any further effort is undertaken, we would want input from the scientific community as to how this subject should be approached, and if indeed NASA is even the proper agency to lead this type of an undertaking. . . .

POSTSCRIPT

Should We Expand Efforts to Find Near-Earth Objects?

In the debate over the risks of NEO impacts on Earth, there are a few certainties: They have happened before, they will happen again, and they come in various sizes. As Mike Reynolds says in "Earth Under Fire," *Astronomy* (August 2006), the question is not whether impacts will happen in the future. "It's just a matter of when and how big the object will be." Many past craters mark the Earth, even though many more have been erased by plate tectonics and erosion. See Timothy Ferris, "Killer Rocks from Outer Space," *Reader's Digest* (October 2002). Ivan Semeniuk, "Asteroid Impact," *Mercury* (November/December 2002), says that, "If there is one question that best sums up the current state of thinking about the impact hazard, it is this: At what size do we need to act? In the shooting gallery that is our solar system, everyone agrees we are the target of both cannonballs and BBs. The hard part is deciding where to draw the line that separates them. For practical reasons, that line is now set at 1 kilometer. Not only are objects of this diameter a global threat (no matter where they hit, we're all affected to some degree), they are also the easiest to spot. Under a mid-1990s congressional mandate, NASA currently funds search efforts to the tune of about $3.5 million per year . . . 'The existing commitment to 1 kilometer and larger is to retire the risk,' says Tom Morgan, who heads NASA's NEO group. 'By the end of this decade we'll be able to tell you if any of these objects presents a threat in the foreseeable future.'" However, as Richard A. Kerr notes, "The Small Ones Can Kill You, Too," *Science* (September 19, 2003). See also Russell L. Schweickart and Clark R. Chapman, "Better Collision Insurance," *American Scientist* (September–October 2005). The risks are very well reviewed in Alan W. Harris, "Chicken Little Was Right! The Risk from an Asteroid or Comet Impact," *Phi Kappa Phi Forum* (Winter/Spring 2006).

What if a "killer rock" does present a threat? In September 2002, NASA held a workshop on *Scientific Requirements for Mitigation of Hazardous Comets and Asteroids*, which concluded "that the prime impediment to further advances in this field is the lack of any assigned responsibility to any national or international governmental organization to prepare for a disruptive collision and the absence of any authority to act in preparation for some future collision mitigation attempt" and urged that "NASA be assigned the responsibility to advance this field" and "a new and adequately funded program be instituted at NASA to create, through space missions and allied research, the specialized knowledge base needed to respond to a future threat of a collision from an asteroid or comet nucleus." The results of the workshop appeared as *Mitigation of Hazardous Impacts due to Asteroids and Comets* (Cambridge University Press, 2004).

The Organization for Economic Cooperation and Development (OECD) Global Science Forum held a "Workshop on Near Earth Objects: Risks, Policies and Actions" in January 2003. It too concluded that more work is needed. In May 2005, the House Science Committee approved a bill to establish and fund a NASA program to detect and assess near-Earth asteroids and comets down to 100 meters in diameter. See also David H. Levy, "Asteroid Alerts: A Risky Business," *Sky & Telescope* (April 2006).

Given political will and funding, what could be done if a threat were identified? There have been numerous proposals, from launching nuclear missiles to pulverize approaching space rocks to sending astronauts (or robots) to install rocket engines and deflect the rocks onto safe paths (perhaps into the sun to forestall future hazards). Several alternatives are discussed in Justin Cunningham, "Collision Course," *Professional Engineering* (December 14, 2005). However, Bill Cooke, "Killer Impact," *Astronomy* (December 2004), warns that for the foreseeable future, our only real hope is evacuation of the target zone. All proposed methods require a stronger space program than any nation now has. Lacking such a program, knowing that a major rock is on the way would surely be little comfort. However, given sufficient notice—on the order of decades—a space program could be mobilized to deal with the threat.

ISSUE 13

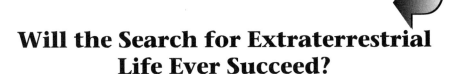

Will the Search for Extraterrestrial Life Ever Succeed?

YES: Seth Shostak, from "When Will We Detect the Extraterrestrials?" *Acta Astronautica* (August 2004)

NO: Peter Schenkel, from "SETI Requires a Skeptical Reappraisal," *Skeptical Inquirer* (May/June 2006)

ISSUE SUMMARY

YES: Radio astronomer and SETI researcher Seth Shostak argues that if the assumptions behind the SETI search are well grounded, signals of extraterrestrial origin will be detected soon, perhaps within the next generation.

NO: Peter Schenkel argues that SETI's lack of success to date, coupled with the apparent uniqueness of Earth, suggest that intelligent life is probably rare in our galaxy and that the enthusiastic optimism of SETI proponents should be reined in.

In the 1960s and early 1970s, the business of listening to the radio whispers of the stars and hoping to pick up signals emanating from some alien civilization was still new. Few scientists held visions equal to Frank Drake, one of the pioneers of the search for extraterrestrial intelligence (SETI) field. Drake and scientists like him utilize radio telescopes—large, dish-like radio receiver-antenna combinations—to scan radio frequencies (channels) for signal patterns that would indicate that the signal was transmitted by an intelligent being. In his early days, Drake worked with relatively small and weak telescopes out of listening posts that he had established in Green Bank, West Virginia, and Arecibo, Puerto Rico. See Carl Sagan and Frank Drake, "The Search for Extraterrestrial Intelligence," *Scientific American* (May 1975) and Frank Drake and Dava Sobel, *Is Anyone Out There? The Scientific Search for Extraterrestrial Intelligence* (Delacorte Press, 1992).

There have been more than 50 searches for extraterrestrial radio signals since 1960. The earliest ones were very limited. Later searches have been more ambitious, culminating in the 10-year program known as the High Resolution Microwave Survey (HRMS). The HRMS, which began on Columbus Day of

1992, uses several radio telescopes and massive computers to scan 15 million radio frequencies per second. New technologies and techniques continue to make the search more efficient. See Seth Shostak, "SETI's Prospects Are Bright," *Mercury* (September/October 2002), and Monte Ross, "The New Search for E.T." *IEEE Spectrum* (November 2006).

At the outset, many people thought—and many still think—that SETI has about as much scientific relevance as searches for Loch Ness Monsters and Abominable Snowmen. However, to Drake and his colleagues, it seems inevitable that with so many stars in the sky, there must be other worlds with life upon them, and some of that life must be intelligent and have a suitable technology and the desire to search for alien life too.

Writing about SETI in the September–October 1991 issue of *The Humanist,* physicist Shawn Carlson compares visiting the National Shrine of the Immaculate Conception in Washington, D.C., to looking up at the stars and "wondering if, in all [the] vastness [of the starry sky], there is anybody out there looking in our direction. . . . [A]re there planets like ours peopled with creatures like us staring into their skies and wondering about the possibilities of life on other worlds, perhaps even trying to contact it?" That is, SETI arouses in its devotees an almost religious sense of mystery and awe, a craving for contact with the *other.* Success would open up a universe of possibilities, add immensely to human knowledge, and perhaps even provide solutions to problems that our interstellar neighbors have already defeated.

SETI also arouses strong objections, partly because it challenges human uniqueness. Many scientists have objected that life-bearing worlds such as Earth must be exceedingly rare because the conditions that make them suitable for life as we know it—composition and temperature—are so narrowly defined. Others have objected that there is no reason whatsoever to expect that evolution would produce intelligence more than once or that, if it did, the species would be similar enough to humans to allow communication. Still others say that even if intelligent life is common, technology may not be so common, or technology may occupy such a brief period in the life of an intelligent species that there is virtually no chance that it would coincide with Earth scientists' current search. Whatever their reasons, SETI detractors agree that listening for extraterrestrial signals is futile. Ben Zuckerman, "Why SETI Will Fail," *Mercury* (September/October 2002), argues that the simple fact that we have not been visited by extraterrestrials indicates that there are probably very few ET civilizations and SETI is therefore futile.

In the selections that follow, Seth Shostak defends SETI and argues that if the assumptions behind the search are reasonable, the search will succeed, perhaps within the next generation. Peter Schenkel, a retired political scientist, argues that SETI's lack of success to date, coupled with the apparent uniqueness of Earth's history and suitability for life, suggests that intelligent life is probably rare in our galaxy. It is time, he says, "to dampen excessive SETI euphoria and to adopt a . . . stand, compatible with facts."

YES

Seth Shostak

When Will We Detect the Extraterrestrials?

Abstract

It has been more than four decades since the first, modern SETI experiment. Many hundreds of star systems have been observed in the radio over wide bandwidth and with impressive sensitivity, and the entire sky has been surveyed in a more restricted mode several times. Optical SETI experiments are underway, and have already scrutinized several thousand nearby stars, looking for nanosecond light pulses.

Still, there is no confirmed signal detection. Given the anticipated improvement in both telescopes and digital electronics applied to SETI, what is the time scale for making such a discovery? In this paper we investigate the rate of stellar surveillance by targeted radio SETI experiments for the foreseeable future, and conclude that it is likely that—if the principal assumptions underlying modern SETI are reasonable—a detection will occur within a single generation.

Introduction

When will SETI succeed is a perennial question which does not, and some would say, cannot, engender reliable answers.* The search has a long history compared with historical exploration efforts, which were typically a decade or so in length—Columbus' four voyages extended over a dozen years, and Cook's reconnaissance of the South Pacific (three voyages) spanned eleven years. In contrast, the first SETI experiment was more than forty years ago (Project Ozma). As has been pointed out, the searches since 1960 have been quite intermittent, and amount to less than two years of continuous observation at sensitivities and spectral coverage comparable to today's experiments. Nonetheless, many SETI researchers are inclined to make the Copernican assumption that our temporal location in the search for signals is mediocre,

---

*To avoid the ambiguity which some researchers ascribe to the word "success" in SETI, we define it as the unambiguous detection of an artificial, extraterrestrial signal.

and that another few decades, or thereabouts, will be necessary for success. Others speak of SETI as a multi-generational project, and encourage a mind-set sympathetic to the "long haul." It is the author's own experience that the most common response by scientists engaged in SETI, when queried as to how long success will take, is to answer with the approximate number of years until their own retirement.

Given the myriad uncertainties of the SETI enterprise, is there any reason to believe that a better prediction could be made, or are such "gut feelings" the best we can hope for? It is the purpose of this brief paper to offer a some-what more quantitative estimate of when SETI might succeed, based on typical assumptions made by the SETI researchers themselves. Of course, these assumptions could be grossly in error, but the merit of this approach is that the timescales presented here are congruent with SETI's own postulates. To the extent that the arguments made for conducting today's SETI experiments are credible, then the sort of predictions presented here of when a signal might be found are similarly worthy of consideration.

Approach

As for any discovery enterprise, the time required to find a sought-for phe-nomenon depends on (a) the frequency with which it occurs, and (b) the speed of the reconnaissance. For SETI searches, the first is, crudely, the num-ber of contemporaneous signal generators (transmitters, if you will), and the second is the rapidity with which our telescopes can survey the sky (or, for targeted search strategies, likely locations on the sky) using spectral coverage and sensitivity adequate to find one of these transmitters.

Since the inception of modern SETI, reckoning the number of celestial transmitters has been done using the Drake Equation. The equation computes N, the number of contemporaneous, galactic transmitting sites, as the prod-uct of the rate at which intelligent societies arise and the length of time they remain in the transmitting state. As noted, these computations are restricted to our own Galaxy, on the assumption that intelligence in other galaxies would not have the incentive to send signals (or provoke replies) that would be millions of years in transit. In addition, some note that intergalactic messaging, even from nearby nebulae, would require untenable power levels: hundreds to millions of times higher than required for communication over typical intragalactic distances. These arguments have not been considered overly persuasive however, since a number of searches for extragalactic transmitters have been made.

Of possibly greater consequence is the Drake Equation's assumption that searches should be directed to stellar systems capable of hosting Earth-like worlds. Interstellar travel is difficult but not impossible, and it's unclear whether truly advanced intelligences would remain exclusively, or even princi-pally, confined to the solar system of their birth. If migration away from the home star is common to technological intelligence, then targeted SETI searches, which are the most sensitive, could miss the most advanced (and possibly the most easily detected) transmitters.

Number of Stars to Search

With these caveats in mind, we begin by taking a conservative position, and consider the number of (galactic) transmitters predicted by Drake's Equation. It is not the provenance of this paper to evaluate the individual terms of this equation; we are only interested in their product, N. A compilation of published estimates assembled by Dick yields a (logarithmic) average of $N \sim 10^5 - 10^6$. (We note that one of Dick's compiled estimates is $N = 0.003$, which, if correct, would mean that it is overwhelmingly likely that there is nothing and no one to find. Among the SETI research community, this is obviously a minority view.) Drake himself is more conservative, and suggests $N \sim 10^4$. In the discussion that follows, we adopt a range of values for N of 10^4 to 10^6.

With this range estimate for N, and assuming a disk galaxy with diameter of ~90,000 light-years and half-power disk thickness (locally) of ~1,000 light-years, we can conclude that the nearest transmitter is 200–1,000 light-years away.

How many suitable targets lie within this distance? There are $\sim 10^{11}$ stars in the Galaxy. Traditionally, 5–10% of these have been considered preferred candidates for harboring intelligence: these comprise, roughly speaking, single F, G or K-type stars at least a few billion years old. The major groups excluded by this historical choice include multiple stars (approximately half of all stars) and M-dwarfs (about 90% of stars). However, recent research has shown that both close double stars and those that are widely separated (tens of AU or more) could host planets in stable orbits. M-dwarfs are presently being reconsidered as SETI targets. It might soon be concluded that only short-lived, massive stars (types A and earlier) can be reliably excluded *ab initio* as SETI targets. Since these comprise only ~1% of all stars, this would mean that virtually the entire stellar complement of the Milky Way would qualify for SETI scrutiny.

However, foreseeable astronomical discoveries may once again narrow the range of interesting stars. The current search for extrasolar planets has shown that ~10% of solar-type stars have detectable worlds, but these are skewed in favor of stars that have higher metallicities. This suggests an obvious target selection criterion. In addition, new space-based interferometers (e.g., NASA's Terrestrial Planet Finder and ESA's Darwin) proposed for deployment in a decade's time will allow not only the direct imaging of Earth-sized worlds, but spectral analyses of their atmospheres. Such techniques could tell us not only which star systems host suitable planets, but could pinpoint worlds that evidence the spectral signatures of life. And, of course, it's still possible that a deeper investigation of the conditions of planets around M-dwarfs could serve to reliably eliminate this very numerous stellar class from consideration.

Consequently, and mindful of this expected progress in our understanding of extrasolar planets, we assume that: (1) for the present decade, all galactic stars remain qualified SETI targets. (2) In the following decade, half of all unobserved stars can be eliminated *a priori* from our SETI target lists, and

(3) in the third decade, 90% of unobserved stars can be eliminated. This is, we propose, a conservative projection of progress in choosing which star systems to observe. Indeed, today's experiments often have more restrictive target lists than we are projecting for 2020 and beyond.

Rate of Target Scrutiny

Having estimated (a) the number of galactic transmitters, and (b) the fraction of star systems that need to be searched, we need only consider the rate at which the search is conducted in order to arrive at our goal: an estimate for when a signal will be found.

We first consider radio searches. Note that large swaths of the celestial sphere have been examined in so-called Sky Survey SETI experiments. The failure (so far) of these experiments to discover a signal, assuming such signals exist, could be due to (a) insufficient sensitivity (note that such sky surveys are typically at least an order-of-magnitude less sensitive than targeted searches, which means that the volume of sky sampled at any given sensitivity level is less by a factor of >60), (b) inadequate spectral coverage, or (c) an inability to monitor specific locations for more than a few seconds, with no facility for making immediate follow-up observations. This precludes detection of all but fully continuous signals.

Targeted searches moderate these shortcomings, but have the disadvantage of being a very slow reconnaissance. This is principally due to the fact that the large telescopes favored for SETI research are only intermittently available. The total number of star systems surveyed to date by the SETI Institute's premier radio search, Project Phoenix (which uses the Arecibo radio telescope), is ~500.

This slow pace of targeted radio searches is about to change. The Allen Telescope Array (ATA), a joint project of the SETI Institute and the University of California at Berkeley, will be a highly sophisticated radio antenna that can be used full-time to make SETI observations. It is anticipated that this instrument will be completed within the current decade. This immediately increases by an order of magnitude the amount of telescope time available for the Institute's targeted searches. In addition, an international consortium is planning the construction of an even larger telescope, the Square Kilometer Array (SKA). If built, this instrument could also be partially dedicated to SETI observations. For the purposes of this paper, we assume that this instrument will double the speed of SETI reconnaissance beginning in the (rather uncertain) year of 2015.

Project Phoenix surveys approximately 50–60 stellar systems annually. The ATA will not only have the benefit of ten times as much observing time as this effort, but will also incorporate multiple beams that allow the simultaneous observation of at least three star systems. In addition, efficiencies in follow-up and wider instantaneous spectral coverage will add at least another factor of 2–3 speed improvement. At a minimum, we can say that, once completed, the ATA will increase the rapidity with which nearby stars are checked for signals by at least two orders of magnitude. In its first year, it will observe considerably more stellar systems than the total investigated by Project

Phoenix. We will (conservatively) assume this number to be 1,000 systems, applicable to the year 2006.

The ATA is conceived as an instrument whose capabilities can be expanded as the cost of digital computation continues to decline. According to Moore's Law, a fact-of-life in the field of computing hardware for three decades, the density of transistors on commercially available chips doubles every 18 months. In more practical terms, this means that the cost of computing is halved each 1-1/2 years. The speed (not necessarily the efficacy) of SETI experiments has historically followed this law. . . .

We can expect, therefore, that at least the speed of stellar scrutiny using the ATA will grow at this exponential rate, at least so long as Moore's Law continues to hold. How long might that be? Various pundits, including Moore himself, point to the fact that the further exploitation of silicon technology will likely hit a physical "wall" at which the dimensions of the transistors become nearly molecular in size. An additional (and perhaps more formidable) barrier to the continued reign of this law is the economic cost of new fabrication facilities and even of the chips themselves. On the other hand, foreseeing this technological barrier has stimulated research into optical and quantum computing, and these approaches are expected by many to not only sustain the pace of improvement, but perhaps to accelerate it.

For the purposes of this paper, we adopt widespread industry predictions that Moore's Law in its current form will continue to hold until 2015. Thereafter, we conservatively assume a decrease by half: doubling of computational power per dollar will take 36 months, rather than 18. The speed of SETI reconnaissance is postulated to follow this technological growth.

Having considered at some length the speed and expected improvements in radio SETI searches, we note that several optical SETI experiments are also underway. These look for short ($\leq 10^{-9}$ sec) bursts of photons that could be produced by, for example, a pulsed laser deliberately targeting our solar system. While optical SETI experiments are still relatively new, several thousand star systems have already been observed, and an instrument dedicated to an optical sky survey of the two-thirds of the sky visible from the northern hemisphere is currently under construction.

Despite these encouraging developments, we will not incorporate them into our estimate of when extraterrestrial intelligence will be found. This is because of the very real possibility that optical signals might be either highly intermittent or sent to only small numbers of targets. However, with not-unreasonable assumptions, optical SETI might succeed very soon. Consider a simple example: suppose that an extraterrestrial beacon is set up to serially target all $\sim 10^{11}$ galactic star systems, briefly illuminating their inner solar systems with a burst of nanosecond pulses once every 24 hours. (This brute-force approach would provide each star with a daily kilobit of data, which might be adequate to serve as a "pointer" to other information being served up by this transmitting society.) The observation time per beam for the planned Harvard-Princeton optical sky survey is ≥ 48 seconds, so that the chance of a detection for every sweep of the northern sky (estimated to take 150 days) is $\sim 3 \times 10^{-4}$ N, or >1 for all our estimates for N.

This sunny assessment assumes that all transmitters are detectable by the sky survey. In fact, optical searches for signals from star systems at great distance need to be sensitive in the infrared to defeat the attenuating effect of interstellar dust. Such systems are not yet operational, as they must be space-based. However, there is no technical reason to doubt that they could be deployed within a decade or two. On the other hand, very low transmitter duty cycles may dictate that an effective optical SETI search will require the use of multiple, or possibly all-sky, detectors. Given the newness of optical SETI, and the lack of a body of historical "assumptions" regarding optical signaling, we will not factor such searches into our estimate of when a SETI detection will be made. This is obviously a conservative approach, assuming that optical SETI has any chance at all to succeed.

When a Detection Will Take Place

We now have in hand the requisite parameters to estimate the likely date of a (radio) SETI detection. . . . [We can plot] the number of targeted star systems observed using the ATA with, eventually, the addition of the SKA. . . . [We can then calculate] the volume of space (specified by a maximum distance) in which we've observed all suitable target star systems [and date when we will have observed enough star systems to expect successful SETI. If $N = 10^6$, the date will be about 2015. If $N = 10^4$, the date will be about 2027.] . . .

We remark that this span of dates for a predicted SETI detection extends less than two dozen years forward. Although SETI searches are sometimes referred to as multigenerational projects, our estimate suggests that this isn't the case: success is within the foreseeable future. Among other things, this justifies the efforts being made to plan for a detection, as well as to consider society's likely reaction and what would be a suitable response (if any).

We have tried to make conservative assumptions in this presentation. In particular, a reconnaissance of extrasolar planets, which would chart out their size, orbit, and whether or not they evidence spectral biomarkers, will eventually tightly focus the interest of SETI researchers, reducing (substantially, one assumes) the number of suitable target systems. We have only made a crude correction for this highly likely development. We have also made no assumption that SETI observations, particularly those that reach beyond a few hundred light-years, will concentrate their attentions on the galactic plane, thereby increasing the efficiency of the search.

While we have reckoned on an exponential improvement in technology that governs SETI search speed over the next two-and-a-half decades, this extrapolation is based on four decades in which this has been demonstrably true. To be on the safe side, we have assumed a slowing of this growth beginning in 2015. Finally, we have taken no account of the likelihood that a detection will be made with radio sky surveys, or using optical SETI techniques.

On the other hand, there are many possible reasons why our assessment that a detection will be made within a generation might be wrong. We have not considered the luminosity function or duty cycle of extraterrestrial transmitters, but have instead assumed that the N transmitters estimated by the Drake

Equation are all detectable by the ATA and SKA. We have not speculated on the possibility that the frequency coverage of our telescopes is inadequate, nor that the signal types to which they are sensitive are the wrong ones. And, indeed, we do not consider that physical laws of which we are still unaware might dictate a completely different approach to interstellar signaling. And, of course, our range of estimates for N are only considered opinion—and some of that opinion [states] that *no* other contemporary, sentient galactic societies exist.

Nonetheless, we reiterate that the intention of this exercise is to improve upon existing "gut feeling" speculation as to when SETI might expect a detection. While there are a myriad uncertainties attendant upon our estimate that this will occur within two dozen years, we have made this prediction using the assumptions adopted by the SETI research community itself. This community builds equipment and uses strategies that it reckons are adequate to find an extraterrestrial signal. It does this based on more than four decades of thought as to how best to prove the presence of extraterrestrial sentience. If such analyses are well grounded, then such proof will not be long in coming.

Peter Schenkel  **NO**

SETI Requires a Skeptical Reappraisal

The possible existence of extraterrestrial intelligence (ETI) has always stirred the imagination of man. Greek philosophers speculated about it. Giordano Bruno was burnt on the stake in Rome in 1600, mainly [for] positing the likelihood of other inhabited worlds in the universe. Kant and Laplace were also convinced of the multiplicity of worlds similar to ours. In the latter part of the nineteenth century Flammarion charmed vast circles with his books on the plurality of habitable worlds. But all these ideas were mainly philosophical considerations or pure speculations. It was only in the second half of the twentieth century that the Search for Extraterrestrial Intelligence (SETI) became a scientifically underpinned endeavor. Since the late 1950s distinguished scientists have conducted research, attempting to receive intelligent signals or messages from space via radio-telescopes. Hundreds of amateur astronomers, members of the SETI-League in dozens of countries, are scanning the sky, trying to detect evidence of intelligent life elsewhere in our galaxy. SETI pioneers, such as Frank Drake and Carl Sagan, held the stance that the Milky Way is teeming with a large number of advanced civilizations. However, the many search projects to date have not succeeded, and this daring prediction remains unverified. New scientific insights suggest the need for a more cautious approach and a revision of the overly optimistic considerations.

The standard argument for the existence of a multiplicity of intelligent life runs like this: There are about 200 to 300 billion stars in our galaxy and probably hundreds of millions, maybe even billions of planets in our galaxy. Many of these planets are likely to be located in the so-called "habitable zone" in relation [to] their star, enjoying Earth-favorable conditions for the evolution of life. The physical laws, known to us, apply also to the cosmos, and far-away stellar formations are composed of the same elements as our solar system. Therefore, it is assumed, many should possess water and a stable atmosphere, considered to be basic requisites for the development of life. Such planets must have experienced geological and biological processes similar to those on Earth, leading to the development of primitive life organisms. Then, in the course of time, following a similar course of Darwin's theory of natural selection, these evolved into more complex forms, some eventually developing cognitive capacities and—as in our case—higher intelligence.

In other words, it is maintained, our solar system, Earth, and its evolution are not exceptional cases, but something very common in our Milky Way galaxy.

Consequently it must be populated by a huge number of extraterrestrial civilizations, many of them older and more advanced than ours.

Considering the enormous number of stars and planets, these seem like fair and legitimate assumptions. It indeed appears unlikely that intelligence should have evolved only on our planet. If many of these civilizations are scientifically and technologically superior to us, contact with them would give mankind a boost in many ways.

These optimistic views are based mainly on the famous Drake formula. . . . It considers the formation of stars in the galaxy, the fraction of stars with planetary systems, the number of planets ecologically suited for life, the fraction of these planets, on which life and intelligent life evolves, and those reaching a communicative stage and the length of time of technical civilizations. On the basis of this formula it was estimated that a million advanced civilizations probably exist in the galaxy. The nearest one should be at a distance of about 200 to 300 light-years from Earth. German astronomer Sebastian von Hoerner estimated a number between ten thousand and ten million such civilizations.

But because of many new insights and results of research in a number of scientific fields, ranging from paleontology, geology, biology to astronomy, I believe this formula is incomplete and must be revised. The early optimistic estimates are no longer tenable. A more realistic and sober view is required.

I by no means intend to discredit SETI; the search for extraterrestrial intelligent life is a legitimate scientific endeavor. But it seems prudent to demystify this interesting subject, and to reformulate its claims on a new level, free of the romantic flair that adorns it.

Years ago, I readily admit, I myself was quite taken in by the allegations that intelligence is a very common phenomenon in the galaxy. In books, articles, and on radio and television I advocated the idea that our world, beset by problems, could learn a lot from a civilization more advanced than ours. But, in the meantime, I became convinced that a more skeptical attitude would do reality better justice. There are probably only a few such civilizations in the galaxy, if any at all. The following considerations buttress this rather pessimistic appraisal.

First of all, since project OZMA I in 1959 by Frank Drake, about a hundred radio-magnetic and other searches were conducted in the U.S. and in other countries, and a considerable part of our sky was scanned thoroughly and repeatedly, but it remained disappointingly silent. In forty-six years not a single artificial intelligent signal or message from outer space was received. Some specialists try to downplay this negative result, arguing that so far only a small part of the entire spectrum has been covered, and that more time and more sophisticated equipment is required for arriving at a definite conclusion. Technological and economic criteria may thwart the possibility of extraterrestrial civilizations beaming signals into space over long stretches of time, without knowing where to direct their signals. Or, they may use communication methods unknown to us. Another explanation is that advanced ETI may lack interest in contacting other intelligences, especially those less developed. The argument of the Russian rocket expert Konstantin Tsiolkovski is often quoted: "Absence of evidence is not evidence of absence."

But neither of these arguments, which attempt to explain why we have not received a single intelligent signal from space, is convincing. True, future search projects may strike pay dirt and register the reception of a signal of verified artificial origin. But as long as no such evidence is forthcoming, the possibility of achieving success must be considered remote. If a hundred searches were unsuccessful, it is fair to deduce that estimates of a million or many thousands ETI are unsustainable propositions. As long as no breakthrough occurs, the probability of contact with ETI is near to zero. The argument that advanced extraterrestrials may not be interested in contact with other intelligences is also—as I will show—highly implausible.

Second, as recent research results demonstrate, many more factors and conditions than those considered by the Drake formula need to be taken into account. The geologist Peter D. Ward and the astronomer Donald Brownlee present in their book *Rare Earth* a series of such aspects, which turn the optimistic estimates of ETI upside down.

According to their reasoning, the old assumption that our solar system and Earth are quite common phenomena in the galaxy needs profound revision. On the contrary, the new insights suggest, we are much more special than thought. The evolution of life forms and eventually of intelligent life on Earth was due to a large number of very special conditions and developments, many of a coincidental nature. I'll mention only some that seem particularly important: The age, size, and composition of our sun, the location of Earth and inclination of its axis to it, the existence of water, a stable oxygen-rich atmosphere and temperature over long periods of time—factors considered essential for the evolution of life—and the development of a carbon-based chemistry. Furthermore an active interior and the existence of plate tectonics form the majestic mountain ridges like the Alps, the Himalayas and the Andes, creating different ecological conditions, propitious for the proliferation of a great variety of species. Also the existence of the Moon, Jupiter, and Saturn (as shields for the bombardment of comets and meteorites during the early stages of Earth). Also the repeated climatic changes, long ice ages, and especially the numerous and quite fortuitous catastrophes, causing the extinction of many species, like the one 65 million years ago, which led to the disappearance of dinosaurs but opened the way for more diversified and complex life forms.

Though first primitive life forms on Earth, the prokaryotic bacteria, evolved relatively rapidly, only about 500 million years after the cooling off of Earth's crust and the end of the dense bombardment of meteorites and comets, they were the only life forms during the first two billion years of Earth's 4.6-billion-year history. Mammals—including apes and man—developed much later, only after the extinction of the dinosaurs 65 million years ago. The first human-like being, the Proconsul, emerged in the Miocene Period, just about 18 million years ago. The Australopithecus, our antecessor, dates only 5 to 6 million years. In other words, it took almost 4 billion years, or more than 96 percent of the age of Earth, for intelligence to evolve—an awfully long time, even on the cosmic clock.

In this regard we should note also the caveat of the distinguished biologist Ernst Mayr, who underscored the enormous complexity of human DNA and RNA and their functions for the production of proteins, the basic building blocks of life. He estimated that the likelihood that similar biological developments may have occurred elsewhere in the universe was nil.

The upshot of these considerations is the following: Because of the very special geological, biological, and other conditions which propitiated the evolution of life and intelligence on Earth, similar developments in our galaxy are probably very rare. Primitive life forms, Ward and Brownlee conclude, may exist on planets of other stellar systems, but intelligent life, as ours, is probably very rare, if it exists at all.

Third is the so-called "Fermi Paradox" another powerful reason suggesting a skeptical evaluation of the multiplicity of intelligence in the galaxy. Italian physicist Enrico Fermi posed the annoying question, "If so many highly developed ETIs are out there, as SETI specialists claim, why haven't they contacted us?" I already expressed great doubt about some of the explanations given [for] this paradox. Here I need to focus on two more. The first refers to the supposed lack of interest of advanced aliens to establish contact with other intelligent beings. This argument seems to me particularly untrustworthy. I refer to a Norwegian book, which explains why the Vikings undertook dangerous voyages to far-away coasts in precarious vessels. "One reason," it says, "is fame, another curiosity, and a third, gain!" If the Vikings, driven by the desire to discover the unknown, reached America a thousand years ago with a primitive technology, if we—furthermore—a still scientifically and technically young civilization, search for primitive life on other planets of the solar system and their moons, it is incredible that higher developed extraterrestrial intelligences would not be spurred by likewise interests and yearnings. One of the fundamental traits of intelligence is its unquenchable intellectual curiosity and urge to penetrate the unknown. Elder civilizations, our peers in every respect, must be imbued by the same daring and scrutinizing spirit, because if they are not, they could not have achieved their advanced standards.

A second argument often posited is that distances between stars are too great for interstellar travel. But this explanation also stands on shaky ground. Even our scientifically and technically adolescent civilization is exploring space and sending probes—the Voyager crafts—which someday may reach other stellar systems. We are still far from achieving velocities, near the velocity of light, necessary for interstellar travel. But some scientists predict that in 200 or 300 years, maybe even earlier, we are likely to master low "c" velocities, and once we reach them, our civilization will send manned exploratory expeditions to the nearest stars. Automatic unmanned craft may be the initial attempts. But I am convinced that nothing will impede the desire of man to see other worlds with his own eyes, to touch their soil and to perform research that unmanned probes would not be able to perform. Evidently, civilizations tens of thousands or millions of years in our advance will have reached near c velocities, and they will be able to explore a considerable part of the galaxy. Advanced ETI civilizations would engage in such explorations not only out of scientific curiosity, but in their own interest, for instance for spreading out and finding new habitats for their growing population, or because of the need to abandon their planet due to hazards from their star, and also because with the help of other civilizations it may confront dangers, lurking in the universe, more successfully than alone. The Fermi Paradox should therefore put us on guard, and foster a sound skepticism. Lack of interest in meeting a civilization such as ours is the least plausible reason why we have not heard from ETI.

A little mental experiment illustrates this point. Carl Sagan held once that intelligent aliens would visit Earth at least once every thousand years. But such visits have not taken place. Even extending this period to a million years, we fare no better. Let us assume an extraterrestrial craft landed on Earth any time during the era of the dinosaurs, lasting about 140 million years. It is only logical to assume the aliens would have returned at reasonable intervals to study our world and these fascinating animals, but also to find out if any one of them evolved the capability of reasoning, higher math, and building a civilization. There would have been reason for much surmise. According to paleontologists, Drake stresses, the dinosaur sauronithoides was endowed with such a potential. It was a dinosaur resembling a bird of our size and weight and possessing a mass of brain well above average, and, Drake speculates, if it had survived for an additional ten or twenty million years, it might have evolved into the first intelligent being on Earth. But it didn't happen, because the dinosaurs went extinct due to a cosmic catastrophe. When *Homo australopithecus*, then *Homo faber* and *habilis*, and lastly *Homo sapiens* evolved, shouldn't that have provoked on the part of visiting extraterrestrials a high level of interest? But no such visits are recorded. Only a few mythological, undocumented and highly suspect accounts of alleged visiting aliens exist. It is fair to assume, if advanced aliens had visited Earth during the past 200 million or, at least, during the past 16 million years, they would have left some durable, indestructible and recognizable mark, probably on the moon. But nothing has been detected. The most likely explanation? No such visits took place! There are no advanced extraterrestrial civilizations anywhere in our vicinity. If they existed, they already would have responded to our world's television signals, reaching some 60 light-years into space—another reason invalidating the claim that our galaxy is teeming with intelligence.

Another argument supporting the skeptical point of view sustained here is the fact that none of the detected planets around other stars comes close to having conditions apt for creating and sustaining life. Since Michel Mayor's Swiss group discovered the first planet outside our solar system around the star 51 Pegasi ten years ago, about 130 other planets have been identified within a distance of 200 light-years. Research results show that most are of gaseous composition, some many times the size of Jupiter, some very close to their stars, very hot and with extremely rapid orbital cycles. So far, not one presents conditions favorable for the development of even the most primitive forms of life, not to speak of more complex species. Again it may be argued that only a very tiny fraction of planets were surveyed and future research might strike upon a suitable candidate. This may well be, and I would certainly welcome it. But so far the evidence fails to nourish optimistic expectations. The conditions in our universe are not as favorable for the evolution of life as optimists like to think.

Even if water or fossils of microorganisms should be found underneath the surface of Mars, the importance of such a finding for the theory of a multiplicity of inhabited worlds would be insignificant. Some astronomers think that Titan, the famous moon of Saturn, may have an ocean, possibly of methane. Primitive life forms may exist in it, but this remains to be seen. Even if it does, the evolutionary path from such primitive forms to complex life as human beings is—as we have seen—a long one, studded with a unique sequence of chance and catastrophes.

I am not claiming that we are probably the only intelligent species in our galaxy. Nor do I suggest that SETI activities are a waste of time and money. Though, so far, they have failed to obtain evidence for the existence of ETI, they enrich man's knowledge about the cosmos in many ways. They helped develop sophisticated search techniques, and they contribute decisively to the perception of man's cosmic destiny. Carl Sagan and Frank Drake, the two most distinguished pioneers of SETI, did groundbreaking work. That their efforts and those of other dedicated SETI experts on behalf of this great cause are tinged with a dash of too optimistic expectation is understandable and profoundly human.

However, in the interest of science and sound skepticism, I believe it is time to take the new findings and insights into account, to dampen excessive SETI euphoria and to adopt a more pragmatic and down-to-earth stand, compatible with facts. We should quietly admit that the early estimates—that there may be a million, a hundred thousand, or ten thousand advanced extraterrestrial civilizations in our galaxy—may no longer be tenable. There might not be a hundred, not even ten such civilizations. The optimistic estimates were fraught with too many imponderables and speculative appraisals. What is required is to make contact with a single extraterrestrial intelligence, obtaining irrefutable, thoroughly verified evidence, either via electromagnetic or optical waves or via physical contact, that we are not the only intelligent species in the cosmos. Maybe an alien spacecraft, attracted by our signals, will decide to visit us some day, as I surmised in my novel *Contact: Are We Ready For It?* I would be the first one to react to such a contact event with great delight and satisfaction. The knowledge that we are not alone in the vast realm of the cosmos, and that it will be possible to establish a fruitful dialogue with other, possibly more advanced intelligent beings would mark the biggest event in human history. It would open the door to fantastic perspectives.

But SETI activities so far do not justify this hope. They recommend a more realistic and sober view. Considering the negative search results, the creation of excessive expectations is only grist to the mill of the naysayers—for instance, members of Congress who question the scientific standing of SETI, imputing to it wishful thinking, and denying it financial support. This absolutely negative approach to SETI is certainly wrong, because contrary to the UFO hoax, SETI (as UCLA space scientist Mark Moldwin stressed in a recent issue of this magazine) is based on solid scientific premises and considerations. But exaggerated estimates fail to conform to realities, as they are seen today, tending to backfire and create disappointment and a turning away from this fascinating scientific endeavor. The dream of mankind to find brethren in space may yet be fulfilled. If it is not, man should not feel sorry for his uniqueness. Rather that circumstance should boost the gratitude for his existence and his sense of responsibility for making the most of it.

POSTSCRIPT

Will the Search for Extraterrestrial Life Ever Succeed?

If the universe is full of intelligent species, why haven't they shown up yet?

Are we in fact alone? Or first? Are the conditions that lead to life and intelligence rare? Are there aliens living in disguise amongst us? Or are we quarantined? Reservationed? Zooed? Or maybe there's nobody there at all—not even us! (Sure, that could be it—if we are just simulations in some cosmic computer.) In *Where Is Everybody? Fifty Solutions to the Fermi Paradox and the Problem of Extraterrestrial Life* (Copernicus Books, 2002), Stephen Webb describes Fermi and his paradox in detail and offers a variety of answers that have been suggested—most seriously, some a bit tongue-in-cheek—for why the search has not succeeded. His own opinion is on the pessimistic side.

The SETI community, however, remains convinced that their effort is worthwhile. *SETI 2020: A Roadmap for the Search for Extraterrestrial Intelligence* (SETI Press, SETI Institute, 2002) is the report of the Search for Extraterrestrial Intelligence (SETI) Science and Technology Working Group, which between 1997 and 1999 developed a plan for the SETI effort through 2020, which will center on multi-antenna arrays, improved multi-channel scanning, and initial efforts to look for infrared and optical signals. The book provides plentiful details, as well as a brief survey of SETI history, the science that backs up the idea that SETI is worth attempting, and the technology that makes SETI even remotely possible.

Naomi Lubick, "An Ear to the Stars," *Scientific American* (November 2002), describes the SETI career of Jill Tarter and discusses new technology being developed for the search. The Terrestrial Planet Finder is discussed by Ray Jayawardhana, "Searching for Alien Earths," *Astronomy* (June 2003). The continuing determination and optimism of the SETI community is described by Richard A. Kerr, "No Din of Alien Chatter in Our Neighborhood," *Science* (February 20, 2004). See also Seth Shostak, "Listening for a Whisper," *Astronomy* (September 2004).

What if SETI succeeds? Frank Drake noted in *Is Anyone Out There? The Scientific Search for Extraterrestrial Intelligence* (Delacorte Press, 1992) that positive results would have to be reported to everyone, at once, in order to prevent attempts to suppress or monopolize the discovery. Albert A. Harrison, "Confirmation of ETI: Initial Organizational Response," *Acta Astronautica* (August 2003), focuses on the need for a response to success but he is skeptical that an effective response is possible; he says, "Foresight and advance preparation are among the steps that organizations may take to prepare for contact, but conservative values, skepticism towards SETI, and competing organizational priorities make serious preparation unlikely." Should our response include sending an answer back to the source of whatever radio signals we detect? H. Paul Schuch, "The Search for Extraterrestrial Intelligence," *Futurist* (May/June 2003), suggests that there may be dangers in such a move. Those dangers are addressed by Ivan Almar and H. Paul Schuch in "The San Marino Scale: A New Analytical Tool for Assessing Transmission Risk," *Acta Astronautica* (January 2007). A few nonscientists have also begun to consider the implications of successful contact. See, for instance, Thomas Hoffman, "Exomissiology: The Launching of Exotheology," *Dialog: A Journal of Theology* (Winter 2004).

Have the results of SETI to date been totally blank? Researchers have found nothing that justified any claim of success, but there have been a few "tantalizing signals." T. Joseph W. Lazio and Robert Naeye discuss them in "Hello? Are You Still There?" *Mercury* (May/June 2003).

ISSUE 14

Is "Manned Space Travel" a Delusion?

YES: Neil deGrasse Tyson, from "Delusions of Space Enthusiasts," *Natural History* (November 2006)

NO: George W. Bush, from "President Bush Announces New Vision for Space Exploration Program," Office of the Press Secretary (January 14, 2004)

ISSUE SUMMARY

YES: Astronomer Neil deGrasse Tyson argues that large, expensive projects such as space exploration are driven only by war, greed, and the celebration of power. The dream of colonizing space became a delusion as soon as we beat the Russians to the Moon, and it remains so.

NO: President George W. Bush argues for his vision of renewed and expanded manned space travel because it improves our lives and lifts the national spirit.

T he dream of conquering space has a long history. The pioneers of rocketry— the Russian Konstantin Tsiolkovsky (1857–1935) and the American Robert H. Goddard (1882–1945)—both dreamed of exploring other worlds, although neither lived long enough to see the first artificial satellite, the Soviet *Sputnik*, go up in 1957. That success sparked a race between America and the Soviet Union to be the first to achieve each step in the progression of space exploration. The next steps were to put dogs (the Soviet Laika was the first), monkeys, chimps, and finally human beings into orbit. Communications, weather, and spy satellites were designed and launched. And on July 20, 1969, the U.S. Project Apollo program landed the first men on the moon.

There were a few more *Apollo* landings, but not many. The United States had achieved its main political goal of beating the Soviets to the moon and, in the minds of the government, demonstrating American superiority. Thereafter, the United States was content to send automated spacecraft (computer-operated robots) to observe Venus, Mars, and the rings of Saturn; to land on Mars and study its soil; and even to carry recordings of Earth's sights and sounds past the distant edge of the solar system, perhaps to be retrieved in the distant future by intelligent life from some other world. (Those recordings are attached to the *Voyager* spacecraft, launched in 1977; published as a combination of CD, CD-ROM, and book, *Murmurs of Earth: The Voyager Interstellar Record,* it is now long out of print.) Humans have not left near-Earth orbit for two decades, even though space technology has continued to develop. The results of this development include communications satellites, space shuttles, space stations, and independent robotic explorers such as the *Mariners* and *Vikings* and—landing on Mars in January 2004—the rovers *Spirit* and *Opportunity* (http://marsrovers. jpl.nasa.gov/overview/).

Why has human space exploration gone no further to date? One reason is that robots are now extremely capable. Although some robot spacecraft have failed partially or completely, there have been many grand successes that have added enormously to humanity's knowledge of Earth and other planets. Another is money: Lifting robotic explorers into space is expensive, but lifting people into space—along with all the food, water, air, and other supplies necessary to keep them alive for the duration of a mission—is much more expensive. And there are many people in government and elsewhere who cry that there are many better ways to spend the money on Earth.

Still another reason for the reduction in human space travel seems to be the fear that astronauts will die in space. This point was emphasized by the explosion on takeoff of the space shuttle *Challenger* in January 1986, which killed seven astronauts and froze the entire shuttle program for over two and a half years, and reinforced by the breakup of *Columbia* on entry February 1, 2003. After the latter event, the public reaction included many calls for an end to such risky, expensive enterprises. See Jerry Grey, "*Columbia*—Aftermath of a Tragedy," *Aerospace America* (March 2003); John Byron, "Is Manned Space Flight Worth It?" *Proceedings* (of the U.S. Naval Institute) (March 2003) (and Richard H. Truly's response in the May issue); and "Manned or Unmanned into Space?" *USA Today* (February 26, 2003), among many others.

In the following selections, astronomer Neil deGrasse Tyson argues that large, expensive projects such as space exploration are driven only by war, greed, and the celebration of power. The dream of colonizing space became a delusion as soon as we beat the Russians to the Moon, and it remains so. The Apollo program was the end of an era, not the beginning that many hoped it would prove. In January 2004, President George W. Bush announced a bold plan to send humans to the Moon and Mars, beginning as soon as 2015. In this speech, he argues for his vision of renewed and expanded manned space travel because it improves our lives and lifts the national spirit.

YES

Neil deGrasse Tyson

Delusions of Space Enthusiasts

Sometimes innovation gets interrupted.

Human ingenuity seldom fails to improve on the fruits of human invention. Whatever may have dazzled everyone on its debut is almost guaranteed to be superseded and, someday, to look quaint.

In 2000 B.C. a pair of ice skates made of polished animal bone and leather thongs was a transportation breakthrough. In 1610 Galileo's eight-power telescope was an astonishing tool of detection, capable of giving the senators of Venice a sneak peek at hostile ships before they could enter the lagoon. In 1887 the one-horsepower Benz Patent Motorwagen was the first commercially produced car powered by an internal combustion engine. In 1946 the thirty-ton, showroom-size ENIAC, with its 18,000 vacuum tubes and 6,000 manual switches, pioneered electronic computing. Today you can glide across roadways on in-line skates, gaze at images of faraway galaxies brought to you by the Hubble Space Telescope, cruise the autobahn in a 600-horsepower roadster, and carry your three-pound laptop to an outdoor café.

Of course, such advances don't just fall from the sky. Clever people think them up. Problem is, to turn a clever idea into reality, somebody has to write the check. And when market forces shift, those somebodies may lose interest and the checks may stop coming. If computer companies had stopped innovating in 1978, your desk might still sport a hundred-pound IBM 5110. If communications companies had stopped innovating in 1973, you might still be schlepping a two-pound, nine-inch-long cell phone. And if in 1968 the U.S. space industry had stopped developing bigger and better rockets to launch humans beyond the Moon, we'd never have surpassed the Saturn V rocket.

Oops!

Sorry about that. We haven't surpassed the Saturn V. The largest, most powerful rocket ever flown by anybody, ever, the thirty-six-story-tall Saturn V was the first and only rocket to launch people from Earth to someplace else in the universe. It enabled every Apollo mission to the Moon from 1969 through 1972, as well as the 1973 launch of Skylab I, the first U.S. space station.

Inspired in part by the successes of the Saturn V and the momentum of the Apollo program, visionaries of the day foretold a future that never came to be: space habitats, Moon bases, and Mars colonies up and running by the 1990s. But funding for the Saturn V evaporated as the Moon missions wound

From *Natural History*, vol. 115, issue 9, November 2006. Copyright © 2006 by Natural History Magazine. Reprinted by permission.

down. Additional production runs were canceled, the manufacturers' special-ized machine tools were destroyed, and skilled personnel had to find work on other projects. Today U.S. engineers can't even build a Saturn V clone. . . .

What cultural forces froze the Saturn V rocket in time and space?

What misconceptions led to the gap between expectation and reality?

Soothsaying tends to come in two flavors: doubt and delirium. It was doubt that led skeptics to declare that the atom would never be split, the sound barrier would never be broken, and people would never want or need computers in their homes. But in the case of the Saturn V rocket, it was delirium that misled futurists into assuming the Saturn V was an auspicious beginning—never considering that it could, instead, be an end.

On December 30, 1900, for its last Sunday paper of the nineteenth cen-tury, the *Brooklyn Daily Eagle* published a sixteen-page supplement headlined "THINGS WILL BE SO DIFFERENT A HUNDRED YEARS HENCE." The contrib-utors—business leaders, military men, pastors, politicians, and experts of every persuasion—imagined what housework, poverty, religion, sanitation, and war would be like in the year 2000. They enthused about the potential of electric-ity and the automobile. There was even a map of the world-to-be, showing an American Federation comprising most of the Western Hemisphere from the lands above the Arctic Circle down to the archipelago of Tierra del Fuego—plus sub-Saharan Africa, the southern half of Australia, and all of New Zealand.

Most of the writers portrayed an expansive future. But not all. George H. Daniels, a man of authority at the New York Central and Hudson River Rail-road, peered into his crystal ball and, boneheadedly predicted:

> It is scarcely possible that the twentieth century will witness improvements in transportation that will be as great as were those of the nineteenth century.

Elsewhere in his article, Daniels envisioned affordable global tourism and the diffusion of white bread to China and Japan. Yet he simply couldn't imagine what might replace steam as the power source for ground transportation, let alone a vehicle moving through the air. Even though he stood on the doorstep of the twentieth century, this manager of the world's biggest railroad system could not see beyond the automobile, tolmhe locomotive, and the steamship. . . .

Three years later, almost to the day, Wilbur and Orville Wright made the first-ever series of powered, controlled, heavier-than-air flights. By 1957 the U.S.S.R. launched the first satellite into Earth orbit. And in 1969 two Americans became the first human beings to walk on the Moon.

Daniels is hardly the only person to have misread the technological future. Even experts who aren't totally deluded can have tunnel vision. On page 13 of the *Eagle's* Sunday supplement, the principal examiner at the U.S. Patent Office, W.W. Townsend, wrote, "The automobile may be the vehicle of the decade, but the air ship is the conveyance of the century." Sounds visionary, until you read further. What he was talking about were blimps and zeppelins. Both Daniels and Townsend, otherwise well-informed citizens of a changing world, were clueless about what tomorrow's technology would bring. . . .

Even the Wrights were guilty of doubt about the future of aviation. In 1901, discouraged by a summer's worth of unsuccessful tests with a glider, Wilbur told Orville it would take another fifty years for someone to fly. Nope: the birth of aviation was just two years away. On the windy, chilly morning of December 17, 1903, starting from a North Carolina sand dune called Kill Devil Hill, Orville was the first to fly the brothers' 600-pound plane through the air. His epochal journey lasted twelve seconds and covered 120 feet—a distance just shy of the wingspan of a Boeing 757.

Judging by what the mathematician, astronomer, and Royal Society gold medalist Simon Newcomb had published just two months earlier, the flights from Kill Devil Hill should never have taken place when they did:

> Quite likely the twentieth century is destined to see the natural forces which will enable us to fly from continent to continent with a speed far exceeding that of the bird.
>
> But when we inquire whether aerial flight is possible in the present state of our knowledge; whether, with such materials as we possess, a combination of steel, cloth and wire can be made which, moved by the power of electricity or steam, shall form a successful flying machine, the outlook may be altogether different.

. . . Some representatives of informed public opinion went even further. The *New York Times* was steeped in doubt just one week before the Wright brothers went aloft in the original Wright Flyer. Writing on December 10, 1903—not about the Wrights but about their illustrious and publicly funded competitor, Samuel E. Langley, an astronomer, physicist, and chief administrator of the Smithsonian Institution—the *Times* declared:

> We hope that Professor Langley will not put his substantial greatness as a scientist in further peril by continuing to waste his time, and the money involved, in further airship experiments. Life is short, and he is capable of services to humanity incomparably greater than can be expected to result from trying to fly.

. . . You might think attitudes would have changed as soon as people from several countries had made their first flights. But no. Wilbur Wright wrote in 1909 that no flying machine would ever make the journey from New York to Paris. Richard Burdon Haldane, the British secretary of war, told Parliament in 1909 that even though the airplane might one day be capable of great things, "from the war point of view, it is not so at present." Ferdinand Foch, a highly regarded French military strategist and the supreme commander of the Allied forces near the end of the First World War, opined in 1911 that airplanes were interesting toys but had no military value. Late that same year, near Tripoli, an Italian plane became the first to drop a bomb.

Early attitudes about flight beyond Earth's atmosphere followed a similar trajectory. True, plenty of philosophers, scientists, and sci-fi writers had thought long and hard about outer space. The sixteenth-century philosopher-friar Giordano Bruno proposed that intelligent beings inhabited an infinitude of worlds. The seventeenth-century soldier-writer Savinien de Cyrano de Bergerac portrayed the Moon as a world with forests, violets, and people.

But those writings were fantasies, not blueprints for action. By the early twentieth century, electricity, telephones, automobiles, radios, airplanes, and countless other engineering marvels were all becoming basic features of modern life. So couldn't earthlings build machines capable of space travel? Many people who should have known better said it couldn't be done, even after the successful 1942 test launch of the world's first long-range ballistic missile: Germany's deadly V-2 rocket. Capable of punching through Earth's atmosphere, it was a crucial step toward reaching the Moon.

Richard van der Riet Woolley, the eleventh British Astronomer Royal, is the source of a particularly woolly remark. When he landed in London after a thirty-six-hour flight from Australia, some reporters asked him about space travel. "It's utter bilge," he answered. That was in early 1956. In early 1957 Lee De Forest, a prolific American inventor who helped birth the age of electronics, declared, "Man will never reach the moon, regardless of all future scientific advances." Remember what happened in late 1957? Not just one but two Soviet Sputniks entered Earth orbit. The space race had begun.

Whenever someone says an idea is "bilge" (British for "baloney"), you must first ask whether it violates any well-tested laws of physics. If so, the idea is likely to be bilge. If not, the only challenge is to find a clever engineer—and, of course, a committed source of funding.

The day the Soviet Union launched Sputnik 1, a chapter of science fiction became science fact, and the future became the present. All of a sudden, futurists went overboard with their enthusiasm. The delusion that technology would advance at lightning speed replaced the delusion that it would barely advance at all. Experts went from having much too little confidence in the pace of technology to having much too much. And the guiltiest people of all were the space enthusiasts.

Commentators became fond of twenty-year intervals, within which some previously inconceivable goal would supposedly be accomplished. On January 6, 1967, in a front-page story, *The Wall Street Journal* announced: "The most ambitious U.S. space endeavor in the years ahead will be the campaign to land men on neighboring Mars. Most experts estimate the task can be accomplished by 1985." The very next month, in its debut issue, *The Futurist* magazine announced that according to long-range forecasts by the RAND Corporation, a pioneer think-tank, there was a 60 percent probability that a manned lunar base would exist by 1986. In *The Book of Predictions,* published in 1980, the rocket pioneer Robert C. Truax forecast that 50,000 people would be living and working in space by the year 2000. When that benchmark year arrived, people were indeed living and working in space. But the tally was not 50,000. It was three: the first crew of the International Space Station. . . .

All those visionaries (and countless others) never really grasped the forces that drive technological progress. In Wilbur and Orville's day, you could tinker your way into major engineering advances. Their first airplane did not require a grant from the National Science Foundation: they funded it through their bicycle business. The brothers constructed the wings and fuselage themselves, with tools they already owned, and got their resourceful bicycle mechanic, Charles E. Taylor, to design and hand-build the engine. The operation was basically two guys and a garage.

Space exploration unfolds on an entirely different scale. The first moon-walkers were two guys, too—Neil Armstrong and Buzz Aldrin—but behind them loomed the force of a mandate from an assassinated president, 10,000 engineers, $100 billion, and a Saturn V rocket.

Notwithstanding the sanitized memories so many of us have of the Apollo era, Americans were not first on the Moon because we're explorers by nature or because our country is committed to the pursuit of knowledge. We got to the Moon first because the United States was out to beat the Soviet Union, to win the Cold War any way we could. John F. Kennedy made that clear when he complained to top NASA officials in November 1962:

> I'm not that interested in space. I think it's good, I think we ought to know about it, we're ready to spend reasonable amounts of money. But we're talking about these fantastic expenditures which wreck our budget and all these other domestic programs and the only justification for it in my opinion to do it in this time or fashion is because we hope to beat them [the Soviet Union] and demonstrate that starting behind, as we did by a couple of years, by God, we passed them.

Like it or not, war (cold or hot) is the most powerful funding driver in the public arsenal. When a country wages war, money flows like floodwaters. Lofty goals—such as curiosity, discovery, exploration, and science—can get you money for modest-size projects, provided they resonate with the political and cultural views of the moment. But big, expensive activities are inherently long term, and require sustained investment that must survive economic fluctuations and changes in the political winds.

In all eras, across time and culture, only three drivers have fulfilled that funding requirement: war, greed, and the celebration of royal or religious power. The Great Wall of China; the pyramids of Egypt; the Gothic cathedrals of Europe; the U.S. interstate highway system; the voyages of Columbus and Cook—nearly every major undertaking owes its existence to one or more of those three drivers. Today, as the power of kings is supplanted by elected governments, and the power of religion is often expressed in non-architectural undertakings, that third driver has lost much of its sway, leaving war and greed to run the show. Sometimes those two drivers work hand in hand, as in the art of profiteering from the art of war. But war itself remains the ultimate and most compelling rationale.

Having been born the same week NASA was founded, I was eleven years old during the voyage of Apollo 11, and had already identified the universe as my life's passion. Unlike so many other people who watched Neil Armstrong's first steps on the Moon, I wasn't jubilant. I was simply relieved that someone was finally exploring another world. To me, Apollo 11 was clearly the beginning of an era.

But I, too, was delirious. The lunar landings continued for three and a half years. Then they stopped. The Apollo program became the end of an era, not the beginning. And as the Moon voyages receded in time and memory, they seemed ever more unreal in the history of human projects.

Unlike the first ice skates or the first airplane or the first desktop computer—artifacts that make us all chuckle when we see them today—the first rocket to the Moon, the 364-foot-tall Saturn V, elicits awe, even reverence. Three Saturn V relics lie in state at the Johnson Space Center in Texas, the Kennedy Space Center in Florida, and the U.S. Space and Rocket Center in Alabama. Streams of worshippers walk the length of each rocket. They touch the mighty rocket nozzles at the base and wonder how something so large could ever have bested Earth's gravity. To transform their awe into chuckles, our country will have to resume the effort to "boldly go where no man has gone before." Only then will the Saturn V look as quaint as every other invention that human ingenuity has paid the compliment of improving upon.

President Bush Announces New Vision for Space Exploration Program

Thanks for the warm welcome. I'm honored to be with the men and women of NASA. I thank those of you who have come in person. I welcome those who are listening by video. This agency, and the dedicated professionals who serve it, have always reflected the finest values of our country—daring, discipline, ingenuity, and unity in the pursuit of great goals.

America is proud of our space program. The risk takers and visionaries of this agency have expanded human knowledge, have revolutionized our understanding of the universe, and produced technological advances that have benefited all of humanity.

Inspired by all that has come before, and guided by clear objectives, today we set a new course for America's space program. We will give NASA a new focus and vision for future exploration. We will build new ships to carry man forward into the universe, to gain a new foothold on the moon, and to prepare for new journeys to worlds beyond our own.

I am comfortable in delegating these new goals to NASA, under the leadership of Sean O'Keefe. He's doing an excellent job. I appreciate Commander Mike Foale's introduction—I'm sorry I couldn't shake his hand. Perhaps, Commissioner, you'll bring him by—Administrator, you'll bring him by the Oval Office when he returns, so I can thank him in person.

I also know he is in space with his colleague, Alexander Kaleri, who happens to be a Russian cosmonaut. I appreciate the joint efforts of the Russians with our country to explore. I want to thank the astronauts who are with us, the courageous spacial entrepreneurs who set such a wonderful example for the young of our country.

And we've got some veterans with us today. I appreciate the astronauts of yesterday who are with us, as well, who inspired the astronauts of today to serve our country. I appreciate so very much the members of Congress being here. Tom DeLay is here, leading a House delegation. Senator Nelson is here from the Senate. I am honored that you all have come. I appreciate you're interested in the subject, it is a subject that's important to this administration, it's a subject that's mighty important to the country and to the world.

From Office of the Press Secretary, January 14, 2004.

Two centuries ago, Meriwether Lewis and William Clark left St. Louis to explore the new lands acquired in the Louisiana Purchase. They made that journey in the spirit of discovery, to learn the potential of vast new territory, and to chart a way for others to follow.

America has ventured forth into space for the same reasons. We have undertaken space travel because the desire to explore and understand is part of our character. And that quest has brought tangible benefits that improve our lives in countless ways. The exploration of space has led to advances in weather forecasting, in communications, in computing, search and rescue technology, robotics, and electronics. Our investment in space exploration helped to create our satellite telecommunications network and the Global Positioning System. Medical technologies that help prolong life—such as the imaging processing used in CAT scanners and MRI machines—trace their origins to technology engineered for use in space.

Our current programs and vehicles for exploring space have brought us far and they have served us well. The Space Shuttle has flown more than a hundred missions. It has been used to conduct important research and to increase the sum of human knowledge. Shuttle crews, and the scientists and engineers who support them, have helped to build the International Space Station.

Telescopes—including those in space—have revealed more than 100 planets in the last decade alone. Probes have shown us stunning images of the rings of Saturn and the outer planets of our solar system. Robotic explorers have found evidence of water—a key ingredient for life—on Mars and on the moons of Jupiter. At this very hour, the Mars Exploration Rover Spirit is searching for evidence of life beyond the Earth.

Yet for all these successes, much remains for us to explore and to learn. In the past 30 years, no human being has set foot on another world, or ventured farther upward into space than 386 miles—roughly the distance from Washington, D.C. to Boston, Massachusetts. America has not developed a new vehicle to advance human exploration in space in nearly a quarter century. It is time for America to take the next steps.

Today I announce a new plan to explore space and extend a human presence across our solar system. We will begin the effort quickly, using existing programs and personnel. We'll make steady progress—one mission, one voyage, one landing at a time.

Our first goal is to complete the International Space Station by 2010. We will finish what we have started, we will meet our obligations to our 15 international partners on this project. We will focus our future research aboard the station on the long-term effects of space travel on human biology. The environment of space is hostile to human beings. Radiation and weightlessness pose dangers to human health, and we have much to learn about their long-term effects before human crews can venture through the vast voids of space for months at a time. Research on board the station and here on Earth will help us better understand and overcome the obstacles that limit exploration. Through these efforts we will develop the skills and techniques necessary to sustain further space exploration. To meet this goal, we will return the Space

Shuttle to flight as soon as possible, consistent with safety concerns and the recommendations of the Columbia Accident Investigation Board. The Shuttle's chief purpose over the next several years will be to help finish assembly of the International Space Station. In 2010, the Space Shuttle—after nearly 30 years of duty—will be retired from service.

Our second goal is to develop and test a new spacecraft, the Crew Exploration Vehicle, by 2008, and to conduct the first manned mission no later than 2014. The Crew Exploration Vehicle will be capable of ferrying astronauts and scientists to the Space Station after the shuttle is retired. But the main purpose of this spacecraft will be to carry astronauts beyond our orbit to other worlds. This will be the first spacecraft of its kind since the Apollo Command Module.

Our third goal is to return to the moon by 2020, as the launching point for missions beyond. Beginning no later than 2008, we will send a series of robotic missions to the lunar surface to research and prepare for future human exploration. Using the Crew Exploration Vehicle, we will undertake extended human missions to the moon as early as 2015, with the goal of living and working there for increasingly extended periods. Eugene Cernan, who is with us today—the last man to set foot on the lunar surface—said this as he left: "We leave as we came, and God willing as we shall return, with peace and hope for all mankind." America will make those words come true.

Returning to the moon is an important step for our space program. Establishing an extended human presence on the moon could vastly reduce the costs of further space exploration, making possible ever more ambitious missions. Lifting heavy spacecraft and fuel out of the Earth's gravity is expensive. Spacecraft assembled and provisioned on the moon could escape its far lower gravity using far less energy, and thus, far less cost. Also, the moon is home to abundant resources. Its soil contains raw materials that might be harvested and processed into rocket fuel or breathable air. We can use our time on the moon to develop and test new approaches and technologies and systems that will allow us to function in other, more challenging environments. The moon is a logical step toward further progress and achievement.

With the experience and knowledge gained on the moon, we will then be ready to take the next steps of space exploration: human missions to Mars and to worlds beyond. Robotic missions will serve as trailblazers—the advanced guard to the unknown. Probes, landers and other vehicles of this kind continue to prove their worth, sending spectacular images and vast amounts of data back to Earth. Yet the human thirst for knowledge ultimately cannot be satisfied by even the most vivid pictures, or the most detailed measurements. We need to see and examine and touch for ourselves. And only human beings are capable of adapting to the inevitable uncertainties posed by space travel.

As our knowledge improves, we'll develop new power generation propulsion, life support, and other systems that can support more distant travels. We do not know where this journey will end, yet we know this: human beings are headed into the cosmos.

And along this journey we'll make many technological breakthroughs. We don't know yet what those breakthroughs will be, but we can be certain they'll come, and that our efforts will be repaid many times over. We may discover resources on the moon or Mars that will boggle the imagination, that will test our limits to dream. And the fascination generated by further exploration will inspire our young people to study math, and science, and engineering and create a new generation of innovators and pioneers.

This will be a great and unifying mission for NASA, and we know that you'll achieve it. I have directed Administrator O'Keefe to review all of NASA's current space flight and exploration activities and direct them toward the goals I have outlined. I will also form a commission of private and public sector experts to advise on implementing the vision that I've outlined today. This commission will report to me within four months of its first meeting. I'm today naming former Secretary of the Air Force, Pete Aldridge, to be the Chair of the Commission. Thank you for being here today, Pete. He has tremendous experience in the Department of Defense and the aerospace industry. He is going to begin this important work right away.

We'll invite other nations to share the challenges and opportunities of this new era of discovery. The vision I outline today is a journey, not a race, and I call on other nations to join us on this journey, in a spirit of cooperation and friendship.

Achieving these goals requires a long-term commitment. NASA's current five-year budget is $86 billion. Most of the funding we need for the new endeavors will come from reallocating $11 billion within that budget. We need some new resources, however. I will call upon Congress to increase NASA's budget by roughly a billion dollars, spread out over the next five years. This increase, along with refocusing of our space agency, is a solid beginning to meet the challenges and the goals we set today. It's only a beginning. Future funding decisions will be guided by the progress we make in achieving our goals.

We begin this venture knowing that space travel brings great risks. The loss of the Space Shuttle Columbia was less than one year ago. Since the beginning of our space program, America has lost 23 astronauts, and one astronaut from an allied nation—men and women who believed in their mission and accepted the dangers. As one family member said, "The legacy of Columbia must carry on—for the benefit of our children and yours." The Columbia's crew did not turn away from the challenge, and neither will we.

Mankind is drawn to the heavens for the same reason we were once drawn into unknown lands and across the open sea. We choose to explore space because doing so improves our lives, and lifts our national spirit. So let us continue the journey.

POSTSCRIPT

Is "Manned Space Travel" a Delusion?

After the *Columbia* tragedy, Stephen L. Petuanch, "No More Shuttles, Please," *Discover* (May 2003), denounced the space shuttle program as too expensive and unsafe. A new generation of shuttles is on the way; see Bill Sweetman, "Space Shuttle: The Next Generation," *Popular Science* (May 2003), and Mark Alpert, "Rethinking the Shuttle," *Scientific American* (April 2003). There are also efforts to develop an affordable spacecraft capable of many safe trips to and from orbit. In October 2004, Bert Rutan's *SpaceShipOne* won the $10 million Ansari X prize by becoming the first private, reusable craft to reach space (though not orbit). See Kathy A. Svitil and Eric Levin, "*SpaceShipOne* Opens Private Rocket Era," *Discover* (January 2005), and Bert Rutan, "Rocket for the Rest of Us," *National Geographic* (April 2005). The next step for private spacecraft is to reach orbit.

When President George W. Bush announced his plan to send humans to the Moon and Mars, beginning as soon as 2015, the reaction was immediate. James A. Van Allen asked "Is Human Spaceflight Obsolete?" in *Issues in Science and Technology* (Summer 2004). Andrew Lawler asked "How Much Space for Science?" in *Science* (January 30, 2004). Physicist and Nobel laureate Steven Weinberg, "The Wrong Stuff," *New York Review of Books* (April 8, 2004), argues that nothing needs doing in space that cannot be done without human presence. Until we find something that does need humans on the scene, there is no particular reason to send humans—at great expense—into space. Indeed, the president's Mars initiative may prove to be no more than a ploy to look visionary and force later presidents to face financial realities. John Derbyshire, "Space Is for Science," *National Review* (June 5, 2006), argues that the expense and hazards of putting humans in space do not justify the benefits when much cheaper automated spacecraft (robots) can make all necessary observations.

The question of whether robots can do the job is particularly relevant because of the success of the Mars rovers, *Spirit* and *Opportunity*. If robots continue to be successful, it seems likely that efforts to promote manned space travel, even from the White House, will meet resistance. Funding for space exploration remains low largely because problems on Earth (environmental and other) seem to need money more urgently than space exploration projects do. The prospects for manned space expeditions to the moon, Mars, or other worlds seem very dim, although Paul D. Spudis, "Harvest the Moon," *Astronomy* (June 2003), asserts that there are four good reasons for putting people at least on the Moon: "The first motivation to revisit the Moon is that its rocks hold the early history of our own planet and the solar system. Next, its unique environment and properties make it an ideal vantage point for observing the universe. The Moon is also a natural space station where we can learn how to live off-planet. And finally, it gives us an extraterrestrial filling station, with resources to use both locally and in near-Earth space." See also Paul D. Spudis, "The New Moon," *Scientific American* (December 2003). Nader Elhefnawy, "Beyond *Columbia:* Is There a Future for Humanity in Space?" *The Humanist* (September/October 2003), says that we cannot ignore the wealth of resources in space. Alex Ellery, "Humans versus Robots for Space Exploration and Development," *Space Policy* (May 2003), maintains that although "robotics and artificial intelligence are becoming more sophisticated, they will not be able to deal with 'thinking-on-one's-feet' tasks that require generalisations from past experience. . . . [T]here will be a critical role for humans in space for the foreseeable future." Carl Gethmann, "Manned Space Travel as a Cultural Mission," *Poiesis & Praxis* (December 2006), argues that costs should not be used to reject manned space travel as a pointless option. The dream and the effort are part of our culture, and we should pursue them as far as we can afford to. Mark Williams, "Toward a New Vision of Manned Spaceflight," *Technology Review* (January 2005), suggests that for prolonged spaceflight, however, humans are so vulnerable to radiation and other space hazards that they may have to be reengineered.

Internet References . . .

Center for Democracy & Technology

The Center for Democracy & Technology works to promote democratic values and constitutional liberties in the digital age.

http://www.cdt.org/

Electronic Frontier Foundation

The Electronic Frontier Foundation is concerned with protecting individual freedoms and rights such as privacy as new communications technologies emerge.

http://www.eff.org

Pew Internet & American Life Project

The Pew Internet & American Life Project explores the impact of the Internet on children, families, communities, the work place, schools, health care, and civic/political life.

http://www.pewinternet.org/

Google Print Library Project

According to Google, the Library Project's aim is to make it easier for people to find relevant books, especially those that are out of print—while carefully respecting authors' and publishers' copyrights. Google's ultimate goal is to create a comprehensive, searchable, virtual card catalog of all books in all languages.

http://books.google.com/googleprint/library.html

The Computer Revolution

*F*ans *of computers have long been sure that the electronic wonders offer untold benefits to society. When the first personal computers appeared in the early 1970s, they immediately brought unheard-of capabilities to their users. Ever since, those capabilities have been increasing. Today children command more sheer computing power than major corporations did in the 1950s and 1960s. Computer users are in direct contact with their fellow users around the world. Information is instantly available and infinitely malleable.*

Some observers wonder about the purported untold benefits of computers. Specifically, will such benefits be outweighed by threats to children (by free access to pornography), civil order (by free access to sites that advocate racism and violence), traditional institutions (will books, for example, become an endangered species?), or to human pride (a computer has already outplayed the human world chess champion)? Does all that time we spend online weaken our connections to our fellow human being? Is privacy vanishing? Should Google be allowed to make the contents of the world's libraries available to all when they search for information?

- Does the Internet Strengthen Social Connections?

- Does the Spread of Surveillance Technology Threaten Privacy?

- Should the World's Libraries Be Digitized?

ISSUE 15

Does the Internet Strengthen Social Connections?

YES: Denise M. Carter, from "Living in Virtual Communities: Making Friends Online," *Journal of Urban Technology* (December 2004)

NO: Jonathon N. Cummings, Brian Butler, and Robert Kraut, from "The Quality of Online Social Relationships," *Communications of the ACM* (July 2002)

ISSUE SUMMARY

YES: Denise M. Carter argues that the Internet enhances or adds to social relationships. In fact, the trust essential to successful relationships may be easier to develop online than offline.

NO: Jonathon N. Cummings, Brian Butler, and Robert Kraut maintain that online communication is less valuable for building strong social relationships than more traditional face-to-face and telephone communication.

It is a truism to say that technologies have social impact, and that that impact can be both far-reaching and unforeseen. Thus the Gutenberg printing press, whose first product was the Bible, wound up contributing to the Protestant Reformation, making public schools essential, creating the scientific and industrial revolutions, and spreading the idea of human rights and thus leading to the American, French, and other revolutions. It also quite shattered what used to be thought of as "community" when most people lived and died within a mile of their birthplace and took the shape of their lives from a single unquestionable religious or civil authority.

Whether these effects were for good or ill depends very much on whom you ask. Most citizens of the modern developed world—the products and beneficiaries of those changes—would surely say they were for good. Some are more skeptical.

When the Internet was new, its partisans promised that it would bring a new age of public participation in political decision-making and link together far-flung people to create a "global village" far more real than anything forecast for television by Marshall McLuhan. However, some people feared that it would be harmful to society. Clifford Stoll claimed the Internet would weaken commitment to and enjoyment of real friendships (*Silicon Snake Oil*, Doubleday, 1995). David Paletz wrote that "the new information technology . . . can inspire populism, but one based on ignorance; it can facilitate the expression of public opinion, but one inspired by demagoguery; it can engender community, but of ethnic, religious, and single-issue groups" ("Advanced Information Technology and Political Communication," *Social Science Computer Review*, Spring 1996). Sherry Turkle feared the Internet would lead to the destruction of meaningful community ("Virtuality and Its Discontents: Searching for Community in Cyberspace," *American Prospect*, Winter 1996). Robert Kraut et al. reported that new Internet users became less socially involved and more depressed ("Internet Paradox: A Social Technology that Reduces Social Involvement and Psychological Well-Being?" *American Psychologist*, 53[9], 1998). Andrew L. Shapiro admitted that the Internet's potential for fostering personal growth and social progress seemed limitless but worried that "customizing our lives to the hilt could undermine the strength and cohesion of local communities . . . shared experience is an indisputable essential ingredient" ("The Net that Binds," *Nation*, June 21, 1999). John B. Horrigan, "Online Communities: Networks that Nurture Long-Distance Relationships and Local Ties," PEW Internet & American Life Project (October 2001), finds that Internet users strengthen their connections to others, expand their social worlds, and increase their involvement with communities, both local and virtual, in a process he calls "glocalization."

Since then, the Internet has grown tremendously. The social impact of online communication is increasingly a matter of global concern. Does it strengthen society by helping people make and keep friends, form "virtual" communities stretching around the globe, and exchange information? Or does it weaken society by drawing people away from face-to-face interactions and local community groups, substituting weak friendships for strong ones, and interfering with the development of mature, good citizens?

Denise M. Carter argues that the Internet enhances or adds to social relationships. In fact, the trust essential to successful relationships may be easier to develop online than offline. For many people, cyberspace has become part of everyday life, to the point that online and offline are no longer distinct and separate. Jonathon N. Cummings, Brian Butler, and Robert Kraut maintain that online communication is less valuable for building strong social relationships than more traditional face-to-face and telephone communication. The overall effect depends on whether online communication replaces or supplements traditional communication.

YES

Denise M. Carter

Living in Virtual Communities: Making Friends Online

Ten years ago social theorists were suggesting that the Internet would revolutionize social relationships. Turkle and Stone both wrote extensively about how the perceived anonymity provided by Computer Mediated Communication (CMC) would allow people to explore alternative aspects of their identity and of themselves like never before. Even Benedikt and Rheingold's early assessments of the revolutionary nature of the Internet led them to believe that it would bring about immense transformations in social life. However, my own research, an ethnography of a Virtual Community called Cybertown suggests that the changes have been much less dramatic than anticipated. Indeed, they are deeply embedded in the existing practices and power relations of everyday life. Markham suggested that users framed their experiences of CMC along a continuum of connection of self. Markham developed three themes along this continuum that helped her to understand online experiences. The first was that of CMC being a tool that facilitates communication, the second that cyberspace was a place to go to be with others, and the third was a way of being that is inseparably woven into lived experiences. It is this third category that is indicative of what Giddens referred to as a revolution in the way we form ties and connections, and that is also reflected in my own research. Despite those early predictions by Benedikt and Rheingold, the Internet has instead become increasingly embedded in everyday lives. Rather than transforming methods of sociability such as friendship, it has enhanced or added to those mechanisms that were already in place in everyday lives. Much of the reason for this has been changes in the ways in which we conceptualize place and space. People are now living in Virtual Communities like Cybertown that do not occupy a geographical place, rather, these communities are wholly mediated through CMC.

This paper begins by examining how a Virtual Community called Cybertown has become one such place where people are actively seeking social relationships online. In part, it achieves this by assessing how people create, negotiate, and reproduce complex virtual social places. Secondly, using traditional theorists like Allan and Jerome it evaluates the friendships that are formed there. By illustrating the similarities between traditional notions of friendship and online friendship, it becomes clear that online friendships are

From *Journal of Urban Technology*, vol. 11, no. 3, December 2004, pp. 109–125. Copyright © 2004 by Taylor & Francis Journals. Reprinted by permission.

formed and maintained in similar ways to those in wider society. Thirdly, it examines how friendships are being moved offline and incorporated into everyday life, and illustrates how people are extending their webs of personal relationships into cyberspace. It is no longer distinct and separate from the real world. It is part of everyday life.

Throughout my research, the two sets of terms real/offline and virtual/online were typically used by respondents quite randomly in conversation. Rather than suggesting a dichotomy between real and virtual, they were simply positional, differentiating between social places—a practice I have chosen to continue throughout this paper. Additionally, acronyms were also often used instead, RL for real life and CT for Cybertown. . . .

A Place Called Cybertown

Cybertown is a very large city. The population on Thursday, October 17, 2002 at 8:07 PM Cybertown Time (CyT) numbered 996,664 registered citizens. Its layout is similar to any other large city in the world, and there are many of the same landscape features: a plaza, a beach, a café, a fun fair, a post office, an employment office, a jail, and the suburbs where the residents live. In the suburbs, the residents live singly in private homes arranged in blocks of about forty houses. Neighborhoods consist of five blocks, or two hundred houses, of which only about half to two thirds are occupied at any one time. Colonies consist of between ten and twenty neighborhoods. People in Cybertown earn "citycash" everyday, which can be spent in the shopping mall on gifts and household goods. In addition, those who work for the city, often policing behavior, can earn extra citycash. Cybertown is a thriving city. However, Cybertown is a city on the Internet, a social world that is no less real for being supported by Internet technologies, and its residents are drawn from all over the world.

Cybertown's citizens actively construct their city as a social space through a combination of two things. First, an individual's subjective experience of those landscapes that make up Cybertown. Secondly, an individual's interaction with other individuals who also occupy those same landscapes, thus supporting Augé's suggestion that places are created when individual practices become collective practices. However, as Crang et al. explain, technologies are not self-contained entities that affect the social; technologies are constituted by the social relations and discourses of everyday life because they are embedded within that life. Hence, it is important that this issue is considered. Similarly, Schaap reminds us that in exploring social phenomena online, we often overlook the fact that the underlying technology is socially constructed. This is apparent in Cybertown where the 3D environment and the spatial organization allow its inhabitants to inhabit a complex digital world that resembles the real world in many ways. This similarity results in Cybertown's alignment with other social worlds, and, as my research demonstrates, facilitates the movement of social relationships between them. The design of Cybertown, therefore, produces the notion that it is a familiar place with recognizable social spaces. As such, it allows people who go there to invest time in social interaction in much the same way as they do in other social spaces with which they are familiar.

During the early stages of my ethnography, I struggled to explain to other researchers why Cybertown was a place. Nowadays, I simply pronounce that it is a place because the people who go there say it is. Consequently, in the same way as Lefebvre argues that rather than space being a priori, a vacuum waiting to be filled, it is produced through social action, then the place that is Cybertown also becomes a social product. Hence, when the people of Cybertown talk about "going there" or "being there" or even "meeting friends there," they are actively producing Cybertown as a social space. It becomes a lived in space where collective and individual practice creates place. As such, it is not a technological construct but a cultural construct, mediated through experience rather than through technology. These ideas are confirmed when talking to Cybertown residents. For example, one Cybertown resident we shall call *mebsuta* explained how Cybertown was just another place to enjoy friends' company, and another resident, *zaniah,* described how she threw a party at her house in Cybertown and that over 20 people came and it lasted about six hours.

Many of the Cybertown residents I spoke to have also moved their relationships offline. Of the 85 inhabitants that I interviewed, 31 had already met other Cybertown residents face-to-face. A further 16 people intended to meet others offline in the future. Another had already spoken on the telephone and eight others said they would like to meet, but they lived too far away. Of the remaining 38, only three said they would never consider meeting anyone outside of Cybertown. In all, 59 percent of the people I spoke to had either met, or were about to meet their Cybertown friends face-to-face. . . .

Friendship

Overwhelmingly, my research in Cybertown has been informed by notions of friendship, because friendship is viewed by residents as an important aspect of the social life of Cybertown. Traditionally, sociologists and anthropologists have studied kinship ties rather than friendship ties. As Bell and Coleman point out, this is partly due to the perceived difficulties involved in describing what constitutes friendship, whereas kinship seems easier to explain. However, in Cybertown, there are no traditional kinship ties. People there do not live in a society based on ties of blood or genealogy although traditional kinship roles are sometimes adopted, for example, "cybermom" or "cyberkid." The private and personal nature of friendship is perhaps best understood when contrasted with the more public, socially prescribed nature of kinship ties. Nevertheless, even drawing comparisons between friendship and kinship does not tell us why people make friends or what purpose this informal network accomplishes. Some theorists like Willmott tend to look at friendship in terms of informal support networks, and their focus is on the influence of class, age, and gender in the development of those friendships. In Cybertown, however, these social distinctions are not clearly defined. Inhabitants cannot see each other, and are, therefore, unable to collect what I call line-of-sight data. In other words, they cannot tell a person's class, age, or gender on first meeting. This information may only be revealed over time as people become more intimate. . . .

Friendship in Cybertown

Giddens suggests that generally intimacy is replacing more traditional bonds of friendship. He uses the notion of pure relationship to elaborate on these changes, describing three core elements involved, freedom, commitment, and intimacy. Pure relationships are not, for Giddens, anchored in the social and economic conditions of everyday life but are free-floating. In pure relationships, the second element, commitment, replaces these external anchors, where Giddens describes commitment as a particular species of trust that has to be earned. He explains that trust partly results from investing confidence in each other and partly from investing confidence in the capability of the mutual bond to withstand future traumas. Giddens maintains that the dynamics of trust in traditional relationships are embedded in criteria outside of that relationship, for example, kinship ties, social duty, or traditional obligation.

The third of Giddens' core elements is intimacy. He maintains that a pure relationship is also focused on intimacy. Again, it is "active trust" within the pure relationship that is important, since active trust brings about disclosure, and disclosure is the basic condition of intimacy. Giddens explains that the only incentives to developing a pure relationship are the rewards that can be gained from it, and outlines intimacy as one of the main rewards. However, although commitment is always actively given, it must always be part of an effort bargain that depends fundamentally on satisfactions or rewards generic to that relation itself. Consequently, individuals commit to the values and practices of a particular friendship, and the friendship is reflexively organized. The pure relationship, therefore, is a social relation which is internally rather than externally referential.

My research demonstrates that friendships in Cybertown conform to these three main aspects of Giddens' thought. First of all, they are free-floating. In other words, they do not rely on external social conditions like gender, race, or age. *Tabit,* one Cybertown resident, explains how, "physical contact is not important in a friendship."

In Cybertown, the process of getting to know someone often begins with quite transitory meetings. Decisions about meeting again and getting to know one another better, or committing oneself to forming friendships are based on whether people enjoy the conversation itself, rather than on external social conditions. In this sense, they are free-floating like Giddens' pure relationships. Two statements are typical of comments made on this subject.

Gianfar, who, at the time of the remark, had lived in Cybertown for thirteen months explained, "I find that we finally judge people for the content of their hearts rather than by the color of their skin, or other social and/or economic standing." Another resident, *Maasym,* suggested that, "online you actually get to know someone inside, without being judged on appearance and everything else wrong with the world today."

These traditional anchors of friendship and kinship are being replaced by commitment based on active trust and disclosure—hence, the value being placed on getting "to know people from the inside out." Trust, as Giddens suggests, is something that is built up over time. The people who go to Cybertown often go there over long periods of time and get to know a wide range of people. This makes being there wrote *sabik,* a resident who had been there for nineteen months, "comfortable."

Kendall suggests that the longer a researcher spends online the easier it is for her to evaluate the authenticity of her informants. Given this, it would seem reasonable to assume that the same must hold true for other individuals online too. For example, Whitty's study of chat rooms reveals that people who spend less time in chat rooms, are more likely to tell lies. Conversely, the more time people spend in chat rooms, the more open they become about themselves. Whitty suggests that this follows a similar pattern in face-to-face relationships where trust develops gradually as people become familiar with one another. In this sense, online relationships are no different from offline relationships.

Since each friendship is unique, both in context and organization, the degree of trust needed to sustain that relationship is negotiable. But as I have already mentioned, in Cybertown, trust is something that must be mediated without face-to-face contact, even though this may seem a difficult thing to achieve. Early cyber theorists like Turkle and Stone suggested that in cyberspace, the self is both fluid and perhaps unknowable. This is partly because of the absence of both visible and audible clues. For example, in everyday life we can see if someone is male or female, young or old. We also talk about liars looking shifty or sounding insincere. In Cybertown, however, as *Gianfar* and *Maasym* have already suggested, the very absence of physical proximity appears to enable trust to build without difficulty and also to be easily sustained. This lack of physical contact does two things. Initially, it removes any preconceived ideas regarding judgements about age, race, gender, etc., allowing a more personal bond of friendship to develop in some cases. Like *Gianfar* and *Maasym, Polaris* explains how he enjoys the company of friends in Cybertown because, "We don't have the extra physical side to deal with. We want to be with each other for who we are not what we look like."

The second thing the absence of physical proximity does is to make people feel safe in their acts of disclosure, removing the embarrassment of confession. Close relationships in Cybertown and elsewhere demand that trust be mutual, otherwise the friendship breaks down. As Giddens says, active trust brings about disclosure, and it is this disclosure that in turn facilitates intimacy. During my time researching in Cybertown, I got to know a resident named *acrux* very well. She explained to me that her intimacy and closeness to her best friend was made much easier because she "lived" in Cybertown. "We're friendly enough for me to be comfortable talking to him. He's close enough to be trusted but not close enough to be clouded by offline issues. He's completely impartial."

For some residents, increased intimacy is a result of a more psychological bonding that enhances their friendships. This more psychological attachment appears to be highly valued. For example, *Jabbah,* who had been living in Cybertown for eighteen months, thought Cybertown relationships were more significant than offline ones because they, "tend to be more emotional and psychological since you cannot see the person's physical characteristics."

Similarly, *Meissa,* who had lived in Cybertown for four months felt that she bonded with her Cybertown friends in a more personal way than her offline friends. In contrast, *Zosma,* who lived in Cybertown for four years and actually visited me in my own home, insisted that friendship online and offline are the same, but suggested that it just takes much longer in real life to get to know people. She also partly agreed with *Jabbah,* who said that in Cybertown, "You get to know each other from the inner person and out; in real life you know people from outside and later inside. So in that way the two are composite. And knowing the inner person first; you see that looks aren't that important."

Interestingly, the fact that many of these friendships are sustainable offline suggests that people are widening their webs of relationships to include those who are no longer dependent on what Willmott called the social patterns that underpin social support. In other words, they are free floating and as such may be moved between different contexts without damage providing that sufficient intimacy and trust have developed.

Moving Friendship Offline

Because online and offline social experiences that occur in social landscapes of the Internet such as Cybertown exhibit similarities and are subject to the same criteria of assessment, they may be interchangeable. This would mean that online relationships can be sustained offline and vice versa. However, as I mentioned earlier, friendships that are appropriate in one setting may be inappropriate in another.

Hence, any decision to meet offline could be problematic and ultimately destructive, a fact that Cybertown residents are aware of. There is an understanding among Cybertown residents that there are common misconceptions about the type of people who use the Internet. Recently, a kind of global moral panic about deviants and the Internet has been amplified by the media. This has emphasized the risk involved with meeting people offline. Despite this, people are learning to trust people they meet on the Internet. As *Acrux*, a 33-year-old Scottish policewoman in her real life, explained, "People who don't use the net a lot don't seem to understand that real friendships can be established online; it's not all mass murderers and psychos."

Similarly, *Lesath,* who had previously been a CB "ham radio" operator, was fairly forthright about meeting her friends offline. She had been doing it for several years.

> Why not meet? General rule of thumb is, if local or in large groups; it's safer . . . also, meeting in public and letting your family or friends know where you are is a wise idea. There are precautions, but no more or less than back in the days of meeting CB buddies off the air for coffee breaks.

Not only did she meet her friends offline, but she is also very happily married to one of them.

> I married one of my online friends (who was strictly a friend, online . . . but over three years or so, we became much more romantically involved offline). Different people view it differently; some are horrified, while others are intrigued and still others don't seem to think it unusual or "different" at all. I am my own person . . . my kids were a little surprised and perhaps apprehensive at first, but they understand who I am . . . and they have come to admit that my choice is the best I've made in a long time. LOL

During my three years fieldwork in Cybertown, I spent many hours chatting to one resident called *Zosma* who was, in effect, my gate keeper as well as my friend. As gate keeper, she had control over key sources and opportunities, and as such she introduced me to many other residents and helped me to find my way around Cybertown. It was *Zosma* who taught me many skills and under her patient tutelage, I learned to "live" life online. Doing fieldwork in Cybertown did not simply mean switching the computer on and typing out words on a keypad. Like Markham, I had to learn how to move, see, and talk because to be present in cyberspace is to learn how to be embodied there. *Zosma*'s help in achieving this state was invaluable, and we became close friends as a result. In September 2002, *Zosma* had planned to fly from her home in Copenhagen to visit another Cybertown friend, *Phad* who lived only fifty miles away from my home, so I invited her to stay with me and my family.

Meeting Zosma

Zosma was the first of four Cybertown residents I met face to face, although she was the only one who stayed in my home, a circumstance I thought I felt confident about because of the length of time I had known her. We had developed a firm Internet friendship, and many details of our everyday lives—jobs, children, families, hopes, and dreams—had been shared, discussed, and dissected. In short, active trust and disclosure over a long time period had moved us towards a relationship of intimacy. Despite this, we were both nervous about our forthcoming meeting and looking back at my field notes for that year, I had questioned both my own and my family's ability to cope. For example, one entry simply said, "I hope *Zosma* is who she says she is;" another said, "What if David (my partner) takes an instant dislike to her?"

Part of our preparation for meeting was to e-mail each other our photographs, and we also exchanged our real addresses (particularly necessary in her case since she was coming to stay with me!). We also arranged to speak on the phone as soon as she landed in the United Kingdom, something I found almost as nerve-wracking as meeting her! We met in Cybertown just a few hours before she left to catch her flight, my field notes observe that "*Zosma* is very nervous," but go on to explain, "Today I had my last conversation before she gets on the plane; she is being picked up by *Phad* at the airport and will ring me when she arrives at his house. It will be the first time I have spoken to her by phone—why am I doing this?"

Our subsequent telephone conversation was surreal; *Zosma* was tired from the flight and later confided how nervous she had been too. In Cybertown, we communicated through text and understood each other very well, yet on the telephone she had an accent, something I hadn't considered. Cryptically, my field notes said, "Done it; it's all OK." What I did not realize until later was that we continued to call each other *dutypigeon* and *Zosma* as we spoke on the telephone.

Finally, the appointed hour of our meeting arrived. I waited at home while *Phad* drove to my house with *Zosma* as a passenger. When she knocked at the door, I went to answer it alone. This was a private moment when we both confronted the truth about each other. I remember looking at her and being very pleased and relieved that she had told me the truth, and that she was exactly like her photograph. It was not until I saw her that I realized how important that particular truth was.

Later, I mentioned in my field notes that it was terrifying to imagine her not telling me the truth about who she was. However, through our use of truth in disclosing our offline identities and physical attributes we had maintained an authentic perception of each other. Failure to do so would have destroyed our friendship and our intimacy would have ended. Throughout the visit, we also continued to call each other by our Cybertown names, to the hilarity of friends and relatives, a strategy I believe is no different from being called "Mum" by my son and Denise by my partner. On reflection, I believe this was yet another strategy for maintaining our perceptions of one another. As Zosma said at the time, "Thank goodness you really are *dutypigeon*."

Zosma and I have remained friends, long after our meeting.

Concluding Remarks

People are constructing and living in new kinds of places on the Internet that are not geographically bounded. Instead, they occupy imaginary landscapes whose construction as a social place is achieved through social action. One of those places is a city called Cybertown. My research indicates that the people who inhabit Cybertown regard it not only as a place where they can meet old friends, but also a place where they can make new friends. Furthermore, to them, Cybertown is not exotic and removed from their everyday life—it is an essential part of it. Going to Cybertown is no more weird and wonderful than going to the local community center.

In addition, online friendships in Cybertown can be evaluated using traditional theorists like Allan and Jerome in much the same way as offline friendship, thus illustrating the many similarities between them. First of all, the friendships formed in Cybertown are informal, personal, and private. Secondly, they are chosen rather than enforced. Third, they are also produced and maintained in similar ways to those in offline life. There are, however, a number of differences.

Online friendships are not initially anchored by the everyday social and cultural construction of gender, age, or race, or by cultural conventions that cover other human relationships like kinship. In contrast, they are what Giddens calls free-floating. Despite this, people living in Cybertown are learning to actively trust each other. In many instances, the free-floating nature of online friendship enables this trust to be achieved more easily by getting to know people from the inside out. Active trust is a major contributory factor in maintaining the commitment and intimacy of online friendship. It is also a major contributory factor in the successful transfer of friendship from one context to another, for example, from online to offline life. Many individuals appear to be extending their webs of personal relationships into cyberspace. As a result, it is no longer distinct and separate from the real world. Cyberspace has become part of everyday life.

Jonathon N. Cummings,
Brian Butler, and Robert Kraut

 **NO**

The Quality of Online Social Relationships

People use the Internet intensely for interpersonal communication, sending and receiving email, contacting friends and family via instant messaging services, visiting chat rooms, or subscribing to distribution lists, among other activities. The evidence is clear that interpersonal communication is an important use of the Internet, if not its *most* important use. For example, both self-report surveys and computer monitoring studies indicate that email is the most popular online application.

Claims regarding the Internet's usefulness for developing social relationships, however, remain controversial. Both personal testimonials and systematically collected data document the deep and meaningful social relationships people can cultivate online.

This evidence, however, conflicts with data comparing the value that people place on their online relationships with offline relationships and with data comparing social relationships among heavy and light Internet users. For example, Parks and Roberts surveyed users of multiplayer environments called MOOs. Ninety-three percent of the users had made friends online, but when asked to compare their online friendships with those offline, respondents rated offline ones higher. Respondents to Nie's national survey reported spending less time with friends and family since going online, with the decline greatest among the most frequent Internet users. And Kraut et al. presented longitudinal evidence to demonstrate that among new Internet users, online time diminished social involvement and psychological well being.

Understanding the impact of the Internet on human social relationships requires two types of evidence. First, we need to know how computer-mediated communication affects the quality of particular social interactions and relationships. Are the online ones better, the same, or worse than those sustained by other means? Second, we need to know how computer-mediated communication affects one's mix of social interactions and relationships. The impact of the Internet is likely to be very different if it supplements communication with existing friends and family, or if instead it substitutes for more traditional communication and social ties.

This article addresses the first question by explicitly comparing online and offline social interaction. We briefly summarize evidence from several empirical studies, all of which suggest that computer-mediated communication, and in

From *Communications of the ACM,* vol. 45, no. 7, July 2002, pp. 103–108. Copyright © 2002 by Communications of the ACM. Reprinted with permission.

particular email, is less valuable for building and sustaining close social relationships than face-to-face contact and telephone conversations. These studies include the following surveys:

- International bank employees who describe the value of particular communication sessions for work relationships;
- College students, using the same methodology, but focusing on personal relationships;
- A longitudinal study of new Internet users; and
- Examination of behavior on email-based listservs.

Comparing Communication over Different Media

One way to evaluate the usefulness of the Internet for developing and maintaining social ties is to ask people to compare particular communication sessions on relevant outcomes. One can then relate the outcomes to features of the communication session (for example, who it was with, the duration, and the modality over which it occurred). This technique has been used to uncover features of conversation that lead to the development of social relationships in face-to-face settings. We apply it to email, telephone, and face-to-face communication among bank employees and university students.

In our 1991 study, 979 employees of a multinational bank reported on their most recent communication conducted over different media. About 81% used email in their jobs, sending an average of 15 messages per week. Respondents evaluated the usefulness of communication episodes using criteria related to the success of work groups, including usefulness for getting work done and for developing or sustaining a work relationship, utilizing a 3-point scale, where 1 meant not very useful and 3 meant very useful. We report data on 5,205 communication episodes that occurred in person, by telephone, or by email. . . .

Respondents reported communication by email to be reliably worse than communication conducted face-to-face or by telephone, both for getting work done and for sustaining work relationships. However, the disadvantages of email were significantly greater for maintaining relationships than for getting work done. These differences among the media remain even when one statistically controls for relevant variables, including respondents' gender, age, job title, daily volume of communication, and experience with email.

One might object that this data comes from the early years of email, although employees in this firm had been using email since the mid-1970s. In addition, one might also object that personal relationships are not central to work activity, although many studies stress their importance for getting work done. To counter these objections, we replicated the original study in 1999 among students at an eastern university. These students used email extensively, estimating a mean of 11 messages per day, and were in a stage in life that stressed the importance of developing personal relationships. Some 39 students completed a diary, recording information about each of 259 communication episodes in which they had participated during a four-hour block—late afternoon to early evening. Students recorded their relationship with their communication partner (relative, friend, acquaintance, or other), its duration, the topic of conversation (schoolwork, personal, or other), and the modality over which it occurred. Respondents evaluated each communication for its usefulness in getting work done, exchanging information, and developing or maintaining a personal relationship. They made their evaluations on 5-point scale.

Like the banking study, students evaluated email communication sessions as an inferior means to maintaining personal relationships compared to those conducted in person ($p < 0.05$) and by telephone ($p < 0.05$), these latter being equal. The students, however, found email to be as good as the telephone and in-person communication for completing schoolwork ($p > 0.10$), and even better for the exchange of information ($p < 0.05$).

Students also estimated the frequency of communication over the different modalities and the strength of their relationship with each of the 148 partners. We created an index of relationship strength by averaging their answers to two questions: "How close do you feel to this person?" and "How often do you get favors or advice from this person" (alpha $= 0.92$). We used linear regression to predict the strength of the relationship from frequency of communication with that partner over the different modalities: email, in-person, and telephone. Frequency of communication across all three modalities was significantly related to the strength of relationship, both directly and once the partner's gender, nature of the relations, length of the relationship, and geographic distance between the parties were controlled statistically. However, communicating in person (Beta s $= 0.36$) and by telephone (Beta $= 0.27$) were both significantly better predictors of a strong relationship than was communication by email (Beta $= 0.15$).

Comparing Internet Versus NonInternet Social Partners

In these studies, respondents selected communication episodes and partners based on the recency of the communication session. This procedure has the advantage of sampling all potential conversations, but may over-represent social relationships not important to the respondents, but are frequent simply because the partners are nearby. Here, we compare the value of using computer-mediated and noncomputer-mediated communication to keep up with partners with whom the respondents have a substantial amount of communication. The data comes from the HomeNet project, a field trial that tracked Internet usage and communication behavior among a sample of 93 households in Pittsburgh during their first year or two online.

Participants answered a series of questions about two individuals with whom they had frequent communication. The first, whom we refer to as the "Internet partner," was the individual outside of their household to whom they sent the most email, as recorded in computer-generated usage logs collected as part of the project. Some 111 respondents answered questions about an Internet partner. The second, whom we refer to as the "nonInternet partner," was the person outside of their household with whom respondents claimed to have the most frequent communication in any modality. Some 125 respondents answered questions about a nonInternet partner. To allow for comparisons between relationships conducted by email and those conducted primarily over other modalities, we limit our analyses here to the 99 respondents who answered questions both about an Internet and a nonInternet partner, and for whom these partners were different individuals.

Respondents indicated each partner's gender and age, duration of acquaintance, role relation (for example, family, friend, co-worker), and geographic proximity (for example, neighborhood, city, state). Participants then rated their frequency of email, face-to-face, and telephone communication: (5-daily, 4-weekly, 3-monthly, 2-less often, 1-never). A 5-point scale indicated psychological closeness with the partner: "I feel very close," "I could freely confide in this person," "This person is important to me," and "I understand this person fully" (alpha = 0.90).

We were interested in three questions: Do people differ in the overall volume of communication they have with the people they keep up with using different modalities? Do they differ in how close they feel toward them? Is communication with a partner over different modalities predictive of differing degrees of psychological closeness?

The number of respondents' communication sessions per month, broken and summed over all modalities, indicate that participants communicated less frequently with their Internet partner (5.2 times/month) than their non-Internet partner (7.2 times/month, $p < 0.001$). . . . Although respondents communicated more by email with their Internet partner ($p < 0.001$), they communicated less using the other modalities ($p < 0.001$ for face-to-face and $p < 0.001$ for telephone). Respondents also reported feeling less close to their Internet partner than to their nonInternet partner ($p < 0.001$).

Using a least squares regression analysis, we predicted psychological closeness from frequency of communication for the nonInternet partner and Internet partner, controlling for sex, age, role relation, duration of acquaintance, and physical proximity. Most notably, frequency of communication was a critical predictor of psychological closeness with the nonInternet partner (Beta = 0.40), but not with the Internet partner (Beta = −0.08). The difference is statistically significant ($p < 0.001$). The weaker association of communication with closeness for the Internet sample is analogous to findings from the student sample.

Social relationships offline involve more communication than those developed online, and thus predicted psychological closeness. Given our cross-sectional data, we cannot tell if communication does not lead to closeness when people are communicating electronically, or if people are exchanging email with people to whom they do not feel close. In either case, they are not getting as much social benefit from email as they do from their other communication activity.

Online Social Groups

The research we described so far concentrates on dyadic relationships between individuals in their online and offline lives. Yet one of the prominent features of the Internet is the presence of larger social collectives, which researchers have called "electronic groups" or "communities." Even before the advent of the Web, the Internet provided an infrastructure for online group-level social behavior, through USENET and email-based distribution lists. In descriptions of social life on the Internet, these electronic or virtual communities are often described as groups where relationships form, and whose members provide each other with companionship, information, and social support.

While existing studies and stories of electronic groups provide insight into the types of social activity that can occur in electronic collectives, the anecdotal nature of this research leaves open the question of what typically happens. Are active, tightly knit electronic groups, in which people form personal relationships and develop a sense of belonging, the norm or are the cases reported in the literature interesting exceptions? To examine this question, we collected data from a sample of 204 Internet listservs. The data shows that, on average, listservs are much more like loosely knit, voluntary organizations than the tightly knit social communities highlighted in prior case studies.

The sample consisted of 204 unmanaged and unmoderated email-based listservs, drawn from a population of approximately 70,000 listservs. An initial random sample of 1,066 was stratified by topic type (work-related, personal, and mixed) to ensure it included a range of topics and member populations. Listservs were dropped from the initial sample if the list owner declined to participate in the study (21%); the listserv was defunct (16%); it had closed membership, generally as part of an organization, course, or task force (15%); or it could not provide membership data in an automated fashion. The final sample consisted of lists evenly divided among those oriented around professional, personal, and academic topics. Based on descriptions of the lists, we were able to classify them as purely electronic or as hybrid, combining both electronic and traditional communications, especially conventional face-to-face meetings. For example, a national list for youth hockey was judged as purely electronic, while the mailing list for a city-specific country dancers' group was judged as hybrid.

For a 130-day period we collected data on each listserv's membership and communication activity. During the observation period, membership was characterized in terms of size (number of members), growth (members entering as a percentage of initial size), loss (members leaving as a percentage of initial size), and net change in size (as a percentage of initial size). Communication activity was measured in terms of volume (number of messages per day) and interactivity (length of discussion threads). In addition, measures of member participation (percentage of members contributing messages and the concentration of message contributions among the active participants) were created for each listserv. . . .

Unlike traditional small groups, listservs have large, fluctuating memberships in which a small core of active participants generates relatively low levels of sporadic communication, whose messages rarely receive a response. Small groups, as described in the social psychological research literature, have between 3 and 15 members, with relatively low turnover. By comparison, the listservs were much larger (median of 64 members), with high churn (22% of original members dropping out annually and double this number joining). In contrast to highly interactive conversation involving almost all group members (typical of small groups), listservs exhibit little communication, with a full 33% exhibiting no communication during the 130-day observation period. Of those that did, the median listserv accrued 0.28 messages per day (or less than 0.0004 messages per subscriber per day). Over 50% of members contributed no messages over the 130-day observation period, and a small number generated most of the messages. Conversation was not interactive. On average, fewer than one message out of three received any response.

The hybrid groups differed little from the purely electronic groups. Though they were significantly smaller, probably reflecting the more limited geographic area from which they could attract members, both types of groups had similar high turnover, low volume of messages, low level of interactivity, and domination by a small proportion of their membership. Regardless of how the hybrid groups acted when they met face-to-face, online they acted like typical weak-tie collectives.

In terms of membership size and change, communication volume and structure, and participation levels, Internet listservs do not appear to be intimate social groups. These findings highlight a bias in prior research on online social activity. While the goal of describing the existence of true social behaviors in online environments has been well served by focusing on highly active and interactive examples of electronic collectives, these cases are not representative of what typically happens. For example, interactivity is a common theme in many descriptions of online social activity. However, our results imply that while interactivity can occur in these contexts, it is the exception, not the rule, when it occurs.

It was not the case that all listservs in this sample had impoverished social behavior, although this was the norm. Nor is it necessarily the case that all types of electronic collectives will look like listservs in terms of the quality of their social behavior. MUDs, MOOs, and Internet Relay Chat are highly interactive, at least among those who actively participate. As is the case with asynchronous media, however, research studying these phenomena has focused on interesting cases (that is, active ones). As a result, we know little about typical behavior in synchronic electronic collectives.

Clearly, there are cases of both synchronous and asynchronous electronic collectives that support the formation of substantial personal relationships and the development of group identity. On the other hand, these types of social activities seem unlikely to occur regularly in the typical listserv, where turnover is high and communication activities is low, noninteractive, and the result of contributions by a small percentage of the membership. This suggests that social places on the Internet where close personal relationships are formed and maintained are rare.

Conclusion

Using the Internet to build social relationships results in social interaction that is wanting, at least when it is explicitly compared to the standards of face-to-face and telephone communication, to social relationships that are primarily conducted offline, and to traditional small groups. We do not assert that online social interaction has little value. Surveys of the general public continually reveal that most people using the Internet value email and other forms of online social interaction. Even in the age of the Web and e-commerce, online social interaction is still the most important use of the Internet. However, in one-to-one comparisons, an email message is not as useful as a phone call or a face-to-face meeting for developing and sustaining social relationships. Listservs are not as valuable as small groups for establishing a sense of identity and belonging and for gaining social support. Relationships sustained primarily over the Internet are not as close as those sustained by other means.

Should these observations be a source of concern? To answer this question, we need additional information not yet available. Our data suggests the Internet is less effective than other means of forming and sustaining strong social relationships. The consequences of using the Internet for social relations, however, depend not only on the quality of the relationships sustained using it, but on opportunity costs as well. Do less-effective email messages substitute for or supplement telephone conversations and personal visits? Do weak social relationships formed online add to one's total stock of social relations or substitute for a more valuable partner? Does the time people spend reading listservs and participating in MUDs add to their social interaction, or substitute for time they would have spent in real-world groups? Only by examining people's full set of social behavior and examining their full inventory of social ties can we assess the net social impact of online social relationships.

POSTSCRIPT

Does the Internet Strengthen Social Connections?

At least one critic criticizes the Internet because it fosters "voluntary" communities based on mutual interests and argues that "learning to make the best of circumstances one has not chosen is part of what it means to be a good citizen and a mature human being. We should not organize our lives around the fantasy that entrance and exit can always be cost-free: Online groups can fulfill important emotional and utilitarian needs. But they must not be taken as comprehensive models of a future society" (William A. Galston, "Does the Internet Strengthen Community?" *National Civic Review*, October 2000). On the other hand, Wade Roush, "Social Machines," *Technology Review* (August 2005), notes that computing devices are now helping "us to be the social beings we are," and Luciano Floridi, "A Look into the Future Impact of ICT on Our Lives," *Information Society* (January/February 2007), finds that if online is not the way to go in the future, certainly the distinction between online and offline will soon disappear and we shall become "inforgs," connected informational organisms. Many people are already well along that path, as attested by the popularity of Second Life (http://secondlife.com/), which like Cybertown lets people live, work, play, buy, and sell in cyberspace. It describes itself as "a 3-D virtual world entirely built and owned by its residents. Since opening to the public in 2003, it has grown explosively and today is inhabited by a total of 2,795,713 people from around the globe." Social networking sites such as MySpace (http://www.myspace.com/) are also immensely popular.

In February 2000, the Stanford Institute for the Quantitative Study of Society released a study by Norman Nie of Stanford and Lutz Erbring of the Free University of Berlin that found that "the more hours people use the Internet, the less time they spend in contact with real human beings," with a quarter of regular Internet users saying it has reduced their in-person or phone time "with friends and family or attending events outside the home." Since time online increases with the number of years one has had Internet access, Nie and Erbring see a potential problem in personal isolation and reduced community participation. James E. Katz, Ronald E. Rice, and Philip Aspden, on the other hand, used telephone surveys from 1995 to 2000 to conclude that Internet users typically have more social contacts and are more involved in their community and in politics ("The Internet, 1995–2000: Access, Civic Involvement, and Social Interaction," *American Behavioral Scientist*, November 2001). Janis Wolak, Kimberly J. Mitchell, and David Finkelhor, "Escaping or Connecting? Characteristics of Youth Who Form Close Online Relationships," *Journal of Adolescence* (February 2003), note that at least with younger people, "girls who had high levels of conflict with parents or were highly troubled were more likely than other girls to have close online relationships, as were boys who had low levels of communication with parents or were highly troubled, compared to other boys." Examining college students, Katie Bonebrake, "College Students' Internet Use, Relationship Formation, and Personality Correlates," *CyberPsychology & Behavior* (December 2002), did not see such differences. Lee Rainie and John Horrigan, in "A Decade of Adoption: How the Internet Has Woven Itself into American Life," *Pew Internet & American Life Project* (http://www.pewinternet.org/PPF/r/148/report_display.asp) (January 25, 2005), note that "For the most part, the online world mirrors the offline world [and the] Web has become the 'new normal' in the American way of life." Donna L. Hoffman, Thomas P. Novak, and Alladi Venkatesh suggest that "normal" is too mild a term in "Has the Internet Become Indispensable?" *Communications of the ACM* (July 2004). Yair Amichai-Hamburger and Adrian Furnham, "The Positive Net," *Computers in Human Behavior* (March 2007), note that "When used appropriately, the Internet may greatly improve the quality of life for its users." Linda A. Jackson et al., "The Impact of Internet Use on the Other Side of the Digital Divide," *Communications of the ACM* (July 2004), suggest that it is still true that neither "normal" nor "indispensable" apply to the poor.

Paul DiMaggio, Eszter Hargittai, W. Russell Neuman, and John P. Robinson say that most of the research on the social impacts of the Internet is flawed, having been performed by nonacademic survey organizations and focused too much on individuals rather than the organizational structure of the Internet itself; more research by academic sociologists is needed. Still, they call the Internet "a potentially transformative technology" and note that it "tends to complement rather than displace existing media and patterns of behavior" (see "Social Implications of the Internet," *Annual Review of Sociology*, 2001).

ISSUE 16

Does the Spread of Surveillance Technology Threaten Privacy?

YES: Julian Sanchez, from "The Pinpoint Search," *Reason* (January 2007)

NO: Stuart Taylor, Jr., from "How Civil-Libertarian Hysteria May Endanger Us All," *National Journal* (February 22, 2003)

ISSUE SUMMARY

YES: Julian Sanchez argues that new technologies make it astonishingly easy to detect transgressions of laws regarding traffic, drugs, weapons, and illegal computer files. Ordinary expectations of privacy are seriously threatened, and we face the need for difficult tradeoffs.

NO: Stuart Taylor, Jr., contends that those who object to surveillance—particularly government surveillance—have their priorities wrong. Curbing "government powers in the name of civil liberties [exacts] too high a price in terms of endangered lives."

The Fourth Amendment to the U.S. Constitution established the right of private citizens to be secure against unreasonable searches and seizures. "Unreasonable" has come to mean "without a search warrant" for physical searches of homes and offices, and "without a court order" for interceptions of mail and wiretappings of phone conversations.

Private citizens who—for whatever reason—do not wish to have their communications with others shared with law enforcement and security agencies have long sought ways to preserve their privacy. They therefore welcomed changes in communications technology, from easily tappable copper wires to fiber optics, from analog (which mimics voice vibrations) to digital (which encodes them). But the U.S. Department of Justice sought legislation to require that the makers and providers of communications products and services ensure that their products remain tappable, and in September 1992, the Clinton Administration submitted to Congress the Digital Telephony Act, a piece of legislation designed to prevent advancing technology from limiting

304

the government's ability legally to intercept communications. For a defense of this measure, see Dorothy Denning, "To Tap or Not to Tap," *Communications of the ACM* (March 1993).

Yet people fear the Internet because it makes a huge variety of information available to everyone with very little accountability. Even children can find sites dedicated to pornography, violence, and hate. Marketers can build detailed profiles. Fraud, identity theft, invasion of privacy, and terrorism have taken new forms. Criminals can use encryption (secret codes) to make their email messages and transmitted documents unreadable to anyone (such as law-enforcement personnel with the digital equivalent of wiretap warrants).

In response the Department of Justice developed an Internet wiretapping system called Carnivore. Before it was abandoned in 2004, many people were disturbed by its invisibility and the potential for abuse in its ability to search Internet traffic without a court order and to search for any key words its operators desired. Similar concerns have arisen in connection with new technologies that make it possible to detect chemicals (drugs and explosives) and other signs of wrong-doing, as well as with the growing presence of streetcorner surveillance cameras (see Brendan O'Neill, "Watching You Watching Me," *New Statesman*, October 2, 2006).

But after September 11, 2001, the War on Terrorism began and every tool that promised to help identify terrorists before or catch them after they committed their dreadful acts was seen as desirable. However, when the Department of Defense's Defense Advanced Research Projects Agency (DARPA) proposed a massive computer system capable of sifting through purchases, tax data, court records, and other information from government and commercial databases to seek suspicious patterns of behavior, the objections returned in force. The Total or Terrorism Information Awareness program soon died although many of its components continued under other names; see Shane Harris, "TIA Lives On," *National Journal* (February 25, 2006). Simon Cooper, "Who's Spying on You?" *Popular Mechanics* (January 2005), argues that we are now subject to massively increased routine surveillance and the collection of personal data by both government and business with very few restrictions on how the data are used. In the following selections, Julian Sanchez argues that the issue is not just computer technology and surveillance of communications and network activity. New technologies make it astonishingly easy to detect transgressions of laws regarding traffic, drugs, weapons, and illegal computer files. "These technologies," he says, "are too powerful to use thoughtlessly." Ordinary expectations of privacy are seriously threatened, and we face the need for difficult tradeoffs. Stuart Taylor, Jr., contends that those who object to surveillance—particularly government surveillance—have their priorities wrong. Curbing "government powers in the name of civil liberties [exacts] too high a price in terms of endangered lives."

YES

The Pinpoint Search

Anyone would consider it a stroke of bad luck to be pulled over for driving six miles per hour over the speed limit, but Roy Caballes had an additional reason to curse his ill fortune. On the November afternoon in 1998 when an Illinois state trooper stopped him, Caballes was carrying 282 pounds of marijuana in his trunk. At first it looked like he'd get off with just a warning. Then another officer pulled up and swept his car with one of the most advanced pieces of technology then available to law enforcement: a drug-sniffing dog named Krott. The pooch uncovered the dope.

Caballes thought the cops didn't have a legitimate reason to bring in Krott, and he fought the search. In 2003 the Illinois Supreme Court ruled that the officers had indeed violated the Fourth Amendment by transforming the traffic stop into a drug investigation without probable cause, or even the weaker "reasonable suspicion." But in the 2005 decision *Illinois v. Caballes*, the U.S. Supreme Court ruled that the dog sniff could not have rendered an otherwise lawful traffic stop unconstitutional unless the dog sniff itself violated Caballes' "constitutionally protected interest in privacy." The Court concluded it did not, citing a 1983 decision in which it ruled that, because a dog sniff reveals only the presence of contraband in which there is no "reasonable expectation of privacy," it isn't a "search" at all. The Supremes sent the case back to Illinois, and Caballes ended up with a 12-year prison sentence.

The dog sniff that caught Caballes is just one crude, old-fashioned example of the search technologies available to law enforcement. A new wave of advanced surveillance tools is capable of detecting not just drugs but weapons, explosives, and illicit computer files, potentially flying under the Fourth Amendment's radar all the while. A handheld scanner picks up stray particles of cocaine on a car during a routine traffic stop. Is that a search? A high-tech camera detects the gun one pedestrian is carrying under his jacket. Is that a search? A forensic analyst finds a single image of child pornography on a computer server containing thousands of files owned by hundreds of users, without ever seeing any other private information. Is that a search?

In a nation whose reams of regulations make almost everyone guilty of some violation at some point, Americans have grown accustomed to getting away with minor transgressions: the occasional joint or downloaded movie or high-speed dash to the airport. For at least some crimes, though, the expectation that our peccadilloes will slip through the cracks may soon be outdated. The

From *Reason Magazine*, January 2007. Copyright © 2007 by Reason Foundation, 3415 S. Sepulveda Blvd., Suite 400, Los Angeles, CA 90034. www.reason.com.

new style of noninvasive but deeply revealing detection—call them "pinpoint searches"—will require rapid adjustments in both legal rules and social mores.

Anatomically Correct Searches

The original pinpoint search, the drug dog's sniff, has built-in limits. A German shepherd is a cumbersome piece of biotechnology, making suspicionless sweeps during routine traffic stops the exception rather than the rule. But chemists and engineers are developing a variety of electronic sniffers that are competing to make Fido's schnoz obsolete.

DrugWipes, for example, are small, swab-tipped devices. Wipe the tip along a surface, or a sample of sweat or saliva, and in two to five minutes a simple indicator window reveals whether drug residue is present. Manufactured by the German firm Securetec, DrugWipes have been used by more than 2,000 law enforcement agencies in the U.S. since the late 1990s, and they're increasingly popular among schools and private employers as well.

DrugWipes have limitations: They're single-use devices, and while the basic model is inexpensive (less than $10 per unit), each picks up only one specific type of drug residue. Even with a relatively low per-unit price, the cost of sweeping a school or a parking lot can mount quickly. For more versatility, cops can turn to General Electric's VaporTracer, a seven-pound handheld particle sniffer that can test for a wide range of drugs and explosives in only a few seconds.

The VaporTracer and its nonportable cousin, the Itemiser, are already used in airports to scan luggage for explosives. With a price tag of $25,000 to $30,000, the VaporTracer is unlikely to become standard issue for beat cops in the near future. (G.E. estimates that about 4,000 are in use worldwide, most for explosive detection.) But researchers are developing ever faster, cheaper, and more sensitive electronic noses.

Among the technologies in the offing is the desorption electrospray ionization scanner. It uses charged droplets to lift particles from a surface and into a mass spectrometer, which can break down and analyze the components of any substance down to the molecular level. It's currently a desktop-sized machine, but its creators, a team of researchers at Purdue University, hope to develop a portable version that can fit in a backpack within a few years. The Purdue team's head, Graham Cooks, guesses such a device might cost about $4,000. That's not exactly cheap, but it's thousands of dollars less than a well-trained drug dog costs.

Meanwhile, scientists at Georgia Tech have developed prototype scanning technologies based on a penny-sized surface acoustic wave chip, which works by measuring disturbances in sound waves as they pass across small quartz crystals. This "dog on a chip" sensor is coated with a thin layer of cloned antibody proteins that bond to a specific molecule, such as cocaine or TNT. The sound waves passing through that sensor can then be compared with an uncoated control crystal: Differences in the waves mean the chip has picked up trace amounts—as little as a few trillionths of a gram—of the target substance.

Handheld scanners aren't the only possible application for such sniffer chips. Metro stations in Washington, D.C., have been fitted with fixed chemical weapon detectors, meant to give advance warning in case of a terrorist attack. Sensors with a range of a few feet could be combined with surveillance cameras to pinpoint passengers who might be worth extra scrutiny.

Police can use new devices to hunt not just for tiny traces of contraband but for larger objects. Millimeter wave (MMW) radiation is all around us. You're emitting it even as you read this article. More important, you're emitting it through your clothes, making it an ideal way to scan for hidden objects that distort or block those waves, whether they're made of metal, ceramic, plastic, or some other composite material—and without any of the health concerns associated with X-rays.

The Federal Aviation Administration began funding MMW research back in 1989. The technology has since been licensed to several commercial firms. Intellifit, for example, has set up MMW kiosks in several malls and clothing stores; they help people find clothing that's a good fit for their frame.

But the primary licensees have been in the security business. In the summer of 2005, a company called SafeView debuted a three-dimensional body scanner, SafeScout, for use in airports and at other security checkpoints. Think of the scene in the 1990 science fiction flick *Total Recall* where California's future governor races behind a panel that exposes, in real time, all the weaponry hidden away among bulging muscles.

In its most intrusive form, an MMW scanner can reveal a rough nude image of its subjects. The models being deployed for most security purposes get around that problem by projecting any objects the scanner detects on a generic virtual mannequin.

Less intrusive is the BIS-WDS Prime, a security camera created by the Florida-based firm Brijot Imaging Systems. Unveiled last spring, the camera pinpoints weapons and suspicious objects at a range of up to 45 feet by comparing hidden objects picked up by its millimeter wave sensor to a database of weapon shapes. The detection process, Brijot claims, takes less than half a second, and the higher-end models will display up to 20 threats simultaneously. (The camera was field tested this summer at New York's Port Authority Bus Terminal and at New Jersey PATH train stations.)

If a search technology based on shape matching still seems a bit low-tech, consider Pulsed Fast Neutron Analysis, which can reveal the molecular composition of a load of cargo without opening its vehicle. In the summer of 2004, U.S. Customs and Border Protection began testing a $10 million, car wash–sized prototype facility at the Ysleta border crossing near El Paso, Texas. It bombards vehicles with high-energy neutrons, which excite the nuclei of atoms, causing the contents to emit gamma rays. Since different elements emit gamma rays at different energy levels, the scanner can infer the chemical structure of the cargo's contents, distinguishing plastic explosives from Play-Doh and table sugar from Colombian White.

Googling for Contraband

In 1996 Michael Adler offered a hypothetical question in *The Yale Law Journal*. Adler imagined a computer worm or virus that could quickly and unobtrusively scan thousands of computer hard drives simultaneously, looking for evidence of illicit files—classified documents, say, or pirated software or child pornography. Would this count as a "search" for Fourth Amendment purposes?

This remained a hypothetical question until 2001, when someone released that worm. Called Noped, the crude Visual Basic Script program would infect PCs by way of an email attachment and (after mailing itself out to everyone in the infected user's address book) scan for images with file names that its author considered suggestive of kiddie porn. If it found a match, it would email law enforcement a list of its findings.

A file name match is too thin a reed on which to hang an investigation, but better technologies can pinpoint specific files on a hard drive. By running a large file through a cryptographic algorithm, it's possible to generate a much shorter unique string of letters and numbers (or close enough to unique for any practical purpose) called a hash value, which can quickly determine whether two files are identical. The National Drug Intelligence Center's Hashkeeper database already contains the hash values of both common commercial software programs and known images of illicit child pornography, making it easy for a trained technician to discern whether a hard drive contains a copy of a particular file.

Orin Kerr, a law professor at George Washington University, literally wrote the book on government searches of computer data: the 2001 Justice Department manual *Searching and Seizing Computers and Obtaining Electronic Evidence in Criminal Investigations*. Kerr says sweeping viral searches would run afoul of existing wiretap laws, which raise more stringent barriers to "unauthorized access" than is imposed by the current judicial interpretation of the Fourth Amendment. Yet he says it's far less clear how the courts would treat digital searches that take place in the course of authorized searches for other material.

Imagine, for example, that a police technician has lawful physical access to a server containing thousands of users' files. He's supposed to be looking for evidence of tax fraud in a specific suspect's documents. Even though the warrant specifies only that user, will it count as an additional "search" if the officer runs a search program on the entire server, designed to alert him only when it locates known child porn? If there's "no reasonable expectation of privacy" when it comes to possessing narcotics, wouldn't the same rule apply to child pornography?

Government investigators may have already caught up with the legal theorists' hypotheticals—searching not for kiddie porn but for terrorist plots. Consider the controversial surveillance carried out by the hyper-clandestine National Security Agency (NSA) following the attacks of September 11, 2001. The first program to be revealed, in December 2005, involved conventional wiretapping, but further leaks hinted that far more sweeping surveillance might be taking place. Voice and text recognition software might be sifting through millions of communications in search of target words or phrases that raised red flags for investigators.

The NSA fired Russell Tice, an intelligence analyst at the agency, in May 2005; he now says he wants to tell Congress about NSA surveillance programs he believes are illegal. While Tice won't discuss specific programs, he notes that the technology exists to filter data and voice traffic on a mass scale, flagging communications where target words or phrases—jihad, say, or the names of known terrorists—are used. With the help of linguistic consultants, he says, intelligence agencies can even zero in on particular accents or speech patterns.

Privacy mavens have long whispered of a program called ECHELON, a massive signals intelligence network rumored to have been developed as a Cold War espionage tool. It supposedly used batteries of high-powered computers, called "dictionaries," to scan voice and data communications for suspicious phrases. While the NSA has never confirmed that ECHELON is real, a 2001 report by the European Parliament concluded that "the existence of a global system for intercepting communications . . . is no longer in doubt."

In a January 2006 speech at the National Press Club, in which he called ECHELON an "urban legend," former NSA head and current CIA chief Gen. Michael V. Hayden asserted that the NSA's warrantless wiretap program, exposed by *The New York Times* in late 2005, "is not a driftnet . . . grabbing conversations that we then sort out by these alleged keyword searches or data-mining tools or other devices. . . . This is targeted and focused." But reports from insiders continue to hint at something far more expansive.

A February *Washington Post* piece described a tiered computer filtering system that initially swept up hundreds of thousands of communications, using increasingly intrusive techniques to winnow the pool down to a far smaller number subject to human examination. In April the Electronic Frontier Foundation disclosed that a former AT&T technician, Mark Klein, had come forward with tales of a "secret room" his erstwhile employer had built at the NSA's behest, in which vast amounts of data were scrutinized by a "semantic traffic analyzer."

And in May *USA Today* revealed that the NSA had created a database compiling information about the calling patterns of millions of Americans. If such analysis was really limited to information about the calls—who phoned whom, when, and for how long—current Supreme Court precedent would not classify the interception as a "search." Less certain, however, is the status of intercepts using ECHELON-style "dictionaries" to probe the contents of some voice and data communications for target words or phrases. "If this approach was used, and hundreds of thousands if not millions of communications were processed in that manner," says Tice, "the argument could be made, well, if a machine was doing the looking and the sucking in, it doesn't matter because that's not monitoring until a human looks at it." Writing in *The New Republic* last February, Richard A. Posner, a judge on the U.S. Court of Appeals for the 7th Circuit, made exactly that argument, suggesting that automated searches do not violate the law "because a computer program is not a sentient being."

Storage Devices and Virtual Files

Courts already have started to tackle some of the questions raised by these new technologies, but not consistently enough for us to predict with confidence where they'll go in the future. In *United States v. Runyan* (2001), the U.S. Court of Appeals for the 5th Circuit ruled that when a woman who had found a few of her husband's child porn files turned his digital storage devices over to police, they had already been "searched." The cops, therefore, didn't perform any additional search when they did a more comprehensive analysis and found more extensive caches of similar material. But in a 10th Circuit case, *United States v. Carey* (1999), the appeals court held that a forensic analyst who was lawfully searching a hard drive in the course of a drug investigation did exceed the scope of the warrant when, after accidentally opening a child porn file, he abandoned the search for drug-related material and started digging for more porn.

Kerr characterizes these as "storage device" and "virtual file" approaches, respectively. The former treats a digital storage medium as though it's a single physical container, like a briefcase or a trunk: Once the lock is lawfully popped, all the contents are subject to observation. With the virtual file approach, a digital storage device is more like a warehouse containing many thousands of individual closed boxes: Police may have the authority to go looking through the warehouse for a few particular containers, but that doesn't mean they may pry anything open willy-nilly. Even under a "virtual file" approach, the logic of *Illinois v. Caballes* suggests that a scan for illicit files using something like the Hashkeeper database, which doesn't technically "open" the file, will not count as a search once police have lawful access to the storage medium.

Kerr has offered his solution, at least in the case of digital searches, in the *Harvard Law Review*. In a June 2006 article he proposes an "exposure theory" of the Fourth Amendment: Any time computer data or information about that data (such as whether it matches certain search criteria) is exposed to human observation via an output device such as a monitor or printer, those data have been "searched" for Fourth Amendment purposes.

This approach would attenuate, perhaps even eliminate, the "plain view" doctrine in the digital realm. That doctrine holds that any evidence uncovered in the course of a lawful investigation is fair game for police, even when the investigation was initiated for a different purpose—as when, for instance, police smell marijuana or spot a gun during a traffic stop. Such a principle would also, in effect, declare Caballes a dead letter online, since it would shift the legal focus to where investigators looked, rather than the amount of additional physical intrusion or the type of information uncovered.

Some want to see Caballes consigned to the dustbin of jurisprudence offline as well. Marc Rotenberg, executive director of the Electronic Privacy Information Center, proposes rolling back the Caballes exception and hewing to a strict version of the standard the Supreme Court articulated in *Kyllo v. United States*, under which any information about certain protected spheres, beyond what an unaided human observer could glean, would be regarded as presumptively private. "Your expectation of privacy really has to be measured against what an unassisted police officer might be able to obtain from you," Rotenberg argues, "not what technology might make possible." Otherwise, he suggests, that expectation will only grow ever weaker as technology improves.

There's another advantage to applying the Fourth Amendment's protections to pinpoint searches: It would create an obstacle to the use of the search power to harass, something that loomed large in the fears of the Founders. For generations, supporters of broad law enforcement powers have claimed that "if you're not guilty, you have nothing to hide." But as the Harvard law professor William J. Stuntz has noted, the Fourth Amendment—and the Fifth Amendment, which protects against self-incrimination—were intended not just as abstract procedural checks but as substantive safeguards against criminalizing certain kinds of activity, such as religious and political dissent. It's harder to prohibit a faith, for example, when police don't have the power to look through citizens' papers or burst into their homes without specific evidence of criminality to cite as grounds for a warrant.

If pinpoint searches are not subject to any judicial oversight, law enforcement agencies will have broad discretion over whom to search and how often to search them. There's ample reason to suspect that such discretion won't always be exercised equitably. Whites and blacks use illicit drugs at similar rates, for example, but blacks make up nearly half of state prison inmates convicted of drug offenses. It is easy to imagine some politically unpopular person or group subject to frequent pinpoint searches for minor drug infractions, zoning code violations, or whatever other commonplace low-grade statute violations new technologies make it possible to detect.

Should We Learn to Stop Worrying and Love Pinpoint Searches?

Despite such concerns, some civil libertarians greet these new technologies with surprising enthusiasm. Jeffrey Rosen, a law professor at George Washington University and the author of *The Unwanted Gaze: The Destruction of Privacy in America* (2001), stresses that such searches avoid some of the central problems the Fourth Amendment's framers worried about. "Privacy people should be unequivocally and unambiguously enthusiastic about technologies that can manage to find illegal activity without intruding on innocent privacy interests," he argues. "The paradigmatic example of an unreasonable search at the time of the framing of the Constitution was the search of private diaries, because you had to look at a lot of innocent and intimate information in order to find potentially illegal information." Pinpoint searches may allow the cop who pulls you over for speeding to scan you routinely for drugs or guns. But they may also mean he'll be less likely to invent a pretext to rifle your glove box, exposing that legal but embarrassing bottle of Viagra. And the subway cop who wants to be sure your backpack doesn't contain a bomb won't need to open it up and see what else you're carrying.

The veteran civil liberties litigator Harvey Silverglate has staked out a position between Rotenberg's and Rosen's. He notes that the Fourth Amendment's clause requiring searches to be "reasonable" is technically separate from the clause outlining the preconditions for a warrant to be issued, and that there are conditions under which courts have ruled warrantless searches to be reasonable. (In addition to the "plain view" exception mentioned earlier, there are exceptions for "exigent circumstance," as when a cop believes a dealer is about to flush his stash or a kidnapper is on the verge of killing his victim.) So you can concede that pinpoint searches really are searches subject to judicial oversight without ruling out the possibility that some searches, under some circumstances, are "reasonable" even without a warrant. Silverglate believes the law will move away from strict warrant requirements for minimally intrusive technologies, such as hand-held explosive sniffers, that are geared to prevent especially severe crimes, such as terrorist attacks. "The courts," he predicts, "are going to say that if some germ or atomic weapon could kill thousands of people, then some methods are going to be 'reasonable' that wouldn't be when you're trying to find a guy smoking pot."

For the most optimistic take on pinpoint searches, turn to the futurist David Brin, author of the 1998 book *The Transparent Society*. Brin believes a world of more perfect enforcement will create democratic pressure to either eliminate or drastically reduce penalties for "victimless" offenses. What matters, Brin avers, is not what the government knows about you but what it can do to you. To those who fear a world in which, for instance, routine speeding infractions are invariably met with stiff fines, Brin ripostes: "Can't you trust your fellow citizens to not want that either?"

Andrew Napolitano, the author of *The Constitution in Exile*, is unconvinced. A legal analyst for Fox News and a former New Jersey judge, Napolitano joins Rotenberg in insisting that a "neutral magistrate" stand between police and the subjects of all government searches. He argues that it's precisely when law enforcement agencies are most tempted to bypass checks on government snooping that the public is least apt to demand adherence to the letter of the law. For proof, he points to many Americans' indifference to—or support of—the NSA's warrantless wiretaps. "When the president can go on TV and get a 57 percent approval rating saying he doesn't care about privacy, he only cares about security," Napolitano concludes, "we may have to count on my black-robed colleagues to protect privacy."

We may hope our elected representatives will either exempt a pothead from pinpoint searches, lighten his punishment to compensate for the new ease of capturing him, or even abandon their long-running war on him altogether. But what about more serious crimes, such as terrorism? Should we allow electronic sniffers to troll through vast haystacks of telecommunications data searching for jihadist needles, in the hope that terrorists will not simply use encryption technology to render such surveillance useless?

Tradeoffs to Come

David Post, a cyberlaw expert at Temple University, hopes we can deploy pinpoint searches in ways that preserve the balance between security and privacy. "The kind of oversight you want in a system like this is very different from what you'd want in the ordinary warrant case," he says. "There you want someone looking at the evidence as it relates to a particular target. Here I want someone who's looking at the system as a whole, an ongoing systemic analysis of a kind that really is new." In Post's model, a panel of legal and technical experts with appropriate security clearances might be granted ongoing oversight responsibilities over an ECHELON-style vacuum-cleaner surveillance program to determine whether it was sufficiently fine-tuned.

Silverglate suggests another way to take advantage of the new surveillance tools while still protecting privacy: establish a "multi-level, tiered approach to electronic searches." At the first level, a filter system overseen by the kind of panel Post imagines sifts through communications, flagging suspicious conversations. Intelligence agents might then listen to brief snippets of conversation selected by the computers but, crucially, without learning the identities of any of the parties to the conversation.

Then, says Silverglate, "based on what the vacuum cleaner picks up, the NSA is going to have to go to a Foreign Intelligence Surveillance Act court and see if they have probable cause to find out the identity of the person on the line." Such an approach might even, paradoxically, make such secret courts, notorious for almost never rejecting wiretap applications, less inclined to defer to intelligence agencies, since instead of being asked whether they are prepared to give terror hunters the benefit of the doubt, judges will already know some of the contents of the communications for which they're being asked to authorize the release of identifying data.

That doesn't solve every problem with such systems, of course. It does not deal with the chilling effect that may occur when speakers begin to watch their words on the phone based on the fear that they will trigger a computer in Fort Meade if they say the wrong thing. And once the necessary infrastructure is set up to use such a system to catch terrorists, it would be both relatively simple technically and powerfully tempting politically to expand it to hunt for the least sophisticated perpetrators of whatever crime is particularly unpopular at the moment.

Whether we adopt the sanguine approach of Rosen and Brin, embrace the strong privacy protections of Napolitano and Rotenberg, or look for a middle path with Silverglate and Post, we will be forced to make difficult tradeoffs. But the debate over how to strike that balance must begin now, before today's prototype rolls off tomorrow's assembly line. These new technologies are too powerful to use thoughtlessly. We're already entering a pinpoint-search world. Now we must decide how to live in it.

Stuart Taylor, Jr.

 **NO**

How Civil-Libertarian Hysteria May Endanger Us All

Someday Americans may die because of Congress's decision earlier this month to cripple a Defense Department program designed to catch future Mohamed Attas before they strike. That's not a prediction. But it is a fear.

The program seeks to develop software to make intelligence-sharing more effective by making it instantaneous, the better to learn more about suspected terrorists and identify people who might be terrorists. It would link computerized government databases to one another and to some non-government databases to which investigators already have legal access. If feasible, it would also fish through billions of transactions for patterns of activities in which terrorists might engage.

But now these goals are all in jeopardy, because of a stunningly irresponsible congressional rush to hobble the Pentagon program in ways that are far from necessary to protect privacy. This is not to deny that, absent stringent safeguards and oversight, the ineptly named "Total Information Awareness" [TIA] program might present serious threats to privacy. It might, for example, subject thousands of innocent citizens and noncitizens alike to unwelcome scrutiny, and might even expose political dissenters to harassment by rogue officials.

But some curbs on potentially dangerous (and potentially life-saving) government powers in the name of civil liberties are not necessary to protect privacy and exact too high a price in terms of endangered lives. Congress's rush to strangle TIA in its infancy is such a case. It makes little more sense than would a flat ban on any and all wire-tapping of phones that might be used by U.S. citizens. Like TIA, wiretapping poses grave risks to privacy if not carefully restricted. So we restrict it. We don't ban it.

The problem with the near-ban on TIA—sponsored by Sens. Ron Wyden, D-Ore., and Charles Grassley, R-Iowa, and known as the Wyden amendment—is that rather than weighing the hoped-for security benefits against the feared privacy costs, and devising ways to minimize those costs, Congress was stampeded by civil-libertarian hysteria into adopting severe and unwarranted restrictions. The Bush administration shares the blame because the person it put in charge of TIA research is Adm. John M. Poindexter, whose record of lying to Congress about the Iran-Contra affair does not inspire trust.

"There are risks to TIA, but in the end I think the risks of not trying TIA are greater, and we should at least try to construct systems for [minimizing] abuse before we discard all potential benefits from technological innovation," says Paul Rosenzweig, a legal analyst at the Heritage Foundation who has co-authored a thoughtful 25-page analysis of the TIA program, including a list of muscular safeguards that Congress could adopt to protect privacy and prevent abuses. Instead of weighing such factors, Rosenzweig says, Congress has "deliberately and without much thought decided to discard the greatest advantage we have over our foes—our technological superiority."

The Wyden amendment seems reasonable enough at first blush. That may be why all 100 senators and the House conferees voted to attach it to the omnibus spending bill that cleared Congress on February 13. The amendment allows pure TIA *research* to continue, if the administration files a detailed report within 90 days or the president invokes national security needs. And the amendment's restrictions on TIA *deployment* have been sold as a temporary move to allow time for congressional oversight.

But such measures, once adopted, are a good bet to become permanent in today's habitually gridlocked Congress, where determined minorities have great power to block any change in the status quo. And the Wyden amendment's impact is likely to be far broader than advertised. It flatly bars *any* deployment of TIA-derived technology, by any agency, with exceptions only for military operations outside the U.S. and "lawful foreign intelligence activities conducted *wholly* [my emphasis] against non-United States persons" (defined to mean nonresident aliens).

The scope of the latter exception is ambiguous. But Rosenzweig fears that it will be read narrowly, and that the Wyden amendment will be read broadly—especially by officials fearful of congressional wrath—as barring virtually *all* uses of TIA technology, even to search the government's own databases for suspected foreign terrorists. This is because virtually all large databases are "mixed": They contain information about U.S. citizens, resident aliens, and nonresident aliens alike.

In any event, the Wyden amendment quite clearly prohibits any use of TIA technology to pursue the unknown but apparently substantial number of U.S. citizens and resident aliens who may be loyal to Al Qaeda, such as suspected dirty-bomb plotter Jose Padilla and the six suspected Yemeni-American "sleepers" arrested in Lackawanna, N.Y., last year. As a technical matter, the FBI, the CIA, and the Department of Homeland Security remain free to develop and deploy similar technology on their own. But they will hesitate to risk charges of evading Congress's will. Not to mention the wastefulness of barring these agencies from building on the TIA technology already developed by the Pentagon.

How did TIA become such a dreaded symbol of Big Brotherism? Part of the reason was well-founded concern that unless strictly controlled, the more exotic uses of TIA, such as surveying billions of transactions involving hundreds of millions of people for patterns deemed indicative of possible terrorist activities, could subject huge numbers of innocent Americans to scrutiny as potential terrorists. But Rosenzweig and others who share these concerns, including officials of the TIA program itself, have already been crafting safeguards. Among them are software designs and legal rules that would block human agents from learning the identities of people whose transactions are being "data-mined" by TIA computers unless the agents can obtain judicial warrants by showing something analogous to the "probable cause" that the law requires to justify a wiretap.

It was largely misinformation and over-heated rhetoric from civil-libertarian zealots—on both the left and the right—that pushed the Wyden amendment through Congress. The misinformation included the false claim that Poindexter would preside over a domestic spying apparatus, and the false suggestion that TIA was poised to rummage through the most private of databases to compile dossiers on millions of Americans' credit card, banking, business, travel, educational, and medical records and e-mails.

To the contrary, Poindexter's job is limited to developing software. And even without the Wyden amendment, TIA would give investigators access only to databases and records—government and nongovernment—that they already have a right to access. Its most basic function would be simply to expedite the kinds of intelligence-sharing that might have thwarted the September 11 attacks, by linking the government's own databases with one another and with any legally accessible private databases. The goal is to enable investigators to amass in minutes clues that now could take weeks or months to collect.

Here's a hypothetical example (adapted from Rosenzweig's analysis) of how as-yet-non-existent TIA technology might help stop terrorists—and how the Wyden amendment might prevent that.

Say the government learns from a reliable informant olmthat the precursor elements of Sarin gas have been smuggled into the United States by unidentified Qaeda operatives via flights from Germany during the month of February. Its first investigative step might be a TIA-based "query" of foreign databases that might help generate a list of possible terrorists. (But the Wyden amendment would bar a TIA-based query for the names of any who might be Americans. And it could be construed as putting entirely off-limits *any* "mixed database" that includes Americans.)

A second step might be a pattern-based query to U.S. government databases to produce a list of all passengers, or perhaps all nonresident aliens, entering the U.S. on flights from Germany during February. (But the Wyden amendment would bar a query for all passengers, and would again pose the mixed-database problem.)

A third query might seek to find which of these passengers' names are also in government databases of known or suspected terrorists. (But the Wyden amendment would pose the same obstacles.)

Fourth, with a list of subjects for further investigation based on these queries, TIA could be used—perhaps after obtaining a judicial warrant—to link to any legally accessible commercial databases to find out whether any of these subjects has bought canisters suitable for deployment of Sarin gas, or rented airplanes suitable for dispersing it, or stayed in the same motels as other subjects of investigation. And so on. (But for the Wyden amendment, that is.)

It is not yet clear whether it is even possible to develop technology powerful enough to do all of this. But it might be possible. Shouldn't we be racing to find out?

POSTSCRIPT

Does the Spread of Surveillance Technology Threaten Privacy?

The basic shape of the debate is simple: surveillance and data collection are useful. Government insists that private citizens do not have the right to act in such a way that they cannot be watched, supervised, and punished if government deems it necessary. The issue gained fresh importance in 2005, when the PATRIOT Act came up for renewal (see "'Trust Me' Just Doesn't Fly," *USA Today* [April 13, 2005]) and the federal 2006 budget for surveillance technology and manpower increased greatly (see http://www.epic.org/privacy/budget/fy2006/). Private businesses have very similar attitudes toward employees and even customers; see Stephanie Armour, "Employers Look Closely at What Workers Do on the Job," *USA Today* (November 8, 2006). The Electronic Frontier Foundation (EFF), the Electronic Privacy Information Center (EPIC), and numerous other groups and individuals insist equally strenuously that the right to privacy must come first.

Carnivore and the Total or Terrorism Information Awareness (TIA) program reflect many fears about the Net—that it is a place where evil lurks, where technically skilled criminals use their skills to fleece the unsuspecting public, where terrorists plot unseen, and where technology lends immunity to detection, apprehension, and prosecution. Other technologies—including such old standbys as radar detectors—give advantages to more ordinary people, and law enforcement has long wished for ways to overcome those advantages. Carnivore and Echelon were milestone attempts in the area of communications, although both have been much criticized. See Nat Hentoff, "1984 Is Here," *Free Inquiry* (Spring 2003), John Foley, "Data Debate," *InformationWeek* (May 19, 2003) and Wayne Madsen, "US Insight—The Secrets of DARPA's TIA: The US Government's Electronic Intelligence Snooping Machine," *Computer Fraud & Security* (May 2003). Nor is the issue solely American. Yves Poullet, "The Fight against Crime and/or the Protection of Privacy: A Thorny Debate!" *International Review of Law Computers & Technology* (July 2004), discusses the issue from the European standpoint and notes that "there is no worse danger than this cyber-surveillance, which hunts a man down in his most intimate space and raises within him a perpetual and haunting fear of exposure." Concerns over the use of surveillance cameras and RFID chips are expressed by Patrick Tucker, "Fun with Surveillance," *The Futurist* (November–December 2006). James Harkin, "You're Being Watched," *New Statesman* (January 15, 2007), thinks that digital tracking technologies may, overall, be a force for good.

In case anyone should conclude that the only surveillance to worry about comes from government and business, "Move Over, Big Brother," *Economist* (December 4, 2004), outlines how surveillance technology—in the form of camera phones and digital cameras—is now available to everyone. People have attached GPS-enabled phones to cars to track spouses or stalk ex-spouses and used camera phones and digital cameras for industrial espionage and identity theft. They have also used them to record crimes in progress and help law enforcement do its job. The full impact on society, whether for good or bad, is not yet clear.

ISSUE 17

Should the World's Libraries Be Digitized?

YES: **Brendan Rapple**, from "Google and Access to the World's Intellectual Heritage," *Contemporary Review* (June 2005)

NO: **Keith Kupferschmid**, from "Are Authors and Publishers Getting Scroogled?" *Information Today* (December 2005)

ISSUE SUMMARY

YES: Brendan Rapple argues that as Google scans, indexes, and makes available for online searching the books of the world's major libraries, it will increase access, facilitate scholarship, and in general benefit human civilization.

NO: Keith Kupferschmid argues that there is no justification in law for Google's massive copying of books. If the Google Print Library Project is allowed to continue, the interests of publishers, authors, and creators of all kinds will be seriously damaged.

When personal computers first came on the market in the 1970s, they were considered useful tools, but their memory was limited to only a few thousand bytes, hard drives were expensive add-ons, and the Internet was two decades away from its present status as a necessity of daily life. But already some people had begun to realize the value of making what had long been available only as print also available in electronic or digital form. Project Gutenberg, founded in 1971 by Michael Hart at the University of Illinois, was busily converting works of classic literature into digital form and making them available on disk. By 1990, a number of small companies were trying to turn electronic publishing into profitable businesses. Almost all are gone, partly because "print on demand" (POD) publishing made it possible to print economically single copies of books stored in electronic form, and partly because the Internet came along and produced an explosion of activity exploiting the new ability to put information of all kinds—including poetry, fiction, comics, and nonfiction of precisely the sort one used to find only on paper—onto "Web pages" that Internet users could access for free. Now, major publishers are making books available in both paper and digital form, and e-books can be downloaded from online booksellers such as Amazon.com.

The Internet Revolution quickly led to the invention of search engines, of which Google is currently the best known and most popular; see Charles H. Ferguson, "What's Next for Google?" *Technology Review* (January 2005). Google's avowed goal is "to organize the world's information and make it universally accessible and useful." Toward this end, it has developed a superlative ability to give those searching for information lists of Web sites, images, scholarly papers, and more. However, though those lists provide access to enormous amounts of valuable information and provide it with speed astonishing to anyone who has ever spent weeks or months researching a topic through a university library, the valuable information is intermingled with a vast amount of garbage. The great flaw of the Internet is that no one checks what goes on Web pages for quality or truth. The traditional publishing industry had its flaws—the vanity presses, for instance, as well as magazines such as the *Weekly World News*—but it had people known as editors who exercised a great deal of quality control. Libraries exerted another level of control through librarians, and the books, magazines, and journals to be found in a university library could generally be trusted. Library collections also extend back for centuries before the Internet existed.

Library collections of course represent a large portion of "the world's information." It was therefore no surprise when Google announced the Google Print Library Project. It would join with a number of large university libraries to scan "millions of books and make every sentence searchable" (see Scott Carlson and Jeffrey R. Young, "Google Will Digitize and Search Millions of Books from 5 Top Research Libraries," *Chronicle of Higher Education*, January 7, 2005). The plan was to begin with older, public domain books, no longer under copyright protection (in the U.S., everything published after 1923 must be presumed to be covered by copyright, meaning that copying requires permission from publishers and/or authors), but to move quickly into copyrighted materials. Older materials would be fully available to Google searchers; copyrighted materials would be available only as short excerpts.

In the following selections, Brendan Rapple argues that the benefits of this effort are enticing. As Google scans, indexes, and makes available for online searching the books of the world's major libraries, it will increase access, facilitate scholarship, and in general benefit human civilization. Keith Kupferschmid argues that there is no justification in law for Google's massive copying of books. If the Google Print Library Project is allowed to continue, the interests of publishers, authors, and creators of all kinds will be seriously damaged.

YES

Brendan Rapple

Google and Access to the World's Intellectual Heritage

I was recently researching the educational views of Vicesimus Knox (1752–1821), headmaster of Tonbridge School, Kent, for thirty-four years. My knowledge of Knox was relatively scant though I knew that his views on liberal education and on the education of females were advanced. Knox was a prolific writer and while his principal educational work was *Liberal Education: Or, A Practical Treatise on the Methods of Acquiring Useful and Polite Learning (1781)*, I realised that his educational views were probably scattered throughout his writings. Less than a year ago my research would have required a laborious and tedious consultation of the multiple microfilm editions of Knox's works owned by my library. Fortunately, however, this library recently purchased *Eighteenth Century Collections Online (ECCO)* a database that aims to include the digital full-text of all significant English-language and foreign-language titles printed in Great Britain during the eighteenth century, together with numerous important works from the Americas. The resource, when complete, will contain the fully searchable text of over 33 million pages from almost 150,000 titles including all the works, as well as variant editions, of Fielding, Burke, Pope, Paine, Franklin, Swift. The titles are based on the authoritative English Short Title Catalogue bibliography, the originals coming from the British Library and other libraries. *ECCO*'s searching capabilities are sophisticated. One may search by precise keywords or phrases, specifying that one wishes to search full text, author, title, date, general subject area and more. The books' pages are presented as digital facsimiles or actual images and from the results list and page view one may link directly to different portions of the work, such as the title page, back-of-book index, list of illustrations, an e-Table of Contents.

My search of *ECCO* with Vicesimus Knox as author retrieved 69 texts, including a number of different editions of his 1781 *Liberal Education*. I then performed an advanced search seeking any text with Knox as author that contained the words 'school' or 'learning' or 'education' anywhere in the work. I also limited these results to any text containing the word 'girl' or 'girls' or 'female' or 'females' or 'woman' or 'women' or 'lady' or 'ladies'. This was much more efficient and productive than browsing through reel upon reel of cumbersome microfilm, though I was still required to do that for Knox's post-1800 works that I did not have available in print. Before leaving the *ECCO*

From *Contemporary Review*, June 2005, pp. 338–343. Copyright © 2005 by Contemporary Review Company Limited. Reprinted by permission.

database I easily located the full-text in digital page image of numerous other eighteenth-century treatises on female education, for example Charles Allen's 1760 *The Polite Lady: Or a Course of Female Education*; the Rev. John Bennett's 1787 *Strictures on Female Education*; Mrs. H. Cartwright's 1777 *Letters on Female Education, Addressed to a Married Lady*; John Moir's 1784 *Female Tuition: Or an Address to Mothers, on the Education of Daughters*; John Rice's 1779 *A Plan of Female Education*; Dublin's Foundling Hospital's 1800 *Rules for Conducting the Education of the Female Children in the Foundling Hospital*.

I found the *ECCO* database so powerful and fascinating that I turned my attention to topics other than female education. It was engrossing to browse through the images of the numerous eighteenth-century editions of Defoe's *Robinson Crusoe*, and I was particularly captivated by the variety and artistic merit of the copious illustrations and the numerous maps delineating Crusoe's voyages. I also came across four editions of *Crusoe* in French. While most of *ECCO*'s 150,000 texts are in English, 443 works are in Welsh, 18 in Dutch, 4322 in French, 76 in German, 429 in Italian, 3712 in Latin, and 45 in Spanish. I was also delighted to access so readily the works of the Edinburgh physician William Cullen and discover his views on nosology, i.e. on the 'systematic arrangement of diseases by classes, orders, genera, and species'. Perhaps I'll sometime investigate in the original text why precisely Cullen made what seems the reasonable claim that 'persons living very entirely on vegetables are seldom of a plump and succulent habit'. I will certainly read the anonymous and scurrilous 1734 text that would undoubtedly not be too congenial to my employers at the Jesuit university where I work: *Love in all its shapes: or, the way of a man with a woman. Illustrated in the various practices of the Jesuits of the Maison Professe at Paris, with divers ladies of Quality and Fashion, at the Court of France.*

Eighteenth Century Collections Online is a wonderful electronic resource that allows one to spend hours in idle enjoyment. For scholars, however, it may become an indispensable tool with the potential to revolutionise radically eighteenth-century scholarship and facilitate innovative multidisciplinary research. It is also an excellent complement to two other powerful electronic databases: *Early English Books Online (EEBO)*, which provides full-text access to nearly every English language book published from the invention of printing to 1700, and *Evans Digital Edition*, the full-text digital collection of books, pamphlets, and broadsides printed in America from 1639 to 1800. Those fortunate in having access to all three databases can utilise an admirable digital collection of full-text imprints from the invention of printing to 1800.

∽◈∾

The resources and research potential provided by these digital full-text databases come at a high price. They are extremely expensive and only more wealthy academic institutions can afford them. However, in December, 2004 many were surprised by a major new initiative announced by Google that may compete with such costly databases. Google is currently working with the libraries of Stanford, Harvard, and Oxford Universities, the University of

Michigan and the New York Public Library to scan books from their collections digitally, include the content into the Google index and then allow users world-wide to search this content in Google. Different arrangements are being made with the five institutions. All seven million volumes in Michigan's library will be scanned, a task that will take about six years. Stanford has agreed to a pilot phased project, though it seems at this point that all its eight million books will be scanned. Oxford's Bodleian Library will contribute an unspecified, though large, number of its pre-1900 public domain works. NYPL will initially contribute only a subset of its non-copyrighted material. About 40,000 of Harvard's fifteen million volumes will be digitised in its pilot project. The pilot will then be evaluated and a decision made about digitising far larger numbers of Harvard's volumes. Though it is currently unclear how many volumes Google will digitise from the five libraries and make available for searching, the final figure might be as high as thirty million. As Google's press release stated, 'Users searching with Google will see links in their search results page when there are books relevant to their query. Clicking on a title delivers a Google Print page where users can browse the full text of public domain works and brief excerpts and/or bibliographic data of copyrighted material. Library content will be displayed in keeping with copyright law'. The new project is an expansion of the Google Print program, which assists publishers in making their books searchable online. Presently Google locates the books found by a Google Print search at the top of the page indicated by an icon of books to the left.

Many are critical of this new initiative. One influential American author on library matters argues that it will be disastrous for Google users to have access to the full-text of only pre-1923 monographs, that is works in the US public domain, the implication being that users will confine their searches to this material and fail to seek out later works. This seems particularly ironic as for years librarians and others have criticised students' tendency to limit their reading to electronic material much of which is of recent vintage and to ignore older works. Michael Gorman, President-elect of the American Library Association, is also quite critical of the Google initiative. As he argued in an op-ed piece in the *Los Angeles Times* (17 Dec., 2004): 'books in great libraries are much more than the sum of their parts. They are designed to be read sequentially and cumulatively, so that the reader gains knowledge in the reading'. He considers that the results of a Google search of these millions of electronic volumes will be an array of disconnected, frequently meaningless parts of books. Jean-Noël Jeanneney, Président de la Bibliothèque Nationale de France, in a *Le Monde* essay (22 Jan., 2005) criticises what he predicts will be the certain bias in favour of Anglo-Saxon and English language material made digitally available in the Google initiative. M. Jeanneney calls on the European Union to build its own comprehensive digital library programme to balance Google's inevitable Anglo-Saxon view 'with its specific coloring with regard to the diversity of civilisations'.

Still, many are applauding the new venture. Reg Carr, the Director of Oxford University Library Services, observed 'Making the wealth of knowledge accumulated in the Bodleian Library's historic collections accessible to as many people as possible is at the heart of Oxford University's commitment to lifelong learning. Oxford is therefore proud to be part of this effort to make information available to everyone who might benefit from it'. The University of Michigan President, Mary Sue Coleman, observed: 'This project signals an era when the printed record of civilization is accessible to every person in the world with Internet access. It is an initiative with tremendous impact today and endless future possibilities'. As a statement from Harvard University Library declared, looking forward to the future greater involvement by Harvard in the project, 'For users outside of Harvard, the larger project would make accessible the full text of a large number of public-domain books. It would also make the copyrighted portion of the Harvard collection searchable. Including works from the vast Harvard library collection in an information location tool available on the Internet would greatly expand the scope and quality of information available to a worldwide audience of knowledge-seekers'.

Many librarians and teachers have for years been critical of the great range of quality of web content to which Google's search engine points, as well as students' frequent difficulty in authenticating and evaluating material they access on the Internet. Moreover, many contend that far too many students, and others, are unwilling to seek and consult material not available on the web, that is most of the world's information. However, Google's adding to the web these millions of books should result in individuals retrieving more quality hits. It is true that many scholars and students utilise the database *WorldCat*, a catalog of almost sixty million records of diverse materials, a high proportion of which are books, held by libraries throughout the world. However, this is a subscription database and those who do not have access to a major university or public library find it difficult to secure the right to use it. Certainly a number of vast, freely accessible online catalogs exist, for example those of the British Library, the Library of Congress, the Bibliothèque Nationale and others, that point to the existence of millions of monographs. However, it is likely that most individuals do not use these catalogues, and certainly far fewer than those who search Google. Some might say that the goal of Google is grandiose, i.e. 'to organize the world's information and make it universally accessible and useful. Since a lot of the world's information isn't yet online, we're helping to get it there. Google Print puts the content of books where you can find it most easily—right in Google search results'. Nevertheless, to the extent that Google makes some, indeed a great deal, of the world's book information accessible on the web, it is indisputably a great boon. It may not be hyperbolic to predict that Google's initiative will create the world's first great virtual library that will be accessible to all with Internet access.'

Google's initiative is, of course, not the first book digitisation project engaged in by libraries and others. Large digitisation programs providing access to full-text monographic material include the University of Michigan's own *Digital Library Text Collection* that currently provides access to over 32,000 texts; Oxford's *Text Archive* that holds several thousand electronic texts and linguistic corpora in a variety of languages; the *Alex Catalogue of Electronic Texts*, a collection of public domain documents from American and English literature as well as Western philosophy; the Electronic Text Center at the University of Virginia that produces an on-line archive of thousands of SGML-encoded electronic texts. Other well-known projects include *Project Bartleby Archive*, *Project Gutenberg*, Berkeley's *Literature@SunSITE*, the *Internet Archive Million Book Project* that has the goal of digitising a million books by 2005. Will such projects, small in scale when contrasted with Google's undertaking, survive? It is not yet clear, though it seems unlikely that they will be able to compete with Google unless their digital texts add value that Google's texts do not.

And what is the future of the large sophisticated digitisation projects discussed earlier, *Early English Books Online, Eighteenth Century Collections Online, Evans Digital Edition/Early American Imprints*? Will libraries continue to expend very considerable funds on full-text collections like these? I think that the answer is yes, at least for the next several years. First of all, they currently exist and scholars want them now. I personally have no wish to indulge my present interest in eighteenth-century female schooling by consulting awkward and inefficient microfilm and microfiche when I have access to databases of digital texts that I can cross-search utilising powerful techniques and that promise to point to new, original, and multidisciplinary research avenues. These databases also have the benefit of being discrete uniform collections. It is unlikely that Google will permit users to select such a distinct body of works that make up, say, *Evans Early American Imprints*, out of all its millions of digitised materials and facilitate advanced searching of this sub-group. Nevertheless, I believe that Google is raising the bar for future digitisation projects. The latter's survival will surely depend on what value, for example scholarly essays, biographical materials, annotations, timelines, bibliographies, images, sound, video etc., they add to mere digitised text to create more attractive packages.

Far from being a destroyer of the written word, the Internet, with Google as a leading vehicle, will prove to be its great support and egalitarian promulgator. In recent months the notion of 'open access' to research has been much in the news and many practical steps have been taken to make research and scholarship freely available to all. Numerous electronic open access scholarly journals have been established. Many institutions have set up freely accessible digital repositories of scholarly resources. The US National Institutes of Health (NIH) has a new policy to facilitate public access to archived publications resulting from NIH-funded, that is tax payer funded, research. In July 2004 the U.K. House of Commons Science and Technology Committee issued a report recommending 'that all UK higher education institutions establish institutional repositories on which their published output can be stored and from which it can be read, free of charge, online'. In October, 2004 the Open Access Team for Scotland issued a declaration stating 'that the interests of Scotland—for the economic, social and cultural benefit of the population as a whole, and for the maintenance of the longstanding high reputation of research within Scottish universities and research institutions—will be best served by the rapid adoption of open access'. Mention might be made of many other open access initiatives but they all share the goal of supporting free electronic access to scholarly literature.

While most projects focus on providing free access to future scholarship, Google is primarily interested in retrospective coverage, that is making freely available already published material, material that may be hundreds of years old. Still, Google's initiative is very much in the spirit and practice of open access. Indeed, it is a very major open access project, perhaps the most important of all. I have already declared my staunch admiration for the power and scope of such digital full-text databases as *Eighteenth Century Collections Online* and *Early English Books Online*. However, access to these extremely expensive databases is invariably highly restricted. On the other hand, the great potential benefit of Google's plan to digitise millions of the world's books is the democratisation of the dissemination and availability of information and knowledge. Most of the world has no access to major research libraries like those of the United Kingdom and the United States. Indeed most inhabitants of these latter nations themselves do not have ready access to such libraries whether because of reasons of geographic location or certain admission prohibitions. Still, the library situation is much worse in most countries of Africa, Asia, South America and it is unlikely that these countries will ever be able to build libraries on the developed world model. However, it is much more probable that the population of these counties will in the coming years gain greater access to personal or institutional computers that provide Internet access. If Google's promise of digitising and making freely available electronically thirty or more millions of the world's monographs comes to fruition, it will constitute a remarkable vehicle for diffusing in both the developed and developing world much of the world's intellectual heritage. Indeed, it will signal a revolution in the dissemination of information on a par with that of Gutenberg's over five hundred years earlier.

Keith Kupferschmid  **NO**

Are Authors and Publishers Getting Scroogled?

$\mathbf{O}$n Oct. 19, five publishers sued Google claiming that the Google Print Library Project violated their exclusive rights provided by U.S. copyright law. The suit—along with the suit filed by the Authors Guild on Sept. 20—is the culmination of months of debate, pitting publishers and authors against Google. The point of contention is whether Google violates copyright law by digitizing millions of books without the permission of the books' authors and publishers and putting them on its servers to allow them to be searched online.

Over the years, other digitization projects have met with success. For example, the recently announced Open Content Alliance (OCA) is a global collaborative effort of cultural, technology, nonprofit, and governmental organizations that are working to build a permanent archive of multilingual digitized text and multimedia content. Content in the OCA archive will be accessible soon through major Web sites such as Yahoo! and through other search engines.

The OCA will encourage the greatest possible access to and reuse of collections in the archive, while respecting the content owners and contributors. Similarly, Microsoft recently struck a deal with The British Library (BL) to scan 100,000 books from the BL's collection and make them available sometime next year. Unlike Google, however, Microsoft plans to scan copyrighted books only if it first receives permission from the book publishers. Other projects include Project Gutenberg . . . , the U.S. Library of Congress Digital Preservation Program . . . , and Carnegie Mellon's Million Book Project. . . . These efforts all have one thing in common: In each case, the aggregators responsible for digitizing, selecting, organizing, and compiling the content took steps to reach agreement with the copyright owners. Without such agreement, these projects would not have succeeded.

Background on the Google Print Library Project

Google manages two projects intended to make the text of books searchable online. One of the projects is referred to as the Google Print Publisher Program, which is a collaborative effort that enables Google to digitize and make books available for search when Google has received permission from the books' publisher or author. This program—because it operates with the consent of copyright owners whose books are copied by Google—is noncontroversial.

The other project, referred to as the Google Print Library Project, is the focus of lawsuits initiated by The Authors Guild and several publishers. In the Google Print Library Project, which was not disclosed to authors and publishers until earlier this year, Google is working with the libraries of the University of Michigan, Harvard University, Stanford University, and Oxford University as well as the New York City Public Library to digitally scan the books in their collections and make the text of the books searchable online. All of this is done without the copyright owners' permission and is in stark contrast to the approach taken by Google in its Print Publisher Program. Google has not disclosed much information about the internal operations of the Print Library Project. It appears that Google employees will digitally scan the collection of books and then index them using keywords so that they can be searched. When users search for these words, they will be provided with search results that show the title of the book, the number of times the keyword appears in the book, and as many as three "snippets" displaying text from the book that includes those keywords. It is not clear how much text the snippets will display.

But many other questions about the program remain unanswered. For instance, it is not clear how many copies of the books Google will be making and retaining for itself and whether its long-term plans involve uses of the books in addition to those that have been publicly disclosed so far. Google may be making and retaining as many as three or more copies of the book for itself (the scanned copy, the digital copy, and a backup copy). Of course, the libraries will also have a copy. Based on our experiences with other information aggregators, Google is likely to make additional copies while maintaining and operating its database.

And how does Google plan to protect against people abusing its search tool, which could destroy the value of the books? For instance, an individual or a computer program could bombard the Print Library search tool with enough keyword requests to download the heart of a book or substantial portions of it. This so-called gaming of the system occurs frequently with publicly accessible online information. One case was brought against the Internet Archive in which an organization made more than 700 attempts to access Web pages on the Internet Archive Web site. Ninety-two of the attempts were successful at obtaining content.

Similarly, it is not clear what security precautions Google is taking to ensure that its Print Library Project search tool is not hacked in a way that allows the digitized books to be freely downloadable. This past summer, Google shut down its video search tool after it was hacked into and entire movies, such as *The Matrix*, were downloaded.

Once the project became public, numerous groups and publishers cried foul. The first to protest publicly was the Association of American University Presses (AAUP), which issued a public letter to Google containing a list of 16 questions. The questions posed included how long a "snippet" of text will the search engine return in the results, how many digital copies will Google make and store, and how does Google plan to use the copies in the future. AAUP's letter was followed by a similar letter from the Association of American Publishers (AAP) and a position statement by the Association of Learned and Professional Society Publishers (ALPSP), both demanding that Google terminate the project.

In early August, Google announced that it would be suspending the Google Print Library Project until Nov. 1 due to this criticism. Google requested that publishers provide lists of copyrighted books they do not want included in the Print Library Project. Not surprisingly, the book publishers were pleased about the moratorium, but they weren't happy about Google's attempt to shift the burden of identifying what titles Google would not be allowed to copy onto the shoulders of the authors and publishers.

In September, the Authors Guild initiated a class action suit against Google. In the following month, five publishers filed their own suit against Google, charging Google with large-scale, systematic copyright infringement. Then in November, Google's moratorium on scanning books ended, and Google once again began scanning books. While the controversy over the legality of the Google Print Library Project is not an issue that is going to go away soon, it represents a significant challenge to the future of copyright in the online world.

Why the Google Print Library Project Violates Copyright Law

Under copyright law, the copyright owner of a book is granted the exclusive right to control whether others make copies of the book, distribute it, or display it. These rights extend equally to portions of the book. Basically, if a person other than the copyright owner wants to copy, distribute, or display a book or excerpts from it, permission must be granted from the copyright owner.

There are several exceptions to this general rule. The best known is the fair use exception. This exception permits a person who wants to copy, distribute, or display excerpts from a book to do so without first obtaining the copyright owner's permission if that person can prove two things. First, the person must establish that the use is for purposes of criticism, comment, news reporting, teaching, scholarship or research. Second, the person must show that the use qualifies as a "fair use" after considering the following four factors: (1) the purpose and character of the use, including whether such use is of commercial nature or is for nonprofit educational purposes; (2) the nature of the copyrighted work (in other words, whether the book is fiction or nonfiction); (3) the amount and substantiality of the portion used in relation to the copyrighted work as a whole; and (4) the effect of the use upon the potential market for or value of the copyrighted work.

Defining Fair Use

Google defends its right to manage the Google Print Library Project by asserting that its activities are covered by the fair use exception. Before engaging in any fair use analysis, it should be noted that any such analysis in this case will be extremely difficult because of the sheer volume and variety of books and authors at issue. Fair use claims usually involve a work or a handful of works all owned by one or a few authors. This case, however, involves potentially millions of books owned by millions of different authors and publishers. There does not appear to ever have been any case involving fair use that has been applied on such a broad scale to so many works by so many authors and publishers being copied by one entity. That fact alone may be sufficient cause to deny Google's fair use claim.

Google claims that, although it is copying entire books, such copies are allowed as a fair use because it is making only small excerpts of the books available online and the copies made are only intermediate copies. It cites *Kelly v. Arriba Soft Corp.*, an anomalous case decided in 2003 by the Ninth Circuit, for the proposition that such intermediate copying is permissible under fair use. In the Kelly case, defendant Arriba Soft Corp. operated a visual search engine that retrieved thumbnail images of photos that were already posted on the Internet. By clicking on a thumbnail image, a user was presented with a page containing a full-size image that was imported directly from plaintiff Kelly's Web site. The court concluded that the use of the images constituted a fair use because, among other things, Kelly's use of the images was an artistic one, while Arriba's use was as part of a tool that indexes images on the Web, which was unrelated to any artistic purpose.

Here is a list of factors for fair use.

1. Purpose and Character of the Use.   The first fair use factor requires an analysis of "the purpose and character of the use, including whether such use is of commercial nature or is for nonprofit educational purposes." If the use is educational in nature, it is more likely to be a fair use; if it is more commercial in nature, it is likely not to be.

While Google will argue that its motives are wholly altruistic and educational, that simply is not the case. Google is a commercial for-profit enterprise. It initiated this project because it believes it will increase traffic to its Web site, which will eventually increase Google's advertising revenue. Some 98 percent of Google's revenue is generated through advertising. The nature of Google's use here is commercial, and the first factor should fall in favor of the copyright owners.

In Kelly, the court concluded that the first fair use factor favored Arriba because Arriba's use was neither to "directly promote its [Web site] nor . . . to profit by selling Kelly's images. Instead Kelly's images were among thousands of images in Arriba's search engine database."

Unlike in Kelly, Google's use of the books is directly for the purpose of promoting its own site. If that were not the case, Google would have made the books entirely searchable on the libraries' sites (potentially raising different issues) and would not have to retain copies of the digitized books themselves. Instead, Google is requiring that searches take place on its site, which ultimately results in more advertising revenue for Google. The other noticeable difference from the court's holding in Kelly is that, in this instance, the court will not be considering use of just one copyright owner's works "among thousands" of others, but considering all owners of all books digitized by Google.

While Google will likely claim that the purpose of its Print Library Project search tool is educational in nature (because it helps people locate books on topics of interest), that argument could be made in most copyright infringement cases. Certainly, Napster and Grokster (both lost recent well-publicized copyright infringement cases) could have argued that they were merely making content more available to the masses.

Google may also attempt to convince the courts that its copying is "transformative," another consideration under the first fair use factor. The courts consider a transformative use to be a use that is for a different purpose or of a different character than the use of the copyrighted work, and the use does not supersede the need for the copyrighted work. Courts have uniformly held that merely transferring a work from one medium or format to another is not enough to qualify as a transformative use.

In Kelly, the use was found to be transformative because the thumbnail images made by Arriba Soft were for "improving access to images on the [I]nternet" and not for the artistic purposes of the original. Unlike in Kelly, however, Google is not improving access to material already on the Internet; it is creating access to material that is not on the Internet. By creating access and not simply improving it, Google has merely transferred the books from one medium (print) to another (online) and far exceeded what was considered a transformative use even in Kelly.

2. The Nature of the Work.   The second factor—"the nature of the copy-righted work"—likely favors the authors and publishers. This factor looks at whether the books are factual or more creative in nature. The more creative and expressive the book, the less likely the book can be subject to fair use. Application of this factor is not entirely clear since Google will be copying both fiction and nonfiction books. However, the sheer volume of fictional books designated for copying likely leads to the result that this factor will favor the authors and publishers.

3. The Amount of the Works Used.   The third factor—"the amount and sub-stantiality of the portion used in relation to the copyrighted work as a whole"—favors the copyright owner more than any other factor. Google is copying entire books—lots of them—for the project. The court in Kelly acknowledged that "copying an entire work militates against a finding of fair use" but ultimately found that this factor did not favor either party because "if the secondary user only copies as much as is necessary for his or her intended use, then the factor will not weigh against him or her." Unlike in Kelly, Google is making more copies than necessary. All that is necessary is to make and pro-vide the library with a copy, but Google has kept a copy (and likely numerous copies) for itself.

Google also contends that since users will see only small snippets of the book text and not the complete text of the digitized books, these complete text copies are "intermediate copies," which are allowed under fair use. This argu-ment ignores several facts. First, in cases where the courts have allowed the mak-ing of so-called intermediate copies, the copies were deleted immediately after they were used. For example, in Kelly, after Arriba Soft created the thumbnail images from the full-resolution images found online, they immediately deleted any copies of the full-resolution images. Here, Google is retaining permanent copies of the digitized books, so, in fact, they are not intermediate copies at all.

The basic premise of copyright protection is that publishers and authors have the right to control the copying, distribution, and display of their books. The display of the snippet through the Google search engine implicates the reproduction, distribution, and display rights because the snippet is a reproduction of a small portion of the text that is being displayed on users' screens and also is being distributed to them via such displays. Because Google copies the entire book as a precursor to displaying a snippet, Google's copying of the book gives rise to an additional claim of infringement of the reproduction right. This claim applies regardless of whether a snippet is ever displayed. Google would have us focus on the display of the "snippet." The display is important, but, fundamentally, it's the copying of entire books without the explicit permission of authors or publishers that is the first step in the analysis (one which Google is sidestepping).

If, as Google insists, the court may consider only whether a snippet is infringing and not whether the full-text copy of the book is infringing—because the full-text copy from which the snippet is created is what Google terms a "non-infringing intermediate copy"—then the reproduction right will be effectively eviscerated. Under this reasoning, an infringement of the reproduction right could only be possible when there is a corresponding distribution or display. In effect, Google's argument here represents a radical new interpretation of U.S. and international copyright law that undermines the basic premise of copyright law.

4. The Effect on the Market for the Work.   The fourth factor, which is often the most influential on a court's decision, asks whether the use will adversely affect the actual or potential market for the books. This factor looks not only at the user's conduct but, more significantly, at the effect on the market if the use should become widespread. The analysis in Kelly is wholly inapplicable to this case, because in Kelly, there was no actual or potential market for the thumbnail images that competed with Kelly's images. In Google's case, however, there are both actual and potential markets for digitizing these books.

The market for licensing such works to aggregators is on the upswing. As Google has no doubt recognized, the marketplace for information is growing exponentially as users desire access to information faster and easier than ever before. Competition in this marketplace is significant, as aggregators hustle to reach agreement with content providers to put their works online.

Google is trying to become a leader in the information industry by changing the rules, rather than playing by them. While other aggregators generally take great care to first reach agreement with copyright owners to make their content searchable online and then compensate them accordingly, Google is doing neither. If Google succeeds on its fair use claim, it will no longer be necessary for aggregators and others that make nondigital content searchable online to get permission from the owners of that content or to compensate those owners. If upheld, Google's claim will have succeeded in destroying the burgeoning market for information content.

Not only will Google's actions destroy the existing and potential marketplace for information content, they will also succeed in destroying Google's own market. As we know, Google has a counterpart project to its Google Print Library Project, called the Google Print Publisher Program (PPP). Under the PPP, Google reaches agreement with publishers to digitize books and make them searchable and accessible through Google's search engine. If Google's fair use claim is allowed, the PPP will become obsolete. Why would Google take the time, money, and resources to get permission from copyright owners to digitize their content and make it searchable and accessible online if they are allowed to do it legally without making that effort?

From a business standpoint, it would be impossible to justify continuation of the PPP under these conditions, destroying PPP and the value it provides to copyright owners in controlling how their works are made accessible through that program. Even if Google were to continue to operate PPP, it would have little value to book publishers and authors because any negotiating leverage that they would have with Google over how to make their books available would evaporate. If they cannot agree to terms, Google will simply make their books available through the Google Print Library Project.

Holding fair use in favor of Google would turn copyright on its head. It would allow not only Google but countless other less reputable entities to engage in wholesale copying of copyrighted works for the purposes of making those works—or portions of them—accessible online. In essence, the rights of writers and publishers would likely cease to exist in the online world.

Implied License

Google's other claimed legal justification for the PPP is that it has permission—more accurately, implied permission (i.e., an implied license)—to copy any content posted on the Internet for the purposes of allowing people to conduct searches using the Google search engine. Google claims this implied permission emanates from the fact that a Web site operator would not have posted content unless he or she wanted it to be found by users. Google will not copy content located behind a firewall or content located on a Web page that includes an exclusion header telling Google not to copy the Web site. Google is of the opinion that any implied authorization that might exist for Web sites extends to its Google Print Library Project.

If Google's implied license theory holds up in court, the ramifications for publishers and authors, as well as others who create copyrighted works, could be devastating. Google and others could copy any copyrighted content, whether print or digital. Books might be first, but Google (or others) might eventually migrate to copying personal letters and e-mails, print newspapers and magazines, or photographs and video that the authors never intended to be copied or searchable online.

Thankfully, Google's implied license argument seems certain to fail. Even if you assume that Google's implied license theory is correct as applied to Web sites, it does not apply to the books being copied as part of the Google Print Library Project, because (unlike Web site content) the collection of books being copied are not at present generally available at no cost on the Internet. For Google to make these books available, it first has to scan and copy the books and save these digital copies on its servers.

There is no justification for an implied license by the copyright owners of these books that would allow Google to digitize them, save them to its servers, and then make them available for searching.

The Next Step

There appears to be no legal basis justifying Google's massive copying of books to populate its Print Library Project. Nevertheless, digital searching of content—if done correctly—could be of great value to authors, publishers, libraries, users, and Google.

A ruling in favor of Google that allows it to continue to operate the Print Library Project would be a devastating blow to authors and publishers and creators of all kinds and would undermine the purpose and goals of U.S. and international copyright law. As a result, no doubt the interested parties will be watching very closely as the cases filed by the Authors Guild and the publishers proceed toward rulings by the courts. . . .

POSTSCRIPT

Should the World's Libraries Be Digitized?

It is interesting to note that Brendan Rapple finds great value in the ability to search through electronic collections of older documents. The particular collections he mentions are comprised of public domain documents bundled and indexed for searching by "aggregators" who do this work for profit. The Google Print Library Project, by making those same documents searchable for free, threatens the business of these companies, many of which belong to the Software and Information Industry Association, which employs Keith Kupferschmid as vice president for intellectual property policy and enforcement.

Clearly, there is money at stake in this issue, and Google is hardly acting out of the goodness of its heart, for it generates revenue by attaching ads to the search pages generated in response to user queries. Publishers and authors of modern works, still protected by copyright, also see money at stake, and John Sutherland, "A New Chapter for Books," *New Statesman* (November 27, 2006), even says new technologies may mean that books face extinction. Steve Seidenberg, "Copyright Clash," *InsideCounsel* (November 2006), describes how in September 2005 the Authors Guild filed a class action suit on behalf of authors and in October 2005 five major publishers filed copyright infringement suits. Google has invoked the "fair-use" exception to copyright protection to support its use of small excerpts from copyrighted works, but critics insist that because Google is keeping illegal copies of the complete work in its computers, it is violating the law. See also Corinna Baksik, "Fair Use or Exploitation? The Google Book Search Controversy," *Libraries & the Academy* (October 2006). Siva Vaidhyanathan, "A Risky Gamble with Google," *Chronicle of Higher Education* (December 2, 2005), says that what Google is doing is valuable but it is work that should be done by libraries rather than private corporations. Unfortunately, says K. Matthew Dames in "Beyond Google," *Searcher* (September 2006), the legal cases seem likely to be settled out of court, "leaving core legal issues unresolved and information professionals without desperately needed ground rules on how to conduct themselves legally in the digital age." According to George H. Pike, "Legal Update: Where the Lawsuits Are," *Information Today* (January 2007), the lawsuits are not likely to reach the courtroom stage before late 2007.

Hot on the heels of Google, both Microsoft and Yahoo have announced plans to digitize books and make them available. Jessica Dye, "Scanning the Stacks," *Econtent* (January/February 2006), says that "Critics and detractors of these book digitization projects might disagree on the exact shape [the] future of digital content will take, but all agree that the Internet, with its nearly universal availability, unlimited storage capacity, and powerful search capabilities, needs a comprehensive library. As Google, Yahoo!, and Microsoft begin building the foundations of their online collections, the Internet community will be waiting, watching, and reading between the lines."

Internet References . . .

Foundation for Biomedical Research

The Foundation for Biomedical Research promotes public understanding and support of the ethical use of animals in scientific and medical research.

http://www.fbresearch.org

Bioethics.net and The American Journal of Bioethics

Bioethics.net, founded in 1993, was the first bioethics website. Together with *The American Journal of Bioethics* (AJOB), it has grown to become the most read source of information about bioethics.

http://bioethics.net

National Human Genome Research Institute

The National Human Genome Research Institute directs the Human Genome Project for the National Institutes of Health (NIH).

http://www.genome.gov/

The U.S. Department of Energy Human Genome Project

This site offers a huge amount of information and links on genetics and cloning research.

http://www.ornl.gov/techresources/
Human_Genome/elsi/Cloning.html

Ethics

*S*ociety's standards of right and wrong have been hammered out over *millennia of trial, error, and (sometimes violent) debate. Accordingly, when science and technology offer society new choices to make and new things to do, debates are renewed over whether or not these choices and actions are ethically acceptable. Today there is vigorous debate over such topics as the use of animals in research and cloning.*

- Is the Use of Animals in Research Justified?

- Is It Ethically Permissible to Clone Human Cells?

ISSUE 18

Is the Use of Animals in Research Justified?

YES: Josie Appleton, from "Speciesism: A Beastly Concept: Why It Is Morally Right to Use Animals to Our Ends," *Spiked-Online* (February 23, 2006)

NO: Tom Regan, from "The Rights of Humans and Other Animals," *Ethics & Behavior* (vol. 7, no. 2, 1997)

ISSUE SUMMARY

YES: Journalist Josie Appleton contends that a proper relationship to animals means using them for human ends, for humans are the measure of all things.

NO: Philosopher Tom Regan argues that any attempt to define what it is about being human that gives all humans moral rights must also give animals moral rights, and that therefore we have no more right to use animals as research subjects than we have to use other humans.

Modern biologists and physicians know a great deal about how the human body works. Some of that knowledge has been gained by studying human cadavers and tissue samples acquired during surgery and through "experiments of nature" (strokes, for example, have taught a great deal about what the various parts of the brain do; extensive injuries from car accidents and wars have also been edifying). Some knowledge of human biology has also been gained from experiments on humans, such as when patients agree to let their surgeons and doctors try experimental treatments.

The key word here is *agree.* Today it is widely accepted that people have the right to consent or not to consent to whatever is done to them in the name of research or treatment. In fact, society has determined that research done on humans without their free and informed consent is a form of scientific misconduct. However, this standard does not apply to animals, experimentation on which has produced the most knowledge of the human body.

Although animals have been used in research for at least the last 2,000 years, during most of that time, physicians who thought they had a workable treatment for some illness commonly tried it on their patients before they had any idea whether or not it worked or was even safe. Many patients, of course, died during these untested treatments. In the mid-nineteenth century, the French physiologist Claude Bernard argued that it was sensible to try such treatments first on animals to avoid some human suffering and death. No one then questioned whether or not human lives were more valuable than animal lives. In the twentieth century, Elizabeth Baldwin, in "The Case for Animal Research in Psychology," *Journal of Social Issues* (vol. 49, no. 1, 1993), argued that animals are of immense value in medical, veterinary, and psychological research, and they do not have the same moral rights as humans. Our obligation, she maintains, is to treat them humanely.

Today geneticists generally study fruit flies, roundworms, and zebra fish. Physiologists study mammals, mostly mice and rats but also rabbits, cats, dogs, pigs, sheep, goats, monkeys, and chimpanzees. Experimental animals are often kept in confined quarters, cut open, infected with disease organisms, fed unhealthy diets, and injected with assorted chemicals. Sometimes the animals suffer. Sometimes the animals die. And sometimes they are healed, albeit often of diseases or injuries induced by the researchers in the first place.

Not surprisingly, some observers have reacted with extreme sympathy and have called for better treatment of animals used in research. This "animal welfare" movement has, in turn, spawned the more extreme "animal rights" movement, which asserts that animals—especially mammals—have rights as important and as deserving of regard as those of humans. Thus, to kill an animal, whether for research, food, or fur, is the moral equivalent of murder. See Steven M. Wise and Jane Golmoodall, *Rattling the Cage: Toward Legal Rights for Animals* (Perseus, 2000) and Roger Scruton and Andrew Tayler, "Do Animals Have Rights?" *The Ecologist* (March 2001).

This attitude has led to important reforms in the treatment of animals, to the development of several alternatives to using animals in research, and to a considerable reduction in the number of animals used in research. See Alan M. Goldberg and John M. Frazier, "Alternatives to Animals in Toxicity Testing," *Scientific American* (August 1989); Wade Roush, "Hunting for Animal Alternatives," *Science* (October 11, 1996); and Erik Stokstad, "Humane Science Finds Sharper and Kinder Tools," *Science* (November 5, 1999). However, it has also led to hysterical objections to in-class animal dissections, terrorist attacks on laboratories, the destruction of research records, and the theft of research materials (including animals).

In the following selections, journalist Josie Appleton contends that the development of human civilization has been marked by increasing separation from animals. Humans come first, and it is entirely moral to use animals for our own ends. Torturing animals is wrong, but mostly because it reflects badly upon the torturer. Writing in a special issue of the journal *Ethics & Behavior*, philosopher Tom Regan argues that any attempt to define what it is about being human that gives all humans moral rights must also give animals moral rights, and that therefore we have no more right to use animals as research subjects than we have to use other humans.

Josie Appleton

Speciesism: A Beastly Concept: Why It Is Morally Right to Use Animals to Our Ends

In recent years, the animal rights camp has claimed the moral high ground, asserting that it is mere "speciesism" to prioritise human ends over those of mice, cats or primates.

Animal rights activist Peter Singer defines speciesism as "a prejudice or attitude of bias towards the interests of members of one's own species and against those of members of other species." Advocates argue that fighting speciesism is an extension of struggles for human equality: just as we once dehumanised others on the basis of their race or sex, so apparently we now think animals are below us. The argument goes that speciesism, racism and sexism are all examples of "exclusionary attitudes." In *The Political Animal: The Conquest of Speciesism*, Richard Ryder notes that Aristotle thought that animals "exist for the sake of men" while also looking down on slaves and women. No coincidence, says Ryder. According to Ryder, either you are a caring person who recognises the value of other beings, or you are selfish and care only for yourself. He cites "evidence of a link between caring for humans and caring for animals": one study found that opponents of animal rights tended to be male, anti-abortion, have "prejudice against homosexuals" and "exhibited racial prejudice"; another study of US students concluded that "those students who favour animal experimentation tend to be male, masculine in outlook, conservative and less empathetic."

When this argument was first made in the early 1970s it was considered crackpot and insulting. America had recently allowed black citizens the vote; national liberation struggles were setting the world alight; women were burning their bras. Human equality was the priority: nobody was much concerned with improving the conditions of gorillas in the West African jungle. Now the notion of speciesism has gained respectability and kudos, filtering into a variety of professions.

One social worker, David B. Wolf, argues that his colleagues need to reflect on their speciesist attitudes: he notes that the current aim of social work is "to enhance human well-being and help meet the basic human needs of all people," and suggests instead that "the issue of speciesism should be incorporated as a basic element of the profession." An article by a Swedish educationalist critiqued the "oppressive human-animal domination structures" in schools, and deconstructed the speciesism implicit in school textbooks and choices of school trips—she calls for these prejudices to be replaced by "compassion and respect for 'the other,' in the broadest sense of the word." A cultural studies professor suggests a "non-speciesist vision" for reading literature and the arts. Just as historians might read history from the point of the oppressed, he suggests that "The visual arts must be viewed so as to interpret the role of the animals which crouch in the corners of the frame or stare from the owners' lap."

The term *speciesism* hasn't yet entered the popular vocabulary, perhaps partly because it is such a mouthful. But the assumption behind the term—that it is wrong to prioritise humans over animals—has become mainstream. Animal experimentation today has few defenders: at the new Oxford animal lab contractors hide their faces behind balaclavas, and few from the government or scientific community will speak out in its defence. The government backs the lab with funding and security but not with political or moral arguments. Indeed the UK government's draft Animal Welfare Bill sends the opposite political message: the new regulations require pet owners to respect their pets' rights to privacy and provide them with adequate "stimulation," and ban animal "mutilation" such as tail-docking and fish-dyeing. Our everyday relationships with animals are being called into question. The US Association for the Study of Animal Behaviour (ASAB) advises schools against keeping pets because this apparently places children's educational needs above the welfare of animals—if they must, "animal handling should be supervised and kept to a minimum, the animals' needs must remain paramount."

Of course, in practice most of us are speciesist: we eat animals but not humans; we buy pets and keep them locked up in cages; we support animal experimentation in order to save human lives. But increasingly these distinctions lack moral justification. It's time we developed a more human-centred morality, to provide our practical judgements with intellectual support.

Human and Animal Equality

Animal rights activists get the relationship between human and animal equality completely skewed. In actual fact, the idea of the brotherhood of mankind was founded on the basis of uniquely human features. In the Enlightenment, when the notion of human equality was hammered out, it was argued that we should treat one another as equals because we were all rational, self-conscious beings. The German philosopher Immanuel Kant argued that we have to respect other human beings because they are *self-willing*: they are conscious of their existence, so you cannot merely treat them as a means to your end. By contrast, says Kant, "Animals are not self-conscious and are there merely as a means to an end. That end is man." It is because animals are not ends for themselves that humans can treat them as a means to our ends.

The flowering of human consciousness went hand-in-hand with a growing distinction from animals. It is when humans lived in cramped and degraded circumstances that they have felt the most commonality with the beasts. In ancient Egypt, cats and dogs were mummified because they were believed to have an afterlife, and Egyptian Gods had animal heads. Premodern societies often had animal totems, and they saw animals and humans as intertwined through reincarnation. Animals were attributed with agency: some societies tried animals in court, and prayed to fish to return to the rivers. The sense of fellowship with animals corresponded to societies subject to the whims of nature. These circumstances didn't foster brotherly love. Some tribes called themselves "the humans," the implication being that outsiders were not fully human and could be killed with impunity (though it might be forbidden to kill a pig for food).

With ancient Greece, when humanity began to develop a fuller sense of itself and its abilities, animals began to be cast out of the picture. Greek Gods are all human—though they sometimes disguise themselves as animals, as in the myth of Leda and the swan. Human-animal hybrids remained in the form of satyrs and mermaids, but crucially these had human heads and arms and so retained the locus of personality. Theorists of ethics and the good life, such as Aristotle, generally argued that animals lacked reason and so could not be granted justice.

Christianity developed a broader notion of human equality, and a clearer distinction between humans and animals. We are all made in the image of God, says the Bible, even women and slaves, and we are all deserving of equal respect. Christianity respected no holy animals, a point made in the Bible where Jesus casts the swine into the sea. But Christianity understood humanity's distinctness from nature as a *gift* from God. "I have given you all things," says God: "Every moving thing that liveth shall be meat for you."

The Enlightenment philosophers increasingly located the source of human distinction in mankind itself, writing excited essays about the innate "dignity of man" and humanity's capacity for self-development. While fish worshipping corresponded to a feeble control over nature, so this notion of human uniqueness corresponded to a society that was developing science, technology and industry. Our "dominion" over nature came to be seen not as a gift from God but as the product of our own hands.

Defining Humans Down

Those who argue that human beings and animals are equal, devalue humanity. As animal rights academic Paola Cavalieri notes, new notions of animal rights are the result of changing definitions of humans, with a shift from "high-sounding claims about our rationality and moral capacity" to "work on a much more accessible level." The ability to feel pain is the definition of moral worth suggested by Peter Singer (who calls it sentience) and Richard Ryder (who calls it painience). Human beings' superior mental abilities are apparently of no moral consequence: Singer talks about humans' "self-awareness, and the ability to plan for the future and have meaningful relationships with others," but argues that they are "not relevant to the question of inflicting pain—since pain is pain." Here commonality with other human beings (and animals) is based on our central nervous systems. We are all part of a "community of pain," says Ryder. Singer suggests that a human life is worth (a bit) more than an animal's, because we have a slightly higher level of sentience. We should therefore treat sentient animals as we would a mentally handicapped human being.

Others take a behavioural psychological approach. Primate studies have found that they form relationships among members of the group; that they have some kind of memory of events; that they can use twigs and rocks as tools and have different "tool cultures" for different groups; that they can communicate with one another and can learn basic signs to communicate with humans. Here the question of moral value is decided in a laboratory or in field tests, weighed on the basis of cognitive and awareness skills. Humans come out better than chimps, but it is a quantitative rather than qualitative difference. "[Chimpanzees] clearly have some kind of self-concept," writes primatologist Jane Goodall. "The line dividing 'man' from 'beast' has become increasingly blurred."

Finally, others take DNA as their measure of moral value. Studies have shown that we share some 98.4 per cent of our DNA with chimpanzees, and an even greater proportion of our genes. When recent research showed that humans shared a closer evolutionary relationship with chimps than previously thought, calls started for chimps to be removed from the *pan* genus and welcomed into *homo*. Many drew the assumption that shared DNA made chimpanzees into moral agents. "Could a chimp ever be charged with murder?," asked the UK *Daily Mail*.

It seems that we no longer know what it means to be a member of the human club, but have a feeling that it cannot be much. These different definitions of moral worth are entirely arbitrary. Why should a shared gene mean that people are of equal value or that we should respect them? If some historically isolated groups had a notably different DNA should we treat them differently? Why does the possession of basic memory mean that we should respect chimps? The drive behind these arguments is not their logical coherence, but the desire to knock humans off their pedestal. Observations on the sophistication of primate behaviour are punctuated with pokes at human beings: "Who are we to say that the suffering of a human being is more terrible than the suffering of a nonhuman being, or that it matters more?" asks Jane Goodall in a piece about chimp behaviour. "Why is human arrogance so pervasive and where does it come from?," asked Roger and Deborah Fouts in a chapter on primate language use.

The notion of humanity here is based on humility. For Richard Ryder this is a generic capacity for caring, the feminine antithesis to dominating machismo. Surely the Jains would be the most humane of us all, as they walk around apologising to ants and plants if they step on them? But what kind of model of man is that? This is the compassion of subservience: we regret causing other beings pain because we feel that we are not worthy. Genuine compassion, by contrast, is based on a fellowship of feeling: "Any man's death diminishes me, because I am involved in mankind," wrote the sixteenth-century poet John Donne. Humility is no basis on which to build commonality between human beings, who properly face each other eye to eye as upright equals.

How Humans Are Different

Human beings are not just a variation on chimps. What is at question is not *awareness* of our world, but *consciousness*. Humans are the only beings that are an object for themselves: that not only exist but know that they exist; that don't just act, but reflect on their activity. "Man makes himself," is the title of a book on human history by archaeologist V. Gordon Childe. He notes that biological evolution selects characteristics that will be useful for a particular environment—a tough hide for protection, fast running to escape predators, or sharp claws with which to kill. Human beings have virtually no useful biological adaptations: we are slow, naked and thin-skinned. Instead we consciously fashion our own adaptations, from clothes to cars to weapons. Rather than being a product of evolutionary improvement, we improve ourselves.

This is not a question of degree: it is a question of kind. Over time evolution has produced increasingly complex species, which have a greater control over and awareness of their environment—from bacteria to plants to reptiles to primates. Evolution is the equivalent of a plane speeding up on a runway, and then with the emergence of humans it takes off and operates according to completely different laws. Whatever chimps' and gorillas' genetic similarity to humans, they are primarily creatures of evolution. A chimp community from two million years ago would be completely indistinguishable to one today.

The human line separated from chimpanzees around seven million years ago, but it was only with the emergence of modern humans some 50,000 years ago that we notice a qualitative leap. In the intervening period there was a host of different hominid species, many of which died out. Our evolutionary line was marked by an increasingly upright stance, a growth in brain size, and a reduction in robustness of the jaw and teeth. Our hominid ancestors had developed basic tools—mainly hand-held "choppers"—and they probably knew how to use fire and buried their dead, but they were sluggish. With anatomically modern humans there is an explosion in the sophistication of tools, including fish hooks, specialised cutters, spears, bows and arrows, lamps. There is also complex culture such as art, jewellery and religious rituals, which suggest humans trying to explain their world to themselves and to exert control over it. Within a few thousand years, humans had spread from Africa to Siberia, Australia and the Americas, showing that they were the universal animal that could adapt itself to each and every clime.

Who knows what the key ingredient was that allowed human beings to take off. Some scientists suggest that it was a refinement in the vocal tract, allowing a greater range of sounds for speech. Certainly consciousness is intrinsically social: we only become aware of ourselves as individuals by seeing ourselves in the eyes of others; we only have inner thoughts through the common symbols of language. As Kenan Malik has argued, if we were mere individuals "we would possess sensations and experiences, but we could never interpret those sensations or experiences, or make them meaningful."

In the development of humans, there was a weakening of biological adaptation and an increasing reliance on culture. We became upright, leaving our hands free; our hands lost their adaptations for swinging (chimps) or bounding (gorillas) and became primarily for manipulation of tools; our mouths lost their adaptations for tearing food (such as tough tongues and lips, heavy jaws, large teeth) and became sensitive and versatile for speech. The hand and the mouth are the key human organs. Aristotle called the hand the "organ of organs" because of its versatility. Thomas Aquinas looked down on the "horns and claws" and "toughness of hide and quantity of hair or feathers" in animals: "Such things do not suit the nature of man. . . . Instead of these, he has reason and hands whereby he can make himself arms and clothes, and other necessities of life, of infinite variety." Reason, Aquinas said, was "capable of conceiving of an infinite number of things" so it was fitting that the hand had the "power of devising for itself an infinite number of instruments."

Some suggest that we have been in denial about the moral implications of Darwinism for the past 150 years. Richard Ryder argues: "Thanks to Darwin, many of the huge and self-proclaimed differences between humans and animals were revealed to be no more than arrogant delusions. Surely, if we are all related through evolution we should also be related morally." In fact, the opposite is true. First, knowledge of Darwinism shows just how much we have managed to break free of the process of natural selection that holds every other living creature in its yoke. Second, in finding that we evolved rather than were created by God, perhaps we truly became our own gods. After all, what kind of species manages to find out the secret of its own origins?

Crossing the Species Barrier

In purely practical terms, modern society is more distinguished from animals than ever before: we live more than ever in conditions of our own creation, immune from natural pressures of hunger and cold. Yet there is a curious dissonance between practical reality and consciousness. Whereas in the past human beings' practical mastery went hand-in-hand with an expanding consciousness, now the two have come apart. While practical mastery continues apace, it lacks the moral foundations to justify it. As a result, we are effectively living in two worlds: one composed of the things we do, and one of the things we can justify. Behind this lies doubt about the point to human existence. E.O. Wilson's 1978 book *On Human Nature* argued: "We have no particular place to go. The species lacks any goal external to its own biological nature." Wilson perceptively noted how such "evolutionary ethics" were a fill-in for "the seemingly fatal deterioration of the myths of traditional religion and its secular equivalents." It was a loss of faith in our ability to make our own history that encouraged the view that we are just a bundle of nerves and DNA.

Some humans are now trying to cross the species barrier, seeking again a kinship with animals. Indeed such is the real content of many of the primate experiments with chimps and gorillas. Jane Goodall in Gombe National Park was less observing chimps from outside than trying to become one with them, empathising with their courtships and fights and injuries. She writes: "She was too tired after their long, hot journey to set to on the delicious food, as her daughters did. . . . The leader of the patrol, hearing the sudden sound, stopped and stared ahead." Goodall's manuscripts are peppered with "as ifs" and "as thoughs," as she projects human dramas and tragedies on to her subjects. Other primate researchers took chimps into their homes and treated them like human children. Two couples—Roger and Deborah Fouts and Beatrice and Allan Gardener—lived with chimps and taught them to use basic sign language. They gave them presents on their birthday and "candy trees" at Christmas, behaving more as parents and kids than researcher and subject.

This blurring of the boundaries between animals and humans means a loss of moral sense, and a disgust at humanity. We can see this dramatically in *Grizzly Man*, a new film about a man who went to live with grizzly bears in the far reaches of Alaska. Tim Treadwell filmed his life with the bears for 13 years, less observing or admiring them than wanting to be like them. "I love these animals!" he repeatedly cried (they all had names like "Mr Chocolate"). He sought to face up to them on their terms, earning their "respect" and refusing to carry weapons. One of his friends observed: "He wanted to become like a bear, to mutate into a wild animal, connect so deeply that he was no longer human." Behind this lay his contempt for the human world. The narrator noted: "Treadwell speaks of the human world as something foreign. Wild primordial nature is where he felt truly at home." Treadwell was able to feel compassion for a bee ("I love that bee!") but saw human visitors to the area as foreign intruders. Of course, Treadwell's is an extreme example—but perhaps he was only living out the theory of human-animal equality. By turning theory into practical reality we can see its depravity.

We are in a paradoxical situation today, of using our capacity for consciousness and creativity to devalue that consciousness and creativity. Scientists use their ability to analyse DNA to prove that we are little more than chimps. Philosophers use their reasoning powers and the accumulated knowledge of human history to try to prove that humans have no special ethical value. Artists use their creativity to represent human experience as akin to that of animals—with British artist Damien Hirst using flies or animals in formaldehyde to explore human experiences of love and death.

There are severe consequences of holding human life so cheap. For a start, it is demoralising, drumming home the notion that our lives are futile. There are practical implications too. Animal research has produced key medical breakthroughs, from insulin to heart transplants to vaccines. Many of us would now be dead were it not for these discoveries. Now that animal rights concerns hold back research, this will mean needless human deaths in the future. Meanwhile, in wildlife sanctuaries in the developing world the welfare of chimps or tigers is placed above that of local villagers. The biologist Jonathan Marks sums up the crude calculations he heard from a colleague: "A British professor thinks there are too many Asians and not enough orangutans."

Towards a Human-Centred Morality

It is only a human-centred morality that can provide for fertile and equal relationships among human beings. We should relate to each other and respect one another as conscious, rational beings, rather than as DNA databases or collections of nerve endings. Attempts to find equality between humans and animals are founded in a loss of moral compass, and a disgust at humanity. As such, they are antithetical to historic attempts to fight for human equality. Moreover, it is our sense of humans as a common family that means that we can treat those who lack full agency and rationality—such as disabled people and children—with love and respect. These humans live in a network of relationships, and are loved and valued by those around them.

None of this means that we should be nasty to or disinterested in animals. Wanton torture is wrong, though less because of the pain it causes to the animal than because it reflects badly upon the torturer. The same level of animal pain, existing for a clear purpose in a slaughterhouse or a science lab, would be entirely justified. A proper relationship to animals consists in using them in a controlled, conscious manner—for the varied ends of the butcher, the nature photographer, the poet, the scientist, or the pet-owner. These relationships with animals are founded on our different aims and values, and as such are moral. A human-centred approach could mean spending hours in the wild studying animals, or painting and admiring them—but seeing them through a human eye rather than trying to escape our humanity.

What is at question is the position from which we see the world. Taking a bear-centred perspective makes no more sense than a DNA-centred perspective. Humans are the measure of all things: morality starts with us.

Tom Regan  **NO**

The Rights of Humans and Other Animals

Because the theme of this issue lends itself to emphasizing the differences that exist between the participating philosophers, it seems especially important to make a few observations about some fundamental points on which we are all agreed. As will be clear momentarily, our unanimity concerns what we all think is false rather than what we think is true.

Points of Agreement

We all agree that moral judgments—judgments about what is right and wrong, good and bad, just and unjust—are not simply and solely expressions of individual feeling or attitude. Some of the things we say are simply and solely of this sort. For example, if I say "I like coffee," and you say "I like tea," each of us has expressed our personal preference regarding what we like to drink. And about such matters there is, of course, no right or wrong, no true or false, and no thought of justifying or supporting or validating what is said. About matters of taste, things just are the way they are, with different people liking different things.

Moral judgments are not like this. When two people make conflicting judgments about a controversial moral issue—about the morality of abortion, for example—they are not simply and solely saying what they like or dislike, as a matter of personal preference. They are saying something *about abortion,* not something *about their individual response* to abortion. And the person who says that abortion is always wrong is saying something about abortion that contradicts what is said by someone who says that abortion is sometimes morally permissible. As such, and unlike the situation in which different people simply and solely express their feelings or preferences, moral judgments do need to be defended, do need to be justified, do need to be validated. *How* to do this is a question whose possible answer divides the philosophers taking part in this discussion. But *that* this needs to be done—that moral judgments need to be justified, defended, validated—is common ground between all of us.

A second important agreement concerns a second falsehood. Just as some people think (mistakenly, in our view) that moral judgments are simply and solely expressions of personal feelings or attitudes, others think they are statements about a culture's mores. On this view, moral right and wrong are defined by the dominant customs of a culture, at any given period of its history; and because different cultures have different customs, this view, which usually is referred to as *cultural relativism,* concludes that there is no universal right and wrong; rather, there are as many rights and wrongs as there are different cultures with different customs.

The philosophers here, without exception, reject cultural relativism. When Frey denies that human beings have moral rights, he does not think he can be shown to be mistaken if we point out that most Americans disagree with him, any more than the rest of us are inclined to agree that slavery was not wrong among White citizens of the antebellum South, given the prevailing customs of that time and place. Even if it is an exaggeration to say, as Henrik Ibsen is said to have observed, that "the minority is always right," it is too obvious to need argument that the majority sometimes is wrong. We do not defend, justify, or validate a moral judgment by doing cultural anthropology.

Neither do we do this—and here I come to the third and final point of agreement among all of us—by consulting some holy book or by taking instruction from God's will. In saying this, I am not saying that no books are holy or that there is no God. I am only saying that, among the philosophers writing here, we all agree that judgments about moral right and wrong, good or bad, the just and the unjust must be defended, justified, or validated independently of what any God says or wills.

The Nature and Importance of Human Rights

As for our disagreements, it is important to realize that it is not only our respective views about animal rights that divide us. We also are divided when it comes to human rights. Cohen, Beauchamp, and I seem to be of one mind concerning the nature of human rights. (Let me add parenthetically that when I speak of human rights this is shorthand for human *moral* rights; and the same is true when I speak of animal rights: I am referring to their moral rights. Questions involving human or animal legal rights are an entirely separate matter.) Here, briefly, are those points on which I think the three of us agree.

Human rights place justified limits on what people are free to do to one another. For example, the right to bodily integrity disallows physically assaulting another person's body simply on the grounds that others might benefit as a result. To use Cohen's example, one cannot justify the Nazi hypothermia research because what was learned might help other people who suffer from exposure. . . .

There are some things that *morally cannot be done* to the individual even if others stand to benefit as a result of doing it. As Ronald Dworkin said, the rights of the individual "trump" the collective interest. In the moral game, the rights card is the trump card.

Even with these very few comments about rights on the table, I think we should be able to see why Cohen is correct when he says that the idea of animal rights is a very important idea, one fraught with massive potential practical significance. Because if animals have rights—including, for example, the right to bodily integrity and the right not to be made to suffer gratuitously—it is difficult to see how anything less than the total abolition of animal model research could be morally acceptable. In particular, if animals have rights, certain familiar ways of defending animal model research will be silenced. No longer will we want to listen to the long list of benefits attributed to research of this kind. If animals have rights, and if rights are the trump card in the moral game, their rights override any benefits, real or imagined, we have gained, or stand to gain, from using them in biomedical research. So, yes, Cohen is on the money when he states that animal rights is an important idea.

Now, Cohen, Beauchamp, and I agree that humans have rights. And Beauchamp and I agree that animals have rights (although we disagree over what rights they have). It is Frey who disagrees with all of us, maintaining, as he does, that neither animals nor humans have rights. Before going on to state my views concerning animal rights, I want to say something about his views concerning human rights.

Frey's Utilitarianism

Frey is a utilitarian, and a utilitarian of a certain stripe. All utilitarians think that the morality of what we do—whether our acts are morally right or wrong— depends on what happens as a result of the choices we make. Utilitarianism is a forward-looking view. The consequences, results, or effects of our actions determine their morality. And by our actions we should be trying to make the world better, to bring about the best possible consequences or results, in any given situation.

What is best [for] all considered, however, is not necessarily what is best for each individual. Utilitarians are committed to aggregating—to adding and subtracting—the positive and negative consequences experienced by different individuals. This means that one person might lose a lot so that another might gain. . . .

[T]he essential point is that his utilitarianism is, in my view, a fundamentally mistaken way to think about morality. Here is a simple test case that I think makes my point. Some time back four teenage boys raped and in other ways sexually abused a seriously retarded teenage girl. Among other things, as I recall, the boys took special pleasure in invading her body with a broom handle and a Coke bottle.

I assume that no one will question that the abuse this poor girl suffered was wrong. But I hope you will notice that Frey's theory cannot easily explain why it is wrong. After all, there were four boys and just the one girl, and the boys evidently had a very good time. Shuffling along, Frey might suggest that there are other consequences that need to be taken into account—for example, the insecurity experienced by other young girls as a result of what happened to this one, and so on.

But this is not the central point. The central point is that, *before* Frey can pass a moral judgment in this case, his theory requires that we take the pleasures the four boys experienced into account—that we count *their* equal interests equally. By my lights, however, the pleasures experienced by these four boys are *totally irrelevant* to assessing the morality of their actions. More generally, the interests of those who do what is morally wrong have no bearing on the determination of the wrong they do. It is because Frey's view requires that we count these interests, *and weigh them equally with those of the victims of wrongdoing,* that I think his way of thinking is fundamentally mistaken.

Thus, the importance of human rights, in my view. Because if we suppose that this young girl has rights, then the good time had by the boys—the benefits they derived from abusing her—emerges as beside the moral point. Her rights trump their good time; indeed, their good time has no bearing whatsoever on assessing the morality of what they did. If there is a valid way of defending or justifying our moral judgments, I believe that it involves thinking along the lines I have just sketched, crude as that sketch is.

Animal Welfare and Animal Rights

I turn now to the topic of animal rights, beginning with some comments on the distinction between animal welfarists and animal rightists. As the name suggests, animal welfarists are in theory committed to taking the welfare of animals seriously. Animals should not be caused gratuitous physical pain; their psychological wellbeing should not be diminished unnecessarily. These are among the principles that guide a conscientious welfarist.

As such, welfarists can, and some of them sometimes do, call for important reforms, in the name of humane improvements, regarding how humans utilize nonhuman animals. Provided, however, that the welfare interests of these animals are taken into account and counted fairly, we do nothing wrong in principle by utilizing them to advance human interests. In particular, the use of nonhuman animals in biomedical research is in principle morally right, from a welfarist perspective, even if this human endeavor occasionally goes wrong in practice, as when a particular researcher neglects or otherwise mistreats animals in his laboratory.

Animal welfarism, therefore, can be seen to embody the utilitarianism championed by someone like Frey. The many benefits allegedly derived from animal model research outweigh the many harms experienced by the animals. Indeed, if the biomedical community is looking for a coherent spokesperson to defend their activities philosophically, it could well be true that they will not be able to find anyone better than Frey and his utilitarianism.

Animal rightists differ from animal welfarists. Although animal welfarists can have reformist aspirations, animal rightists are necessarily abolitionists. From their perspective, the use of nonhuman animals in scientific research is wrong in principle, not simply occasionally wrong in practice. These animals do not belong in laboratories in the first place: They do not belong there because placing them there, in the hope of gaining benefits for others, violates their rights. Rights being the trump card in the moral game, it is not larger cages, but empty cages, that animal rightists call for.

Whatever we might think of the animal rights–animal welfare debate, it is important to realize that it represents a type of debate that has many logical cousins. The ongoing debate over the justice of the death penalty is an example.

Some people believe there is nothing wrong with capital punishment in principle, even as they acknowledge there certainly have been some things wrong with it in practice. It was not too long ago that convicted criminals were hanged in public, burnt to death, or drowned for offenses that included such crimes as (here I cite North Carolina law) breaking a fish pond, stealing apples, dueling if death ensued, and (most remarkable of all) growing tobacco plants. Over the years, reformers of the death penalty sought to make the setting of the punishment more dignified and the method of execution more humane. Death by lethal injection, carried out in a sterile, hospital-like setting, would seem to represent as far as we might be able to go in the direction of such reforms.

This is not far enough for death penalty abolitionists. Think what one might of their arguments, these critics of capital punishment believe that it is wrong in principle, not merely sometimes grotesquely immoral in practice, and they therefore call for its complete abolition, not merely various "humane" reforms.

Thus does the logic of the animal rights–animal welfare debate mirror the logic of other important, divisive, and enduring social controversies. Other examples include the debates over reforming or abolishing slavery, child labor, and legal access to abortion. That all these controversies differ in important ways from the animal rights–animal welfare debate is too obvious to be denied. My point is not that this debate is like these other controversies in each and every way; mine is the far more modest point that they share a common logic.

Animal Rights

But *do* animals have rights? And if they do, what rights do they have? My answers to these questions are explained in my book, *The Case for Animal Rights* (1983), and it is this work that I recommend to anyone who is interested seriously in what my answers are and why I answer as I do. Concerning the latter point, let me remind you that all the philosophers writing in this issue agree that we do not offer answers to moral questions just by saying how we happen to feel or what we happen to like, or by making reference to the dominant customs in America today, or by citing selected passages in the Bible or some other sacred book. Our moral thinking needs to move in a different direction than those these paths open up to us.

But if not in these ways, how? No easy question, this; certainly not for the philosophically faint of heart. But here is *a* way, although certainly not the only way, to proceed.

Suppose we begin by assuming that humans have rights and ask how we might be able to illuminate or explain why we do. Of course, Frey will protest. You will recall that he denies *both* animal *and* human rights. But you also will recall where, in my opinion, his utilitarianism-without-rights lands him. So, although beginning with the assumption that humans have rights is certainly not noncontroversial, it is a place we can defend using on this occasion—one that, by the way, Beauchamp and Cohen can be counted on as approving, given their agreement that humans do indeed have rights.

If humans have rights, there must be something about being human that helps explain or illuminates why we have them. Put another way, there must be some characteristic or set of characteristics (for brevity's sake, I refer to these possibilities as *C*) that makes the attribution of rights plausible in our case and implausible in the case of, for example, clouds, negative afterimages, and microfungi. The question is: What could this C be?

Possible answers are many. Some, although possibly widely believed, will not pass muster with my fellow philosophers. The idea that C is the soul, and that God endowed us with rights when he endowed us with a soul, rests on a religious basis that we agree is unsatisfactory. A more promising, nonreligious candidate is rational autonomy. It is because humans are rational autonomous agents, and because clouds, negative afterimages, and microfungi are not, that we have rights and they do not.

Suppose we grant this candidate for C for the moment; then we can ask how nonhuman animals would fare. In other words, we can ask, Are any nonhuman animals rational and autonomous? Because if some are, it would smack of prejudice to deny that they have rights but to affirm that we do.

Whether any nonhuman animals are rational and autonomous is a very difficult empirical question, one that we are unlikely to settle on this occasion. My own view, for what it is worth, is that there are many species of animals whose members satisfy these conditions. Nonhuman primates are the most obvious example. Next are the great whales and other mammals. Obviously, where we draw the line that separates those animals who are rational and autonomous from those who are not will be neither easy nor free of controversy. Indeed, it may be that there is no clearly defined line we can draw with confidence, given the abundance of our individual and collective ignorance. However, it is enough for our purposes to recognize that *some* nonhuman animals are like humans in being rational and autonomous. So if rational autonomy explains or illuminates why we have rights, consistency requires that we make the same judgment in the case of these other animals: They, too, would have rights.

There is, however, a problem. Not all human beings are rational, autonomous agents. Infants are not, although most of them some day will be, and older people who suffer from serious mental deterioration are not, although most of them once were. Plus there are those many thousands of humans who, like the young woman raped by the four teenage boys, are seriously mentally retarded throughout their entire lives. In any or all of these cases we have individuals who *are* human beings but who are *not* rational and autonomous. So if C is rational autonomy, it appears that billions of human beings lack rights and, in lacking them, lack the most important card in the moral game. In their case, we cannot say that it would be wrong to harm them in the hope of benefiting others because their rights trump the collective interest. In the nature of the case, they have no rights.

This problem can be avoided by putting forth a different candidate for C. Instead of using what Beauchamp refers to as "cognitive criteria," . . . criteria such as rationality, we might instead rely on noncognitive criteria, criteria such as sentience (the capacity to be able to experience pain and pleasure) or emotion. And this does seem to be a more promising way to think about C, especially because all those humans who were denied rights, given the criterion of rational autonomy, seem to satisfy these noncognitive criteria.

Noncognitive criteria do more than increase the number of human beings who qualify as rights holders. These same criteria also increase the number of nonhuman animals who qualify. Line drawing problems doubtless will persist, but, wherever one reasonably draws the line, it seems evident that there are many more nonhuman animals who are sentient or who feel emotions than there are nonhuman animals who are rational and autonomous.

Although much more needs to be said to complete the argument for animal rights, some features of the central plot emerge from the little that has been said here. We face a choice: *Either* we can set the criteria of rights possession (C) rather high, so to speak, requiring capacities such as rationality and autonomy, *or* we can set the criteria of rights possession lower, requiring noncognitive capacities such as sentience. If we choose the former, some (but not a great many) nonhuman animals arguably will qualify as possessors of rights; but many human beings also will fail to qualify. If we choose the latter alternative, these humans will be enfranchised within the class of rights holders; but so will many nonhuman animals. Rationally, we cannot have it both ways—cannot, that is, rationally defend the view that all and only human beings have rights. Cohen may think he can do this. But for reasons I hope to explain in the future, I believe he is seriously confused and mistaken.

Which choice should we make? Informed people of good will can answer this question differently. I favor a view of rights that enfranchises the most vulnerable humans among us. Infants and young children, the elderly who suffer from degenerative diseases of the brain, the seriously mentally retarded of all ages are the most obvious examples. I do not think those of us who are more fortunate should be free to utilize these human beings—in biomedical research, for example—in the hope that we might learn something that will benefit us or others. Frey's utilitarianism certainly could allow this, which in my opinion is all the more reason not to accept his moral philosophy. If we recognize the rights of these humans, however, we recognize that they hold trump cards that have greater ethical force than what is in the general interest. And that certainly is the position I hold and recommend in their case.

I also recognize, however, that any plausible criterion that would enfranchise these humans within the class of rights holders will spill over the species boundary, so to speak, and enfranchise many hundreds, possibly many thousands of species of animals. That being the case, these animals also must be viewed as holding the trump card in the moral game. And because the rights they have should not be overridden in the name of seeking benefits for ourselves or others, it follows that none of these animals should be in any laboratory for that purpose. From an animal rights perspective, as noted earlier, it is not larger cages, it is empty cages that recognition of animal rights requires.

POSTSCRIPT

Is the Use of Animals in Research Justified?

Much debate about the lethal experiments that were conducted on non-consenting human subjects by the Nazis during World War II, as well as the ensuing trials of the Nazi physicians in Nuremburg, Germany, has established a consensus that no scientist can treat people the way the Nazis did. Informed consent is essential, and research on humans must aim to benefit those same humans.

As these ideas have gained currency, some people have tried to extend them to say that, just as scientists cannot do whatever they wish to humans, they cannot do whatever they wish to animals. Harriet Ritvo, in "Toward a More Peaceable Kingdom," *Technology Review* (April 1992), says that the animal rights movement "challenges the ideology of science itself . . . forcing experimenters to recognize that they are not necessarily carrying out an independent exercise in the pursuit of truth—that their enterprise, in its intellectual as well as its social and financial dimensions, is circumscribed and defined by the culture of which it is an integral part." The result is a continuing debate, driven by the periodic discovery of researchers who seem quite callous (at least to the layperson's eye) in their treatment of animals (see Kathy Snow Guillermo, *Monkey Business: The Disturbing Case That Launched the Animal Rights Movement* [National Press, 1993]), by the charge that animal rights advocates just do not understand nature or research, and by the counter-charge that animal research is irrelevant (see Peter Tatchell, "Why Animal Research Is Bad Science," *New Statesman* (August 9, 2004).

In the February 1997 issue of *Scientific American,* Andrew N. Rowan presents a debate entitled "The Benefits and Ethics of Animal Research." The opposing articles are Neal D. Barnard and Stephen R. Kaufman, "Animal Research Is Wasteful and Misleading" and Jack H. Botting and Adrian R. Morrison, "Animal Research Is Vital to Medicine." Among books that are pertinent to this issue are F. Barbara Orlans, *In the Name of Science: Issues in Responsible Animal Experimentation* (Oxford University Press, 1993); Rod Strand and Patti Strand, *The Hijacking of the Humane Movement* (Doral, 1993); Deborah Blum, *The Monkey Wars* (Oxford University Press, 1994), and Tom Regan, *Empty Cages: Facing the Challenge of Animal Rights* (Rowman and Littlefield, 2005). Adrian R. Morrison provides a guide to responsible animal use in "Ethical Principles Guiding the Use of Animals in Research," *American Biology Teacher* (February 2003). Barry Yeoman, "Can We Trust Research Done with Lab Mice," *Discover* (July 2003), notes that the conditions in which animals are kept can make a huge difference in their behavior and in their responses to experimental treatments.

Reviewing recent developments in the animal rights movement, Damon Linker, in "Rights for Rodents," *Commentary* (April 2001), concludes, "Can anyone really doubt that, were the misanthropic agenda of the animal-rights movement actually to succeed, the result would be an increase in man's inhumanity, to man and animal alike? In the end, fostering our age-old 'prejudice' in favor of human dignity may be the best thing we can do for animals, not to mention for ourselves." An editorial in *Lancet* (September 4, 2004), "Animal Research Is a Source of Human Compassion, Not Shame," insists that the use of animals in biomedical research is both an essentially humanistic endeavor and necessary. Assistant professor of anesthesiology and radiology at the University of Pittsburgh Stuart Derbyshire writes in "Vivisection: Put Human Welfare First," *Spiked-Online* (June 1, 2004), that the use of animals in research is justified by the search for knowledge, not just the search for medical treatments, and reflects a moral choice to put humans first. John J. Miller, "In the Name of the Animals," *National Review* (July 3, 2006), equates U.S. animal rights activists to terrorists and says that their activities delay or prevent medical progress and disrupt the nation's economy. This view has resulted in legislation designed to fight "animal activist extremism by closing loopholes and increasing penalties in federal law dealing with criminal acts against animal enterprises [including] animal research organizations, farms, zoos and pet stores"; see "Anti-Terrorism Bill Passes," *DVM: The Newsmagazine of Veterinary Medicine* (January 2007).

Charles Colson and Anne Morse agree that the animal rights movement assaults human dignity in "Taming Beasts," *Christianity Today* (April 2003). Yet the idea that animals have rights too continues to gain ground. Steven M. Wise finds in *Drawing the Line: Science and the Case for Animal Rights* (Perseus, 2002) that there is a spectrum of mental capacities for different species, which supports the argument for rights. Niall Shanks, in "Animal Rights in the Light of Animal Cognition," *Social Alternatives* (Summer 2003) considers the moral/philosophical justifications for animal rights and stresses the question of consciousness. Jim Motavalli, in "Rights from Wrongs," *E Magazine* (March/April 2003), describes with approval the movement toward giving animals legal rights (though not necessarily human rights). Erin E. Williams and Margo Demello, *Why Animals Matter: The Case for Animal Protection* (Prometheus, 2007), link the mistreatment of animals in labs, slaughterhouses, and other venues with the mistreatment of immigrants and workers.

You can find the benefits of the use of animals discussed on a number of Web sites. Begin with Americans for Medical Progress (http://www.amprogress.org). For lists of specific benefits, visit Michigan State University at http://www.msu.edu/unit/ular/biomed/biomed_index.htm and the Pennsylvania Society for Biomedical Research at http://www.psbr.org/society/ABOUT.htm.

ISSUE 19

Is It Ethically Permissible to Clone Human Cells?

YES: Julian Savulescu, from "Should We Clone Human Beings? Cloning as a Source of Tissue for Transplantation," *Journal of Medical Ethics* (April 1, 1999)

NO: David van Gend, from "Prometheus, Pandora, and the Myths of Cloning," *Human Life Review* (Summer/Fall 2006)

ISSUE SUMMARY

YES: Julian Savulescu, director of the Ethics Program of the Murdoch Institute at the Royal Children's Hospital in Melbourne, Australia, argues that it is not only permissible but morally required to use human cloning to create embryos as a source of tissue for transplantation.

NO: Physician David van Gend argues that not only is the cloning of embryonic stem cells morally indefensible, but recent progress with adult stem cells makes it unnecessary as well.

In February 1997 Ian Wilmut and Keith H. S. Campbell of the Roslin Institute in Edinburgh, Scotland, announced that they had cloned a sheep by transferring the gene-containing nucleus from a single cell of an adult sheep's mammary gland into an egg cell whose own nucleus had been removed and discarded. The resulting combination cell then developed into an embryo and eventually a lamb in the same way a normal egg cell does after being fertilized with a sperm cell. That lamb, named Dolly, was a genetic duplicate of the ewe from which the udder cell's nucleus was taken. Similar feats had been accomplished years before with fish and frogs, and mammal embryos had previously been split to produce artificial twins. It was not long before researchers successfully cloned monkeys and other animals. But the reactions of the media, politicians, ethicists, and lay-people have been largely negative. Dr. Donald Bruce, director of the Church of Scotland's Society, Religion and Technology Project, for example, has argued at some length about how "nature is not ours to do exactly what we like with."

Many people seem to agree. In 1994 the U.S. National Advisory Board on Ethics in Reproduction called the whole idea of cloning oneself "bizarre . . . narcissistic and ethically impoverished." Arthur Caplan, director of the Center for Bioethics at the University of Pennsylvania, wonders, "What is the ethical purpose of even trying?" Conservative columnist George Will asks whether humans are now uniquely endangered since "the great given—a human being is the product of the union of a man and a woman—is no longer a given" and "humanity is supposed to be an endless chain, not a series of mirrors." Leon R. Kass, "The Wisdom of Repugnance," *The New Republic* (June 2, 1997), argues that human cloning is "so repulsive to contemplate" that it should be prohibited entirely.

Others go further. President Bill Clinton asked the National Bioethics Advisory Commission (see http://bioethics.georgetown.edu/nbac/), chaired by Harold T. Shapiro, president of Princeton University, to investigate the implications of this "stunning" research and to issue a final report by the end of May 1997. He also barred the use of U.S. funds to support work on human cloning. The commission's report called for extending the ban and called any attempt to clone a human "morally unacceptable" for now. Many countries besides the United States agreed, and bans on cloning research were widely imposed.

Yet, says J. Madeleine Nash in "The Case for Cloning," *Time* (February 9, 1998), "hasty legislation could easily be too restrictive." Cloning could serve a great many useful purposes, and further development of the technology could lead to much less alarming procedures, such as growing replacement organs within a patient's body. See Arlene Judith Klotzko, "We Can Rebuild . . . ," *New Scientist* (February 27, 1999). Some of these benefits were considered when George Washington University researchers, using nonviable embryos, demonstrated that single cells could be removed from human embryos and induced to grow into new embryos. If permitted to develop normally, the cells would grow into genetically identical adults. The resulting adults would be duplicates, but only of each other (like identical twins), not of some preexisting adult.

Did Dolly represent something entirely new? For the very first time, it seemed more than science fiction to say it might soon be possible to duplicate an adult human, not just an embryo. But when ethicist John A. Robertson spoke at the National Bioethics Advisory Commission conference held in Washington, D.C., March 13–14, 1997, he said, "At this early stage in the development of mammalian cloning a ban on all human cloning is both imprudent and unjustified. Enough good uses can be imagined that it would be unwise to ban all cloning and cloning research because of vague and highly speculative fears."

In the following selection, Julian Savulescu argues, in part, that because cloned embryos have no moral value beyond that of the cells from which they are cloned, and because human suffering can be relieved, it is not only permissible but morally required to use human cloning to create embryos as a source of tissue for transplantation.

In the second selection, physician David van Gend takes strong exception to the idea that embryos—cloned or not—have no moral value. The cloning of embryonic stem cells, he says, is morally indefensible. In addition, recent progress with adult stem cells makes it unnecessary.

YES

Julian Savulescu

Should We Clone Human Beings?

Introduction

When news broke in 1997 that Ian Wilmut and his colleagues had successfully cloned an adult sheep, there was an ill-informed wave of public, professional and bureaucratic fear and rejection of the new technique. Almost universally, human cloning was condemned. Germany, Denmark and Spain have legislation banning cloning; Norway, Slovakia, Sweden and Switzerland have legislation implicitly banning cloning. Some states in Australia, such as Victoria, ban cloning. There are two bills before congress in the US which would comprehensively ban it. There is no explicit or implicit ban on cloning in England, Greece, Ireland or the Netherlands, though in England the Human Embryology and Fertilisation Authority, which issues licences for the use of embryos, has indicated that it would not issue any licence for research into "reproductive cloning." This is understood to be cloning to produce a fetus or live birth. Research into cloning in the first 14 days of life might be possible in England.

There have been several arguments given against human reproductive cloning:

1. It is liable to abuse.
2. It violates a person's right to individuality, autonomy, selfhood, etc.
3. It violates a person's right to genetic individuality (whatever that is—identical twins cannot have such a right).
4. It allows eugenic selection.
5. It uses people as a means.
6. Clones are worse off in terms of wellbeing, especially psychological wellbeing.
7. There are safety concerns, especially an increased risk of serious genetic malformation, cancer or shortened lifespan.

There are, however, a number of arguments in favour of human reproductive cloning. These include:

1. General liberty justifications.
2. Freedom to make personal reproductive choices.
3. Freedom of scientific enquiry.
4. Achieving a sense of immortality.

5. Eugenic selection (with or without gene therapy/enhancement).
6. Social utility—cloning socially important people.
7. Treatment of infertility (with or without gene therapy/enhancement).
8. Replacement of a loved dead relative (with or without gene therapy/enhancement).
9. "Insurance"—freeze a split embryo in case something happens to the first: as a source of tissue or as replacement for the first.
10. Source of human cells or tissue.
11. Research into stem cell differentiation to provide an understanding of aging and oncogenesis.
12. Cloning to prevent a genetic disease.

The arguments against cloning have been critically examined elsewhere and I will not repeat them here. Few people have given arguments in favour of it. Exceptions include arguments in favour of 7–12, with some commentators favouring only 10–11 or 11–12. Justifications 10–12 (and possibly 7) all regard cloning as a way of treating or avoiding disease. These have emerged as arguably the strongest justifications for cloning. This paper examines 10 and to some extent 11.

Human Cloning as a Source of Cells or Tissue

Cloning is the production of an identical or near-identical genetic copy. Cloning can occur by fission or fusion. Fission is the division of a cell mass into two equal and identical parts, and the development of each into a separate but genetically identical or near-identical individual. This occurs in nature as identical twins.

Cloning by fusion involves taking the nucleus from one cell and transferring it to an egg which has had its nucleus removed. Placing the nucleus in the egg reprogrammes the DNA in the nucleus to replicate the whole individual from which the nucleus was derived: nuclear transfer. It differs from fission in that the offspring has only one genetic parent, whose genome is nearly identical to that of the offspring. In fission, the offspring, like the offspring of normal sexual reproduction, inherits half of its genetic material from each of two parents. Henceforth, by "cloning," I mean cloning by fusion.

Human cloning could be used in several ways to produce cells, tissues or organs for the treatment of human disease.

Human Cloning as a Source of Multipotent Stem Cells

In this paper I will differentiate between totipotent and multipotent stem cells. Stem cells are cells which are early in developmental lineage and have the ability to differentiate into several different mature cell types. Totipotent stem cells are very immature stem cells with the potential to develop into any of the mature cell types in the adult (liver, lung, skin, blood, etc). Multipotential stem cells are more mature stem cells with the potential to develop into different mature forms of a particular cell lineage, for example, bone marrow stem cells can form either white or red blood cells, but they cannot form liver cells.

Multipotential stem cells can be used as

1. a vector for gene therapy.
2. cells for transplantation, especially in bone marrow.

Attempts have been made to use embryonic stem cells from other animals as vectors for gene therapy and as universal transplantation cells in humans. Problems include limited differentiation and rejection. Somatic cells are differentiated cells of the body, and not sex cells which give rise to sperm and eggs. Cloning of somatic cells from a person who is intended as the recipient of cell therapy would provide a source of multipotential stem cells that are not rejected. These could also be vectors for gene therapy. A gene could be inserted into a somatic cell from the patient, followed by selection, nuclear transfer and the culture of the appropriate clonal population of cells in vitro. These cells could then be returned to the patient as a source of new tissue (for example bone marrow in the case of leukaemia) or as tissue without genetic abnormality (in the case of inherited genetic disease). The major experimental issues which would need to be addressed are developing clonal stability during cell amplification and ensuring differentiation into the cell type needed. It should be noted that this procedure does not necessarily involve the production of a multicellular embryo, nor its implantation in vivo or artificially. (Indeed, cross-species cloning—fusing human cells with cow eggs—produces embryos which will not develop into fetuses, let alone viable offspring.)

A related procedure would produce totipotent stem cells which could differentiate into multipotent cells of a particular line or function, or even into a specific tissue. This is much closer to reproductive cloning. Embryonic stem cells from mice have been directed to differentiate into vascular endothelium, myocardial and skeletal tissue, haemopoietic precursors and neurons. However, it is not known whether the differentiation of human totipotent stem cells can be controlled in vitro. Unlike the previous application, the production of organs could involve reproductive cloning (the production of a totipotent cell which forms a blastomere), but then differentiates into a tissue after some days. Initially, however, all early embryonic cells are identical. Producing totipotent stem cells in this way is equivalent to the creation of an early embryo.

Production of Embryo/Fetus/Child/Adult as a Source of Tissue

An embryo, fetus, child or adult could be produced by cloning, and solid organs or differentiated tissue could be extracted from it.

Cloning as Source of Organs, Tissue and Cells for Transplantation

The Need for More Organs and Tissues

Jeffrey Platts reports: "So great is the demand that as few as 5% of the organs needed in the United States ever become available." According to David K C

Cooper, this is getting worse: "The discrepancy between the number of potential recipients and donor organs is increasing by approximately 10–15% annually." Increasing procurement of cadaveric organs may not be the solution. Anthony Dorling and colleagues write:

> "A study from Seattle, USA, in 1992 identified an annual maximum of only 7,000 brain dead donors in the USA. Assuming 100% consent and suitability, these 14,000 potential kidney grafts would still not match the numbers of new patients commencing dialysis each year. The clear implication is that an alternative source of organs is needed."

Not only is there a shortage of tissue or organs for those with organ failure, but there remain serious problems with the compatibility of tissue or organs used, requiring immunosuppressive therapy with serious side effects. Using cloned tissue would have enormous theoretical advantages, as it could be abundant and there is near perfect immunocompatibility.

There are several ways human cloning could be used to address the shortfall of organs and tissues, and each raises different ethical concerns.

1. Production of Tissue or Cells Only by Controlling Differentiation

I will now give an argument to support the use of cloning to produce cells or tissues through control of cellular differentiation.

The fate of one's own tissue.   Individuals have a strong interest or right in determining the fate of their own body parts, including their own cells and tissues, at least when this affects the length and quality of their own life. A right might be defended in terms of autonomy or property rights in body parts.

This right extends (under some circumstances) both to the proliferation of cells and to their transmutation into other cell types (which I will call the Principle of Tissue Transmutation).

Defending the Principle of Tissue Transmutation
Consider the following hypothetical example:

Lucas I   Lucas is a 22-year-old man with leukaemia. The only effective treatment will be a bone marrow transplant. There is no compatible donor. However, there is a drug which selects a healthy bone marrow cell and causes it to multiply. A doctor would be negligent if he or she did not employ such a drug for the treatment of Lucas's leukaemia. Indeed, there is a moral imperative to develop such drugs if we can and use them. Colony-stimulating factors, which cause blood cells to multiply, are already used in the treatment of leukaemia, and with stored marrow from those in remission in leukaemia before use for reconstitution during relapse.

Lucas II   In this version of the example, the drug causes Lucas's healthy skin cells to turn into healthy bone marrow stem cells. There is no relevant moral difference between Lucas I and II. We should develop such drugs and doctors would be negligent if they did not use them.

If this is right, there is nothing problematic about cloning to produce cells or tissues for transplantation by controlling differentiation. All we would be doing is taking, say, a skin cell and turning on and off some components of the total genetic complement to cause the cell to divide as a bone marrow cell. We are causing a differentiated cell (skin cell) to turn directly into a multipotent stem cell (bone marrow stem cell).

Are there any objections? The major objection is one of practicality. It is going to be very difficult to cause a skin cell to turn *directly* into a bone marrow cell. There are also safety considerations. Because we are taking a cell which has already undergone many cell divisions during terminal differentiation to give a mature cell such as a skin cell, and accumulated mutations, there is a theoretical concern about an increased likelihood of malignancy in that clonal population. However, the donor cell in these cases is the same age as the recipient (exactly), and a shorter life span would not be expected. There may also be an advantage in some diseases, such as leukaemia, to having a degree of incompatibility between donor and recipient bone marrow so as to enable the donor cells to recognise and destroy malignant recipient cells. This would not apply to non-malignant diseases in which bone marrow transplant is employed, such as the leukodystrophies. Most importantly, all these concerns need to be addressed by further research.

Lucas IIA In practice, it is most likely that skin cells will not be able to be turned directly into bone marrow cells: there will need to be a stage of totipotency in between. The most likely way of producing cells to treat Lucas II is via the cloning route, where a skin cell nucleus is passed through an oocyte to give a totipotent cell. The production of a totipotent stem cell is the production of an embryo.

Production of an embryo as a source of cells or tissues. There are two ways in which an embryo could be a source of cells and tissues. Firstly, the early embryonic cells could be made to differentiate into cells of one tissue type, for example, bone marrow. Secondly, differentiated cells or tissues from an older embryo could be extracted and used directly.

Are these permissible?

In England, the Royal Society has given limited support to cloning for the purposes of treating human disease. The Human Genetics Advisory Commission (HGAC) defines this as "therapeutic cloning," differentiating it from "reproductive cloning." Both bodies claim that embryo experimentation in the first 14 days is permitted by English law, and question whether cloning in this period would raise any new ethical issues.

Cloning in this circumstance raises few ethical issues. What is produced, at least in the first few days of division after a totipotent cell has been produced from an adult skin cell, is just a skin cell from that person with an altered gene expression profile (some genes turned on and some turned off). In one way, it is just an existing skin cell behaving differently from normal skin cells, perhaps more like a malignant skin cell. The significant processes are ones of *cellular multiplication* and later, *cellular differentiation*.

If this is true, why stop at research at 14 days? Consider the third version of the Lucas case:

Lucas III   The same as Lucas IIA, but in this case, Lucas also needs a kidney transplant. Therefore, in addition to the skin cell developing blood stem cells (via the embryo), the process is adjusted so that a kidney is produced.

The production of another tissue type or organ does not raise any new relevant ethical consideration. Indeed, if Lucas did not need the kidney, it could be used for someone else who required a kidney (if, of course, in vitro maturation techniques had been developed to the extent that a functioning organ of sufficient size could be produced).

Consider now:

Lucas IV   In addition to the blood cells, all the tissue of a normal human embryo is produced, organised in the anatomical arrangement of an embryo. This (in principle) might or might not involve development in a womb. For simplicity, let us assume that this occurs in vitro (though this is impossible at present).

Is there any morally relevant difference from the previous versions? It is not relevant that many different tissues are produced rather than one. Nor is the size of these tissues or their arrangement morally relevant. If there is a difference, it must be that a special kind of tissue has been produced, or that some special relationship develops between existing tissues, and that a morally significant entity then exists. When does this special point in embryonic development occur?

The most plausible point is some point during the development of the brain. There are two main candidates:

1. when tissue differentiates and the first identifiable brain structures come into existence as the neural plate around day 19.
2. when the brain supports some morally significant function: consciousness or self-consciousness or rational self-consciousness. The earliest of these, consciousness, does not occur until well into fetal development.

On the first view, utilisation of cloning techniques in the first two weeks to study cellular differentiation is justifiable. The most defensible view, I believe, is that our continued existence only becomes morally relevant when we become self-conscious. (Of course, if a fetus can feel pain at some earlier point, but is not self-conscious, its existence is morally relevant in a different way: we ought not to inflict unnecessary pain on it, though it may be permissible to end its life painlessly.) On this view, we should use the drug to cause Lucas IV's skin cells to transmutate and remove bone marrow from these. What is going on in Lucas IV is no different, morally speaking, from cloning. If this is right, it is justifiable to extract differentiated tissues from young fetuses which have been cloned. . . .

I cannot see any intrinsic morally significant difference between a mature skin cell, the totipotent stem cell derived from it, and a fertilised egg. They are all cells which could give rise to a person if certain conditions are obtained. (Thus, to claim that experimentation on cloned embryos is acceptable, but the same experimentation on non-cloned embryos is not acceptable, because the former are not embryos but totipotent stem cells, is sophistry.)

Looking at cloning this way exposes new difficulties for those who appeal to the potential of embryos to become persons and the moral significance of conception as a basis for opposition to abortion. If all our cells could be persons, then we cannot appeal to the fact that an embryo could be a person to justify the special treatment we give it. Cloning forces us to abandon the old arguments supporting special treatment of fertilised eggs.

Production of a Fetus

If one believes that the morally significant event in development is something related to consciousness, then extracting tissue or organs from a cloned fetus up until that point at which the morally relevant event occurs is acceptable. Indeed, in law, a legal persona does not come into existence until birth. At least in Australia and England, abortion is permissible throughout fetal development.

Production of a Child or Adult as a Source of Cells or Tissues

Like the production of a self-conscious fetus, the production of a cloned child or adult is liable to all the usual cloning objections, together with the severe limitations on the ways in which tissue can be taken from donors for transplantation.

Many writers support cloning for the purposes of studying cellular differentiation because they argue that cloning does not raise serious new issues above those raised by embryo experimentation. Such support for cloning is too limited. On one view, there is no relevant difference between early embryo research and later embryo/early fetal research. Indeed, the latter stand more chance of providing viable tissue for transplantation, at least in the near future. While producing a cloned live child as a source of tissue for transplantation would raise new and important issues, producing embryos and early fetuses as a source of tissue for transplantation may be morally obligatory.

Consistency

Is this a significant deviation from existing practice?

1. Fetal Tissue Transplantation

In fact, fetal tissue has been widely used in medicine. Human fetal thymus transplantation is standard therapy for thymic aplasia or Di George's syndrome. It has also been used in conjunction with fetal liver for the treatment of subacute combined immunodeficiency.

Human fetal liver and umbilical cord blood have been used as a source of haematopoietic cells in the treatment of acute leukaemia and aplastic anaemia. Liver has also been used for radiation accidents and storage disorders. The main problem has been immune rejection.

One woman with aplastic anaemia received fetal liver from her own 22-week fetus subsequent to elective abortion over 20 years ago.

Fetal brain tissue from aborted fetuses has been used as source of tissue for the treatment of Parkinson's disease. Neural grafts show long term survival and function in patients with Parkinson's disease, though significant problems remain.

Fetal tissue holds promise as treatment for Huntington's disease, spinal cord injuries, demyelinating disorders, retinal degeneration in retinitis pigmentosa, hippocampal lesions associated with temporal lobe epilepsy, cerebral ischaemia, stroke and head injury, and beta thalassemia in utero using fetal liver. Fetal pancreas has also been used in the treatment of diabetes.

Fetal Tissue Banks

Indeed, in the US and England, fetal tissue banks exist to distribute fetal tissues from abortion clinics for the purposes of medical research and treatment. In the US, the Central Laboratory for Human Embryology in Washington, the National Diseases Research Interchange, and the International Institute for the Advancement of Medicine and the National Abortion Federation, all distribute fetal tissue.

In the UK, the Medical Research Council's fetal tissue bank was established in 1957 and disperses about 5,000 tissues a year.

2. Conception of a Non-Cloned Child as a Source of Bone Marrow: Ayala Case

Not only has fetal tissue been used for the treatment of human disease, but human individuals have been deliberately conceived as a source of tissue for transplantation. In the widely discussed Ayala case, a 17-year-old girl, Anissa, had leukaemia. No donor had been found in two years. Her father had his vasectomy reversed with the intention of having another child to serve as a bone marrow donor. There was a one in four chance the child would be compatible with Anissa. The child, Marissa, was born and was a compatible donor and a successful transplant was performed.

A report four years later noted: "Marissa is now a healthy four-year-old, and, by all accounts, as loved and cherished a child as her parents said she would be. The marrow transplant was a success, and Anissa is now a married, leukaemia-free, bank clerk."

Assisted reproduction (IVF) has been used to produce children to serve as bone marrow donors. It is worth noting that had cloning been available, there would have been a 100% chance of perfect tissue compatibility and a live child need not have been produced.

Objections

While there are some precedents for the proposal to use cloning to produce tissue for transplantation, what is distinctive about this proposal is that human tissue will be: (i) cloned and (ii) deliberately created with abortion in mind. This raises new objections.

Abortion Is Wrong

Burtchaell, a Catholic theologian, in considering the ethics of fetal tissue research, claims that abortion is morally wrong and that fetal tissue cannot be used for research because no one can give informed consent for its use and to use it would be complicity in wrongful killing. He claims that mothers cannot consent: "The flaw in this claim [that mothers can consent] is that the tissue is from within her body but is the body of another, with distinct genotype, blood, gender, etc." Claims such as those of Burtchaell are more problematic in the case of cloning. If the embryo were cloned from the mother, it would be of the same genotype as her, and, arguably, one of her tissues. Now at some point a cloned tissue is no longer just a tissue from its clone: it exists as an individual in its own right and at some point has interests as other individuals do. But the latter point occurs, I believe, when the cloned individual becomes self-conscious. The presence or absence of a distinct genotype is irrelevant. We are not justified in treating an identical twin differently from a non-identical twin because the latter has a distinct genotype.

In a society that permits abortion on demand, sometimes for little or no reason, it is hard to see how women can justifiably be prevented from aborting a fetus for the purpose of saving someone's life. And surely it is more respectful of the fetus, if the fetus is an object of respect, that its body parts be used for good rather than for no good purpose at all.

It Is Worse to Be a Clone

Some have argued that it is worse to be a clone. This may be plausible in the sense that a person suffers in virtue of being a clone—living in the shadow of its "parent," feeling less like an individual, treated as a means and not an end, etc. Thus cloning in the Ayala case would raise some new (but I do not believe overwhelming) issues which need consideration. But cloning followed by abortion does not. I can't make any sense of the claim that it is worse to be a cloned cell or tissue. These are not the things we ascribe these kinds of interests to. Cloning is bad when it is bad for a person. Likewise, arguments regarding "instrumentalisation" apply to persons, and not to tissues and cells.

Creating Life with the Intention of Ending It to Provide Tissue

Using cloning to produce embryos or fetuses as a source of tissue would involve deliberately creating life for the purposes of destroying it. It involves intentionally killing the fetus. This differs from abortion where women do not intend to become pregnant for the purpose of having an abortion.

Is it wrong deliberately to conceive a fetus for the sake of providing tissue? Most of the guidelines on the use of fetal tissue aim to stop women having children just to provide tissues. The reason behind this is some background belief that abortion is itself wrong. These guidelines aim to avoid moral taint objections that we cannot benefit from wrong-doing. More importantly, there is a concern that promoting some good outcome from abortion would encourage abortion. However, in this case, abortion would not be encouraged because this is abortion in a very special context: it is abortion of a *cloned* fetus for medical purposes.

But is it wrong deliberately to use abortion to bring about some good outcome?

In some countries (for example those in the former Eastern bloc), abortion is or was the main available form of birth control. A woman who had intercourse knowing that she might fall pregnant, in which case she would have an abortion, would not necessarily be acting wrongly in such a country, if the alternative was celibacy. When the only way to achieve some worthwhile end—sexual expression—is through abortion, it seems justifiable.

The question is: is the use of cloned fetal tissue the best way of increasing the pool of transplantable tissues and organs?

An Objection to the Principle of Tissue Transmutation

Another objection to the proposal is that we do not have the right to determine the fate of all our cells. For example, we are limited in what we can do with our sex cells. However, we should only be constrained in using our own cells when that use puts others at risk. This is not so in transmutation until another individual with moral interests comes into existence.

Surrogacy Concerns

At least at present, later embryonic and fetal development can only occur inside a woman's uterus, so some of the proposals here would require a surrogate. I have assumed that any surrogate would be freely consenting. Concerns with surrogacy have been addressed elsewhere, though cloning for this purpose would raise some different concerns. There would be no surrogacy concerns if the donor cell were derived from the mother (she would be carrying one of her own cells), from the mother's child (she would be carrying her child again) or if an artificial womb were ever developed.

Should We Give Greater Importance to Somatic Cells?

I have claimed that the totipotent cells of the early embryo, and indeed the embryo, do not have greater moral significance than adult skin cells (or indeed lung or colon or any nucleated cells). I have used this observation to downgrade the importance we attach to embryonic cells. However, it might be argued that we should upgrade the importance which we attach to somatic cells.

This is a *reductio ad absurdum* of the position which gives importance to the embryo, and indeed which gives weight to anatomical structure rather than function. If we should show special respect to all cells, surgeons should be attempting to excise the very minimum tissue (down to the last cell) necessary during operations. We should be doing research into preventing the neuronal loss which occurs normally during childhood. The desquamation of a skin cell should be as monumental, according to those who believe that abortion is killing persons, as the loss of a whole person. These claims are, I think, all absurd.

Yuk Factor

Many people would find it shocking for a fetus to be created and then destroyed as a source of organs. But many people found artificial insemination abhorrent, IVF shocking and the use of animal organs revolting. Watching an abortion is horrible. However, the fact that people find something repulsive does not settle whether it is wrong. The achievement in applied ethics, if there is one, of the last 50 years has been to get people to rise above their gut feelings and examine the reasons for a practice.

Permissive and Obstructive Ethics

Many people believe that ethicists should be merely moral watch-dogs, barking when they see something going wrong. However, ethics may also be permissive. Thus ethics may require that we stop interfering, as was the case in the treatment of homosexuals. Ethics should not only be obstructive but constructive. To delay unnecessarily a good piece of research which will result in a life-saving drug is to be responsible for some people's deaths. It is to act wrongly. This debate about cloning illustrates a possible permissive and constructive role for ethics.

Conclusion

The most justified use of human cloning is arguably to produce stem cells for the treatment of disease. I have argued that it is not only reasonable to produce embryos as a source of multipotent stem cells, but that it is morally required to produce embryos and early fetuses as a source of tissue for transplantation. This argument hinges on:

1. The claim that the moral status of the cloned embryo and early fetus is no different from that of the somatic cell from which they are derived.
2. The claim that there is no morally relevant difference between the fetus and the embryo until some critical point in brain development and function.
3. The fact that the practice is consistent with existing practices of fetal tissue transplantation and conceiving humans as a source of tissue for transplantation (the Ayala case).
4. An argument from beneficence. This practice would achieve much good.
5. An argument from autonomy. This was the principle of tissue transmutation: that we should be able to determine the fate of our own cells, including whether they change into other cell types.

This proposal avoids all the usual objections to cloning. The major concerns are practicality and safety. This requires further study.

The HGAC and The Royal Society have broached the possibility of producing clones for up to 14 days: "therapeutic cloning." Those bodies believe that it is acceptable to produce and destroy an embryo but not a fetus. Women abort fetuses up to 20 weeks and later. We could make it mandatory that women have abortions earlier (with rapid pregnancy testing). However, we do not. Moreover, while the decision for most women to have an abortion is a momentous and considered one, in practice, we allow women to abort fetuses regardless of their reasons, indeed occasionally for no or bad reasons. If a woman could abort a fetus because she wanted a child with a certain horoscope sign, surely a woman should be able to abort a fetus to save a person's life.

I have been discussing cloning for the purposes of saving people's lives or drastically improving their quality. While we beat our breasts about human dignity and the rights of cells of different sorts, people are dying of leukaemia and kidney disease. If a woman wants to carry a clone of her or someone else's child to save a life, it may not be society's place to interfere.

David van Gend

 **NO**

Prometheus, Pandora, and the Myths of Cloning

One of the earliest human trials in regenerative medicine was conducted on a crag high in the Caucasus around the dawn of time. Or not strictly human, since Prometheus was a Titan. But for fraternizing with humans he was pegged out on a high rock where the eagle of Hephaestus ate his liver out each day, and it grew back each night.

With remarkable scientific insight, although without specifying the key role of hepatic stem cells, the Greeks observed that the liver is the one internal organ that has a capacity for vigorous regrowth after trauma.

Prometheus was being punished for his beneficence to humans—for teaching them arts practical and aesthetic, and worst of all for stealing the secret fire of Zeus to give humans comfort in their caves and supremacy over the animals.

To call scientists "Promethean" seems to me a compliment. Their role is to benefit humankind by their labours—and scientists who labor in the field of regenerative medicine using adult stem cells are most authentically Promethean.

The proper term for scientists who violate norms of human relationships and ethics, unleashing destructive forces upon us, is not "Promethean" but "Pandoran." She was the other chapter in Zeus's punishment of Prometheus. Pandora was asexually reproduced, "forged on the anvil of Hephaestus," essentially a laboratory creation like the modern clone. Irresistibly packaged, she wowed the impressionable brother of Prometheus, who accepted her gift of a mysterious box—which, upon being opened, released all sorts of corrupt and harmful things into the world. It is said that one thing only remained in Pandora's box after all the noxious things had emerged: hope, groundless and unreasonable hope.

With cloning, modern Pandorans raise unreasonable hope with their attractively packaged deceit. With obscure motives, they threaten forms of harm to humanity that we are only beginning to understand.

Keeping the lid on Pandora's box is still possible if we can show clearly why cloning is both redundant and wrong.

From *Human Life Review*, Summer/Fall 2006, pp. 15 16, 21 27. Copyright © 2006 by David van Gend. Reprinted by permission. Notes omitted.

Why Cloning Is Redundant

A patient of mine with advanced Parkinson's disease hopes to be the first man treated with stem cells from the back of his nose. He is among the dozens of patients with various genetic illnesses whose stem cells have been collected for research at the Griffith University Adult Stem Cell Centre, here in Queensland, Australia.

There are cautious, very cautious, grounds for hope for my patient, given that Griffith has successfully used these adult stem cells to treat Parkinson's in rats, and is planning primate trials. If all goes well, human trials will follow.

His case is an example of the true state of stem-cell science, as opposed to its political distortion. In the public mind embryonic stem cells and cloning are the main event, whereas in reality they are a conjurer's sideshow. Adult stem cells are now safely used in 72 human conditions . . . embryonic stem cells remain both unusable and dangerous. The cloning lobby dreams of creating "patient-specific stem cells" for research; adult-stem-cell researchers have already achieved that goal.

Australian cloning advocate Professor Alan Trounson has recently clarified that cloning is not about cell therapies for Parkinson's or spinal injury, but is limited to the modest research goal of creating patient-specific cells for studying disease and developing drugs. That is an important clarification, since the media still pretend that embryonic stem cells, cloned or otherwise, can be used as magic bullets for direct "cell therapy." That has always been false—since, among other things, the risk of tumors inherent in the use of embryonic cells rules out human application. Trounson's revised prospectus for cloning is more honest: "It's not about cells for therapy. This is about cells that give us an opportunity to discover what causes a disease and whether we can interfere with that."[1]

Fine—but even that more realistic goal for cloning has been made redundant, since that is exactly the research capacity Griffith has now achieved with adult stem cells. They possess an expanding range of patient-specific stem cells, easily obtained from patients, readily transformed into the required cell type (brain, muscle, kidney, liver) and useful for genetic study of the disease and development of drugs. These adult stem cells are superior for research because they are cheap, ethically uncomplicated, and free of the genetic damage caused by cloning. And only adult stem cells can be used safely for direct cell therapy without the risk of tumor formation and immune rejection.

Cloning has been left for dead, and Griffith Professor Alan Mackay-Sim has written its obituary telling the Lockhart enquiry into Australia's cloning laws that "it is probable that such stem-cell lines as these will render therapeutic cloning irrelevant and impractical."

If that view is correct, what possible justification is there for pursuing cloning? . . .

Why Cloning Is Wrong

Here is the dual desecration of "research" cloning: not just that a human life is wrongfully killed for the benefit of others, but that a human life is wrongfully created outside of any normal human setting.

To clone is to generate a living human embryo with no mother—think of that! Only an emptied-out female egg is used, with no trace of the mother's genetic identity. And no father, either—for the donor of DNA is not father to the clone, but is instead its identical twin, and could be as anonymous a donor as a piece of human tissue from the laboratory fridge.

Cloning creates a subclass of humans who are nobody's children. Anonymous artifacts, not beloved offspring; scientific objects with no mother or father to defend their interests. The bonds of belonging are broken: A human being is created outside the circle of human kinship and care.

And yet the cloned offspring is a child like any other; if it were allowed to be born, we would care for it as any other orphan. As Australia's religious leaders have pointed out, it would be a lesser evil to let a cloned embryo be born as a child—even considering the sociological distress and genetic disease it will suffer. The greater evil is the one proposed: that it will be created but never allowed to be born, remaining a mere laboratory animal, meat for the consumption of science.

That is not to condone the obvious abuse of "live-birth" cloning. Let Dolly the sheep, Matilda the lamb, or Snuppy the puppy be part of the freak show of cloning, but not a human child. But it is to be clear that the act of asexual reproduction of a human being, regardless of whether the clone lives for days or for years, is an abuse in itself—violating the essential bonds of "blood and belonging" that every human individual needs, willfully creating the world's first absolute orphan. That is a desecration of humanity, and must be condemned as such.

In Australia in 2002, our Parliament was united in condemning cloning—but in 2006, the debate has been reopened. We are at a different stage of the debate than the U.S.; in 2002, we banned cloning but lost the argument over the use of "surplus" IVF embryos, which are now available for research. At that time we argued that there was no good way out for the "surplus" embryos. We advised that it would be a lesser evil to let the current frozen generation of embryos die—acknowledging our shame in allowing them to be stockpiled in the first place, and ensuring it never happened again. We said it was a greater evil to set up a permanent industry exploiting human embryos, since demand would ensure supply: IVF clinics would ensure the ongoing creation of surplus embryos to feed the drug companies.

Our argument failed. In the U.S., there does not appear to be a fixed deadline at which frozen embryos must be thawed out, so they are not so clearly "going to die anyway"; more vividly, the U.S. practice of adopting frozen embryos further negates that fatalistic argument. In Australia, by contrast, the argument that the doomed embryo "may as well be used for research" (in the context of wild claims of miracle cures from the use of embryonic stem cells) carried the majority vote. The prime minister, a fair-minded man, spoke for the misled majority: "I could not find a sufficiently compelling moral difference between allowing embryos to succumb in this way and destroying them through research that might advance life-saving and life-enhancing therapies. That is why, in the end, I came out in favor of allowing research involving excess IVF embryos to go ahead."

But importantly, an ethical line in the sand was drawn between using IVF embryos that were "going to die anyway" and deliberately creating new embryos specifically for destructive research. The PM made this distinction: "It is also my very strong belief that human embryos should not be created for any purpose other than IVF treatment." On this principle a ban on creating embryos "by any means other than by the fertilization of a human egg by human sperm" was passed unanimously by Parliament.

On the same principle, there was a majority vote (non-binding) against all forms of human cloning at the United Nations last year. One delegate expressed the principle as: "No human life should ever be produced to be destroyed for the benefit of another." They saw the inhumanity of creating a cloned human embryo—identical to you or me at that stage of life—with the sole intention of exploiting it for science. Likewise, the creation of a human embryo purely for research is expressly prohibited in Article 18 of the European Convention on Human Rights and Biomedicine.

Australia's Prohibition of Human Cloning Act 2002 provided for periodical review of the legislation, and in late 2005 a six-person committee, handpicked under the auspices of a pro-cloning cabinet minister, predictably recommended overturning the unanimous vote of Parliament and allowing research cloning. This committee acknowledged that cloning creates a human embryo, which could be born as a baby like any of us. But they callously reasoned that the cloned embryo does not really "matter" to anybody, since nobody intends to bring it to birth—therefore let it be cut up for stem cells, used for drug testing, even hybridized with animals, provided it is killed by the age of 14 days.

The question of whether the embryo "matters" goes straight to the heart of this debate. This is the dividing line for public opinion in every legislature around the world. Interestingly, the question is no longer whether the embryo is a human life, but whether that human life "matters." In the words of our Senate report from the 2002 debate: "There is in fact little disagreement that the embryo is a human life and that its life commences at fertilization. The difficulties arise in specifying exactly in what sense it is to be considered 'a life,' and hence what significance should be attached to it."

The committee referred to an earlier Senate report that had reviewed "the biological facts of the matter" and concluded: "Two universally accepted attributes are that the fertilized ovum has 'life' and that it is genetically human (i.e. it is composed of genetic material entirely from the species homo sapiens). It is also generally agreed that it is an entity (a centrally organized unit which has a purposeful independent function as opposed to an organ or tissues). It also has developmental potential."

One can agree on the bare facts—that the embryo is a living individual member of our species—but whether that individual life "matters" depends on the worldview one brings to the debate. And faced with this key question—the meaning of a human life in all its embryonic simplicity—the cultural divide shows up most starkly.

A citizen who believes, as C. S. Lewis put it, that human life is "a transient and senseless contortion on the idiotic face of infinite matter" is unlikely to grant great meaning to a mere embryonic contortion. If ultimately we are all just strangely complex lumps of meat floating in time, then the embryo is just a very small lump of meat, devoid of real meaning.

For those citizens whose worldview gives a deeper context to human life, even the life of the embryo has meaning. To those who share the Christian theory of life, all of us matter, even the "littlest of these His brethren," precisely because we matter to God. Size and age are not a measure of human meaning; what matters is that the individual life is known and loved in God.

On this understanding, a new name is spelled out at conception and written on the palm of God's hand—even if the font is too small for us to read. That name, that genetic identity, will take a lifetime to be fully expressed, but it is the same name we carry for our whole existence: a new character scripted into our vast mystery play, which no other character has the right to erase.

It is vital to engage in the battle for the meaning of the human embryo, for even if there is no hope of persuading card-carrying nihilists, there is always the muddled middle of fellow citizens who can be convinced one way or the other. All future policy on cloning, human-animal hybridization, prenatal eugenics, transgenic manipulation, and other as yet unimagined abuses depends on the dominant view of what the human embryo is, and therefore how we are bound to treat it.

There are four key arguments demeaning the human embryo, which can be rebutted in interesting ways.

First, there are the recurrent dismissive comments that the embryo is "smaller than the full stop at the end of this sentence" (which, being translated into American, refers to a "period"). On this, we should play the scientists on their own ground, reminding them that, according to their own theories, the Universe itself was once "smaller than a period." To cosmologists, the fact that such a tiny entity as the embryonic Universe contained within itself the capacity to unfold into this vast and fruitful cosmos is not a cause for contempt, but intellectual wonder. We need similar eyes of understanding, not of ignorant contempt, when we contemplate the embryonic human. This tiny entity, like the embryonic Universe, is unfolding into the vast and fruitful cosmos of a human being, and deserves a comparable response of intellectual wonder. The only event in the physical world comparable in complexity and wonder to the Big Bang is human conception, which creates the only entity that can know, and therefore in a sense transcend, the Universe itself. The embryonic human is in that sense a greater being than the embryonic universe.

Second, the logic of the culture of death will work backwards from abortion to argue that since the fetus does not matter, the embryo matters even less. . . .

Care is needed here. Policy on how we treat embryos is formed in an entirely different context from policy on abortion. Abortion is portrayed as an act of self-defense against the threatening intruder in the womb. In no way is the laboratory embryo threatening the mother. In the case of the cloned embryo, there is no mother to threaten. Abortion is portrayed as an assertion of moral autonomy over one's private life, often in the context of emotional crisis, while policy on embryonic research is a coldly calculated decision by public committees. The two types of policy must be kept widely separated, and the meaning of the embryo considered on its own merits.

Third, there is the argument that the embryo cannot be considered an individual human being until the stage of possible "twinning" has passed. This is generally taken to be about 14 days of embryonic life. Until that time, we cannot know if the embryo is going to end up as one "entity" or two, which surely casts doubt on its moral status. I admit to finding this a very muddled argument, and it is the phenomenon of cloning itself that finally clears the fog. For with cloning you or I can now undergo "twinning" well past day 14—in fact, tomorrow, if you like. Does that mean that your moral status as a true, unambiguous "individual" today is in question, just because tomorrow you might have split off an identical twin? Is your current "soul" somehow diminished because you have twinned yourself into a clone? The problem is no different for the embryo: If it splits off a twin at day 14 it has merely cloned itself into an identical embryo, a twin that is 14 days younger than the original embryo. So, again, there is a positive way to look at the early embryo: It is a wonder, a marvel, and if it splits off a twin, that is just greater cause for celebration: We now have two marvels, two wonders. At the very least we are looking at one embryonic human; there is the happy chance of a second, younger human being arising a few days later from the phenomenon of natural cloning, or twinning, but that is no cause for downgrading the significance of either life.

Fourth and finally, there is the argument that so many embryos are "wasted" naturally that they surely cannot be considered to have a full human status—even, for some sensible Christian people, full spiritual status in the eyes of God. Estimates vary wildly for embryonic loss, but even if the figure is 30 percent I do not see how the problem is any different from the similar "wastage" of infants in the part of Africa I was born in. Does the fact that some 30 percent died in infancy (including some children of my early missionary ancestors) mean they were not truly human? With all due respect, if God has a problem with taking seriously the moral status of embryos because so many are "wasted," He has the same problem with these wasted African infants, or with the high percentage of Chinese babies wasted through female infanticide. And I remain unconvinced as to why a higher spiritual status should be granted to those of us who, through good luck and good environment, happen to have persisted longer on this earth. None of us matter, in the Christian understanding, unless we matter to God, and it seems wise to give the benefit of the doubt to the most embryonic of these His brethren.

Conclusion

Cloning is wrong.   It violates our humanity and the bonds of love and care to manufacture offspring who have no mother or father. It violates the most basic ethical prohibitions to create an embryo with the intention of destroying it in research. Only the parent-child relationship is the legitimate and humane context in which to create a human embryo.

Cloning is redundant. Once we have rejected it on ethical grounds, the great consolation is that we do not need cloning anyway; adult stem cells will get us the good things of stem-cell science, leaving cloning "irrelevant and impractical." But we must remember that the scientific argument is strictly secondary: Even if there were additional scientific benefits from cloned-embryo stem cells over the new disease-specific adult stem cells (and there appear not to be) cloning must still be rejected on grounds of basic human-ity: fundamental respect for the dignity of a living member of the human species, which rules out creating such a life with its destruction in mind.

In the magnificent new field of regenerative medicine, we can and must be diligent Prometheans, while keeping the lid locked on Pandora's deceitful and dehumanizing gift.

POSTSCRIPT

Is It Ethically Permissible to Clone Human Cells?

Although the cloning debate became vigorous only after the cloning of an adult animal, it is worth stressing that most of the discussion now centers on the cloning of embryos in order to obtain stem cells that can become any cell type or tissue found in the body. The hope is to be able to replace defective cells and cure disease. Ian Wilmut, "The Case for Cloning Humans," *The Scientist* (April 25, 2005), argues that cloning human embryos may offer the best way to understand and treat difficult diseases; Wilmut's team received a license to clone human embryos in February 2005. For a good overview of the stem cell issue, see Rick Weiss, "The Power to Divide," *National Geographic* (July 2005). See also Ronald Bailey, *Liberation Biology: The Scientific and Moral Case for the Biotech Revolution* (Prometheus, 2005).

Leon Kass develops his objections to cloning in "Preventing a Brave New World," *The Human Life Review* (July 2001), and *Life, Liberty and the Defense of Dignity: The Challenge for Bioethics* (Encounter, 2002). He gains support from Mary Midgley, who in "Biotechnology and Monstrosity: Why We Should Pay Attention to the 'Yuk Factor'," *Hastings Center Report* (September October 2000), argues that intuitive, emotional responses to things such as cloning have a significance that must not be dismissed out of hand. In *Our Posthuman Future: Consequences of the Biotechnological Revolution* (Farras, Strauss & Giroux, 2002; paperback Picador, 2003), Francis Fukuyama argues for limits on cloning and genetic engineering in order to protect human nature and dignity. David Gurnham, "The Mysteries of Human Dignity and the Brave New World of Human Cloning," *Social & Legal Studies* (June 2005), agrees that cloning threatens human dignity. As a result of such arguments, the United States has banned the use of federal funds for reproductive cloning and severely limited the cloning of embryos to obtain stem cells for either research or treatment purposes. However, some states (e.g., California; see Nigel Williams, "California Ramps Up Stem Cell Plans," *Current Biology* [March 2005]) have chosen to develop their own state-funded research programs. In other countries, progress has been more rapid. See Susan Mayor, "UK and Korean Teams Refine Techniques for Human Cloning," *BMJ: British Medical Journal* (May 28, 2005).

Speaking to the National Bioethics Advisory Commission (whose report was summarized by chair Harold T. Shapiro in the July 11, 1997, issue of *Science*), Ruth Macklin, of the Albert Einstein College of Medicine, said, "It is absurd to maintain that the proposition 'cloning is morally wrong' is self-evident. . . . If I cannot point to any great benefits likely to result from cloning, neither do I foresee any probable great harms, provided that a structure of regulation and oversight is in place. If objectors to cloning can identify no greater harm than a supposed affront to the dignity of the human species, that is a flimsy basis on which to erect barriers to scientific research and its applications." Nathan Myhrvold argues in "Human Clones: Why Not? Opposition to Cloning Isn't Just Luddism—It's Racism," *Slate* (March 13, 1997), that "Calls for a ban on cloning amount to discrimination against people based on another genetic trait—the fact that somebody already has an identical DNA sequence." There are reasons why cloning—at least of embryonic cells—should be permitted. According to Thomas B. Okarma (interviewed by Erika Jonietz, "Cloning, Stem Cells, and Medicine's Future," *Technology Review*, June 2003), they hold great hope for new and useful medical treatments. And according to Robin Marantz Henig, "Pandora's Baby," *Scientific American* (June 2003), when other reproductive technologies such as *in vitro* fertilization were new, they faced similar objections; now they are routine, and it is likely that someday cloning will be too. Daniel J. Kevles agrees; in "Cloning Can't Be Stopped," *Technology Review* (June 2002), he said that if human cloning can but succeed, it will "become commonplace . . . a new commodity in the growing emporium of human reproduction." Seymour W. Itzkoff, in "Intervening with Mother Nature: The Ethics of Human Cloning," *The Mankind Quarterly* (Fall 2003), calls objections to cloning and related issues "reactionary" and notes that "The cloning of humans and the stem cell production issue are . . . the tip of the iceberg, the slippery slope, or any other metaphor that points to the growing impact of scientific research that could undercut the twentieth-century ideological opposition to viewing human behavior as biologically/genetically determined."

So far, the result of the debate is that research continues but under various regulatory and funding restrictions. See Charles C. Mann, "Braving Medicine's Frontier," *Technology Review* (September 2005). Work with adult stem cells has so far proved disappointing, but see Agneta M. Sutton, "'Yes' to Adult Stem Cells," *Southern Medical Journal* (December 2006). Hopes have also been raised by the discovery that stem cells can be obtained from the amniotic fluid surrounding a fetus in the womb; see Constance Holden, "Versatile Stem Cells Without the Ethical Baggage?" *Science* (January 12, 2007).

Contributors to This Volume

EDITOR

THOMAS A. EASTON is Professor of Science at Thomas College in Waterville, Maine, where he has been teaching since 1983. He received a B.A. in biology from Colby College in 1966 and a Ph.D. in theoretical biology from the University of Chicago in 1971. He has also taught at Unity College, Husson College, and the University of Maine. He is a prolific writer, and his articles on scientific and futuristic issues have appeared in the scholarly journals *Experimental Neurology* and *American Scientist,* as well as in such popular magazines as *Astronomy, Consumer Reports,* and *Robotics Age.* His publications include *Focus on Human Biology,* 2d ed., coauthored with Carl E. Rischer (HarperCollins, 1995), *Careers in Science,* 4th ed. (VGM, 2004), and *Taking Sides: Clashing Views on Environmental Issues,* 13th ed. (McGraw-Hill Contemporary Learning Series, 2008). Dr. Easton is also a well-known writer and critic of science fiction.

AUTHORS

JOSIE APPLETON is convenor of the Manifesto Club, a new association aiming to put human aspirations back into politics. She is also a journalist who writes for a variety of publications.

RONALD M. ATLAS is graduate dean, professor of biology, professor of public health, and co-director of the Center for Health Hazards Preparedness at the University of Louisville.

JOHN BALBUS is a program director at Environmental Defense in Washington, D.C.

MICHAEL BEHAR is a freelance writer and editor based in Washington, D.C. His beat includes environmental issues and scientific innovations.

DAVID L. BODDE is professor and senior fellow at the International Center for Automotive Research, Arthur M. Spiro Center for Entrepreneurial Leadership, at Clemson University.

LEWIS M. BRANSCOMB is the Aetna professor of public policy and corporate management emeritus and former director of the Science, Technology, and Public Policy Program in the Center for Science and International Affairs at Harvard University's Kennedy School of Government.

JOSEPH BURNS, Irving Porter Church Professor of Engineering and Professor of Astronomy at Cornell University, is a member of the National Research Council's Solar System Exploration Survey Committee.

GEORGE W. BUSH is the current president of the United States.

BRIAN BUTLER is an assistant professor of business administration at the University of Pittsburgh.

GEORGE CARLO is a public health scientist, epidemiologist, lawyer, and founder of the Health Risk Management Group. He is chairman of the Carlo Institute and a fellow of the American College of Epidemiology, and he serves on the faculty of the George Washington University School of Medicine. Dr. Carlo has published numerous research articles, commentaries, chapters in books, and health policy papers addressing issues in the health sciences, and he is frequently consulted for television, radio, and newspaper interviews pertaining to public health issues.

DENISE M. CARTER recently completed her doctorate in social anthropology at the University of Hull, UK. She is particularly interested in how the Internet transforms the ways people live and becomes ever more embedded in everyday lives.

KAREN CHARMAN is a journalist specializing in environmental issues. She is also the managing editor of the journal *Capitalism Nature Socialism*.

GREGORY CONKO is the director of food safety policy at the Competitive Institute. He is the coauthor, with Henry I. Miller, of *The Frankenfood Myth: How Protest and Politics Threaten the Biotech Revolution* (Praeger, 2004).

JONATHAN N. CUMMINGS is an assistant professor of management at the Massachusetts Institute of Technology.

RICHARD DENISON is a senior scientist at Environmental Defense in Washington, D.C.

KYLE D. DIXON is senior fellow and director, Federal Institute for Regulatory Law & Economics, The Progress & Freedom Foundation. He has also worked at the Federal Communications Commission, most recently as special counsel for broadband policy.

KAREN FLORINI is a senior attorney at Environmental Defense in Washington, D.C.

ROBERT KRAUT is the Herbert A. Simon Professor of Human Computer Interaction at Carnegie Mellon University.

KEITH KUPFERSCHMID is the vice president for intellectual property policy and enforcement for the Software & Information Industry Association (SIIA).

LAWRENCE LESSIG is the C. Wendell and Edith M. Carlsmith Professor of Law at Stanford Law School. His latest book is *Code: Version 2.0* (Basic Books, 2006).

DR. JOHN H. MARBURGER, III, is the science adviser to the president and director of the Office of Science and Technology Policy. He has also served as director of Brookhaven National Laboratory, the third president of the State University of New York at Stony Brook, and a University of Southern California professor of physics and electrical engineering.

ANNE PLATT McGINN is a senior researcher at the Worldwatch Institute and the author of "Why Poison Ourselves? A Precautionary Approach to Synthetic Chemicals," *Worldwatch Paper 153* (November 2000).

MICHAEL MEYER, the European editor for *Newsweek International*, is a member of the New York Council on Foreign Relations and was an Inaugural Fellow at the American Academy in Berlin. He won the Overseas Press Club's Morton Frank Award for business/economic reporting from abroad in 1986 and 1988 and was a member of the *Newsweek* team that won a 1993 National Magazine Award for its coverage of the Los Angeles riots. He is the author of *The Alexander Complex* (Times Books, 1989), an examination of the psychology of American empire-builders.

HENRY I. MILLER is a research fellow at Stanford University's Hoover Institution. His research focuses on public policy toward science and technology, especially biotechnology. He is the coauthor, with Gregory Conko, of *The Frankenfood Myth: How Protest and Politics Threaten the Biotech Revolution* (Praeger, 2004).

DAVID NICHOLSON-LORD is an environmental writer, formerly with *The Times, The Independent,* and *The Independent on Sunday*, where he was environment editor. He is the author of *The Greening of the Cities* (Routledge,

1987) and of *Green Cities—And Why We Need Them* (New Economics Foundation, 2003), a member of UNESCO's UK Man and the Biosphere Urban Forum and of the Urban Wildlife Network executive and a trustee of the National Wildflower Centre. He also teaches environment in the journalism faculty at City University, London.

BRENDAN RAPPLE is the Collection Development Librarian in the O'Neill Library of Boston College.

TOM REGAN, emeritus professor of philosophy at North Carolina State University, is considered the philosophical leader of the animal rights movement in the United States. His latest book is *Empty Cages: Facing the Challenge of Animal Rights* (Rowman & Littlefield, 2004).

DONALD R. ROBERTS is a professor in the Division of Tropical Public Health, Department of Preventive Medicine and Biometrics, Uniformed Services University of the Health Sciences.

JULIAN SANCHEZ is a contributing editor to *Reason* magazine.

JULIAN SAVULESCU is director of the Ethics Unit of the Murdoch Institute at the Royal Children's Hospital in Melbourne, Australia, and an associate professor in the Centre for the Study of Health and Society at the University of Melbourne. He has also worked as a clinical ethicist at the Oxford Radcliffe Hospitals, and he helped set up the Oxford Institute for Ethics and Communication in Health Care Practice.

PETER SCHENKEL is a retired political scientist interested in the question of what contact with advanced aliens would mean to humanity.

MARTIN SCHRAM is a syndicated columnist, television commentator, and author. His publications include *Mandate for Change,* coedited with Will Marshall (Berkley Books, 1993) and *Speaking Freely: Former Members of Congress Talk About Money in Politics* (Center for Responsive Politics, 1995).

SETH SHOSTAK is a senior astronomer at the SETI Institute and the author of *Sharing the Universe: Perspectives on Extraterrestrial Life* (Berkeley Hills Books, 1998).

JEFFREY M. SMITH is the author of *Seeds of Deception: Exposing Industry and Government Lies About the Safety of the Genetically Engineered Foods You're Eating* (Yes! Books, 2003). He studies the risks of GM foods.

SIR NICHOLAS STERN, is head of the British Government Economics Service and adviser to the British government on the economics of climate change and development.

STUART TAYLOR, JR., is a senior writer and columnist for *National Journal* and a contributing editor at *Newsweek.*

MIKE TREDER is executive director of the Center for Responsible Nanotechnology, a nonprofit research and policy group based in New York City.

NEIL DeGRASSE TYSON is the director of the Hayden Planetarium at the American Museum of Natural History. His latest book is *Death by Black Hole and Other Cosmic Quandaries* (Norton, 2007).

THE UNION OF CONCERNED SCIENTISTS (UCS) is an independent non-profit alliance of more than 100,000 concerned citizens and scientists. It was founded in 1969 by faculty members and students at the Massachusetts Institute of Technology who were concerned about the misuse of science and technology in society. Their statement called for the redirection of scientific research to pressing environmental and social problems. From that beginning, UCS has become a powerful voice for change.

THE UNITED KINGDOM'S NATIONAL RADIATION PROTECTION BOARD JOINED THE HEALTH PROTECTION AGENCY (HPA) as its Radiation Protection Division (http://www.hpa.org.uk/radiation/) on April 1, 2005. The mission of the HPA is to provide better protection in the UK against infectious diseases and other dangers to health, including chemical hazards, poisons, and radiation.

DAVID VAN GEND is a physician and secretary of the Queensland, Australia, branch of the World Federation of Doctors Who Respect Human Life.

MICHAEL J. WALLACE is executive vice president of Constellation Energy, a leading supplier of electricity to large commercial and industrial customers.

SCOTT WALSH is a project manager at Environmental Defense in Washington, D.C.

EDWARD WEILER is NASA's Associate Administrator for space science.

STEVEN WEINBERG holds the Josey Regental Chair in Science at the University of Texas at Austin, where he is a member of the physics and astronomy departments. His research has earned him the Nobel Prize in Physics (1979), the National Medal of Science (1991), and the Benjamin Franklin Medal of the American Philosophical Society (2004). He is a member of the U.S. National Academy of Sciences, Britain's Royal Society, the American Philosophical Society, and the American Academy of Arts and Sciences. He has written over 300 articles on elementary particle physics and numerous books, of which the latest is *Glory and Terror—The Growing Nuclear Danger* (New York Review Books, 2004).

Index